Kate Williams fell in love with the eighteenth century whilst studying for her BA at the University of Oxford. She has an MA from Queen Mary, University of London and a DPhil from the University of Oxford. She is also a lecturer and TV consultant, appearing regularly on BBC and Channel 4 programmes to discuss her work. She lives in London.

JOSEPHINE

DESIRE, AMBITION, NAPOLEON

KATE WILLIAMS

arrow books

Published by Arrow Books 2014

2 4 6 8 10 9 7 5 3 1

First published in Great Britain in 2013 by
Hutchinson
Random House, 20 Vauxhall Bridge Road,
London SW1V 2SA

www.randomhouse.co.uk

Addresses for companies within The Random House Group Limited can be found at:
www.randomhouse.co.uk/offices.htm

The Random House Group Limited Reg. No. 954009

A CIP catalogue record for this book
is available from the British Library

ISBN 9780099551423

The Random House Group Limited supports the Forest Stewardship
Council® (FSC®), the leading international forest-certification organisation.
Our books carrying the FSC label are printed on FSC®-certified paper.
FSC is the only forest-certification scheme supported by the leading environmental
organisations, including Greenpeace. Our paper procurement policy can be found at
www.randomhouse.co.uk/environment

Typeset in Bembo by Palimpsest Book Production Limited,
Falkirk, Stirlingshire

Printed and bound in Great Britain by
CPI Group (UK) Ltd, Croydon CR0 4YY

Contents

List of Illustrations

1. Empress Josephine (1763-1814) 1808 (oil on canvas), Gerard, Francois Pascal Simon, Baron (1770-1837) / Chateau de Fontainebleau, Seine-et-Marne, France / Giraudon / The Bridgeman Art Library.

2. La Pagerie. R.Ziff / Travel-Images.com.

3. Alexandre de Beauharnais. Unknown French painter of the David circle.

4. Gerard, Francois (1770-1837): Portrait de la reine Hortense de Digitale Beauharnais (1783-1837) enfant. Elle est la fille de l'imperatrice Josephine de Beauharnais et la mere du futur Napoleon II, 18eme siecle. Avignon, Musee Calvet. peinture © 2013. White Images/Scala, Florence.

5. Portrait de Son Altesse Impériale le prince Eugène Napoléon. (C) RMN-Grand Palais (musée des châteaux de Malmaison et de Bois-Préau) / Michèle Bellot.

6. Visite de Joséphine à son mari Alexandre à la prison du Luxembourg en 1794. (C) RMN-Grand Palais (musée des châteaux de Malmaison et de Bois-Préau) / Daniel Arnaudet.

7. Letter to Josephine de Beauharnais, 1795-6 (pen & ink on paper), Bonaparte, Napoleon (1769-1821) / Private Collection / Photo © Christie's Images / The Bridgeman Art Library.

8. Portrait of Theresa de Cabarrus (1773-1835) also known as Madame Tallien, printed by Boussod, Valadon and Company, 1895 (coloured litho), Isabey, Jean-Baptiste (1767-1855) (after) / Bibliotheque Nationale, Paris, France / Giraudon / The Bridgeman Art Library.

9. Paul Francois Nicolas, Vicomte de Barras, from 'Histoire de la Revolution Francaise' by Louis Blanc (1811-82) (engraving), French School, (19th century) / Private Collection / Ken Welsh / The Bridgeman Art Library.

10. Ci-devant Occupations, or Madame Talian and the Empress Josephine Dancing Naked before Barrass in the Winter of 1797, published by Hannah Humphrey in 1805 (etching with aquatint), Gillray, James (1757-1815) / © Courtesy of the Warden and Scholars of New College, Oxford / The Bridgeman Art Library.

11. Portrait of Napoleon I Bonaparte (1769-1821) by Andrea Appiani, oil on board, 1796, Appiani, Andrea the Elder (1754-1817) / Pinacoteca Ambrosiana, Milan, Italy / De Agostini Picture Library / © Veneranda Biblioteca Ambrosiana - Milano / The Bridgeman Art Library.

12. Three Graces (marble), Canova, Antonio (1757-1822) / Hermitage, St. Petersburg, Russia / Cameraphoto Arte Venezia / The Bridgeman Art Library.

13. Napoleon I (1769-1821) on the Bridge of Arcole (oil on canvas), Gros, Baron Antoine Jean (1771-1835) / Hermitage, St. Petersburg, Russia / The Bridgeman Art Library.

14. The Empress Josephine, 1806 (oil on canvas), Lefevre, Robert (1755-1830) / Apsley House, The Wellington Museum, London, UK / © English Heritage Photo Library / The Bridgeman Art Library.

15. Premier Empire : 'Vue du chateau de Malmaison, facade sur le parc' 1805. © Photo Scala, Florence.

16. View of the Wooden Bridge on the River near the Statue of Diane, from 'Views of Malmaison', engraved by Louis Garneray (1783-1857) (aquatint), Garneray, Auguste Simon (1785-1824) (after) / Bibliotheque des Arts Decoratifs, Paris, France / Archives Charmet / The Bridgeman Art Library.

25. Robe de cour de l'impératrice Joséphine. (C) RMN-Grand Palais (musée des châteaux de Malmaison et de Bois-Préau) / Gérard Blot.

26. Le diademe (couronne) de l'imperatrice Josephine de Beauharnais (Marie-Joseph-Rose de Tascher de la Pagerie) (1763-1814). 1804-1809. White Images/Scala, Florence.

27. Hortense de Beauharnais (1783-1837) (oil on canvas), Richard, Fleury Francois (1777-1852) / Fondation Dosne-Thiers (Musee Frederic Masson) Paris, France / Giraudon / The Bridgeman Art Library.

28. Portrait en pied d' Hortense de Beauharnais, reine de Hollande (1783-1837) et son fils Napoleon Charles, 1807. © Photo Scala, Florence.

29. Imperial Botany, or: a peep at Josephine's collection. The Bodleian Libraries, the University of Oxford, Curzon b. 30 (83).

30. Imperial Botany, or: a peep at Josephine's collection. The Bodleian Libraries, the University of Oxford, Curzon b. 30 (83).

31. Imperial Botany, or: a peep at Josephine's collection. The Bodleian Libraries, the University of Oxford, Curzon b. 30 (83).

32. Divorce statement of Emperor Napoleon Bonaparte (1769-1821) and Empress Josephine (1763-1814) 9th January 1810 (pen & ink on paper), French School, (19th century) / Archives du Ministere des Affaires Etrangeres, Paris, France / Archives Charmet / The Bridgeman Art Library.

33. Marie Louise (1791-1847) and the King of Rome (1811-32) (oil on canvas), Gerard, Francois Pascal Simon, Baron (1770-1837) / Château de Versailles, France / Giraudon / The Bridgeman Art Library.

34. Vue du château de Navarre. (C) RMN-Grand Palais (musée des châteaux de Malmaison et de Bois-Préau) / Daniel Arnaudet.

35. Napoleon I (1769-1821) on the Imperial Throne, 1806 (oil on canvas), Ingres, Jean Auguste Dominique (1780-1867) / Musee de l'Armee, Paris, France / Giraudon / The Bridgeman Art Library.

Prologue

1 December 1804.

It was the most important night of Josephine's life.

Parisians and men and women from all over France were taking their positions along the route in the darkness, dignitaries from across the world had arrived, the gold coaches were prepared, and the imperial robes were hanging ready for the supreme hero. The next day, Napoleon was to be crowned Emperor of France and all its territories. The little Corsican soldier would be 'His Imperial Majesty'.

All France thought Josephine overwhelmed with happiness, but inside the grand palace of the Tuileries she was afraid. She was about to pull off the most audacious plan of her life.

Everything was riding on how she conducted herself in what would be the most important test of her life so far. If she succeeded, she would be crowned Empress, first woman of the world and the consort of the greatest man the century would ever see. But if she failed, she would be condemned to disgrace, humiliation and poverty. She was forty, she had been Napoleon's wife for eight years, and he was talking of annulling their marriage.

Napoleon had once been obsessed by his 'little Creole'. But he mourned the lack of an heir, and now that he was the ruler, every woman in the empire was offering herself to him. When Josephine fell into jealous rages, he left the room, bored by her tears. And as he knew, because he had married her in a civil ceremony, she would not be too difficult to put aside.

The Imperial Majesty, so decisive on everything, was unsure about his Empress. His family whispered to him that marrying a foreign princess would boost his grandeur – and produce an heir. And yet Josephine was very popular with the French people and Napoleon saw her as his good-luck charm. He was also a deeply loyal man. 'How can I put away this excellent woman just because I am becoming great?' he fretted. Perhaps, he thought, he would wait until after he was crowned.

Then he made one crucial mistake. He confided his concerns to Josephine. She responded calmly. Then she plotted. Pope Pius VII and his entourage were visiting and Napoleon had asked Josephine to act as hostess. She was a celebrated diplomat, and he was proud of her graceful, charming ways. She seized the opportunity to win Pius over to her side.

By 1 December, the night before the coronation, Josephine was ready to strike. She begged the Pope for a private audience and assumed her prettiest, gentlest manner. She confided to him that she felt quite distraught, violently worried about her soul, and only he could help her. She simply had to tell him her secret: the marriage had only been a civil union and so they were living in sin in the eyes of God. She was afraid, she told him, so desperately afraid, that the Emperor was destined for hell.

Pius was prompted to action by her tears and gently whispered worries. He marched straight to the Emperor and blustered that he refused to crown a sinful man. Declaring himself shocked that his Imperial Majesty had not confessed the truth to him, he announced that he must be immediately married in a religious ceremony. Napoleon pleaded and bullied, but Pius would not relent. The imperial pair must be united by a priest or he would refuse to conduct the coronation.

Josephine sat demurely and waited for her plan to succeed. She had lingered until the very last minute to tell Pius, so that Napoleon did not have the time to argue the Pope into a compromise. The supreme Emperor was forced into a corner. Either he agreed to marry or the coronation would be delayed. Finally, grudgingly, he gave in. A makeshift altar was created in his study and the couple were secretly married that evening by one of Pius's cardinals. Napoleon kicked and fumed, while Josephine smiled.

She had won. She was Napoleon's wife before God. It would be almost impossible for him to set her aside. She, the 'little Creole', would be Empress of France.

That night, Josephine savoured her triumph. She had beaten everybody – Napoleon's spiteful family, the politicians who whispered against her and all the actresses and duchesses who had tried to usurp her. They would all have to watch her be crowned.

At 10am on 2 December, the imperial coach set out from the Tuileries Palace for Notre-Dame. A giant concoction of gleaming gilt, it was drawn by eight splendid white horses and topped with a magnificent crown borne by four sculpted eagles. Napoleon and Josephine sat resplendent, just visible in their sumptuous coronation robes through the long glass windows. Crowds lined the route, along pavements that seemed to have been sprinkled in gold.

Josephine had never looked more beautiful. She wore a long, white satin gown heavily embroidered in gold and the shining ringlets of her hair were arranged around a fabulous diadem of leaves made from 1000 diamonds and adorned with pearls. Her necklace and earrings were sapphires and emeralds surrounded by cut diamonds and on her finger she wore a ruby – the symbol of joy and 'so perfect a personification of elegance and majesty'.

At Notre-Dame, Napoleon received his crown from the Pope. He placed it on his head and then waited as Josephine advanced towards him. She knelt to him and clasped her hands, as if praying to him. Then Napoleon moved towards her and placed his crown on her head, gently so as not to disturb her priceless diadem.

Josephine – impoverished Creole, widow, semi-courtesan and mistress – was now Empress of all France. She had won.

Or so she thought.

Marie-Josèphe-Rose de Tascher de La Pagerie grew up a carefree girl on Martinique, became a kept mistress in Paris and ended as the most powerful woman in France. She was no great beauty, her teeth were black, and she was six years older than her husband, but one twitch of her skirt could enthral into slavery the man who terrorised Europe. She became the perfect consort, skilled at pleasing the crowds and reading Napoleon's mood all the while. She was soft power to his hard power: she excelled at all the roles of patronage, diplomacy and etiquette that he could not. As a heroine of the Terror and a former aristocrat, she legitimised him in the eyes of the people as a defender of the Republic, and her kindness and gentle mien made people forget his brutality and rudeness.

She pretended that she had no desire for power. Feigning meekness, she would say she was 'not born for such grandeur'. But really she wished for ascendancy over all those who had snubbed her.

Josephine's proofs of her victory were her incredible possessions: her sumptuous wardrobe, her artworks and her jewellery box spilling more diamonds than Marie Antoinette's. Her home, Malmaison, was a work of art. Complete with Swiss alpine chalet and greenhouse, her gardens had hundreds of varieties of flowers never before grown in France. The house was furnished with priceless paintings and statues Napoleon had stolen for her from all over the world. Josephine was one of the most powerful and energetic art collectors in history. She was a second Catherine the Great, using art to shore up her rule and create her power. A mistress, a courtesan, a Revolutionary heroine, a collector, a patron and an Empress, she was, in the words of one of her friends, 'an actor who could play all roles'.[1]

To win, Josephine would do anything – abandon friends, undermine her enemies and inform on her rivals. She would even sacrifice her daughter.

1
La Pagerie

One day in the spring of 1763, a young woman climbed to the top of a hill on a plantation in the south of the island of Martinique. Six months pregnant with her first child, Rose-Claire de Tascher de La Pagerie was twenty-six, a scion of one of the greatest families on the island, and not easily intimidated. The last seven years of her life had seen battles with the British for the island. French forces had filled the nearby port, Fort-de-France, fighting bitterly. The French settlers on Martinique huddled in their homes, terrified of losing their land to soldiers or slave rebellions. Her handsome husband had defended the island and she was deeply in love with him. Finally, in early 1763, the British and French signed a treaty – Martinique would be French. Rose-Claire clambered up the hill, accompanied by her slaves, and watched the British ships on the horizon sail away. She patted the swell of her stomach, convinced that she was carrying a boy.

Three months later, on 23 June 1763, Rose-Claire's first child was born. Marie-Josèphe-Rose de Tascher de La Pagerie had only narrowly escaped being born British. 'Contrary to our hopes, it has pleased God to give us a daughter,' wrote Rose-Claire on the occasion of the little girl's birth. 'My own joy has been no less great. Why should we not take a more favourable view of our own sex?'[1] But the child was a terrible disappointment to the rest of the family. Rose-Claire's husband, Joseph de Tascher de La Pagerie, desired a boy who, one day, might haul the family into gentility. Her family wished for a boy to take over the land. Marie-Josèphe was not valuable as a girl, intended at best for an early marriage to one of the local landowners, then life as a busy matron to half a dozen children.

Tiny Martinique, barely forty miles across and fifteen miles wide, was 4000 miles and several weeks' sailing from France – and remote from the motherland. The French fought for its lush lands, but saw the place as a cash cow and the people who lived there as provincial and ill-educated. Some families came out from France to make their fortune there, but rather ashamedly, for the capital, Fort Royal, now Fort-de-France, was no bastion of culture. 'Everyone hurries to get rich in order to escape a place where men live without distinction, without honour.'[2] The women were indolent, while the men struggled to resist the temptations of drinking island rum, gambling and duelling. Children were raised to take over plantations, as masters or wives, and never leave the Caribbean.

Josephine was the name that Napoleon would give her. Marie-Josèphe was known to her family as Yeyette, or Rose when they were being very formal. She was born into a dynasty in decline. Her mother, born Rose-Claire des Vergers de Sannois, was a member of a wealthy plantation family, and a descendant of both Pierre Bélain d'Esnambuc, who had established the first French colony on the island in 1635, and Guillaume d'Orange, who had defended the colonials from the Dutch Navy's attempt on the island in 1674. Rose-Claire was a proud member of an elite family – the Sannoises owned swathes of land on Martinique and her father was a true *grand blanc*, one of the prosperous landowners who retained near-absolute control over the island.

Rose-Claire should have married a son of another wealthy family But she was still unmarried at the shockingly advanced age of twenty-five, when most other girls had been married for eight or so years and were already mothers. When the rather poor Joseph-Gaspard de Tascher de La Pagerie asked for her hand, she was delighted at the prospect, and her parents had no choice but to agree. Joseph was a charmer with an eye for the ladies. His father, Gaspard-Joseph, had been a steward on the plantations, with a reputation for irresponsibility and hedonism. Thanks to his skill at making connections, Gaspard managed to install his son in a position at the French court, as a page at the Palace of Versailles. The young man returned after three years, elegant, polished and in search of a rich wife.

Newly married, the ill-matched pair settled in their home, the place where Rose-Claire had lived for most of her life, a large and beautiful plantation near the little village of Trois-Îlets in the south-west of Martinique. Habitation de La Pagerie, as it became known, was 1230 acres of highly fertile land, bordered by lush hills. Cocoa, coffee, cassava and cotton flourished on the slopes, while sheep and cows grazed on rich green pastures and field after field of sugar cane surrounded the house. The River La Pagerie snaked through the grounds. Like most plantations, it was self-sufficient and had its own carpenters and iron-mongers, as well as a flourmill, sawmill and hut for treating injuries and illness. Over 300 exhausted, often sick slaves tended the sugar, the cows and the cocoa, all of them crammed into poky hovels near the main house. Almost as soon as Joseph turned his hand to management, the plantation's fortunes began to decline. 'He means well,' his brother said of him, 'but he must be pushed.'[3]

Yeyette, the future Empress of France, had, as she herself claimed, a 'spoilt childhood'.[4] Her parents, grandparents and unmarried aunt let her do as she pleased. Her home was a large plantation house, a single-storey, white wooden dwelling with large windows open to the air. Like all plantation houses, it was in the centre of the grounds to allow the owner to see the labour of his slaves. There were over 400 plantations on the island and La Pagerie was comparatively small and humble, but it was pretty to look at – for the white inhabitants, at least. Nestled around three sides was a sheltered veranda decked with blossoms. Around it were outbuildings, including the stone building that housed the kitchen, and a pretty garden, overhung with tamarind, mango and frangipani trees, surrounded by a floral hedge. All that remains of the domestic buildings is the kitchen, for, as was customary, it was built of stone rather than wood. Although it is now part of the museum and without all the paraphernalia of saucepans and pots, its sheer size indicates how much food even a small family and their attendants would require.

Yeyette grew into a pretty, happy child with limpid amber eyes and a beautiful complexion. Like all plantation children, she had a black wet nurse (a custom that shocked the French). The little girl spent her days with her nurse, Marion, and her maids, Geneviève and Mauricette, who devoted themselves to her care. Anxious to preserve their position as house servants, they obeyed Yeyette's every whim and treated her like a princess.

'I ran, I jumped, I danced, from morning to night; no one restrained the wild movements of my childhood,' Yeyette rhapsodised.[5] Her sister, Catherine, arrived on 11 December 1764, and the two were playmates, hiding behind bushes and making toys out of sticks. Few other inhabitants on the plantation were so free. Sugar was an exacting master – as soon as one crop was harvested, it was ready to be planted again. The underfed slaves worked from six in the morning until seven at night throughout the year, digging, planting, reaping, and then beginning once more. Gangs of them toiled under the broiling sun, moaning as they were whipped by the lash. As soon as the cane was harvested, the slaves worked urgently for up to eighteen hours a day to extract the juice. In the sugar mill, at the centre of the property, female slaves pushed the cane through rollers to crush it. Cutlasses were kept on hand, for the slaves frequently caught their arms in the machinery and the quickest way to free them was to cut off the arm. Elsewhere, in the *sucrerie* or *purgerie* (the sugar house), the slaves struggled in the terrible heat of the boiler room to press the juice into thick sugar syrup.

Martinique was the third stop on the fatal and repetitive voyages of the slave trade. African men and women were captured and sold on the Ivory Coast in exchange for gold, tobacco, guns, gunpowder or cloth, and were then crammed into ships bound for France. In France, the ships took on supplies required in the Caribbean and set off, full of slaves and books, gowns and furniture. When little Yeyette went to the port, she saw the slaves being taken off the ships and hauled to market, branded, shackled and then set to work. Emptied of their human cargo, the ships were loaded up with bundles and crates and sent back to France, where eager ladies awaited sugar for their tea and cocoa for their stores.

The children of slaves were the possession of the mother's owner, and slaves were not permitted belongings of their own, or even to pass down a family name. The punishments allowed in colonial French society were severe – ranging from brutal beatings to brandings to being burned alive. Slaves could be covered in honey and placed on anthills to be stung to death, shot (although owners thought this a waste of bullets), drowned or thrown into ovens. The average life expectancy of a slave was twenty-five.

Yeyette heard the slaves cry out as she skipped in the garden. When she and her family sat indoors, dining on fish, roast meats, pastries and sweet fruit, the red flames of the slaves' fires shimmered at the windows, and their songs rang through the night. The air of the plantation was always slightly sweet, and during syrup-making time it was thick with the smell of burned sugar. She played with the slave children of her own age, fond of one-legged Boyoco and Timideas, who was sickly. Yeyette's daily life was bound up with the slaves and she did not question it. Slaves, she thought, were the way of the world.

About forty slaves had the better luck to work directly for the family as maids, cooks, laundresses and manservants. For the families, they were both friend and foe, the serpents in the bosom they feared might turn to poison or the knife in a moment of rage – or, for the women, seduce their husbands. Female slaves were accepted as a sexual resource for the colonial men. Some of Yeyette's closest slaves were probably also her relations. Her devoted mulatto nurse, Marion, could have been the daughter of her grandfather or perhaps the overseer, and her delicate maid, Euphémie Lefèvre, who travelled with her to Paris and whom she supported for the rest of her life, was very likely the daughter of Joseph, her father. Euphémie was her day-to-day companion, her maid and her friend.

The slave owners lived in fear that their slaves would rise against them. They worried about the *marrons* or runaways, who hid out in the hills and plotted revenge, or they fretted about murder – indeed, Yeyette's mother would later prosecute one of her house slaves for attempting to poison her. The news of the abolitionist movement, gaining credibility in France, infuriated the *grands blancs*, who became increasingly defensive. Across the rest of the world, there was a growing sense that slavery was unfair and cruel. The British and French economies were reliant on the produce of the Caribbean islands, but Quakers and other religious groups had long been suggesting that the price was too high to pay. One later cartoon showed drops of sugar as slaves' tears in ladies' cups of tea. In 1771, John Somersett, a slave who had been brought to Britain by an American customs officer, escaped and was recaptured. After a highly publicised trial, it was declared illegal to hold and remove him against his will. In Britain (if not the wider British Empire) a man could not be a possession. The question of whether slavery should be abolished was swirling in settler society, even though they tried to ignore it.

Creoles, the name given to whites born in the Caribbean, had a reputation in France for being pleasure-loving, lazy, sensual, capricious – and possessed of arcane sexual skills. It was a reputation that an older Josephine assiduously cultivated, but it was true of her personality. While she was running wild in the grounds of La Pagerie, her future friends in France were ruled by strict discipline in chilly houses, told to sit up straight, dressed in stiff frills for visits by adults, and kept to a rigid timetable of lessons and plain food.

Rose-Claire had little time for educating Yeyette and Catherine. They lived in a paradise of pleasure and their lives were unintellectual, ill-disciplined and free. Yeyette ran about with Euphémie and Marion, wearing the loose cotton dresses that were customary for colonial children, and discovering lizards and butterflies, picking flowers and the fruit that hung heavy on the trees. As she grew older, she rode around on her Spanish pony, took long walks to the hills and splashed in the sea like a dolphin. She sucked on sugar cane plucked from the fields, and drank the syrup so enthusiastically that she gave herself a cavity in her front incisor. In adulthood, her teeth gave her pain and to hide them she smiled with her lips pressed close, looking enigmatic and mysterious to those who did not know the truth.

She adored her home, but her father was less content. After living off his father for years, he had expected to be cosseted by his wife's family. To his horror, he found that Rose-Claire and her parents wished him to be the head of the family, stewarding La Pagerie through crises and devoting himself to its care. He was both incompetent and unlucky at business, with no aptitude for the dreary tasks of supervising the overseer, checking the books and keeping careful accounts of what was bought and sold, along with an inability to befriend fellow traders. His health was poor, he hated the heat, suffered frequent bouts of malaria and resented his wife for not having a son. Marooned owing to bad roads, La Pagerie received few visitors outside of feast days, and Joseph became consumed by nostalgia for the balls and soirées of Versailles. Soon he was hardly ever at home and instead threw himself into gambling at cards and nights with mistresses in the capital. 'He spends his time in his charming Fort Royal where he finds more pleasure than he does with me and his children,' Rose-Claire wrote to Edmée, her husband's sister.[6] She was pregnant again and yearning for a boy. 'I hope with all my heart that it will be the little nephew you desire; perhaps that will give his father a little more love for me,' she said.

On 13 August 1766, it was hurricane season and lowering dark clouds obscured the horizon. Soon rain was battering the trees and winds of up to 100 miles an hour were slashing the island. In the middle of the night, three-year-old Yeyette was woken and seized from her bed by Marion. Joseph, Rose-Claire, baby Catherine and a few domestic slaves hurried to shelter in the first floor of the sugar house. There Yeyette and her family crouched, hands over their ears, trying to block out the screams of their slaves as their dwellings were torn in two by the rapacious winds.

For two days, Martinique was battered by the storm. When the winds abated and the family emerged, they saw nothing but devastation. They had lost everything. The dead bodies of slaves lay strewn across the ground and their homes had been entirely destroyed. The trees were flattened, the crops wrecked and most of the animals killed. Their grand plantation house was reduced to scraps of wood. The only remnants of their grandeur were the stone outbuilding used as the kitchen and the sugar house, where they had so wisely sheltered.

The destruction was terrible – 440 people dead, hundreds more injured, and close to fifty ships wrecked off the coast. The island's crops of sugar, coffee and cocoa had been wiped out and whole villages wrecked. People had lost their lives, their homes and their ambitions for the future. In nearby Trinité, the wind tore a church from its foundations, threw it into the air and smashed it to the ground. During the storm, houses, trees and cattle soared up towards the clouds, only to fall crashing into the wet soil or the raging sea. One family found themselves using the door of their house as a raft, holding on until they could be rescued.

Joseph gazed at his home in despair. He could not contemplate the work that had to be done. The family adopted the upper floor of the sugar house as their living quarters, and built a veranda over the south side. It was meant to be their residence for six months or so. A few weeks later, Rose-Claire went into labour and they all prayed for a son. The child was Marie-Françoise or 'Manette'. Once more, Joseph had been saddled with another useless mouth. He railed at the poor hand life had dealt him.

The defeat of the island broke the heart of Rose-Claire's father, and he died six months later. The family had expected great wealth in his will, but there were only debts and Joseph did not have the gumption to investigate any possible mistakes in the accounts. The young husband now had a family of dependent women – a mother-in-law, sister-in-law, wife and three daughters. Fortunately, he had an efficient overseer in Monsieur Blanque, who ensured that the slave quarters were rebuilt and the sugar-processing buildings restored. But even though all the crops were replanted, the estate dwindled and Joseph spent more time than ever gambling and squiring mistresses in Fort Royal. Soon there were only 150 slaves and sugar production was less than half what it had been. Angry, frustrated and left alone for long periods, Rose-Claire watched her childhood home collapse into ruins.

Joseph never had the money or the energy to rebuild their wooden house, and so the upper floor of the *purgerie* became their permanent home. No genteel family would ever live over the workrooms, and Yeyette's reputation among her friends fell sharply with her father's failure to build a proper home.

With the hurricane, the death of grandfather Sannois, and the birth of a third daughter, the family's situation was dire. Oblivious, Yeyette continued skipping through the sugar canes, playing with her nurse under the breadfruit trees and riding her pony.

From the age of six the daughters of the great plantation families were sent to France to be educated. Their families wished them to acquire polish and escape the merciless tropical diseases that killed so many children before the age of twelve. In Paris, Joseph's sister Edmée was eager to take Yeyette, but her father declared he could not afford to send her. She dodged disease. At the age of seven, she caught a severe bout of smallpox but recovered and was left unmarked.

In the same year on the other side of the world, the Dauphin, Louis-Auguste, was married to the fourteen-year-old Maria Antonia of Austria. She was met by officials on an island in the Rhine, stripped of her fine Austrian wedding clothes, re-dressed in French gowns, and sent to Versailles. 'Meeting with Madame la Dauphine,' Louis wrote in his hunting journal of their first encounter at the Chateau de Compiègne. Two thousand people died in the fashionable avenue of the Champs-Élysées after a crush at a fete to celebrate their marriage.

The young Princess was flung into a world of pomp, etiquette, formality and treacherous courtiers. 'Everything depends on the wife,' her mother, Maria Teresa, had told her, 'if she is willing, sweet and *amusante.*' Four years later, Louis XV died of smallpox, tears rolling down his cheeks after sending away his favourite mistress, Madame du Barry. Then the palace resounded with a thunderous rushing noise as hundreds of courtiers left the King to hurry to the presence of Louis-Auguste and Marie Antoinette, now King Louis XVI and the Queen of France.

Marie Antoinette, barely seven years older than Yeyette, became the primped young queen of Versailles, surrounded by dozens of servants and her favourites, the dizzy, soft-hearted Princesse de Lamballe and the sensual Comtesse de Polignac. Giggling at card parties, her tiny figure swamped by heavy brocades, hooped skirts and trains, she piled her hair three feet high and topped it with feathers, ribbons and diamonds. Her mother chastised her for 'following fashion to excess'.[7] But the Queen could not stop powdering her hair, decking herself with precious stones and covering her face with lead paint and rouge. She ordered four new pairs of shoes a week and three yards of ribbon every day so that her *peignoir*, or dressing gown, was always tied with fresh ribbon. A palace of exquisite, exotic desserts that no one ever ate, hairstyles that took days to perfect and courtiers bent obsessively on guessing the Queen's every whim, Versailles was a labyrinth, the jewel in the French crown – and much of the money to pay for it came from the sugar islands of the Caribbean.

France at the time was riven by inequality. Peasants and labourers worked with little respite and for a few coins. Life expectancy across the board was very low thanks to the appalling rate of child mortality, and the average age of death was around twenty-five – the same as the slaves in the Caribbean. At the top were the nobles living in grand style through the rents from land tilled by peasants and tenant farmers – and then, above the nobility, was Versailles, a great iced palace built from the toil of thousands of hands. The island of Martinique barely crossed the mind of Marie Antoinette, choosing shoes and demanding her maid adjust the position of her ribbons. But Martinique thought obsessively about her. Society gossip on the island was all about Versailles, the fashions of Paris and the favourites of the Queen.

Yeyette turned ten in 1773 and Rose-Claire decided to send her to boarding school in Fort Royal. After a long journey by canoe, she arrived at her new home, accompanied by Marion, her nurse. They took a carriage past brothels, slums and shebeens, and then to the grandeur of colonial buildings and the Governor's House. In the midst of it all was the Maison de la Providence, a convent school for young ladies, founded in 1763 in an attempt to instill proper morals in the lax girls of the island and prepare them to be 'wives, mothers and mistresses of plantations', who would embed proper Christian tenets in their husbands and children.

Yeyette awoke at five, dressed herself in the red and blue striped cotton uniform, and began two hours of supervised prayers. Then teachers from France, under the beady eye of the Mother Superior, instructed the girls in arithmetic, drawing, embroidery, penmanship and geography. Rose-Claire was still ambitious for her daughter and the girl was given extra lessons in dancing and painting. She had Wednesday and Saturday afternoons off for gossiping and giggling with the other *filles de la Providence*, and one day in town per month, when she usually visited her grandmother. The main purpose was that a young lady would befriend a circle of other girls and thus be introduced to their brothers or male relations – and find herself a plantation husband. Fortunately for Yeyette, the education was light, for she had little interest in applying herself. 'Her voice is sweet, she plucks prettily at the guitar, and, showing a general aptitude for music, she could with proper instruction perfect her singing, playing and dancing,' her father wrote – but her music remained a mere 'aptitude'.[8]

Yeyette left school at the age of fourteen, knowing little more than when she had arrived. She began to attend gatherings at other plantations or balls at the Governor's House in Fort Royal. Attended by their house slaves, young ladies gowned in white and finely-dressed gentlemen paraded on the lawn before entering the humid ballroom to dance to the music of the slave orchestra under bouquets of flaming tropical flowers. Yeyette was a popular girl to flirt with but not to marry, for, in the words of one man, she was 'fused with grace, more seductive than beautiful', entrancing and magnetic, but 'the family in real life lives in mediocrity'.[9] Many girls her age were already married, but, without property, she was not sought after. But Yeyette wished for more than marriage to a plantation son. Seduced by her father's nostalgic stories about Paris and Versailles, she had ambitions for more. She wanted to go to France.

Yeyette was fifteen when she and two friends decided to visit the local witch. Euphémie David lived in the hills near La Pagerie, mixing potions, telling stories and promising to cure all ills. She kept a healthy trade – in a world of disease and sudden violence, few could resist the pull of the occult. The old woman clutched the hand of each girl in turn. The first, she said, would marry a planter and live a contented life. The second, a distant cousin of Yeyette's, would live a scandalous life and be captured by pirates. Yeyette was destined to marry one man in France, but unhappily, and then wed a 'dark man of little fortune', who would 'cover the world with glory' and make her greater than a queen. Even so, she would die unhappy and often yearn for the ease of life on Martinique.[10] It seems too convenient to be plausible, but Josephine would later refer to it intently, and even brought it up in newspaper interviews long before she became Empress.[11] Most likely, the sorceress saw her yearning for adventure and guessed that she was destined for a new life in France – one that would not necessarily bring happiness.

France seemed like an impossible dream. But then Yeyette's aunt, Edmée, wrote to suggest that one of the La Pagerie girls be sent over to marry her lover's son, Alexandre. He was seventeen, born just over three years before Yeyette, handsome and eager for a Creole bride. As the eldest, Yeyette was the obvious choice.

The Tascher de La Pagerie family had a poor reputation, and Joseph's sister, Désirée (whom her family called Edmée), was a scandalous figure. In 1757, François de Beauharnais arrived on Martinique as the Governor. His wife, a wealthy Saint-Domingue heiress, took an immediate fancy to the nineteen-year-old Edmée, and moved her in as her companion. The forty-two-year-old Governor fell passionately in love with Edmée and made her his mistress. Ambitious and amoral where her brother was quiescent and parasitic, she did as she liked. In order to hide their liaison, Beauharnais (who had declared himself a marquis), found her a husband, Alexis Renaudin, a handsome young King's Musketeer. He had been recently released from prison for the attempted poisoning of his wealthy plantation father, but Beauharnais was impatient and the marriage was arranged in 1758.

The Governor was so obsessed with arranging the wedding of his lover that he ignored the plight of the nearby island of Guadeloupe. The British attacked and Beauharnais delayed for three months before responding to the requests of the lieutenant-in-command for assistance.

He was lazy, too cautious and preoccupied with enjoying Edmée after her wedding to Renaudin (for he could take her freely, since if she fell pregnant the child would be seen as her husband's). By the time his fleet reached Guadeloupe, the British had won. For such appalling dereliction of duty, he was called back to France. He refused to leave immediately and instead whiled away his last months on the island fondling Edmée. Realising that he was a cuckold, Renaudin angrily abandoned her and hurried to France to arrange a legal separation. She followed after him in an attempt to seize a financial settlement, having ensured that her brother's marriage to Rose-Claire was arranged before she left. Beauharnais and his wife followed soon after, leaving their three-month-old son Alexandre with Edmée's mother.

In France, the discarded Madame de Beauharnais retired to a country estate. The Marquis wangled a generous pension from the King and set up home in Paris with Edmée, who was now separated from her husband. The two women wrote to each other affectionately until Madame de Beauharnais died. When Alexandre was five, he was sent to Paris to live with his father and Edmée, and he became as fond of her, he said, as if she was his own mother. Parisian society despaired – adultery was all very well, but it was immoral to live together. Still, the Marquis adored his much younger lover and his wealth protected them from cruel comments, in public at least.

When Edmée was thirty-eight, after nearly twenty years with her lover, she began to think about securing her future. The Marquis was a sickly sixty-two and she would be left virtually penniless on his death, as his estate and that of his wife would go to Alexandre. She wanted to keep this money for herself and suggested Alexandre marry her niece, in the hope that the couple would care for her after her husband's death. Alexandre agreed, for he needed to marry in order to come into his inheritance. Creole girls were in demand as brides for aristocratic families in search of cash, and they had a reputation for beauty and sensuality. Alexandre had only one proviso: he wished his wife to be very young.

The Marquis wrote to Joseph de La Pagerie telling him that Alexandre did not want Yeyette, since, 'my son, who is only seventeen and a half finds that a young lady of fifteen is too close in age to his own.'[12] He asked for Catherine, but she had recently died from a strain of yellow fever. Instead, Joseph offered Manette, eleven and a half, a girl equipped, he cheerfully wrote, with health, gaiety and 'a figure that will soon be interesting'.[13]

The family fell into uproar. Manette was hysterical at the thought of leaving her home, and her mother felt she could not permit her to marry so young. Yeyette was tearful and furious. She had dreamed of Paris for as long as she could remember – and now Manette was taking her place. She begged her father to take her instead. Otherwise, she had nothing to anticipate but a dreary future as a planter's wife. Yeyette, normally so pliable and indolent, was passionately set on travelling to France. Her father relented.

'The oldest girl, who has often asked me to take her to France, will I fear be somewhat affected by the preference which I appear to give to her younger sister,' he wrote. He continued that Yeyette had 'very fine skin, lovely eyes, good arms, and a surprising gift for music. She longs to see Paris and has a very sweet disposition. If it were left to me, I would bring the two daughters instead of one, but how can one part a mother from both her remaining daughters when death has just deprived her of a third?'[14]

Back in Paris, Edmée was growing desperate. She wanted the marriage agreed at once, before Alexandre's guardians dissuaded him. 'We must have one of your children,' she wrote. 'Come with one of your daughters or with both of them, but hurry.'[15] The Marquis sent a letter authorising the publication of the marriage banns on Martinique. Alexandre's name had been added, but the space for the bride's name was blank. By the time the letter arrived, Joseph's decision had been made for him. Poor Manette had so exhausted herself from crying that she fell ill with a fever and her mother refused to let her go. When Alexandre heard the news he was not ecstatic. 'Surely it is not your intention to have me marry this young lady if she and I should feel mutual dislike for each other?' he wrote to his father. Still, he was obedient. 'I feel sure after the description that has been given that she will charm me.'[16]

Yeyette was to be married. But, having won his battle, her torpid father dragged his feet. It was not until six months later that the priest stood in the church of Notre-Dame de la Martinique and announced the forthcoming marriage between Alexandre-François, Chevalier de Beauharnais, and Marie-Josèphe-Rose de Tascher de La Pagerie. Then Joseph again delayed over the journey. For years, he had said he longed to return to France – and now he did not wish to go.

He ignored his sister's pleas for urgency. He was ill, the journey was expensive – and travel was growing more dangerous by the day. After the uneasy truce shortly before Yeyette's birth, hostilities between Britain and France had begun again, and Martinique was under siege. Moreover, the hurricane season was approaching, making it unsafe to travel by sea.

Aunt Edmée pushed and demanded until finally, accompanied by her father, her aunt Rosette and her maid Euphémie, Yeyette embarked for France in September 1779. But Joseph forgot to tell his sister that they were leaving. Yeyette was sixteen, barely educated, pretty and thoughtless. Her every thought was directed towards her forthcoming marriage.

2

Sophistication

*a*lexandre de Beauharnais was slender, strong jawed and handsome. As languidly aggressive as a character in the forthcoming
novel *Les Liaisons Dangereuses*, he was already an arch seducer
by the age of seventeen. He felt the world was his for the taking. In
August 1779, just before Yeyette departed from Martinique, he wrote
to his stepmother that he was 'going into the country' with a 'wife of
a sub-lieutenant in the navy, a charming woman'. He was not planning on conversation. 'I count on spending two days there, and in
that short space of time I shall do everything possible to succeed.'

He won his prize. His new mistress, Marie Françoise-Laure de
Girardin de Montgérald, Madame de Longpré, was from a Martinique
family, twenty-nine and the mother of a child. Stylish and tempera-
mental, she had captivated her youthful lover. 'Yes indeed, the chevalier
has tasted happiness. He is loved by a charming woman who is the
object of all the aspirations of the garrison of Brest and the district.'[1]
He expected Edmée to congratulate him. Entranced by Laure's conversation, enthralled by her sexual experience, he barely gave a thought
to the girl who was travelling to see him. To Alexandre, love meant
sex and conquest, and life was about enjoying himself.

A spoiled, much beloved child, Alexandre had been raised by his
father and Edmée to believe he was destined for greatness. Until the
age of five, he had lived on Martinique, and then was sent to his
indulgent father and his mistress in France. In 1775, after taking him
and his elder brother François to Germany, his tutor, Patricol, was

offered a position in the household of the two nephews of the Duc de La Rochefoucauld. A leading figure of the Enlightenment, the Duc was friends with Voltaire and Lafayette and a fervent abolitionist. Alexandre grew up in the Duc's Parisian palace and his country chateau, listening to debates about freedom, and learning to hide his desires beneath a patina of elegant diffidence. 'What astonishes me most in him, and greatly displeases me, is the extreme care that he takes to hide, and the ease with which he disguises, the feelings of his heart,' rued Patricol.[2] A modern teacher might say Alexandre was deceptive and shallow.

At sixteen, Alexandre achieved a commission in the Sarre Infantry Regiment, which was commanded by the Duc. His passion for women hit new heights. They were to him 'trophies of war'.[3] He wrote lists of all the women he had ensnared, comparing their various features and titles. Stationed with the unit, he seduced ladies of the town and regimental wives – always eagerly acquainting his stepmother Edmée with his every success. By the age of seventeen, having long lost his innocence, he preferred older, married women, since they were more nonchalant and skilled at verbal sparring. Laure – bored, sensual, teasing and glamorous – was perfect.

While Yeyette travelled to France, Laure gave Alexandre a piece of news. She was pregnant with his child.

Yeyette expected her journey to be terrifying. Only a year before, her cousin Aimée had disappeared on the high seas, and her party believed she had been kidnapped by pirates. Yeyette and her party took places on a naval store ship, *Île de France*, heading to the mainland in a convoy led by the *Pomone*. The weather was rough, and the storms were so bad that the passengers believed they would die. Joseph and his daughter were hopelessly seasick and terrified of battle at sea, for they were repeatedly harassed by British ships.

In spite of sickness and the British, Yeyette arrived at the large naval port of Brest, on the west coast of France, on 12 October 1779. Overwhelmed by the bustle, the cold and the dreary autumnal skies, the family retrieved what remained of their baggage and took lodgings in town. The French sophistication she had dreamed of was nowhere to be found. Brest was one of the two major naval bases, a practical town of bars, brothels and supply shops Worse still, her father was ill and exhausted. He had forgotten to write to his sister before departing to say they were coming. Then he waited a week to write to her to say that they had arrived and did not send the letter until 20 October.

Edmée had expected much more warning and had to rush to depart, seizing Alexandre and hurrying him to Brest. The young soldier was furious about the lack of notice. From the start, he was ill-disposed and ready to find fault with the Creole girl he thought too old to be properly biddable.

Still sick and suffering from the journey, Yeyette readied herself to meet her fiancé. Euphémie dressed her mistress's hair and she pinched her cheeks for colour. Yeyette thought she looked enchanting, and remembered how men had admired her at the Governor's balls. As soon as she saw Alexandre she was delighted. Nineteen and very hand-some, he was superb in his uniform of white with silver buttons and facings. Unlike her shabby father, he was precise in his appearance, with hair perfectly powdered and drawn back at the nape of his neck. She admired his piercing blue eyes and prominent nose. Everything about him corresponded with the strictures of male beauty at the time – except for the fact he was of rather less than average height.

Yeyette held out her hand, bright with excitement. Alexandre looked at her in shock. He was obsessed by appearances and already a little jaded by too much experience with women, and Mademoiselle de La Pagerie was not what he had expected at all. He had anticipated a dusky beauty, all languorous grace and a sensual smile, as well as French sophistication. He saw a plump girl with a thick Creole accent and a clumsy manner. Yeyette barely understood fashion and she was ill at ease with the heavy brocade gowns and high hairstyles she was expected to wear. She looked like a child in her mother's clothes.

Alexandre could barely smile. It was even worse when Yeyette spoke. Lightly educated, lacking in sophistication and without style, the girl who had run wild in the baking sun belonged in the schoolroom, not at a soirée. She was a poor comparison to his glamorous mistress, Laure – Yeyette had neither beauty nor accomplishments and her deportment was terrible.

The young soldier was used to seeing women practically swooning at his smile, so Yeyette's fascination with him had no novelty. It was obvious that the girl was eager to please, and that she was a virgin. But he had little desire to take her to his bed. Still, he respected his stepmother, Edmée, and there was no turning back. Over the following days together he tried hard to love Yeyette. Certainly, she was so in love with him that she seemed as though she would be docile. Perhaps, he thought, some schooling in manners from Edmée, and time spent with a dressmaker, might shroud her rougher edges. 'Mademoiselle de La Pagerie may perhaps appear to you less pretty than you had expected,' he wrote to his father, 'but I think I may assure you that her amiability and the sweetness of her nature will surpass even what you have been told.'[4] He thought Yeyette was a ridiculous name. She must henceforth be Marie-Josèphe-Rose, the woman whom Napoleon would call Josephine.

Josephine was too blinded by infatuation to understand that her fiancé was immune to her charms. Edmée took whirlwind charge. She told her niece that all was proceeding marvellously, and then took her brother to visit a notary in Brest. She encouraged him to sign a document agreeing to the marriage and ceding all control to her. Ill and lazy, he agreed, even though his sister now had the right to decide the dowry and could mortgage all the La Pagerie property in order to fulfil it.

On 2 November, the party set off for the 300-mile journey to Paris. Josephine was in love. She had, Edmée wrote to the Marquis, 'all the feelings that you could wish her to have toward your son, and I have observed with the greatest satisfaction that she suits him'.[5] The young bride-to-be gazed from the carriage window at countryside that was so unlike Martinique, and imagined her life with her new husband.

As they travelled, the route began to fill up. Carriages of fine ladies, soldiers on horseback, farmers driving their livestock and labourers looking for work all crammed onto the bumpy road towards the great, gated city. An unthinkably huge, bustling place of 600,000 souls, a place of incredible luxury and awful poverty in one, Paris was an eye-opener for anyone, let alone a plantation girl from far-off Martinique.[6]

Finally, Josephine arrived at the city she had dreamed of with such fervour. Elegant houses bordered the streets, servants trotted along with messages, ladies descended from carriages to enter the shops or the homes of their friends. The smell of the streets was so intense that many visitors fainted on their first visit. Hardened by her awful sea journey, Josephine stared through the window, gathering in every sight until they arrived at the rue Thévenot, her marital home.

It was a thin, two-storey house near modern-day Les Halles. Once fashionable, the area was now rather down-at-heel. Formerly the home of the Marquis's grandmother, the house had fallen into disrepair and it had not been renovated for the young couple because no one realised they were coming. Still, it was grand and imposing, with reception rooms hung with heavy chandeliers and tapestries. It all seemed a long way from her rooms in the sugar house at La Pagerie.

The Marquis and Edmée had quit their stylish apartment in the rue Garancière to live with the newly-weds. They all crowded into the narrow, gloomy house. Josephine missed the beautiful scenery of Martinique all the more – when she opened the window, she could smell the pungent stench of the tanneries. On nearby streets, butchers set up open stalls and threw their waste meat into the middle of the road.

Edmée was determined not to lose any time. She put out orders for the wedding trousseau, arranged for the banns to be read in three different churches, and on 10 December, the marriage contract was signed. In the house on the rue Thévenot, Joseph agreed to give his daughter the incredible dowry of 120,000 livres, a sum chosen by his sister. The bride offered presents and furniture given to her by friends and relations on Martinique – generously valued at 15,000 livres. Edmée donated a summer house at Noisy-le-Grand and all its furnishings, as well as a sum of money due to her from the will of a relative. Alexandre brought an annual sum of 40,000 livres, from the family estates in France and Saint-Domingue.

With such money, the young couple would be so rich that no one could snub Josephine for her countrified ways. But their wealth existed only on paper. There was no arrangement to bring the furniture from Martinique, and Edmée had a life interest in her gifts to Josephine, so she would not be able to use them until her aunt died. Edmée had assessed Joseph's contribution on the basis of the value of the properties in the Caribbean, but the sum was impossible. He could hardly afford his expenses in Paris, and he was supposed to give the couple 6000 a year as interest on their dowry. In reality, the newly-weds would be living off Alexandre's money and borrowed cash.

On 13 December 1779, Josephine was married. The chill, dark church at Noisy-le-Grand was filled with Alexandre's friends and relations, and dominated by her new father-in-law, the Marquis. She was virtually alone. Her father was too ill to attend and she was given away by a distant cousin. Euphémie, her maid and probably her half-sister, was the only person she knew well. Her position of dependence and inferiority could hardly have been clearer. On the register, her wobbly and childlike 'M.J.R. Tascher de La Pagerie' now appears poignant, the sole feminine signature among fourteen names.[7] Alexandre had conferred on himself the title of Vicomte, even though he was not yet entitled to it. Josephine was now the Vicomtesse de Beauharnais. That night, Alexandre took her to his bed, and forced himself to do his duty. After their first night together, Josephine only adored her husband more intensely.

'The union is your doing, their happiness must be your work also,' the bride's mother wrote to Edmée.[8] It was an optimistic view of Madame Renaudin's powers. La Pagerie had been poor preparation for the cruelty of Josephine's new world. Parisian ladies discussed the philosophy of Montesquieu or the labyrinthine politics at court. Josephine – who had never seen an opera, knew nothing of poetry, and could not comment on art – was out of her depth. At dances, she was shy and lumpen and people laughed at her behind their hands.

She refused to give in to sadness. Full of the *joie de vivre* of youth, she reminded herself that she was married to a handsome man her school-friends would envy. She was anxious to see fashionable society and be a good wife to her husband. Every day she waited excitedly for her invitation to court, since it was customary for aristocratic brides to be introduced to the Queen. She longed to see the Versailles her father had extolled. The decision eventually came: because the Marquis had created a newfangled title, and the family had been fined before for claiming false titles, the couple would have no place at Versailles. Alexandre was furious at the insult and great with resentment at the King and Queen.

He despaired of his wife's coarse manners, but her intense need for him and her fervent adoration suited his egotistic soul. It also made him complacent and convinced he could treat her as he chose. Mortified by her provincial behaviour, he left her at home when he visited his friends and relations for dinners and soirées. He found her childish, too dependent and her incessant questions annoyed him. He did not like her maid, Euphémie, and thought her too unsophisticated (perhaps he also thought the family resemblance too obvious). Josephine's lustrous chestnut hair, pretty eyes and gentle heart had no effect on him. He called her an 'object who has nothing to say to me', and quickly returned to his regiment.[9] 'Instead of spending my time at home with a creature with whom I can find nothing in common,' Alexandre wrote to Patricol, his former tutor, 'I have to a great extent resumed my bachelor life.' Laure de Longpré was by then heavily pregnant with his child, and he had fallen in love with her. 'I have until now attached myself only to persons incapable of inspiring a violent passion,' he wrote of his conquests before Laure. 'I have never experienced true love.'[10]

With her husband away, the young Vicomtesse de Beauharnais was lonely, unoccupied and perpetually cold. The chilly, airless rooms at rue Thévenot were impossible to heat. Her father remained unwell, and she was still a little afraid of her aunt. She wrote to her husband rebuking him for not writing. He replied accusing her of trying to 'poison the pleasure which I take in reading what you write by reproaches which my heart does not deserve'.[11] She begged him for attention, railed at her unhappiness, and upbraided him for leaving her alone. He responded with anger. 'She has become jealous,' he fumed, 'and wants to know what I am doing.'[12]

Fatigued by her begging and unhappiness, Alexandre decided to embark on a project of reforming his wife. In public, Josephine was socially embarrassing and her slight education had not given her the resources to amuse herself while alone. She needed to acquire the semblance of an accomplished and educated mind, and interests that might distract her from her complaining. He had a plan to 'recommence your education and repair by my zeal, the first fifteen years of your life which has been so tragically neglected'.[13] Under the supervision of aunt Edmée, the Vicomtesse would be put to work studying history and geography, learning by rote the works of the great poets, and reading the theory of drama. Alexandre also wished to correct her poor posture and hired a dancing master in an attempt to instill his wife with the poise and grace required of a Parisienne.

Josephine promised to work hard and Alexandre rewarded her with rapturous praise. 'I am delighted at the desire to improve yourself which you have demonstrated to me,' he puffed. 'You will acquire knowledge that will raise you above others, and combining wisdom with modesty, will make you an accomplished woman.'[14] He was too hopeful.

Josephine had taste and sensitivity but her mind was too ill-disciplined to absorb her studies without a great effort of will, and this she was too lazy to attempt. She had a kind heart and a generous manner, but these counted for little in a time when accomplishments and elegance were the definition of female excellence. In her husband's eyes, she corresponded to the most unfortunate Parisian prejudices about ignorant Creoles.[15] His wife was hopeless at everything – and worse still, without money.

Josephine learned little poetry and her dancing did not improve. Exasperated, Alexandre became even more intensely attached to Laure de Longpré. Any thought of separation from Laure induced in him 'the deepest despair'.[16] In the spring, she gave birth to their son, and her triumph over his heart was complete.

But Josephine had a card up her sleeve. By early 1781, after a successful winter visit from her husband, she was quite sure she was pregnant. Alexandre was pleased by the news and he made plans to leave his regiment for the birth. But he was soon disenchanted with her once more, exasperated by her disgraceful reluctance to improve herself. 'If my wife really loved me, she would make the effort . . . to acquire the qualities which I admire and which would bind me to her,' he fumed to Patricol.[17]

After little more than a year of marriage, Alexandre and Josephine were on the brink of separation. Patricol applied himself to reuniting them and wrote to Edmée encouraging her to tell her niece to restrain her jealous demands: 'brusqueness and bossiness are two of the worst ways to attract to her a husband'. It was wise advice, but Josephine could not control her emotions. Pregnant, lonely and afraid, she became despondent and needy.

On 3 September 1781, eighteen-year-old Josephine gave birth to a boy, baptised Eugène Rose. Alexandre was thrilled by his legitimate son. But within a month, he lost patience with his wife again and was affronted by the appointment of Euphémie as his child's nurse. Edmée decided to send him away on an Italian tour in the hope that his travels might mature him, and time away from Laure de Longpré might encourage him to appreciate his wife. Josephine was left alone once more. She was struggling to manage on the money her aunt and father-in-law chose to give her. She began to run up debts, using the goods and money in her marriage contract as security.

Alexandre returned in the summer of 1782 to find that his father-in-law, Joseph, stepmother and aunt had travelled to Martinique. The little family then took a lease on their own house, on the rue Neuve Saint-Charles. Alexandre was delighted with their new home, and pleased by Eugène, now a bonny toddler. He felt more kindly towards Josephine and she quickly fell pregnant again.

Alexandre decided his wife was a little improved from her first days as his fiancée. He had developed a passion for intellectual freedom and debating a future France, one with a constitution and a political government. He took her to the salons of Paris, the ideas factories of the pre-Revolution era. Choderlos de Laclos's novel *Les Liaisons Dangereuses* had erupted into social life – and everyone discussed its political inferences. Even Marie Antoinette read it in secret. In the exciting furnace of new ideas, women were prominent, celebrated and powerful. Josephine listened and participated, but could not help feeling jealous as she watched her husband flirt with everyone but her.

After a few weeks with his wife, Alexandre yearned to be with Laure again. He crept away from Paris in the middle of the night, writing to Josephine on the journey to ask for her pardon for 'having left you without farewell, for having gone away without warning, for having fled without having told you again, a last time, that I am all yours'.[18] At Brest, he found no letter waiting for him. 'Love for my wife and the love of glory both hold the absolute sway in my heart,' he lied crossly. 'If I yield to the latter it is for your future good and for that of your children.'[19] It was, of course, not at all a quest for soldierly distinction – he was going to spend time with Laure. He informed her that Laure de Longpré's father had died on Martinique and Laure would be accompanying him on the ship.

'Kiss little Eugène with all your heart and guard his little brother,' Alexandre wrote as he waited to depart, certain that the child in her womb was a son.[20] He was less pleased with Josephine's failure to write to him. 'This neglect is inconceivable,' he seethed. 'If, as I begin to fear, our marriage turns out decidedly badly, you will only have yourself to blame.'[21] Used to nurturing older women, who cooed over his cares, he felt aggrieved and deserted. Friendless, worrying about money, pregnant and the mother of a young child, Josephine could not provide the support he needed. He scribbled melodramas onto the paper. 'Amidst the risks of war and of the seas, where I go to seek death, I shall without sorrow and without regret see a life taken from me whose moments will have only been reckoned in misfortunes.'[22] His was the classic strategy of attacking the spouse as a way of blotting out his own guilt.

At the end of December, Alexandre finally set sail and divided his time between upbraiding Josephine and playing lotto with Laure. 'I was often bored by the game but amply recompensed by the pleasure which I derived from the journey,' he wrote to his wife, enjoying rubbing salt in the wound.[23]

Alexandre arrived on Martinique in January 1783 and was appalled. He had not seen the island since he was five and had cherished dreams of orderly tropical beauty. Instead he found chaos and impropriety. 'The morals, the multitude of people of colour, in their indecent costumes, their manner of living, their dwellings, the appearance of libertinage, all this has amazed me.'[24] He was deeply disappointed by La Pagerie. Instead of a fine house surrounded by a bustling plantation, he found his in-laws huddled in the sugar house, struggling to control malcontent slaves. Manette, the girl he had first desired, was now fourteen, and very ill.

Peace negotiations had begun in London the week before his arrival, and Alexandre found there was little glory to be had on Martinique. Initially, he tried to be a good son-in-law, talking of a marriage between Manette and one of his fellow officers. 'Your mother loves and always misses you,' he reported to his wife.[25] But he soon lost interest, and after only two days at La Pagerie he returned to Fort Royal and threw himself into the social life of the island, accompanied by Laure de Longpré. In the daytime, tired and a little sick from wine, he dwelled on his annoyances with his wife. Hurt and angry at his slights and his continuing affair with Laure, Josephine had stopped writing. Alexandre was predictably aggressive.

'Finally I have proof of your inconstancy! With my own eyes, I have seen the proof! Yes, with my own eyes, I have seen that you have written to your parents, and me, I alone have been forgotten,' he scrawled. 'Should you want information about me, my father will always know my news and through him, if you are curious you can find out what country I am living in . . . I am abandoned!'[26]

At eight months pregnant, his wife was unlikely to be enjoying affairs, but still he worked himself into paroxysms of jealousy. 'You know my character, boiling, torrid, my desires are as a lively as are my sentiments and passions.'[27] On 10 April 1783, Josephine gave birth to a little girl, Hortense-Eugénie. Struggling for money and already receiving demands for her debts, she sold jewellery to pay for the baptism. She sent word of the birth to her parents, but not to her husband.

Laure de Longpré heard the news and worked her snakelike charms. She suggested that because the baby had arrived two weeks early, she was not his child. Alexandre drove himself into a frenzy of hatred. Drumming his heels on Martinique, dissatisfied and ill at ease, he decided his wife was as licentious as her father. It was immediately clear to him: he was married to a whore.

Alexandre went on the hunt for evidence. He questioned Josephine's friends and family and tried to bribe and blackmail the slaves on the plantation to tell stories against her. 'Such totally base conduct and vile methods, how can this be the behaviour of a man of culture and good birth?' Rose-Claire wrote in despair to the Marquis. 'I would never have thought that he would have let himself be led around so, by Mme de Longpré. She has turned his head completely.'[28] He even threatened to kill Brigitte, one of the family's most trusted house slaves, if she did not give him the information he wanted. 'M. le Vicomte used all his means to extract something unfavourable about the conduct of my mistress,' Brigitte recorded.[29] In Alexandre's mind, his wife was shockingly wicked. Scratching his wound over and over, he demanded corroboration of his wild fantasies.

Josephine, far away in France, heard nothing of Alexandre's activities. She continued unaware, wrapped up in her new baby, hoping that her husband would grow tired of Laure. After a few months in the lush lands of her beloved Martinique, he might return contented.

3

'Beneath all the sluts in the world'

On a fine August day in 1783, twenty-year-old Josephine was sitting with her son and daughter in the drawing room of the summer house at Noisy-le-Grand. She was told that a visitor had arrived to see her. Into the room swept Laure de Longpré, returned from Martinique – sophisticated, glamorous and ten years her senior, she was sleek with pleasure in triumph. She handed Josephine a letter from Alexandre. Nothing could have prepared her for its contents.

Josephine read and learned that her husband had been gathering evidence against her, and he was quite sure of her depravity. 'In spite of the despair in my soul and the fury which overwhelms me, I will contain myself,' Alexandre wrote. 'I will tell you coldly, that you are in my eyes the vilest of creatures and my period in this country has revealed to me your abominable behaviour.' The Creole heritage that had been such an attraction was now evidence of a propensity to vice that she had enthusiastically indulged. He told her he knew all about her affairs with other men. 'As to repentance, I do not even ask it of you, you are incapable of it,' he cried. 'A woman, on the eve of her departure, who can take a lover into her arms when she knew that she is affianced to another, has no conscience; she is beneath all the sluts in the world.' And he believed that she had continued her dreadful licentiousness in France. What, he wondered, 'shall I think of this last child, arriving eight months and a few days after my return from Italy?' He was, he puffed, 'forced to accept her, but I swear to all the heavens that she belongs to another; it is a stranger's blood that courses through her veins!' Alexandre was merciless. 'Never, never shall I put myself in danger of being so abused again. Remove yourself to a convent as soon as you receive this letter.' He would not be moved. 'I will see you once and once only on my return to Paris, to discuss practicalities . . . but, I repeat, no scenes and no protestations.'[1]

Madame de Longpré glided away, smiling in victory. Josephine was sick with shock. Her husband hated her. She was about to lose everything: her husband, home and, since men took the custody of children, Hortense and Eugène as well. Edmée and the Marquis were horrified by the letter. Entirely dependent on Alexandre, since his inheritance paid for the house in which they lived, they promised her they would try to intervene. But the letters from his father and stepmother only angered him. When he arrived in France in September, he was incensed to hear that Josephine had not yet left their house. Writing from a property owned by Laure, he said that it would be quite impossible for them to live together because he would be forever 'tortured by the perpetual images of the wrongs of which you know I am aware'. She had two alternatives: go to a convent or return to the Caribbean. And he was not going to listen to his family: 'tell my father and your aunt that their efforts will be useless.'[2] He could not divorce her, but he would exile her, and then proceed to live as he pleased. At twenty, Josephine's future looked bleak.

'Come back to your little country,' begged her mother, 'our arms are always open to welcome you . . . and console you for the injustice you have suffered.'[3] But Josephine knew that if she left for La Pagerie, she would have to leave her children with Edmée. And she would be nothing on Martinique but a burdensome daughter on a struggling plantation, unable to marry again even if any man was to take an interest in her. At the end of November 1783, she took up residence in the Panthémont Convent in the rue de Grenelle in Saint-Germain. Eugène and Euphémie went with her. Hortense was left behind as she was too young to be separated from her wet nurse. In nearly four years of marriage, Alexandre had spent a mere ten months with his wife.

Josephine, with the assistance of her aunt Edmée, chose a particularly fashionable convent, dedicated to housing women of aristocratic background. Thomas Jefferson's two daughters were attending the attached convent school, after assurances that the girls would be exempt from religious instruction. Side by side with the nuns lived ladies of great hauteur, some staying temporarily within the walls because their fathers or husbands were away; others, like Josephine, had been abandoned. These lady boarders paid modest sums to rent anything from a small chamber to a grand, six-roomed apartment with its own kitchen. They could leave the convent, receive visitors and behave as they pleased.

In December, Josephine met the court adjudicator to discuss her marriage. She showed him Alexandre's enraged letters from Martinique and talked of his unfaithfulness. As she told him, even her father-in-law believed her the wronged party. 'It is not possible for the complainant to submit to such indignities,' the adjudicator ruled.[4] The provost of Paris ordered that she remain in the convent while the legal process of separation began and that Alexandre should pay maintenance for his children and various costs. Alexandre did not. Instead, he demanded that the lease on the house in Neuve Saint-Charles was sold, refused to pay her bills and asked for money from her – including the sum she received after selling her jewellery to pay for Hortense's baptism.

The Panthémont ladies were fashionable aristocrats, more used to the dressmaker and the salon than Bible reading. They amused themselves as they had done in the outside world, with dancing, couture and debate. Josephine, hitherto such a poor student, was finally willing to learn. Understanding that she had nothing but her charms to rely on, and by watching the women around her, she grasped the art of graceful movement and conversational allure. She softened her voice and lost her accent, practised the art of whispered suggestion and developed a husky, slow tone of voice that became one of her chief attractions. She learned to cover her mouth with her handkerchief when she laughed, to hide teeth ruined by too much sugar as a child. She lost weight and discovered how to enhance her rather clumsy figure with clinging dresses, shawls and perfect carriage.

Changes in fashion helped. Bored with the stiff gowns, Marie Antoinette's dressmaker, Madame Bertin, had encouraged the Queen to eschew the hoops and brocade on more formal occasions and assume a simpler look. The Queen had begun losing her hair after the birth of her eldest son in 1781, and a plainer coiffure, popularised by the painter Elisabeth Vigée Le Brun, became à la mode. The new draped gowns and softly curling natural coiffure suited Josephine's face and figure perfectly.

The Panthémont women passed on their secrets. Josephine learned to make the best of herself with creams, lotions, whitening potions for the face and hands and oils for the hair. She probably added dye to brighten the colour of her hair and smoothed lead-based white paint on her cheeks. Other women traced their veins with blue pencil to suggest the opacity of the skin, but Josephine's skin was a little too dusky for such pretences. She added a little shading with kohl and elderberries and even applied soot to her eyebrows and long lashes. And she learned the art of rouge.

In Britain and other parts of Europe, red face paint was frowned upon as the tool of courtesans, but no French lady of style saw herself as dressed without her rouge. By 1781, French women were using two million pots of rouge a year. Court ladies wore heavy swathes of it, leading down from the sides of their eyes to their lips, while gentry wives placed small spots of rouge in the middle of the cheek. Josephine was covering herself with toxins, for the best rouge was made from vermilion, ground from cinnabar (mercury sulphide) or creuse, produced by dousing lead plates in vinegar. Some died from smearing their faces with lead-based potions – the beautiful Maria Gunning had died in Britain at the age of twenty-seven from excessive use of make-up.

To a twenty-first-century observer, French eighteenth-century women would look strange, for there was little colour on the eyes (apart from maybe a spot of rouge, which cannot have been flattering) while the cheeks flamed with false-looking red. Rouge was battle paint – it recalled sexual flush and made women look more doll-like. Josephine's annual expenditure on rouge alone would soon amount to well over 3000 francs.[5]

At twenty-one, she was not a great beauty or even 'precisely pretty'.[6] She was about five foot – a respectable height for a woman – and slender, with slim hips but a slightly broad back. She had small, attractive feet, thanks to a childhood without shoes. The foot was an intensely erotic part of a woman's body, since it was so infrequently seen after skirt lengths dropped as soon as a girl was fifteen or so – a dainty ankle was often more likely to drive men wild than a generous bosom. The new style of flowing gown more easily revealed the foot and Josephine made sure to expose hers at every opportunity.

The Vicomtesse charmed with her beautiful, low voice and the easy, sensual grace she had learned so carefully at the convent. She had chestnut-brown, curling hair, delicate features and a small mouth. White paste concealed her dark complexion. Her most appealing features were her lashes, luxuriant and fluttering around her luminous eyes, glowing a little green, a little amber, and stopping men in their wake. Women pondered the nature of her attraction. Men saw it immediately. She made them think of the boudoir.

In early 1785, Alexandre seized Eugène from the convent. Josephine wrote to the provost of Paris to complain and the Vicomte and Vicomtesse were called to appear at the Châtelet. In March, the affair was settled. Josephine won. Under the terms of the separation, she would be allowed to live anywhere she chose and use any moneys of her dowry. Alexandre was to give her 5000 livres a year and 1000 a year for Hortense until the age of seven and 1500 after, and she would live with her mother until marriage. Eugène would be taken by his father after the age of five, but he would spend summers with his mother. Hot-headed Alexandre also had to eat humble pie. The authorities found no evidence for his accusations of immorality and forced him to sign a document withdrawing his accusations, and admit that 'he was wrong to write the said lady the letters of 12 July and 20 October of which she complains and which he admits were inspired by the passions and anger of youth.'[7] Josephine had been declared innocent. Yet it was a straw victory. She was in an impossible position, a woman without male support, unable to marry again.

She soon joined the Marquis and aunt Edmée at their new home in Fontainebleau. Then a rather countrified village, around thirty-five miles south-east of Paris and surrounded by lush forest, Fontainebleau was entirely dominated by the King's hunting seat of the same name, a huge and ornate palace greatly extended by Francis I and Henry II. The village was transformed during the hunting season as the court arrived and the aristocracy took houses. Josephine, her face whitened, her cheeks rouged, resplendent in a flowing gown and soft coiffure, could finally play the role of the Creole who was as sensual as Martinique itself. In just over a year, she had metamorphosed from a gauche schoolgirl into a sophisticated seductress — and she needed a man to seduce.

In Fontainebleau, Josephine had a small but pleasing social circle of minor aristocrats, rounds of card parties, promenades and sometimes even a ball. Eugène was sent to live with Alexandre. Josephine had expected to lose her son and was stoic about it, but Euphémie mourned him. His tutor sent a letter putatively from him to the woman who was most probably his aunt, saying 'there was no need for six pages to express to you my eternal gratitude for the care and kindness you have shown towards me.'[8]

Josephine's debt collectors had left her alone after the news of her marriage settlement, but in Fontainebleau they began to return. Alexandre did not pay her allowance. She begged her father for money, but he was barely able to pay any of the 6000 livres a year he had promised her on marriage. 'You know me well enough, my dear Papa,' she wrote to him, 'to be quite sure that if it were not for an urgent need for money, I would speak of nothing but my fondest sentiments for you.'[9] The Marquis de Beauharnais had installed him to administer his properties on Martinique, and Joseph was failing miserably at turning them to profit, or even keeping them running as they were. The Marquis sent letters instructing him and offering suggestions, but the revenue kept falling. And the Marquis himself was no longer as rich as he once was, as his pension from the government had been cut. There was little left for Josephine and her daughter.

The King liked to hunt three or four times a week, and, nobles from all over the country arrived in Fontainebleau to follow his procession. There were weeks of spectacles, games and dancing. Josephine wanted to find her way into the court. She immediately made sure to befriend François Hüe, chief clerk of the royal hunt, and was soon given the rare privilege of following the hunt, which had not been permitted to her husband. She was not allowed to approach the King, but she could attend his sumptuous feasts and enjoy the games. The Vicomtesse was on her way to social success.

The court Josephine encountered in the first hunting season of 1786 was troubled. Marie Antoinette was thirty and had recently given birth to her fourth child, Princess Sophie Hélène Béatrice. The baby was fragile and Louis Joseph, the Dauphin, was often ill. The Queen was criticised for spending millions of livres on fripperies, as well as a palace for her children at Saint-Cloud and a fantasy version of farm life at Petit Trianon at Versailles, with a model village of twelve houses, windmills and dovecotes and a dairy made of marble with silver pails for the milk. There, she and her ladies could play at being country girls admiring perfectly groomed sheep.

Scabrous cartoons suggested that the Swedish nobleman and avid visitor to Versailles, Count Axel von Fersen, was Sophie's father.[10] Parisians snapped up cartoons depicting Louis XVI as a fat, stupid, cuckold, while his immoral Queen manipulated France for Austrian desires. Marie Antoinette was shown surrounded by her sexual favourites, dallying with her lesbian lover, the Princesse de Lamballe, in a vitiated, spendthrift court.

The previous summer, Marie Antoinette had received a letter from a jeweller, Charles Auguste Boehmer, in which he proffered his gratitude and explained that the finest set of diamonds would soon be in her possession. Marie Antoinette asked Madame Campan, her Lady of the Bedchamber, to interpret the meaning of this letter, but she could not. The Queen decided it was irrelevant and discarded it.

Boehmer was referring to an impossibly ornate necklace of nearly 650 diamonds, which he had long been trying to sell for the astronomical sum of a million and a half livres. Cardinal de Rohan, who hoped to win the favour of Marie Antoinette, had advanced some of the money after she met him secretly outside the palace one night and told him he would indeed gain her favour if he did so. The necklace was sent. When Boehmer went to demand the rest of the money from Marie Antoinette, she said she did not have the necklace and had never asked for it.

The King requested an explanation from Cardinal de Rohan, and he produced a note signed by Marie Antoinette accepting the jewels. It was found that the note had been forged by a con woman who had paid a woman of low virtue to imitate the Queen at the night-time meeting, and had then seized the necklace. The Cardinal was arrested and tried by the Parlements of Paris, which acquitted him on the grounds that he had been duped by the con woman. Marie Antoinette declared her innocence, yet even those who believed her were deeply troubled by the fact that any man could think the Queen would buy a necklace in secret – and meet up after dark to discuss it, like a pros-titute loitering in the shadows. The presses worked overtime producing caricatures attacking the woman who was ruining the country with her demand for luxurious goods. She and her vast, bloated palace of Versailles became the scapegoat for France's economic hardship and the excessive power of Austria and the German states. By the time Josephine encountered the hunt, the Affair of the Diamond Necklace was still dividing the courtiers.

The French court was hated in Paris, but at Fontainebleau they forgot everything and abandoned themselves to celebration. There was splendour, ritual and a tradition of courtship and gallantry to ladies. The huge caravan of the court wanted young, beautiful women, and the Vicomtesse de Beauharnais was perfect.

Josephine was invited to soirées, balls, concerts and parties thrown by members of the court. She delighted in the glamorous company, the lavish breakfasts laid out under the trees and the rush of the horses. Exhilarated from following the hunt and excited by the proximity to royalty, she often came home drenched with rain, glowing with the exercise, and eager to return. It was her first chance for carefree pleasure since she had arrived in France, but such liberty came at a cost. She needed funds for dresses, jewels and entertaining, as well as visits to Paris. Without a husband or family, there was only one way for a pretty woman to find money. Josephine was determined to exploit her youth. As one friend wrote, since she was desperate to have the 'luxurious enjoyments of her era', she found that her 'attractiveness gave her certain advantages'. She did not care about polite society and indeed 'defied public opinion rather overtly'.[11] The Vicomtesse was playing a dangerous game.

She began to depend on the kindness of her older gentlemen friends, such as the banker Denis de Rougement, who invited her to stay with him in Paris. She cultivated the Chevalier de Coigny, who was twenty years her senior, and the married Comte de Crenay. Men of her own age, she had found, were difficult and demanding. Older gentlemen petted her, appreciated her charms, gave her handsome presents of jewels and paid her for her time.

In 1786, Josephine was spending rich men's money, but her newly adopted country was verging on bankruptcy. The government could not borrow any more. The Controller General asked the King to call an Assembly of Notables – 144 members of the aristocracy, Church and government – and inform them that taxes must be raised. The Assembly demanded that there should be a supervisory commission of finance, and that it must be distinct from the royal government. The King responded by dismissing the Assembly. The provincial governments and that of Paris declared that only the Estates General, not called since 1614, could pass such demands.

The aristocracy continued gaily on the road to debauchery. In the midst of it all, Josephine made a snap decision to travel to Martinique. Denis de Rougemont lent her 6000 livres, she borrowed another 1000 from her aunt and sold some of her possessions, and bought a passage on the *Sultan* for herself, Hortense and Euphémie.

It was not a good time to leave France. Eugène was due to arrive to see her for his summer visit, Edmée was unwell, and they would be travelling to Martinique during hurricane season, through seas thick with hostile British ships. Hortense later declared that her mother was thinking of her own 'ageing mother, who she hoped to see one last time'.[12] Josephine also wanted to secure funds from her estates. But there was more to her voyage than money and family feelings. She had been the mistress of various men and was most likely fleeing because the scandal had become heated and she thought it best to absent herself for a while. If Alexandre heard any unfortunate intimations he might spread gossip against her, or even try to take Hortense. After a year of living on the periphery of the ruinously expensive French court, Josephine was in debt and in trouble, and she needed to escape.

The *Sultan* arrived on 11 August 1788. She was delighted to see her family and the slaves waiting for her at La Pagerie. Initially, she remained quietly at the plantation. Little Hortense took easily to the role of *grande dame*. One day she found some copper coins to distribute among the slaves – and was chastised by her grandmother for playing at being superior when she was only a child. After a year, Josephine began to spend more time at the balls and receptions of Fort Royal, riding high on the cachet gained from Fontainebleau. She wrote to aunt Edmée asking her to send a dozen fans and a muslin ball gown.

On Martinique, social unrest was growing. The slaves saw newspapers, heard the talk of the freed slaves, and overheard the huddled conversations of their masters. They also learned that America was in the process of abolishing slavery, and that across Europe there were fierce debates about emancipation. Soon anti-slavery literature was circulating throughout the Caribbean. The freed Martinique blacks were forming committees and demanding parity with the whites.

On 31 August 1790, a slave rebellion began in Saint-Pierre and became a revolt when underprivileged whites and dispossessed soldiers joined the ranks of the protest. The turbulence spread and soon Fort Royal was in uproar. Josephine's uncle was seized and the slaves took over the fort. She decided that she and Hortense should leave at once. Along with Euphémie, they hurried to the port and embarked on *La Sensible*. As they ran, a cannonball landed a few feet from them.

Josephine set off on her long journey back across the Atlantic, forced to wear makeshift clothes made from material in the ship's store. The slaves were defeated not long after she left. The ringleaders were beaten to death in public, and their heads propped on posts around the island. But the seeds for change had been sown. Martinique would never be the same again.

France, too, had been altered forever in just two years. Josephine's world had been turned upside down.

4

Revolution

hile Josephine danced at Fort Royal balls, Versailles had been struck with gloom. 'Death of my son at one in the morning,' Louis XVI wrote in his diary. The seven-year-old Dauphin died on 4 June 1789, emaciated and covered in sores. Baby Sophie had already died. By the end of the year, the King was a man besieged. The winter of 1789 had been the most severe in living memory. Josephine's friends skated on frozen ponds and enjoyed hot drinks in front of the fire while the poor suffered, scrabbling for firewood and eating scraps of stale bread in desperation. Over 20,000 beggars wandered in search of food in the area around Versailles. The government gave 12,000 of them work labouring in the hill at Montmartre, for the tiny sum of 20 sous a day.

On 4 May 1789, the first meeting of the Estates General was held: it was composed of the Church, the nobility and the third estate – lawyers, merchants and professional men. Alexandre de Beauharnais became the representative for Blois, his ancestral town. When the Estates General was reconstituted into the National Assembly on 17 June, he became a key player, allying himself with the group of liberal nobles petitioning for reform. Aggrieved at his previous exclusion from court, he threw himself into his role. Finally, he felt, somebody was listening to him.

On 11 July, the King dismissed Jacques Necker, court financial adviser and father of Madame de Staël. When the news reached the streets, the theatres closed and armed men marched through the city, chanting

Necker's name. The violence continued. On 14 July, the King wrote '*rien*' in his hunting journal, meaning he had failed to catch any prey that day. In Paris, an armed crowd of over 100,000 attacked the Bastille, freeing the prisoners and killing the governor. The Duc de Liancourt came to Versailles to report the news to the King while he was in bed. 'Is it a revolt?' asked the King. 'No, Sire,' replied the Duc. 'It is a revolution.' Alexandre and his fellow deputies were delighted by the fall of the Bastille, for it meant that revolution was truly coming. The next day, some of the most hated courtiers – such as the Queen's confidante, the Duchesse de Polignac – agreed to flee, but the King and Queen refused to leave. Against a summer of bread riots and bloody demonstrations, the King and his courtiers continued to hunt and feast on champagne breakfasts.

On Monday 5 October, the King was hunting in the woods near Versailles. He had shot over eighty animals when he was told that a large group of working women had left Paris that morning to demand grain and flour from their sovereign – as well as concessions to democracy. The King ordered his granaries to open their stores, but the crowd would not be pacified. As night fell, they were demanding the bodies of the sovereigns. At four o'clock in the morning, the palace apartments were invaded, and by midday the King and Queen were being taken to the capital surrounded by the chanting mob, the heads of their guards planted on sticks and waved around the royal couple. At the palace, the only sound to be heard was the closing of doors and shutters. Locked up and deserted, the ghost court at Versailles stood in its ornamental gardens and wooded parks, a hated relic of a monarchy that was breathing its last.

'Kings who become prisoners are not far from death,' the Queen told Madame Campan.[1] At the dilapidated Tuileries Palace in Paris, the King paced the rooms and the Queen tried to give her children the impression of normality. They decorated their apartments with furniture and ornaments from Versailles and drapes were strewn over the damp patches on the walls and the rotting wood of the doorframes. In Versailles, the royals had been distant figures, seeing nothing but brocaded gowns, powdered hair and gilded furniture. At the Tuileries, dirty, toothless faces pressed up against their windows and their carriage was pelted with mud whenever they drove out.

Alexandre and his fellow deputies proposed that the King cede military command to the National Assembly, and drafted other changes that attempted to install equality into French life, including the abolition of a hereditary monarchy. The National Assembly confiscated the Church lands, which constituted nearly ten per cent of France. Plum positions in the Church, government and military were opened up to the population, rather than being reserved for the aristocracy. Alexandre was made one of the secretaries of the Assembly. The venal, womanising soldier and minor aristocrat considered too insignificant to follow the hunt was now a man of leadership, one of the rulers of Revolutionary France.

On 29 October 1790, Josephine, Euphémie and Hortense disembarked from *La Sensible* at Toulon after a difficult crossing. France had changed entirely. Every village and town was still festooned with banners and garlands and the tributes of liberty, and the trees in the squares wore red caps of liberty. Even the language was different: people were increasingly calling each other 'tu', though by 1792 the accepted form of address was 'citoyen' and 'citoyenne'.

The walls and houses of Paris were covered in red caps, ribbons and slogans. At Fontainebleau, the hunting shelters and fine horses stood untouched. The workshops of the perfumiers were quiet, the Sèvres factory made porcelain nobody bought, and embroiderers, saddle makers and hairdressers sat glumly unemployed, while lemonade makers and patissiers scrabbled for the scraps of aristocratic work.

Josephine took up lodgings at 953 rue Saint-Dominique, just off the fashionable Boulevard Saint-Germain. She lived with Désirée Hosten, a fellow Creole with a thirteen-year-old daughter, who loved to play with Hortense. Euphémie was also with her, along with Hortense's faithful governess Marie de Lannoy, and Josephine's new dog Fortuné, an ill-tempered, cross-faced but loyal pug. At her new home she received the sad news that her father had died, fifty-five and bankrupt.

Madame Hosten was truly a woman of Revolutionary sympathies. Josephine learned from her the new way to survive: how to dress, behave and speak like a person from the working classes (or an aristocratic notion of such a person). Josephine – who hated the strict regimes of dress and etiquette and had never been able to speak in a properly affected manner – was in her element. In a reaction against Versailles, the women of the 1790s were no longer beribboned ornaments wearing corsets so pointed that they could not sit down in a carriage. They hid their jewellery under their beds and gave the hoops from their dresses to their children as toys. The decorative woman with a fan was a hated symbol of the parasitic aristocratic society. Finally, Josephine could cut up the flouncy, boned gowns she loathed.

The young Citoyenne Beauharnais now wore simple gowns striped in red and blue for the city of Paris, plain bonnets and jewellery made of iron and steel. Her hair curled unpowdered around her face – the new orthodoxy was that flour should be feeding the poor, not adorning the coiffures of the upper classes.[2] She still kept a little rouge on her cheeks, but the simple style was much more suited to her careless elegance. She was in fashion and – in certain lights – beautiful. She was the ideal Revolutionary woman: plainly dressed, practical and very informal. She had everything necessary – except zeal for the dismantling of royal and aristocratic privilege. She thought the treatment of Louis XVI and Marie Antoinette was more horrifying than gratifying. But she kept her views quiet and everyone believed her a friend of the Revolution. All she had to do was appear hopeful for the future.

A new Parisian salon society sprang up to replace the court. The city was alive with cabals, discussions and meetings of the men making the decisions, and as the wife of Alexandre, she had a new cachet and could enter any salon she desired. Anything seemed possible and the people imagined a new country, free of aristocratic privilege and royal oppression, emerging phoenixlike from the ashes of the Revolution. 'The nation was seized with hopes for boundless happiness,' wrote Madame de Staël, and 'one has never seen both so much life and so much intellect.'[3] Her salon was vital in directing government policy. There Josephine encountered men who were shaping her country, and who would also transform her life, including the ruthless former priest Abbé Sieyès and the limping bishop turned Republican Charles Maurice de Talleyrand, who had tried to seduce Madame de Staël to pursue his ambition. The thirty-six-year-old aristocrat, expelled from the Church for keeping a mistress, had persuaded the King to make him a bishop and thus survived the Revolution. Talleyrand was the most skilled and devious politician Josephine would ever meet.

Newly dressed in her plain striped gowns, she was granted entry to every salon, congratulated, admired, invited to balls, operas, country picnics and receptions. Josephine, who had not been presented at court, was an ideal example of a woman excluded by the petty snobbery of

Versailles, and the perfect victim. She was in demand, and she spent money as if there was no tomorrow.

Underneath all the sparkling chat, the cheering and the caps of liberty, France was bankrupt. The crowds were prowling and unwilling to wait much longer for the bread they had been promised.

At 10.30pm on Monday 20 June, the two surviving children of the King and Queen were carried out of the Tuileries, half asleep and disguised in heavy woollen dresses, and bundled into a coach with their governess. The young Princess asked her brother what he thought they were doing. 'I suppose to act a play,' he replied, 'since we have got these odd costumes.'⁴ The King and Queen, the King's sister Elisabeth and their escorts joined them, all disguised as servants in shawls and pulled-down hats. Louis's crown and robes were stuffed into the baggage under the seats. The King had finally agreed to flee Paris and head to the border, where royalist troops and foreign armies would protect him and allow him to demand concessions.

The plan was that the royals would pretend to be the servants of a noblewoman, the Baroness de Korff, played by the governess. The King would act the part of a valet. At the city walls, the party transferred to a large, custom-made coach guarded by three men in bright yellow livery.

At 11 pm on the following night, the ill-disguised set of servants arrived at the small town of Varennes-en-Argonne, where they searched desperately for fresh horses. The huge coach and the yellow-clad guards made them conspicuous. They were recognised and captured, only twenty-five miles from the fortified royalist town of Montmédy, where they had hoped to be safe.

When the news came through of the royal flight, Alexandre was on his second day as President of the Assembly. He dispatched riders to retrieve the royal party and announced that the Assembly should sit continuously until the runaways were caught.

On 25 June, the royal family were dragged back through Paris in front of crowds of spectators. Madame Campan attended the Queen on her return to the Tuileries and found that her hair had turned entirely white.

Alexandre de Beauharnais was the hero of the hour. The flight of the King was a turning point. The moderates who had espoused the idea of a constitutional monarchy – or a king with limited powers over an elected form of governance – felt terribly betrayed. Those on the left were confirmed in their notion that the King and Queen were dangerous traitors who had intended to reach Austria and then wage war on France. The members of the powerful pro-Revolution Jacobin club – who hoped for equality, along with their working-class supporters, the *sans-culottes* – were infuriated. Marie Antoinette was cast as a corrupt plotter, a woman who would betray the country without compunction.

In September 1791 the constitution, so long in formation, was signed by the King. Louis had only the right of veto and the country would be governed by a Legislative Assembly, elected by three-quarters of the adult male population. 'The Revolution is ended!' the people cried. Fireworks and bonfires lit up the sky. A hot-air balloon floated over the Champ de Mars, billowing ribbons of red, white and blue. The Champs-Élysées was strewn with illuminations from the Tuileries and everybody was encouraged to celebrate. 'It seemed that the Revolution had been completed,' said Madame de Staël.[5]

The crowds cheered the fireworks but they were still angry. 'There is nothing to be done with this assembly, it is a gathering of scoundrels, madmen and fools,' wrote Marie Antoinette.[6] The salon aristocrats of Josephine's circle lived in a gilded bubble. The twenty theatres of Paris were full every night and the balls and receptions continued. The aristocrats genuinely believed that once the King's power and spending were reduced, the people's anger would be assuaged and life would return to normal. They expected to retain their privileges and see a large chunk of the money and luxury that had once been the preserve of Versailles.

On 20 June 1792, the anniversary of the flight to Varennes, the guards let a mob into the Tuileries gardens. They stormed into the King's apartments with pikes and hatchets and threw a red cap on his head. For two hours, they danced and sang and forced him to drink the health of the country, while the Queen clutched her children in terror. By the evening, order was restored but all the doors had been broken, furniture smashed and the drapes torn down. The King and Queen were like animals in a zoo, and they had no escape.

Later in the summer of 1792, the jubilation dispelled and the newly borrowed money had run out. With the King and Queen imprisoned, the people needed someone to blame for their poverty. They turned their attention to the aristocrats. The parading crowds shouted, 'We will hang all the aristocrats.' Members of the Versailles court were arrested and imprisoned. Alexandre left Paris to serve in the army at Blois. Josephine and her friends became very afraid and redoubled their efforts to appear ordinary and citizenlike.

The government hoped that the imprisonment of the royal family might pacify the people. On 9 August, the National Guard were sent to the Tuileries to take the King and his family to prison. They butchered the courtiers and 500 Swiss Guards, along with hundreds from their own side who were mistaken in the confusion. The gravel was left stained with blood and strewn with limbs. 'What a lot of leaves!' was the King's only comment as he left. After a stop in a convent, the royal family were taken to the Tower of the Temple near the Bastille. 'We shall never return,' said Marie Antoinette's intimate, Princesse de Lamballe, the fluffy blonde so hated by the populace.

Within a month Jacobin and *sans-culottes* mobs had set upon the prisons and killed many of the remaining courtiers, as well as hundreds of ordinary farmers, maids, shopkeepers and children, in what became known as the 'September Massacres'. Josephine and her children hid in their house, thankful that she had never attended court. She was near enough to the prisons to hear the screams as 1600 men, women and children were tried by ad hoc tribunals and either released or hacked to death. Crowds came to stare at the new, swift piece of killing equipment set up in front of the city hall. An afternoon with 'Madame la Guillotine' became a popular entertainment as people gathered to watch, clutching 'programmes' of who was to be killed.

They were hungry for blood. The Queen's darling, Princesse de Lamballe, was put in front of a hastily assembled trial. When she refused to proclaim her hatred of the royal family, she was thrown to the crowds, raped, killed, assaulted again and then her breasts were sliced off. The jubilant mob propped her head on a pike, her innards on another, and paraded her through Paris, and even took her head to a hairdresser to arrange her golden locks. They then ushered her head to the Tower, so the Queen could give her lips one last kiss. The horrific sight of the Princesse's head on a pike popping up at the windows was too much for the hardened guards and they hurried to close the shutters so the Queen could not see it. The mob paraded throughout the afternoon and later abandoned the head, which was retrieved by a kindly citizen who asked to give the last remains of the Princesse a proper burial.

No one was safe. The Prince of Salm, a friend of both Josephine and Alexandre, offered to take Eugène and Hortense to his country estate and then away from France. The children were told they were taking a brief summer holiday. Eugène, who was used to separation, was excited by travel but nine-year-old Hortense missed her mother intensely. 'I am touched by your regrets at being away from your mother; but my dear it is not for long,' Josephine wrote. 'I hope that the Princess [of Salm] will return in spring, or I will come and collect you.'[7]

The rest of Europe gazed on France in horror. Catherine II of Russia was encouraging active intervention, and Austria, Spain, Prussia, Saxony and Sweden were in favour. On 20 April, France had declared war on Austria. Alexandre, serving with the army in Strasbourg, was furious when he heard that his children had been sent away, for he felt it was their duty to remain in Paris. He demanded the Prince of Salm return them. Alexandre then sent Eugène to school in Strasbourg and told Josephine she could keep Hortense at home.

On 26 December 1792, the trial of Louis XVI began. On 15 January 1793, he was found guilty of collaboration with counter-Revolutionary forces. At 2pm on Sunday 20 January, thirty-eight-year-old Louis was told that he would die the next day. He begged for three days in order to prepare his soul, but was refused. Marie Antoinette asked that she and the children spend the night with him, but Louis told them he needed peace to ready himself. The children were so hysterical that he only persuaded them to leave him by saying he would see them in the morning. On the morning itself, he crept away silently because he could not bear to wish them goodbye.

At around the same time Louis was informed of his fate, a guillotine was set up in the Place de la Revolution (formerly Place Louis XV and now the Place de la Concorde). During the night, flakes of snow fell onto the blade. By the morning, there was a great crowd, rubbing their ice-cold fingers and buying hot rolls from the sellers who wove through the throng. At 10.15, the King arrived wearing grey breeches, a pink waistcoat and a brown silk coat, elaborately neat, his hair as perfectly coiffed as if he were in Versailles. Refusing to allow the executioner to tie his hands, he climbed onto the platform, took off his coat and waistcoat and began to speak: 'My people, I die an innocent man,' but his voice was swamped by the noise of the drums. He was compelled to kneel, the blade was brought down and his head tumbled into the basket. Spectators dipped their handkerchiefs in the blood as souvenirs.

Marie Antoinette waited, hoping she might see him one last time, until she heard the crowds below shout out that he was dead. One of the guards brought her a gift from him – his wedding ring engraved with 'M.A.A.A., 19 Aprilis 1770', from the days when she had been Marie Antoinette, Archduchess of Austria.

'A great nation had that day soiled its history with a crime for which the future would hold it guilty,' said Madame de Staël.[8] Almost overnight, the aristocrats were no longer congratulating themselves on intellectual endeavour. Instead they trembled in fear for their lives.

Starving dogs stalked the city. Left to their own devices after the deaths or flights of their masters, they drank the blood in the gutters and threatened anyone who dared venture out. Soldiers were sent to kill them, and the people of Paris covered their ears at the sound of scattered shots. Three thousand canine carcasses lay around the streets, until the authorities came to collect them – using the confiscated carriages of the aristocracy and piling them high with dead dogs.

At the beginning of March, the first pro-monarchy uprising took place in the Vendée area. The Committee of Public Safety was instituted as the government, and in July, Maximilien de Robespierre was elected to its ranks. With his installation, France careered towards disaster.

The National Convention had proposed that slaves be freed in the French dominions. A settler representative at the Assembly declared that he and his fellow white islanders would 'rather die than assent to this infamy!' He was uncompromising in his threats. 'If France sends troops for the execution of this decree, it is likely that we will decide to abandon France.'[9] In 1793, the plantation owners made a pre-emptive strike. Rather than submit to a France abolishing slavery, they gave up their island to Britain. Josephine's home was now British. The news hit her finances hard. When the British fleet blocked traffic there was no chance of receiving money from her family or the estates belonging to Alexandre. The kindness of men sufficed again. She borrowed from friends, and also engaged in black-market trading with a network selling Parisian goods to Belgium.

Matters went little better for Alexandre. In 1793, he was appointed commander-in-chief of the army, but his election coincided with terrible failures. On 23 July, the Austrians recaptured Mainz and the French general was forced to retreat, leaving 20,000 troops behind to be killed. Alexandre offered his resignation, and it was promptly accepted on the basis that he had 'neither the strength nor the moral energy necessary in a General of the Republican army'.[10] The previous day, the Convention had decreed that no one of aristocratic birth could hold office.

The failures of the Austrian campaign reminded everyone of their former Queen, still locked up in the Temple. On 1 August, wearing a plain black gown, her belongings reduced to little more than a hand-kerchief and some smelling salts, Marie Antoinette was taken to a cell in the public prison of the Conciergerie. There the jailers showed off Prisoner 280 to the eager public for money. She held her head high, accepted favours from still-loyal shopkeepers and hoped that her relations would come to rescue her. But the Committee of Public Safety believed that the only way to bind the working classes to the Republic was to execute the Queen.

On Monday 14 October 1793, she was brought in front of the Revolutionary tribunal. Gaunt, white-haired and dressed in her thread-bare black gown, thirty-eight-year-old Marie Antoinette was put on trial for treason – accused of giving money to her brother, the Emperor of Austria, of engaging in orgies and other terrible acts. She denied everything. 'If I have not replied, it is because Nature itself refuses to respond to such a charge laid against a mother,' she said, when accused of incest with her son. Composed and dignified, she felt sure she would be exiled as a punishment. At nearly four in the morning, she was handed her verdict and forced to read it aloud. She was found guilty on every charge.

At 7am on the 16th, her faithful maid came to her cell and tried to give the doomed Queen some food. Marie Antoinette donned a plain white gown while the warders watched, her hair was hacked off and her hands were bound, despite her protests that her husband had not suffered a similar humiliation. As she passed the Tuileries, her eyes filled with tears. At 12.15 the crowd jeered as her head fell into the basket. When her body arrived at the mass graveyard where her husband was buried, it received no special treatment. The gravediggers were on their lunchbreak, so the head and body of the Queen were left lying on the damp grass.

The city was a terrible, ghoulish place, as ravaged and sick as if it had been hit by the Black Death. People denounced employees, neighbours, friends and lovers, and were constantly afraid of being accused of treason, plotting or anti-Republican feeling. Almost the entire company of the Comédie-Française was imprisoned for suspicious behaviour. Women were dragged to the guillotine from childbed, husbands and wives were so eager to save their skins that they cheered the deaths of their loved ones.

The gay salons were over and women dressed drably, all the better not to be noticed. Notre-Dame was renamed the Temple of Reason, the churches were destroyed, their statues of saints smashed into pieces, bronzes stolen and melted down. A new Republican calendar was instituted at the end of 1792, which had a rest day every ten rather than every seven days. Robespierre declared there would be a new religion: the cult of the Supreme Being. Streets called after saints would now be renamed – after vegetables, agricultural implements or patriots of the past. The Convention voted in the 'Law of Suspects', ordering the arrest of all those who had by remarks – or even connections – shown themselves 'the partisans of tyranny'. Anyone in aristocratic circles was at risk of arrest. Josephine quickly left the rue Saint-Dominique for Croissy, a quiet town near Paris, where she hoped to keep a low profile. She and Madame Hosten took the Maison Rossignol, an elegant house decorated in Louis XIV style, formerly the home of Madame Campan, who still lived nearby. Josephine declared herself a citoyenne of the Republic and arranged for Eugène to train as an apprentice with a local carpenter and for Hortense to practise dressmaking.

Life at Croissy was calm and as safe as anywhere could be in the circumstances. Josephine gazed out of her windows at a grand chateau concealed by tall trees and parks. It was owned by local aristocrats, the Molays, and called Malmaison. She became close friends with Madame Campan, the former First Lady of the Bedchamber. She also met Jean-Lambert Tallien, the twenty-five-year-old radical deputy in the

Committee of Public Safety, vulpine, clever and always ready to change sides. Otherwise, she lived quietly.

But Josephine was too confident. The Committee's attentions had turned to the Beauharnais family, and ordered the arrest of Alexandre's intently royalist brother, François. Josephine wrote begging for clemency for François's estranged wife Marie – and, by extension, for herself and Alexandre. As she knew, once one family member was taken, the rest would usually follow. She proposed her Revolutionary credentials. 'If he [Alexandre] was not a republican, he would have neither my esteem nor my affection. I am an American and I know only him of his family . . . my household is a republican household; before the Revolution, my children could not be distinguished from *sans-culottes* and I hope they will be worthy of the Republic.'[11]

Josephine's description of herself as an American rather than a slave-owning Creole was almost ludicrous. 'I write to you frankly as a genuine *sans culotte*,' she wrote from her fine villa, her jewels stowed in boxes upstairs. Eugène and Hortense might have been plainly dressed but they, like their mother, were a long way from *sans-culottes* – the often ragged people of the Revolutionary mob. There was no reply and Josephine did not achieve the meeting she sought. By March 1794, Alexandre had been arrested on suspicions of intending to undermine the state. He was taken to prison at the Luxembourg, then Les Carmes. Jacques-Louis David, painter and arch Revolutionary, signed the warrant for his arrest. 'Every day I was brought hundreds of them to sign and in the heat of the moment, I did not even read everything I signed,' he later said.

Josephine busied herself writing to various people trying to free her husband. By doing so, she secured her own fate. The Committee for Public Safety received a letter denouncing Josephine and Madame Hosten for running a 'gathering place for suspected persons'. The writer told the Committee: 'Beware of the former Vicomtesse de Beauharnais who has secret dealings and connections with government offices.'[12] On Easter Sunday, late at night, citoyens Lacombe and George arrived to search the home of Josephine and Madame Hosten. The men conducted their mission with care. 'After the most scrupulous search,' they reported, 'we have found nothing contrary to the interests of the Republic; on the contrary, a multitude of patriotic letters which can only commend the citoyenne.'[13] But their fair treatment was immaterial.

The next day the women were arrested. Josephine could not bring herself to wake her children. 'I could not bear to see them cry,' she told their governess, Mademoiselle de Lannoy.[14] She and Madame Hosten were taken to Les Carmes, the most infamous prison in Paris. Alexandre was already there, desperate and ill. At thirty, Josephine was doomed. No one expected to get out of Les Carmes alive.

Previously a convent, Les Carmes had quickly become dirty and infested with rats and lice. The walls were still spattered with blood after the September Massacres. Three hundred inmates waited there to die. Josephine shared a cell on the first floor with other women, including the Duchesse d'Aiguillon, and hundreds of mice. They overlooked the garden, but the windows were barred and they saw little daylight. The fetid mess from the latrine buckets overflowed in the corridors, and the place reeked of human misery. Many prisoners had given up hope and sat barely dressed, hardly able to wash themselves or care about their surroundings. Outside, as they knew, the streets around the guillotine ran constantly red with blood. Josephine yearned for her children. She wrote to Hortense, 'I embrace you both from the bottom of my heart.'[15]

The prisoners were suffering, but at least there was food. At meal times in the refectory – first the men and then the women – each prisoner was given a half bottle of wine and as much stale bread as they could manage. In the afternoon husbands and wives, mothers and sons could snatch a few hours together as the prisoners were sent out into the courtyard for fresh air. Josephine had many friends there, including the Prince of Salm, who had been captured after he came to the city to return Hortense and Eugène.

The day after she arrived, Josephine saw her husband in the recreation area. He had become rapturously devoted to one of Josephine's cellmates, the blonde widow of a general, Delphine de Custine, whom he called the 'queen of roses'. But still he was devastated – if not surprised – to see his wife in prison, and concerned that his children were left unprotected.

In the afternoons, the prisoners would chat, walk and play cards in the recreation area. The Revolutionary Tribunal usually came to collect those chosen to be guillotined in the morning, although the carts came back for others in the afternoon. The prisoners were brave: it was convention that they should simply wave goodbye to their companions with a sanguine air. After all, every man and woman who watched a victim being taken away knew that he or she might be taken tomorrow. The end of the recreation period was a momentary relief, since the Tribunal tended not to come at night.

Josephine cut her hair short, like many of the women, to avoid the executioner cutting her hair at the moment of death. Short hair was also more practical in a lice-ridden prison where there was little chance to wash, but, most of all, the women wanted the dignity of cutting their own hair when they chose. Within a week of arriving at the prison, Josephine's health and spirits were low. She wept desperately and was deeply distressed every time she saw an acquaintance hauled off by the Tribunal. She used the tarot cards to try and see how long she had left.

Her only succour was the comfort of her friends. As the weeks wore on, some prisoners sat huddled alone, afraid of conversing in case they were accused and guillotined for conspiracy. Josephine always tried to keep talking. It stopped the pain. The beautiful and daring Grace Elliott, former mistress of the Duc d'Orléans, decided she was 'one of the most accomplished and one of the most amiable women I have ever met'.[16] She thought Josephine had been on the side of the Revolutionaries but now had completely reversed her sympathies. Josephine also befriended the glamorous twenty-year-old Thérésa Cabarrus, the mistress of Jean-Lambert Tallien. They had met when he was sent to extend the Terror into Bordeaux. She returned to Paris with him and was promptly imprisoned. Thérésa, in contrast to the other unhappy prisoners, taught Josephine how to find hope.

In Les Carmes the moral strictures of the outside world were forgotten. With no idea how much longer they would live, people seized love where they could. It was easy enough to bribe one's way out of a cell, steal through the darkness and creep onto the pallet of another. Everybody wanted to forget their pain, but the women had a motive: if a female prisoner was pregnant, her name was removed from the list of those to be guillotined and she would briefly be allowed out of prison for the birth.

Josephine fell in love with the handsome young General Lazare Hoche, somewhat her junior at twenty-seven, charismatic and commanding, with a curly mop of black hair. Imprisoned after his enemies in the army denounced him, he was a good catch. As a valued prisoner, he had his own cell, where he ate excellent food and drank fine wines. He had married a pretty sixteen-year-old, Adelaide Dechaux, just over a week before he was imprisoned. He was still in love with her, but he could not resist the febrile atmosphere of the prison. Josephine soon seduced him into an intense affair. She was free to spend her time with Hoche and deploy all her weapons: her alluring way of speaking, the soft touch of her hands, her flirtatious conversation. Night after night, she crept to his cell. But after twenty-six days, he was transferred to the Conciergerie for interview and trial.

With Hoche seemingly on the way to the guillotine, Josephine felt hopeless. Certain she would never escape, she craved her children. They had hit upon the clever idea of sending messages via their mother's cross but intelligent pug, Fortuné. He dashed under the prison gate, negotiated the rats and found his mistress, who then took the messages from under his collar. The letters, as Josephine said, 'did me much good'.[17] The siblings had sent a heart-rending letter to the Tribunal, begging for the release of their parents, but it was merely placed in a file and forgotten.

One day, a woman bearing a note from Josephine came to Mademoiselle de Lannoy asking that the children be given to her for a few hours. She then hurried them to the prison and they stood in a courtyard. A window opened and they saw their mother and father. Hortense cried out in happiness, which alerted a sentry and the woman rushed the children away.

On 22 June, a new law was passed denying any of the accused either a defence or the right to cross-examination. There would be no need for solid evidence. With this, the worst stage of the Terror was unleashed. Men and women, rich and poor, were tried in groups of fifty and speedily dispatched.

On 21 July, Alexandre was called to the Conciergerie for his trial. As he told his wife, a group of prisoners had been interrogated and had named him. 'I am the victim of several villainous calumnies brought against me by several aristocrats, so-called patriots.' He felt the injustice of being judged a 'bad citizen'. He sent a lock of hair for the children and wrote Josephine a touching letter, aware as he scratched out every word that his own death made hers inevitable.

I have no hope of seeing you again, my friend, nor of embracing my dear children. I shall not tell you of my regrets: my tender affection for them and the brotherly attachment that binds me to you can leave you in no doubt as to the feelings with which I take leave of life . . . Farewell, my friend, comfort yourself with my children, console them by enlightening them, and above all teaching them that it is on account of virtue and civic duty that they must efface the memory of my execution and recall my services to the nation and my claims to its gratitude. Farewell, you know those whom I love, be their comforter and by your care make me live longer in their breasts. Farewell, for the last time in my life, I press you and my dear children to my breast.[18]

Alexandre appeared in front of the Revolutionary Tribunal on 23 July, with forty-eight others. All but two were declared guilty. The next day, he was taken to the guillotine, along with the Prince of Salm. Alexandre's head rolled into the basket as the crowds around the Place de la Nation cheered. Josephine was a widow.

She collapsed when she heard the news and retired to her cell. Josephine knew she would be next. 'My children, your father died on the scaffold and your mother will die there too,' she wrote. She recalled life on Martinique and then launched into praise of Alexandre, who 'having made me the happiest wife was to make me the most glorious and unfortunate mother. Oh my dear Alexandre! How brief and beautiful those moments we were together and how the days which drag on since death destroyed them seem heavy and long.'[19]

Her time was running out.

Five nights after Alexandre's execution, the prisoners heard terrifying sounds: the drums of the call to arms and the cries and shouts of those taken away. Josephine and the other prisoners barricaded the prison as well as they could. Next morning, the guard came in for her trestle bed. One of her cellmates, the Duchesse d'Aiguillon, demanded to know if she would receive a better bed. 'No, no, she will not need one,' he replied with a terrible smile, 'because they are going to come to take her to the Conciergerie, and from there to the guillotine.'[20]

The women burst into tears. Josephine calmly, as the Duchesse recalled, 'told them that their pain was entirely irrational, that not only would I not die, but that I would be *Queen of France*'. The Duchesse thought she had gone mad, but humoured her by asking if she had appointed her household. '"Ah! It is true, I was not thinking about that. Well my dear, I shall appoint you lady of honour, I promise you."' The women wept even harder.

That afternoon, when Josephine took the Duchesse to the window to console her, they saw a peasant woman making gestures at them, clearly desperate for them to understand. Josephine gazed at her without comprehension as the woman repeatedly picked up her skirts. 'I called out to her: *Robe!* She made a sign to show that I was right; then she picked up a stone and put it in her skirts, which she showed us again lifting up the stone with the other hand: *Pierre!* I called out to her again.' At this the woman made a movement as if cutting her throat and then began to dance.[21] Josephine stared: *Robe? Pierre.* Then she understood. Robespierre was dead. 'You see,' she said to her cellmates, 'I will be the *Queen of France.*' She was given back her bed and spent 'the best night in the world'.[22]

On 26 July, Thérésa Cabarrus had sent Jean-Lambert Tallien a dagger and a letter condemning him for failing to rescue her. 'I die in despair at having belonged to a coward like you,' she wrote. Whether it was the letter or the fear that he would soon follow his mistress to prison, Tallien decided on action. The next day, Robespierre was in mid-flow addressing the Convention when Tallien leaped up, waving the dagger and crying, 'Down with the dictator!' It was a signal to his fellow plotters Paul de Barras and Louis Fréron to rise up behind him.

The deputies turned on Robespierre and he fled to the Hôtel de Ville. Barras stormed the building and Robespierre was dragged away. He tried to shoot himself but only succeeded in shattering his jaw. He was left bleeding on a table in the Committee for Public Safety, then moved to the same cell that Marie Antoinette had occupied. Hundreds of Parisians followed his cart to the guillotine. Robespierre, always immaculately dressed, stood in front of a furious crowd, his jaw held together with bandages, his blue coat spattered in blood. The people cheered as he was guillotined.

The Jacobins were now the new enemies. Barras, Tallien and Fréron were the heroes. Tallien became the president of the Convention.

The Terror was over. Through the incredible revolving door of eighteenth-century France, a new political system was in charge: Thermidor. Founded on the hope of equality, it has left little to history, conserved only as the name of a lobster recipe.

In Les Carmes a few days later, Josephine was told that she would walk free. She was among the first to be chosen, thanks to the personal intercession of Tallien. When she received the news, she fainted. She had lost her husband and many of her friends. She had been in prison for three and a half months and her health was ruined.

Fortunately, she was not entirely alone. General Hoche had also escaped the guillotine, and he wished to resume their affair.

5

The height of good manners to be ruined

On 6 August 1794, with little more than the dress she stood up in, Josephine emerged into a France that had changed forever. With Robespierre dead, people streamed onto the streets, no longer afraid to speak to each other. They saw a city in ruins. Paris was derelict and neglected, rubbish piled high and weeds grew through the cracks in the roads. Animals ran wild and beggars huddled in corners. The grand houses had been entirely despoiled: not only the furniture and mirrors from the interiors but the lead from the roofs and glass from the windows had been snatched and sold. Bands of robbers and pickpockets scoured the streets and murder was par for the course.

Josephine took an apartment on the rue de l'Université for herself and her children, sharing with another female friend, Madame de Krény (Madame Hosten was still in prison). She began borrowing to survive. All her possessions at the rue Saint-Dominique were still sealed away and unavailable to her, as the property of the state. She needed gowns, jewellery, crockery and supplies. She threw herself into the arms of General Hoche, who whiled away his time with her, handing her money as he left.

Josephine had tried hard to conserve her beauty in prison. But it had been a hopeless quest. She was slender and her skin was fine, but her hair had thinned, her teeth were ruined, and she was often wracked with nervous illness. At thirty-one, she had to use every aid of beauty she could find to ensure Hoche's affections. Luckily, she still had her sensual arts. Hoche wrote to his child-wife Adelaide, telling her that he was unavoidably detained in Paris. Josephine confided in him her fears about her son and he offered to take Eugène on tour with him.

'We are free,' cried one newspaper, 'our thoughts, our intentions, will no longer be poisoned.'[1] Even though Robespierre was dead, the people could not forget the atmosphere of denunciation and suspicion, and it was impossible to feel at ease in conversation with friends, even at home. Parisians were grateful to Tallien and his allies, but they did not trust them.

The British were still blockading Martinique, but Josephine managed to find someone travelling to New England who would take a letter for her. 'You have without doubt heard about all the awful things that have befallen me,' she wrote to her mother. 'I've been widowed for four months! My only consolations are my children and you, dear mother, for my support. My most cherished wish is that we will be reunited one day.'[2] In the wastes of Paris, poverty-stricken and desperate, she found it hard to feel grateful for her survival. 'My children now only have my support and I cling to life only to make them happy,' she wrote. As a PS, she added, 'Greetings to all the slaves on the plantation', and sent a kiss to her wet nurse.[3]

Josephine begged her mother to send letters of credit or supplies of sugar via Hamburg. French currency had been devalued by a third – and anyone who had sugar or coffee could sell it on the street for a high price. She wrote again and again to her family, begging for money while living on loans and credit. In the ruins of post-Terror Paris, only the moneylenders were getting rich. One friend gave her food, another gave her petticoats and skirts.

Paris had turned into, as one Swiss traveller put it, a 'giant flea market'.[4] The gangs sold their booty, families tried to earn money from their belongings and neighbours ransacked the homes of anyone who had not returned from prison. Everywhere on the streets were carts selling furniture, curtains, tapestries, floor coverings, saucepans and plates. There were piles of children's toys for sale at street corners and stacks of clothes balanced on makeshift tables near the river. Agents acting for the Russians were investigating what could be bought cheap, and men sent by the Prince of Wales had snapped up paintings, bronzes and furniture from Versailles. Josephine, unable to retrieve her belongings, spent excessively on new tables, chairs and drapes for her home.

Around her all the Parisians who had survived were throwing

themselves into amusement, unsure how long the peace would last. 'It is impossible to die of hunger with more gaiety,' sighed Baron de Frénilly.[5] Thirteen theatres reopened, gambling dens welcomed revellers throughout the night, and over a thousand new dance halls were set up, as well as dining and drinking halls. The rich feasted on the new dish of Lobster Thermidor, while the poor fought over bread. The courtesans who had disappeared during the Terror came out in force. The city was full of women in bright dresses, sauntering arm in arm and taking clients back to the deserted parks stalked by hungry cats.

Those who had suffered imprisonment were immediately at the top of the social tree. 'It was the height of good manners to be ruined,' declared Baron de Frénilly, 'to have been suspected, persecuted, and, above all, imprisoned.' Those who had not been imprisoned were suspected of having bribed their way out of it – or of manoeuvring to put others in their place. 'People greatly regretted that they had not been guillotined.'[6] Survivors like Josephine attended 'victims' salons' and 'victims' luncheons'.

The most exclusive invitation of all was to the *Bals des victimes*. Only those who had been imprisoned or had relations who had died in the Terror were permitted to attend. Women wore chemise-style gowns, cropped their hair, as the prisoners had done at Les Carmes, and wore thin red ribbons around their necks to recall the cut of the blade. When guests entered the ballroom, they had to bow their heads, in imitation of the head dropping from the guillotine. The fashionable short hairstyle was called the '*coiffure à la victime*'. Josephine, so long excluded and often ridiculed, was now *à la mode*. Everyone in Paris wanted to meet a victim, especially a pretty one without a husband.

A young Corsican soldier, newly arrived from the provinces, was struck by the Bacchanalian frenzy. 'Everyone is determined to make up for their sufferings,' twenty-two-year-old Napoleon Bonaparte wrote to his brother Joseph. He had thought himself destined for a stellar career but had fallen out with his paymasters and all seemed lost. On half pay without a commission and virtually friendless, he tried to write a romantic novel and goggled at Parisians trying, because they were afraid of the future, 'not to miss a single pleasure of the present'. He was most struck by the glamorous females. 'Women are everywhere, in the theatres, the promenades, the bookshops,' he told Joseph. 'Here alone they deserve to rule; all men are mad for them, think of nothing but them, live only for them. A woman needs to live in Paris for six months to know her due, to know what her empire is.'[7] He gazed at women like Josephine, knowing they would never take notice of him.

Josephine's passport suggested that she was three years younger than she was. She wanted to start again. And for this, she needed money and protection. She begged Hoche to divorce Adelaide, but he dithered between his teenaged wife and his mistress. On 21 August, he was appointed commander-in-chief of the army on the coast of Cherbourg. He offered to take thirteen-year-old Eugène with him on campaign. Josephine drew confidence from this act of kindness that he would return and choose her.

Hoche travelled to Cherbourg and began his command on 1 September. Josephine sent him passionate letters, pouring out her heart and trying to persuade him to marry her. He replied diligently, but he was growing tired of her demands for money and her inability to save a penny.

Always a strong believer in spending money to gain more money, she was throwing her purse around more excessively than ever. Carriages were now incredibly rare – but Josephine hired one and paraded around the city in style. She was hugely in debt to moneylenders and the banker Jean Emmery. She wrote to her family, 'I hope that you have received the tender expressions of your poor Yeyette and that of her children; she really needs support from you, her heart is battered and she has been deprived for a long time. We have no hope of existence but your generosity.'[8] It was an impossible demand, and Josephine realised that she would have to find the money herself.

In December, the Seine iced over. Wolves howled on the outskirts of the city. With roads submerged in snow, Paris was stranded and its citizens suffered greatly. What little food there was to buy was expensive since maximum price laws had been abolished and inflation was soaring. Every tree in the Bois de Boulogne and the parks of the Tuileries was chopped down for firewood. Women threw themselves in the Seine over the shame of being unable to provide for their children. The ranks of streetwalkers swelled to 30,000 as desperate girls did anything they could to buy food. The government instituted rationing – one quarter of a pound of black bread, made from a bitter mix of peas and chestnut flour. At one in the morning, starving men, women and children began queuing outside the bakeries. At seven o'clock, they started tearing at each other as they tried to grab the tiny loaves. In the wealthier classes, guests took their own bread and candles with them to dinner parties. Josephine was one of the few exempted from this custom on account of her extreme poverty.★

The streets were stalked by the Muscadins, young aggressive men who attacked anyone they thought of as Republican and threw their caps of liberty to the ground. Savage purges began of the Jacobins and anyone accused of being a *sans-culotte*. Barras, Tallien and the rest could barely see past ensuring their own political and physical survival. In the lawless, poverty-stricken city, missing thousands of its men to conscription, the corrupt and the venal flourished as they made money from profiteering and speculating on state assets that had been quickly sold off. Thousands of émigrés had left behind estates, houses and businesses. Those who remained creamed off the best for themselves. Dishonest men willing to enforce their desires with violence could make a fortune in a month.

Josephine needed to join the circles of those who were making money in the post-Terror world – the moneylenders, arms profiteers, bankers and the men of the political elite. She was still alluring, despite her travails in prison. A travel document of the time listed her as 'height five feet, nose and mouth well made, eyes orange, hair and eyebrows dark brown, face long, chin somewhat prominent'.[9] She began to cement her friendship with Thérésa Cabarrus, twenty-one-year-old heroine of all Paris. Tall and very beautiful with deep brown eyes and dark hair, Thérésa had a charming personality, more charisma than the entire Comédie-Française, and a love of fame that made her the new idol of the age.

For many, lovely Thérésa was entirely responsible for the downfall of Robespierre. She was invited everywhere, applauded at the theatre, followed in the street, and called 'Our Lady of Thermidor' for her bravery. She was followed around by a group of Thermidor loyalists, dressed up in brightly coloured jackets with long hair curling around their shoulders and speaking in an affected drawl. Josephine and Thérésa were soon fast friends. Josephine called her 'little one' and acted as her witness at her wedding to Tallien on 26 December 1794.

★ In 1795, the livre was replaced by the franc, worth 7 livre, 3 deniers. The new currency added to the financial chaos. Indeed, many people continued to refer to money as 'livres' – especially when referring to large sums or property transactions.

Josephine spent much of her time at Thérésa's cottagelike home, La Chaumière, near the rural area of the Champs-Élysées. At Thérésa's parties champagne flowed and politicians, bankers, generals, actresses and courtesans danced together. As the founder of Thermidor, Tallien was the hero, and presiding over it all was his lover, in outfits that were barely decent. By the winter, Josephine was standing next to her, often in a similarly diaphanous gown to add to the effect. As a confidante of Thérésa, her credit increased and she was able to borrow more money. But she was most of all in a position to meet Thérésa's friends and dance with them, drink with them – and then invite them to visit her at the rue de l'Université.

The newspapers were preoccupied with Thérésa. Also billowing from their pages was Juliette Récamier, the delicate seventeen-year-old beauty who was limpid and shy where Thérésa was brash. She was the wife of a wealthy, elderly banker, although some gossiped that she was really his illegitimate daughter, whom he had married when she was fifteen to ensure she took his estates if he were killed. It was unlikely, even though the marriage was not physical and he treated her like a daughter. 'I am not in love with her,' he wrote, 'but I feel for her a genuine and tender attachment . . . she possesses germs of virtue and principle such as are seldom seen so highly developed at so early an age.' Whatever the truth, he encouraged her to host salons and delighted in her reputation as one of the most beautiful women in Paris. He poured money into her glittering entertainments as she held court among men of power – speaking so softly that they had to lean in close to hear her. Another newspaper favourite was Fortunée Hamelin, eighteen and newly married. A glamorous Creole, her long hair and tiny waist made her entrancingly attractive, even though she had, according to one contemporary, the face of a bulldog.

Seductive, a survivor of prison, stylish and somewhat lacking in morals, Josephine fitted in perfectly. She, Thérésa, Fortunée and Juliette became known as the *Merveilleuses*, the fashion plates, the stars. Some called them the 'Graces'. Taking the fashion for prison-chemises and short hair to the extreme, they flaunted their lovely figures in transparent gowns. If couture at Versailles had been stiff corsets and the post-Revolution period simplicity and restraint, Thermidor was decadent nakedness. The overthrown Queen had been palely pretty and blonde, and Thermidor wanted a different look. Josephine, like Thérésa and Fortunée, was dark-haired and dusky-eyed.

The *Merveilleuses* curled their hair tight around their heads, put flowers behind their ears, donned sandals on bare legs and wore filmy puff-sleeved dresses scooped low over the bosom. Unsuited to the muddy streets of Paris – or indeed for venturing outside, other than in high summer – the gowns were best worn at evening parties. Every curve of the body was exposed, and any dancer could feel the warm flesh of his partner as they proceeded around the floor. Unlike the torturous gowns of Versailles, the Thermidor frocks were easy to whip off. Despite the Paris chill, dresses had become so diaphanous that people said the '*sans culottes* had given way to the *sans chemises*'. Fortunée Hamelin once walked down the Champs-Élysées with her breasts entirely on show.

Otherwise, Thérésa wore the most eye-popping outfits. She preferred short, see-through Grecian gowns, split at the thighs, the cloth dipped in scented oil to mould itself to her body. 'It is not possible to expose oneself more sumptuously,' Talleyrand exclaimed of her.[10] Her arms jangled with gold bracelets and she wore gold rings on her toes. At one party at La Chaumière, she wagered a man that her entire dress would not weigh more than two six-franc pieces. In front of her forty guests, she removed every scrap of clothing – including her bracelets and shoes. She won the bet.

Josephine was sought after by men and women alike. As one news-paper reported, 'An event talked of in the Paris Salons! Alteration in the style of hair-dressing affected by Mesdames Tallien and Beauharnais!'[11] She cared about the matter, writing on one occasion to Thérésa:

I think it of importance that our head-dresses should in all respects be alike. I now state for your information that I propose wearing a red handkerchief in my hair, tied in the Creole fashion with three locks on each side of the head. That which is a presumption on my part is quite natural on yours, as you are younger, and, if not hand-somer, still of a much fresher complexion . . . We are, however, attempting a bold thrust and must drive the *trois Bichons* and the *Bretelles Anglaises* [rival women in society] to despair. You fully under-stand the effects of this conspiracy, the necessity for secrecy, and the wonderful effects which must attend it.[12]

All of them were noticed at the theatre, followed by crowds, and discussed in minute detail at society gatherings. For Josephine, however, it was a risky game: the other *Merveilleuses* were married and over ten years younger, nearer to Hortense's age than her own. Baron de Frénilly declared her the sort of woman who could remain for fifteen years at the age of thirty.[13] Even so, thirty was excessively old in the new world of the 1790s. She knew that if she spent her time with youthful girls of twenty-one, potential suitors would think her a similar age. Prison had ruined her health but it gave her a claim to fame and notoriety. Thanks to the horror of Les Carmes and her ability to flatter her way into the affections of celebrated young women, she had become the most expensive mistress in the land.

At one of Thérésa's parties, Josephine was introduced to the man who would change her life. At forty, Paul François, Vicomte de Barras – former soldier and civil servant, and Tallien's successor as president of the National Assembly – was Thermidor's most powerful man and one of the wealthiest individuals in the country. Handsome, with dark hair and green eyes, he was clever and dishonest. After overthrowing Robespierre, he had the reputation of a hero but his fellow politicians denounced him as untrustworthy, cruel and a hypocrite for surrounding himself with 'the most corrupt of aristocrats, lost women, ruined men, cheaters at cards, courtesans and speculators. He was like an exotic potentate: magnificent and dissolute.'[14] In attaching herself to Barras, Josephine was aiming high.

After meeting him in the winter, she wrote asking for his help to assist a young *sans-culotte* man. It was a typical act of kindness to someone who would have once been her enemy. The request was also an excuse: she said she had not had the pleasure of seeing him for a long time, reproached him for forgetting an acquaintance, and asked him to visit her in her apartment. The widow Beauharnais was issuing a clear invitation.

By the following spring, she was Barras's established mistress and her money worries were over. 'Along with all that is seductive and captivating', declared an anonymous pamphlet about her, probably written by the Marquis de Sade, Josephine had 'a usurer's avidity for money, which she squanders with the alacrity of a gambler and a love of luxury grand enough to swallow up the revenue of ten provinces'.[15] Barras paid the rent on her home, discharged her debts and gave her everything she desired, including a country residence in Croissy. In return, she lavished him with attention. Since Eugène was with General Hoche and Hortense was staying with her aunt Edmée, Josephine was free to direct her every waking hour to him. Barras wanted her to be complaisant, sexually adventurous and an exhibitionist. She was expected to arrange parties for him at which nothing was forbidden.

Less than a year after she had been released from prison, the widow of nearly thirty-two with poor teeth was presiding over the most powerful table in Paris. Once a week, she travelled to her country estate in Croissy and the stage would be set for an incredible celebration. Her neighbours watched astounded as carts of meat, game, exotic fruits and flowers arrived at her door, despite the food shortages. Soldiers arrived later, escorting Barras himself.[16] He and his fellow heroes were behaving like kings, and they desired a harem to entertain them.

With the drink flowing and the *Merveilleuses* wearing barely any clothes, Croissy evenings sometimes degenerated into orgies. On one occasion, Josephine, Thérésa and Fortunée undressed during the soup course and Thérésa dipped her breast into Barras's champagne glass. While the guests were eating salad, Fortunée used a small napkin to perform an erotic dance. The dessert was handed round and then Thérésa dropped to her hands and knees and imitated 'the undulations of an African panther'. By the cheese course, Josephine was on Barras's knee and fondling him in front of everybody. The other guests tripped off with each other to the bedrooms.[17]

In later life, consumed with bitterness against Josephine and her husband, Barras declared her a 'lewd Creole' and blustered that she 'derived none of her attractions from nature, but everything from art, the most refined, the most provident' used by the courtesans of Greece and France. She was motivated only by money, he thought. She never loved 'except from motives of interest', even though she gave the impression to those who possessed her that 'she was conquered by them and had freely given herself'. He flourished that she would have 'drunk gold from the skull of her lover'.[18] The truth was that Josephine was hungry for both love and money.

After years of privation, she had finally found security. She reaped the rewards of her new life. She enrolled twelve-year-old Hortense in an exclusive girls' school, the Institut National de Saint-Germain, run by Madame Campan. An enclave of aristocratic civilities, the school was a haven for refugees from Versailles – such as Jean-Baptiste Isabey, Marie Antoinette's miniaturist, who was now the tutor in drawing.

Madame Campan trained girls to be accomplished young ladies with perfect etiquette. There was no notion of learning a trade useful to the state, as there had been during the Revolution. Life, once more, was all about exquisite manners and show.

Unlike her mother, a lax pupil with the nuns in Fort Royal, Hortense was diligent and quick-witted (rather to the envy of some of the other girls) and excelled in the curriculum of languages, history, geography, drawing, music and dancing. Latin was not included and maths, as in all girls' schools, was an extra subject that parents had to request. Hortense had private harp lessons and excelled with Isabey at drawing and painting.

When Eugène returned from accompanying Hoche on tour, he was sent to an elite academy for young men. Josephine then took a large house on 6 rue Chantereine, which she rented (with Barras's money) from an actress friend, Julie Carreau. Developers had been buying up areas of the city and building brash new houses for the bankers, moneylenders and speculators. Now the rue de la Victoire in the ninth arrondissement, the rue Chantereine had recently been converted from marshland into one of the most fashionable new districts. The house came with stables and a coach house and Josephine needed a staff of coachman, manservant, cook, chambermaid and maid, as well as Mademoiselle de Lannoy, governess to her children for their occasional visits. Only a few months after becoming Barras's mistress, Josephine was rich.

She dipped into Barras's pot of money for decorations. The sheer muslin curtains, typical of Martinique, were perhaps not the most pragmatic choice for her dining room. She covered the chairs in pale blue nankeen and displayed classical ornaments, including an Etruscan silver urn. Excited by her decorating, she forgot to buy enough practical goods and there was a shortage of spoons, cups and plates.

In the summer of 1795, the Convention appointed Barras in charge of the troops engaged to defend it. He liked to pick out people down on their luck and vault them into privilege, for he thought it gave him more control over them. Among them, he chose an obscure and poor young Corsican general by the name of Napoleone Buonaparte. Society, so far, had entirely ignored him.

6

'What strange power you have over my heart'

It was the early autumn of 1795. The chandeliers glowed above a table heavy with food, perfumed flowers adorned the vases, wine flowed into crystal goblets. Barras seated Napoleon next to Josephine, who appeared at her best in the soft candlelight, her gown clinging to her bosom. They fell deep into conversation. Unlike every woman the young soldier had met, she neither mocked nor ignored him. Instead, she listened to him talk of his military victories and praised his successes. Napoleon was dazzled by her sophistication. 'I was not immune to the charms of women,' he said, 'but I had not had good fortune with them; and my character rendered me shy before them. Madame de Beauharnais is the first to have reassured me. She said flattering things about my military talents, one day when I found myself seated next to her. Her praise intoxicated me; I addressed myself only to her.' Impulsive and decisive, he had fallen in love, and after that evening, 'I followed her everywhere; I was passionately in love with her.'[1] Ill at ease in society and without an object of devotion, Napoleon had found an ambition and a goal: to seize his patron's mistress.

That night was his first meeting with Josephine, but he had seen her from afar and, like everybody in society, he knew of her reputation. Josephine, the exotic Creole, the survivor of Les Carmes, was discussed in the salons and feted in the newspapers. From a distance, she was a glittering prize – close up, she was gentle, seductive and elegant. Her days as a gauche bride long behind her, she was the epitome of delicacy and mystery, her smile the promise of sensual delights. Napoleon was immediately her slave.

'It was chez Barras that I saw my wife for the first time,' Bonaparte later recalled.[2] In his attempt to keep the little Corsican on his side, Barras enlisted his secret weapon: Madame de Beauharnais. Anyone could understand Napoleon's attraction to her. Josephine was a real Parisienne, an aristocrat who held everything he wanted: position, social cachet, sophistication and a true Revolutionary past. As his friend from the military academy at Brienne, Louis-Antoine de Bourrienne, put it, she would 'aid him in achieving his ambition', since through her, he would have access to the most influential people in society.[3] And, simply, he was captivated. 'She was a real woman,' Napoleon said, enthusiastically praising her rear end.[4]

Born on 15 August 1769, six years Josephine's junior, Napoleon was a fighter from the cradle. Named for an uncle who had died in the battle for Corsica against the French, he was the second child of his parents' marriage to survive. In 1764, handsome eighteen-year-old Carlo Buonaparte had married Maria Letizia Ramolino, aged thirteen and intelligent, entirely uneducated and very strong-willed. Initially Corsican nationalists, the Buonapartes changed sides when the French took over the island a year before Napoleon's birth. Carlo changed his name to Charles de Bonaparte and, as overdressed as a peacock, befriended the Comte de Marbeuf, the commander-in-chief of the French forces on Corsica. He later travelled to France to wait around at Versailles for favours and money. Letizia, virtually alone on Corsica, raised her eight children with a strict hand. 'To the manner in which she formed me at an early age,' Napoleon said, 'I principally owe my subsequent elevation.'[5] Severe on laziness and venality, she had no compunction about whipping her offspring. Napoleon prided himself on never crying out.

In later years, he talked up his poverty. 'We never bought anything except what was absolutely necessary, such as clothes and furniture,' he said.[6] He was not entirely truthful: his mother's dowry was thirty-one acres of land, a mill and a bakehouse, and his father was successful at gaining favour for the family. By the rough and ready standards of Corsica, they were wealthy, with a shuttered stone house on the route to the port, shared with other Bonaparte family members, and a small country home, as well as the mill and the bakehouse. They spent a lot on appearances: as Napoleon's mother said, 'Better to have fine clothes and a grand salon and to eat dry bread in secret.'[7]

Napoleon did not learn French until he was nine. Corsica was linguistically, culturally and historically Italian. Letizia resented speaking French and her son would always pronounce certain words in the Italian fashion. 'I have a presentiment that one day this small island will astonish Europe,' declared Jean-Jacques Rousseau.[8] He meant that its compact size and isolation made it the ideal laboratory to try out his social theories of the primitive man. Corsica was mocked, looked down on as a humble farming island with meagre culture.

Napoleon was a tough, assertive, aggressive child, intelligent and fizzing with suppressed anger. At the age of seven, he was sent to a Jesuit school where he learned to read, write and add, as well as a little Latin and ancient history. He spent his time there destroying his surroundings, pulling out the stuffing from chairs, scratching tables and tearing leaves off plants. Marbeuf encouraged Charles to put his children forward for a scheme in which the offspring of impecunious members of the elite could apply for scholarships at French schools. In 1778, Napoleon won a place at the Military School of Brienne, the lowest ranked of the ten military academies where noble sons were trained for the army. Charles took his son to Brienne while on his way to pay his respects − alongside other Corsican nobles − to the new King Louis XVI and Marie Antoinette. Napoleon's elder brother Joseph, bound for the priesthood, wept copiously at their parting, but Napoleon only let slip a single tear.

At Brienne, the little king of the Bonaparte family was brought down to earth with a bump. Graceless, foreign, with a heavy Italian accent, small and ugly, an island boy on a scholarship, Napoleon was a target for the bullies. His fellow schoolboys shouted that the Corsicans were cowards, called him '*paille au nez*', or straw nose, and laughed at his height and his waddling little body. 'I'll make you French pay for this,' he cried. He became preoccupied with joining the army, so much so that when an inspector suggested he was not yet ready, he considered applying to the British navy.

Life at Brienne was harsh. There were no visits home unless a parent was gravely ill, and no holidays other than a fortnight's break at the end of the summer, when the boys were taken on walks in the barren countryside around the school. Among the other boys was Bourrienne – who would become his secretary – but Napoleon later claimed that he had few friends because friendship took up time. The teachers were poorly trained and the inspection reports noted laziness in the twenty staff and 150 students, and widespread insubordination. The vice principal prided himself on dashing through Mass in nine minutes. Napoleon was bad at singing, deportment and music and awful at dancing, but he tried hard in ancient history and geography and had a real aptitude for mathematics. 'That child will never be good for anything but geometry,' he later recalled people saying.[9] In 1782, he told an inspector that he wished to devote his life to science and produce a theory of electricity or a new model of the cosmos.

In 1784, he had his chance to escape. Just as he was due to graduate, the Ministry of War was looking for students with a talent for mathematics. Fourteen-year-old Napoleon was selected to attend the École Royale Militaire in Paris. Unlike ramshackle Brienne, the École Militaire was luxurious, with meals served by waiters, thirty professors and staff from grooms to wigmakers and shoemakers. Unfortunately for Napoleon, he still had to take the dreaded dancing lessons. He did, however, learn plenty of maths and took useful classes in fortification. The boys at the École Militaire were the *crème de la crème*, too occupied with their studies to mock Napoleon for his accent, but they were not friendly to him and he felt excluded and looked down on. He emerged with a lifelong chip on his shoulder regarding the aristocracy, to whom everything came easily. His graduation report noted he was hard-working and 'capricious, proud and extremely egotistical'.[10]

In 1785, Charles died of stomach cancer. Napoleon barely mourned his father. He promptly informed his mother that he was now the head of the family, as his elder brother was wedded to the Church. Thirty-five-year-old Letizia and four of the younger children – the youngest, Jérôme, was only a baby – were now essentially dependent on his wage (the middle two, Lucien and Maria Anna, known as Elisa, were on scholarships). Letizia was excused church as she had so much domestic work. As the breadwinner, Napoleon had to work harder to qualify as an artillery officer and cram into a few months preparation that would normally take two years. At sixteen he graduated forty-second out of fifty-eight in his class. He was then sent as a second lieutenant in the La Frère Regiment in southern France.

Already shy of women, he was the only new recruit who did not visit a brothel in Lyons on the way.

Life in the garrison town was undemanding. Napoleon spent his copious free time reading rapaciously. As he put it, 'I conquered rather than studied history.'[11] He ate one meal a day to save money and sent every spare penny to Letizia. In September 1786, he took an extended leave and finally returned home for the first time in eight years, and met the four younger siblings who had been born after his departure, Louis, Pauline, Caroline and Jérôme. He asked for further leave on the grounds of illness, but returned in late 1787 to Paris. He encountered a pretty girl working the red-light district of Palais Royal. The expensive women took rooms overlooking the arcades, while the cheaper girls like her were forced out in all weather to find clients. Napoleon asked her how she had become a streetwalker and stood with her, feeling so vigorous, he declared, that he did not feel the cold. He took her to a nearby hotel, and lost his virginity. After wasting a further six months on Corsica at the beginning of 1788, he returned to his regiment.

In 1789 the Revolution broke, and Napoleon, bored of quelling bread riots, went back to Corsica hoping to win political influence on the island. He had little success and returned to France in 1791. He hedged his bets: he joined the Jacobin Society on 3 July and publicly celebrated Louis XVI's birthday in August. As the Terror spread, Napoleon left for Paris and took his sister, Elisa, out of her school at Versailles. On the journey south to Corsica, their coach was frequently halted by Revolutionaries demanding their passports and instructing them to shout 'Vive la Nation!' The people clapped Napoleon on the back, shabby in his army uniform. In Marseilles, Napoleon felt safe: he and his sister spent a month there and then travelled in leisurely fashion to Corsica. For Napoleon, his early twenties were a time of dodging responsibility. He had little interest in romance, as he wrote in his *Dialogue on Love*, 'I do more than dispute the existence of Love. I consider it to be actually as injurious to society as to the personal happiness of mankind.'[12]

In 1793, the political situation on Corsica exploded. The Corsican Assembly deemed the Bonapartes traitors and exiled them for good. Napoleon and his banished family fled to Toulon, where he wrote a Republican pamphlet and finally found his spirit. Toulon had been attacked by the British, and Napoleon, the budding politician, used his contacts with the president of the Revolutionary committee and was given the post of commander of artillery, after the previous holder had been wounded. It was the first of his impressive promotions. He took a key role in the rescue of Toulon and impressed Paul de Barras, then at Nice with the army. Barras spotted his talent and after the French won Toulon he encouraged his promotion to brigadier general.

By 1794, his brother Joseph had long given up the priesthood and was on the verge of marriage to a Marseilles girl, Julie Clary. He introduced Napoleon to her plump, cheerful sixteen-year-old sister Désirée. Napoleon called Désirée by her middle name 'Eugenie', and he was more practical than romantic, telling her what books she should read and how she could improve her manners. He considered marrying her, since she brought a large dowry, but was not affected by particular feelings for her. He held fast to his belief that love weakened the man.

He received orders to join the Army of the West, suppressing the protests of royalists in the Vendée. He would have been under the command of Josephine's lover, Lazare Hoche, a man strict about taking unpaid leave. There was no glory in the Vendée, and Napoleon travelled to Paris to argue his position. Following a furious unresolved argument, after his leave period expired, he was living in a cheap hotel, existing on a tiny allowance sent by Joseph. He tried to meet anyone of influence, knocking on doors and demanding introductions, but was often turned away.

Depressed and miserable, Napoleon looked sickly, he rarely bothered to comb his hair and his uniform was shabby. At the age of twenty-six, his career seemed over. He wrote despondent letters to Joseph and Désirée, and seriously contemplated suicide. 'I will end up not stepping aside when a carriage passes,' he wrote dolefully to Joseph.[13] 'Life is a mere dream that fades.'[14]

Paris in the summer of 1795 was food for cynicism. The only winners after the Terror were the get-rich-quick speculators and black marketers, profiteers, military contractors and bankers. Thermidor was a regime that protected property, enshrined the supremacy of those with money and allowed them to get richer by buying public monopolies for a song, snapping up handsome estates previously owned by aristocrats and the extensive lands once owned by the Church. 'There is one thing alone to do in this world and that is to keep acquiring money and more money, power and more power,' Napoleon said.[15]

He wandered the streets and started work on a romantic novel, *Clisson et Eugénie*, a doomed love story that reflected a young man's eager desire to experience passion, having repeatedly read Goethe's *Sorrows of Young Werther*. Clisson, 'born for war', meets two sisters and falls in love with the younger, Eugenie. He gives up the army for her, but is then called back. When wounded, he sends his aide to tell Eugenie, but she falls in love with the aide. Clisson decides to die in battle, writing to her, 'At twenty-six I have exhausted the fleeting pleasures of fame.'[16]

Napoleon had taken up his pen as a romantic novelist but the fates were aligned differently. Paul de Barras saw in him a man who would do anything to be on the winning side. Barras's friends were baffled by the great man's fascination with the swarthy Corsican, 'Who is this Bonaparte? Where has he served? Nobody has ever heard of him.' The vitiated society men laughed at 'Barras's little protégé'. 'At that stage in his life,' wrote Laure Permond, 'Bonaparte was ugly.'[17]

At just over five foot three, he was not excessively small (the average Frenchman was about five foot six), but gave the impression of short stature because of his slumped posture and skinny chest.[18] Underfed, with a yellowing complexion, grey eyes and a protruding nose and chin, he was almost unpleasant to look at. In an age when the ideal of male beauty was dark curls and lustrous eyes, Napoleon's lank, greasy hair and small eyes made him a joke, and revealed him – to snobbish Parisians – as of lowly stock. He refused to waste money on gloves, his boots were dirty and his fingernails were black. Even worse, his French was still heavily accented and hesitant. He had a bad case of scabies, contracted at Toulon, and his hands were covered in red spots, which he was always scratching. Dress and behaviour meant everything, even after the Revolution, and Napoleon was scruffy, dirty and rude. He had little idea of social niceties, and tended to smile at the wrong moment or burst into laughter for no reason. Most of the time he was too awkward to say anything, but when he did speak it was usually a crude joke. Profoundly frustrated that he could not impress people as he wished, he retreated into bouts of temper and sulking.

Barras took Napoleon to the salons of Madame Tallien and Madame de Staël and to various parties. 'He was just a little general who was unhesitatingly dubbed a fool by all those who knew him,' said Madame de Chastenay. Bonaparte mused to his brother that 'a mad desire to get married will take possession of me'.[19] He was so frantic to be accepted that he proposed marriage to Laure Permond's mother, fourteen years his senior. He even considered the gold-digging courtesan, Grace Elliott, whom Josephine had met in prison.[20]

Napoleon was young, lustful for power and fascinated by the women who spurned him. Parisian ladies, he wrote to Désirée Clary, were as 'beautiful as old romances and as learned as scholars . . . all these frivolous women have one thing in common, an astonishing love of bravery and glory'. He observed them like a scientist, evaluating their characteristics. 'Their toilette, the fine arts and their pleasures take up all their time. They are philosophers, lovers, courtesans and artists.'[21] Admiring but excluded, he was more than ready to fall in love with the first of these fabulous creatures who deigned to show him any attention. At the fateful dinner in 1795, he was captured wholesale. After one evening with her, he was entirely devoted to Madame de Beauharnais.

Josephine's interest in Napoleon was utterly baffling to her friends. The ladies in the salons, the *Merveilleuses* and the women who wished to be like Josephine could not comprehend her willingness to humour the skinny little Corsican, who was six years her junior. But she was drawn to his ambition and intelligence, although she would not be his lover. She told Barras that 'she believed she could do better than him'.[22]

In October 1795, pro-royalist sentiment flared in the streets of Paris. In what became known as the 13 Vendémiaire, royalist supporters rose up and declared allegiance to the émigré army of the Comte d'Artois, then marching towards the capital. Barras put Napoleon in charge and he suppressed the riots with swift brutality. Hundreds of royalists were killed.

Barras and his allies used the violence to declare the need for a new political system, the Directory: five men in overall charge, presiding over the Council of Elders and the Council of Five Hundred. Barras quickly emerged as the leader. 'The memory of the terror today serves the friends of despotism,' said Madame de Staël.[23]

Barras resigned as Commander-in-Chief of the Army of the Interior and put Bonaparte, the inexperienced soldier who had been practically expelled from the army, in his place. At only twenty-six, Napoleon, dubbed General Vendémiare, was wealthy and celebrated. He moved to an expensive new house, took headquarters at the Place Vendôme and used a private box at the Opéra. He immediately started enriching his family – and redoubling his appeals to Josephine.

★   ★   ★

'When General Bonaparte fell in love with Mme de Beauharnais, it was love in all the power and strength of the term,' said his friend Auguste de Marmont. 'It was apparently his first passion and he felt it with all the vigour of his nature.'[24] Although he continued writing to his putative fiancée, Désirée, he was a man devoted.

Now that Napoleon was the military hero of Thermidor, Josephine became more enthusiastic about his advances. She wrote to him seducing his attention.

> You no longer come to see a friend who is fond of you. You have quite deserted her. This is a mistake, as she is tenderly attracted to you. Come to lunch with me tomorrow, *septidi*. I want to see you and talk to you about matters that will interest you. Good night, *mon ami, je vous embrasse*.[25]

Napoleon replied immediately. 'I cannot imagine the reason for the tone of your letter. I beg you to believe that no one desires your friendship as much as I do, no one could be more eager to prove it.'[26]

Josephine held out against Napoleon's pleadings for intimacy, but not for long. By December 1795 they were lovers. He scribbled his passion at seven o'clock in the morning, enraptured after their first night together.

> I wake up filled with thoughts of you. Your image, and the intoxicating pleasures of last night allow my senses no rest. Sweet and thrilling Josephine, what strange power you have over my heart! Are you annoyed with me? Are you unhappy? Are you upset? My soul is broken with grief and my love for you denies me repose. But how can I rest any more, when I submit to the feeling that overwhelms my very self, when I drink from your lips and from your heart a soothing flame? Yes! One night has taught me how short your portrait falls short of the reality! You start at noon: in three hours I shall see you again. Till then, a thousand kisses, *mio dolce amore*, but give me none back for they set my soul on fire.[27]

Napoleon's letter is a masterstroke of ardour – and somewhat different to the letters from his rival Lord Horatio Nelson to his mistress Emma, Lady Hamilton, telling her he thought of her so much 'I could not touch even pudding', and he had felt jealous on the last night and dreamed he had hit her with a 'big stick'.[28] In France, it was the age of the sentimental letter writer, of the outpouring of emotion, ruled by the fervent (although rather less explicit) letters in books such as Rousseau's *La Nouvelle Héloïse*. Napoleon threw all his emotions into his letters, high on sexual obsession. He scrawled hard, breaking holes through the paper with his pen, covering the words with blots because he was so impatient to write to her. Near-illegible and misspelled, his words burn with the fire in his soul for Josephine, her husky voice, clinging dresses and boudoir promises. As with his fiancée, Napoleon decided not to address his lover by her given name, instead feminising her middle name. He called her the name she would always be known by - Josephine.

Gone were all his notions that love was merely a 'social passion'. With Josephine, he was overturned, consumed and fascinated and could think of nothing but her. Poor Désirée wrote letters but they languished on his desk, barely touched.

Napoleon was immediately in thrall to Josephine's small waist and high bosom, her fine skin, delicate movements and low voice. In bed, he was delighted by her, baffled and excited by her repertoire of techniques and her flattering interest in him. Josephine recognised that Napoleon was a man who was always ambitious for theatre. She dressed up for him, doused herself in the scents he liked and embodied the role of the temptress. She decorated her chamber with absolute care, covering the walls with gilt and mirrors. In the old days, she had learned the hard way how to be a perpetual mistress to a man: willing, inventive, compliant. Her early roués had been only too familiar with such tricks – mirrors and shadowy postures in candlelight, bedroom acrobatics (Napoleon praised her 'zig-zags'), and perfume in the hidden hollows of the body. He had never encountered these tricks and he could not believe his luck. Josephine knew how to feign pleasure. As he later wrote to her, he never 'forgot those visits' to the 'little black forest'.

Napoleon had a fascination with make-up, partly because it was something his mother would never have used. Josephine, who bathed daily and whose dressing table groaned with pots of powder and skin whitener, was his ideal. She even made her own cosmetics – one she used in a 'very secret' ritual in her daily toilette, perhaps a form of the 'facial varnish' popular at the time to stretch out the skin and minimise wrinkles.

Her small hands and feet were the most exquisite imaginable (he was obsessed with hands and feet and was now very vain about his own). To him, she was the ultimate in beauty.

Almost as soon as they became lovers he was demanding that she marry him, throwing himself at her feet and falling into rages when she refused. Shy and nervous around women, conscious of his failings as a lover, he was convinced only she could understand him. Josephine's softness, her lack of education, her pliability, indolence and excessive femininity made her his dream lover. Even her failure to live within her means was erotic, yet another indication of how she needed the firm hand of a man. Her readiness to forgive slights and wrongs made her a good match for him. No woman who bore grudges could have lived with Napoleon.

He was also wildly jealous. One evening he announced he would use the cards to read the futures of the guests attending a party. He told Madame Tallien that she would experience 'a thousand follies'. When he came to General Hoche, he delivered what was, for a soldier, the ultimate insult: 'General, you will die in your bed.' He hated any man who admired Josephine – except Barras.

Napoleon wished to be the all-powerful man in every aspect of his life. Josephine looked up to him and asked for his advice. When he whipped himself up into a rage with her, she acted out the supplicant, weeping and pleading for mercy. She was a naturally lachrymose woman in a sentimental age, sometimes weeping three times a day, and Napoleon was swept away by the erotic tableau of her in tears. 'I keep remembering your kisses, your tears, your lovely jealousy,' he said.[29] Tears were proof of her emotion and her femininity, and Josephine's ability to turn on the waterworks was vital to her power over him. 'I was not born with a heart that could bear the sight and sound of weeping,' he said.[30] He found the image of her sobbing on her knees unbearably arousing. 'Ah! Tears!' he said, cynically, 'Woman's only weapon.'[31] Josephine's tears were a weapon he craved. He had a deep-seated need to watch her acting out the role of humiliated maiden – nothing bolstered his sense of masculinity more. With his instinct for drama, he loved to stir up terrible rows and push her to hysterical tears, and then forgive her, the lovers clinging to each other in passionate reconciliation.

'Bonaparte is all day in adoration before me as though I was a goddess,' Josephine wrote.[32] His sexual obsession with her was entrancingly novel, after a series of jaded men like Barras. But she had been broken in to the ways of love by her failed marriage. As a teenager on the ship over from Martinique, she too had been alight with ideas about romantic destiny derived from books and the enthusiasm of youth. After the cruelties of Alexandre and her treatment at the hands of her lovers and keepers in the years after her separation, Josephine had become a woman who did not have the luxury of believing in love. Romance and sex were to her a way of gaining status and security, the bargains that a woman had to make to survive. Over the years she had learned charm and sophistication, while forgoing her excitement, her joy in the new and her desire to lose herself to another. She had not been looking to fall in love, but for a man to support her and her children. Napoleon interested her and she loved him, in her way, but she no longer believed that passion could change her life.

Napoleon was sensual in his letters, but in person he could be rough and abrupt. He knew virtually nothing of polite conversation and instead expected Josephine to listen to him describing military plans. Although he adored her and was entirely in thrall to her sexuality, he had little interest in her thoughts or opinions and did not wish for much repartee. He was the type of man with whom a woman could feel terribly lonely, even as he caressed her.

Paul de Barras did not care that he had lost his mistress. When he had instructed Josephine to please Napoleon, he had only meant for her to ensure the soldier would remain by his side. But he had grown disillusioned with her, for she was both expensive and increasingly dependent on him. He thought Napoleon could support her and felt that they would both be more loyal to him if they believed they owed their happiness to him. He encouraged Napoleon to ask her to marry him. 'You have the rank, the talent to become a hero,' Barras said, 'but you are poorly connected; without fortune, without relations.' Barras explained that, as Napoleon put it, Josephine was valuable because she was part of 'both the old regime and the new' and would 'make people forget my Corsican name, would make me wholly French'.[33] To be 'wholly French' was Napoleon's ambition, and if he thought that Josephine could give him such a prize, he would have offered marriage even if she had been plain and twice his age. He promptly proposed.

She consulted her friends on whether to marry Bonaparte. The ladies thought him a joke, others worried that a military life was insecure and that a financier or a statesman would be a better bet. Josephine's lawyer was dismayed when he heard that her groom would offer her only the tiny sum of 1500 francs a year. She was aware that Napoleon's family did not approve of her. On top of it all, Hortense was unenthusiastic. She first met Napoleon at a dinner at the Luxembourg Palace − she was sitting between him and her mother and he was so desperate to talk to Josephine that Hortense had to give up, lean back and listen to his trumpeted chatter flying over her head. Afraid of losing her mother, she begged her not to marry him.

Josephine wrote to a friend, probably Madame de Krény, in a state of indecision.

> Do you like him? You will ask me. − But . . . No. − You feel cool about him then? − No; but I find myself in a lukewarm state which I do not like . . . Taking a side has always seemed tiring to my Creole nonchalance, I find it far easier to follow the will of others.
>
> . . . I admire the general's courage, the breadth of his knowledge of everything, of which he speaks equally well; the quickness of his mind, so he understands the thoughts of others almost before they have been expressed; but I am afraid, I admit, of the empire he seems to want over all those who surround him. His scrutinising gaze has something strange about it which I cannot explain.
>
> Finally, the thing that should please me, the force of passion, of which he speaks so much and which means one cannot doubt his sincerity, is exactly what stops me offering the consent that I am just as often on the point of giving.[34]

The strength of 'this affection which almost seems to render him delirious' discouraged her. She worried that if he fell out of love with her he would resent her. She had, after all, seen so many men infatuated with her but who then grew cold.

But the 'Widow Beauharnais', as she signed herself, could not remain single forever. Barras would not marry her. General Hoche was still visiting her over the winter, but showing no signs of divorcing his wife.

Josephine made up her mind. She agreed and said yes to his passion, to his obsession with her, to the small financial settlement and the role of a military wife. Napoleon, overjoyed, saw himself as beginning a new life with his prize by his side. In a signed contract both parties agreed that there would be no joint property or goods and neither would be responsible for the debts of the other.

In his letters Napoleon was the impassioned lover, but he had enquired into the status of Josephine's accounts and decided the wedding was to be swift and practical. There could be no church service for the friend of the Directoire, but there would also be no dinner or reception, as Josephine would have had if she had married a financier. A week previously, Napoleon had been made commander-in-chief of the French Army of Italy, and still he had no desire for a celebration. Josephine did not invite her children, or the Marquis de Beauharnais and aunt Edmée or her female friends. Napoleon's family were absent, disapproving from afar. Désirée heard the news and told him she was heartbroken. 'You have made me unhappy for the rest of my life,' she wrote. 'I shall never promise myself to another.'[35]

7

'The single object in my heart'

Josephine's second marriage was a quiet affair in a dingy town hall. Once stylish, the Hôtel du Mondragon was situated in a small road off the Avenue de l'Opéra and was serving as the town hall of the second municipal district of Paris. The grand panelling on the walls was faded and the great chandelier had fallen into disrepair.

Josephine arrived at the arranged time of 8pm on 9 March 1796. She wore one of her cherished muslin dresses with a tricolour sash. Napoleon had not yet arrived. Josephine waited in a room on the second floor reserved for civil marriages, watching the faces of the witnesses, Tallien and Barras, darken as the candles sputtered and died.

Napoleon still did not appear. There was nowhere to sit, no refreshments, and the registrar, Charles Leclercq, grew increasingly annoyed. Finally, he declared the wait insupportable and retired to bed, instructing his subordinate to take the ceremony. Josephine waited patiently. At ten o'clock, they heard the front door creak and then the unmistakeable noise of Napoleon clambering up the stairs. He burst into the room, accompanied by an aide. He had been drawing up military plans for the Army of Italy, so inspired by his own genius and so caught up in his imagination that he had entirely forgotten the time, he said. He was quickly forgiven and the ceremony was conducted by Leclercq's minion, Antoine Lacombe, his eyes nearly closing in the light of the one remaining candle.

Napoleon had made his power clear to Josephine: she must wait for him. Still, he found a way to make it up to her – the marriage certificate added eighteen months to his age and knocked four years off hers, making him twenty-eight and her a few months short of twenty-nine. He gave her a gold and enamel medallion engraved 'To destiny'.

To later observers, the wedding was flagrantly flawed. Because of the difficulty of obtaining documents from abroad, the officials waived the need for certificates of baptism and instead took sworn statements. Josephine's birth date was given as 1767, and Napoleon as having been born on 5 February 1768 (not 15 August 1769), which would have made her a child at the time of her first marriage and Napoleon only a month younger than his brother, Joseph. Still worse, his aide had not reached the age of majority and so should not have been a witness. There was doubt that Lacombe was qualified to conduct the marriage.

Napoleon declared it all excellent and whisked Josephine back to 6 rue Chantereine. He hoped for a night of passion, but Fortuné had other plans. In the bedroom, Josephine's mulish pug perched on the bed and would not be moved. As Napoleon recalled, 'I was told frankly that I must sleep elsewhere or share the bed with him.' Josephine was not in the mood to be merciful. 'Take it or leave it,' she said.[1] Napoleon tried to thrust the dog aside and the pug promptly bit him on the shin.

The day after the wedding, the Bonapartes drove to Saint-Germain to break the news to Eugène and then Hortense. Eugène was cool and Hortense wept. Napoleon treated them gently, wandering over the grounds, and asking them about their studies. He promised Madame Campan that he would enrol his sister Caroline at her school. 'Assure them that I love them as if they were my own children,' he wrote to Josephine.[2] It was not hard to love the two Beauharnais teenagers. Eugène was a good-looking young man, dutiful, gentle and obedient, with a strong sense of responsibility. His rather small stature was pleasing to his stepfather. No intellectual, he was hard-working and naturally contented. Hortense was the pet of Madame Campan's school, already tall, pretty, with beautiful, thick fair hair and fine skin, she was lively and gay, and excellent at her studies, with a particular skill for drawing and singing. Napoleon put her weeping down to youthful mood swings and was confident he would win them both over.

Josephine had been single for eight years and on her second day as a married woman, she was wishing Napoleon farewell. On 11 March, he played the general all day and then, that evening, briefly seized his bride in his arms, gathered his belongings and climbed into a carriage bound for Italy. In his baggage were 8000 livres in gold coins – and a miniature of his beloved. He longed for her to come to Italy. Unfortunately, the Directory had withheld Josephine's passport and she could not travel. They wished Napoleon's mind to be concentrated on the task in hand.

Napoleon set off, obsessively planning military strategy and passionately scribbling to Josephine in his spare moments. 'You are the constant object of my thoughts,' he wrote to her a few days after his departure. 'My mind is exhausted imagining what you are doing. If I see you sad, my heart is torn and my grief mounts. If you are gay and lively with your friends, I am full of reproaches.' As he put it, 'I am not easy to make content.' He foreswore his ego for her. 'The illnesses, the passions of men influence me only when I imagine them touching you, my love.' He signed off with 'a thousand kisses'.[3]

After a week's travelling, Napoleon paused to visit his mother in Marseilles. Josephine had written her a sweet letter of introduction, but Madame Letizia was not impressed. The family had all preferred Désirée Clary, who was docile and easily influenced. The notorious and famously extravagant Madame de Beauharnais, a fashion plate who already had two children, was far too old. Indeed, she was only thirteen years Letizia's junior. Napoleon was already the family's main breadwinner and they saw Josephine as a threat to their own chances of becoming rich through him. Still, Letizia accepted she had no choice and wrote a reply to Josephine, with Napoleon standing at her shoulder to dictate the words. Josephine, her soft voice, her tears and her 'zig-zags' had won. Napoleon had chosen the woman most likely to annoy his family and staked a claim for independence.

On 27 March, he arrived in Nice and greeted his senior officers. He stood in front of the raggle-taggle group of soldiers and promised them land, riches and victory. As he travelled, he thought of his wife.

Not a day has passed without my loving you, without holding you in my arms. Every time I drink a cup of tea, I curse the glory and ambition that keeps me from the soul of my existence. In the middle of business, at the head of my troops, reviewing the camps, my wonderful Josephine is the single object in my heart, occupation of my soul, absorbs my thoughts.[4]

The letters flooded into the rue Chantereine. Josephine's responses were rather slower. When they arrived, they inspired Napoleon with glee.

How can you think, my darling, of writing me like this? Don't you think I'm in a bad enough state as it is without further increasing my sadness and confounding my reason? What eloquence, what feeling you portray; they are fiery, they inflame my poor heart! My incomparable Josephine, away from you there is no joy – away from you the world is a wilderness in which I am alone and without experiencing the bliss of unburdening my soul. You have robbed me of more than my soul, you are the only thought of my life.[5]

All Napoleon's untapped literary ability came pouring out in the letters. 'By what art have you learnt to entrance all my faculties, to concentrate in yourself my spiritual existence – it is witchcraft, dear love, which will only end with me. To live for Josephine, that is the story of my life.'[6] She had never read anything so romantic, so heavy with longing. Napoleon was experiencing the exhilarating pleasure of pure physical passion. It was first love in every sense of the word. He sent her letters spilling love, and mused on the meaning of life. 'What means the past? What are we? What magic fluid surrounds and hides us from the things we most need to know?'[7]

He threw a tantrum when he thought her cool. 'I am not happy with your last letter, it is as chilly as one from a friend. I have not found that fire which kindles your looks, and which I have sometimes believed I found there.'[8] Napoleon had a policy of bundling his letters into a basket and would read them a few weeks later, on the principle that only a fifth would need answering by then.[9] But he seized Josephine's letters the minute they arrived, devoured them for details about her. He could hardly believe she was his wife. Even though the old addresses of Monsieur and Madame had returned, his early letters in the campaign were directed to Citoyenne Beauharnais, then Citoyenne Bonaparte care of Citoyenne Beauharnais.

Napoleon was always begging for more. 'If you loved me, you would write twice a day. But you have to chat with your gentlemen callers at ten in the morning and then listen to the empty gossip and silly nonsense of a hundred dandies until an hour past midnight.' He complained that in 'countries with any morals', women were home at ten and 'write to their husbands, think of them, live for them'.[10] He could have easily found such a biddable woman. He chose Josephine – independent, difficult and cool – because he adored a challenge. And he was her sexual slave. 'A kiss to the heart, then lower, much, *much lower.*'[11]

Napoleon's military campaign was patchy. He played down his failures in his letters to Barras and the Directory. On 21 April, Barras wrote to Josephine with the news that nearly 4000 enemy soldiers were imprisoned or killed. Two days later, Napoleon wrote to Josephine describing his victories and asking her to join him. 'Come quickly. I warn you: if you are late, you will find me ill.'[12] He informed her that Junot, his aide, was returning to Paris to deliver the flags of victory to the Directory, and she should return with him. If she did not, 'I will suffer misery without remedy.'[13] He sent an enthusiastic recommendation of Junot: 'he will breathe in your temple, you will maybe give him the unique and inestimable favour of a kiss on the cheek.'[14]

Josephine was content in Paris with her friends and had no desire for the hardships of travel. Her father-in-law, the Marquis de Beauharnais, and aunt Edmée were due to be married in June, and her children would return for the summer holidays. She was spending thousands of francs on renovating the house at rue Chantereine, employing the fashionable architect Vautier to redecorate the house entirely and create new furniture. She covered the walls with a sickly-sweet décor worthy of Madame de Pompadour, mistress of Louis XV, with Pompeian frescoes, pink little cupids, roses, mirrors and swans. Her bedroom was painted with swans and pink roses and adorned with bronze chairs and a new harp. Next door was a dressing room entirely covered with mirrors. She bought a fine mahogany table for the dining room and matching chairs, along with two marble-topped side tables. She had a free hand: Napoleon had approved her plan to redecorate and only suggested she 'put portraits of yourself everywhere'.[15]

Moreover, Josephine had a new-found celebrity to exploit. As the wife of a military hero she was cheered and feted, poets wrote long verses to her and she was besieged with presents and invitations. Merchants extended her credit. She, not Madame Tallien, was now the most sought-after woman in Paris, the guest everyone desired at their dinners and parties. In May, the Directory threw a ball to celebrate Napoleon's victories. 'Vive la citoyenne Bonaparte!' cried the people as they saw her. Another woman cried out that she was 'Notre Dame des Victoires'. The name 'Our Lady of Victories' stuck and was Josephine's until her death.

With such accolades and stardom, she had no desire to trek to Italy. Napoleon's letter to her was wildly passionate, the words written so hard that the paper had been torn. 'My life is a perpetual nightmare,' he wrote. 'I have lost more than life, more than happiness.'[16] He blamed 'perfidious friends' for keeping her away from him. 'I hate everybody who is near you.'[17] He would not hold back. 'To die without being loved by you, to die without that certainty, is the torment of hell.'[18] When he saw that the glass covering his miniature of Josephine was broken, he cried, 'my wife is either very ill or unfaithful'.[19]

General Murat was sent to persuade Josephine to leave for Italy. She told Murat she had been unwell – with symptoms similar to pregnancy. A man fixated by his virility, Napoleon was thrilled. 'I wish I could see your little stomach,' he blustered, 'it will make you look fascinating.'[20] Unfortunately, Josephine's fevers, headaches and irregular menstruation were not caused by pregnancy. She was only thirty-three but her health had been wrecked by her period of imprisonment and her menstrual cycle was irregular and often absent. Her reproductive health would not have been strengthened by her years as a kept mistress using contraceptive procedures such as noxious douches. She was probably infertile by the time of her marriage. In the years to come, Napoleon would hanker after the return of her 'little red sea', and she would lie to him about its frequency.

Josephine's letters reduced to a trickle. In June, she sent only two, of three lines each. Poor Napoleon begged for more. 'As if a pretty woman would give up her habits, her friends, Madame Tallien, a dinner with Barras and Fortuné.'[21] He gained victories, but dolefully sought after his Josephine. 'It's impossible that you inspired a limitless love and don't share it.'[22] As his friend, Marmont, said of him, 'He spoke frequently of her and his love, with the effusion, ardour, and the delusions of extreme youth.'[23] 'Without you, I am useless here. I will leave the chase after glory and serving the country to others.' It was all a picture of romantic despair. 'A thousand daggers are ripping my heart to bits,' he roared.[24] He dreamed of being her shoes and her gown. When she still did not reply, his letters grew wilder and Josephine threw them aside, weary with his 'delirium'. Once, she read out a letter in which he fretted about a rival and threatened he would take an Othello-style revenge. She simply laughed and said, 'He is funny, Bonaparte.'[25] Napoleon cried out about lovers, desperate for reassurance. 'Stay in Paris, have lovers – let everybody know it.'[26] She did not send him particular denials.

Napoleon was no fool, although people often took him for one. Usually correct in his judgements, he was hardly ever wrong about Josephine. 'Our Lady of Victories' was having an affair. In April, she had met a handsome soldier, Hippolyte Charles, when he had accompanied General Leclerc to call on her. Twenty-three and eager to please, a lieutenant in the Hussars, a gambler, man about town and a dandy, Hippolyte was rather small but extraordinarily good-looking, with a chiselled face, fine blue eyes and dark hair, and was very pernickety about his dress. Men sneered that he was a coxcomb, a hairdresser dancing attendance on the ladies. He was immediately a part of the circle of victory heroines. 'We are all smitten, Mmes Récamier, Tallien, Hamelin have all lost their heads, the man is so handsome,' Josephine wrote to Talleyrand. 'I think that there is no one in the world who ties his cravat with more aplomb.'[27] Few men could have provided a greater contrast with scruffy, ugly Napoleon. Hippolyte asked questions about fashion and hairstyles and always knew the latest gossip. He revelled in jokes, never a forte of Napoleon's, and played schoolboy pranks, throwing glue into General Junot's scabbard and pretending to be a Creole in Josephine's salon. As a young soldier at the Battle of Valmy, he had been nicknamed *l'Eveille* because of his talent to amuse – he woke everybody up.

Hippolyte pursued Josephine avidly, but with languid charm rather than the wild passion of Napoleon. Unlike her husband, who cheerfully rode roughshod over her opinions, Hippolyte was more deferential and liked to listen to Josephine converse. By the summer, they were having an affair. The man all her friends wanted was too enticing a conquest. Instead of writing to her husband, she was spending her mornings and afternoons with the best-dressed man in Paris.

Through Hippolyte, Josephine had also found a terribly risky way of making money. There was very little cash in the government coffers to fight the wars against Austria and so companies sprang up that would supply horses, uniforms and weapons and accept the money much later, usually with interest added. One of these was owned by Louis Bodin of Lyons. The companies fleeced the government and Bodin was one of the worst. Invoices were changed after submission and men in the field would open boxes and find blunt, rusty weapons. Instead of horses, he sent donkeys seized from French peasants. Despite such shocking practices, Bodin continued in business, because he paid bribes to the ministers and generals in charge. He used Hippolyte to pursue the relationship with army paymasters – and his employee's relationship with the wife of the man who made all the decisions was a gift to him (it is not impossible that Hippolyte chased her to further his career). Josephine took kickbacks from Bodin for smoothing relations with her husband's colleagues. She earned money to pay off her debts and buy herself elegant outfits that she could wear at balls as the Lady of the Victories.

All the while, Napoleon groaned for her presence. Josephine was hesitant, and the government was still withholding permission for her to travel. Finally, in May, the Directory wrote to Napoleon. 'It is with great reluctance that we yield to the desire of citoyenne Bonaparte to join you. We were afraid that the attention she would give you would distract from the glory and safety of your country.'²⁸ But it was too late; Josephine was in love with Hippolyte.

On 15 May, Napoleon entered Milan in triumph. At a dinner on the previous night, the hostess commented on his youth. He shrugged that he was indeed 'not very old at present – twenty-seven', but he would be much older in twenty-four hours as he would gain Milan (or *mille ans*).²⁹

He declared that he wished for Italian unification, but he presided over an orgy of looting. Carts of paintings, bronzes, statues and jewels were packed up by his soldiers and sent back to France. On 6 May, he had asked the Directory 'for a few reputable artists to take charge of choosing and transporting all the beautiful things we shall see fit to send to Paris'.³⁰ Artists and scholars, including Antoine Gros, arrived and drew up lists of prizes. Every conquered city and state surrendered its treasures. The Pope handed over twenty-one million francs worth of gold, a hundred paintings and *objets d'art*, and eighty-three statues, including the breathtaking *Apollo Belvedere*. Napoleon also took 500 manuscripts, including one by Virgil that had belonged to Petrarch and contained his notes (Bonaparte had initially wanted 2000 but the artists suggested he moderate his demands). The Duke of Parma gave up Correggio's *Dawn* and fifteen other pieces, including the same artist's *Madonna di San Geralamo*, much to the distress of the people of Parma. Napoleon personally demanded Raphael's *Madonna di Foligno* from Perugia. Venice lost its bronze horses from the Piazza San Marco. Works by Giorgione, Raphael, Leonardo, Lippi and Titian, among others, all created to glory the Italian city state, were seized by Napoleon and packed off to France. Private citizens found their walls devoid of paintings when they finally returned to the homes they had fled.

Nearly every week saw congratulatory articles in the French press, some written by Bonaparte himself, about the brilliant seizures of art in Italy. He and his soldiers claimed lofty ideals: true art belonged in France, the land of liberty and the home of man's cultural patrimony, rather than in the corrupt Italian state. He had received a command from the Directory that he should send back art 'in order to strengthen and embellish the reign of liberty'.[31] He knew it humiliated Italy to lose its art – and he wanted it for himself. Just as millions of the francs he stole went into his own pocket (possibly only a fifth of the money made its way back to the government), he was seizing works of art for the Louvre, the Directory and most of all for Josephine. Italy made her a true collector.

But still she did not write. Napoleon howled into the silence. 'I received a courier who left Paris on 27 May, and I have had no response, no news of my *bonne amie*. Could she have forgotten me or forgotten that there is no greater torment than not to have a letter from *mio dolce amore*? They gave me a great party here; five or six hundred elegant and beautiful ladies tried to charm me; none had that sweet and harmonious face which I have engraved on my heart. I saw only you, I thought only of you!'[32] He asked after the progress of her pregnancy. 'I imagine constantly that I see you, with your little round tummy.'[33] Josephine read the letter and set it aside. 'You know that I have never been in love before, that Josephine is the first woman I have adored,' he wrote to his brother. 'If she doesn't love me any more, there is nothing left for me.'[34]

By June, Napoleon had endured enough. He said he would leave at once for Paris. Josephine ignored the letter and continued dallying with Hippolyte. Enraged, Napoleon threatened the Directory that he would return home. 'I hate all women. I am in despair!' he roared to Barras. His paymaster needed Napoleon to win victories in Italy, and he swung into action. On 24 June, Barras informed Josephine she would have to travel immediately. He threw her a grand dinner at the Luxembourg Palace two days later, and then pushed her into a carriage. Josephine wept and protested and wore the expression of someone about to be sent to the scaffold.

Still, she had one consolation. In the first carriage, along with her cross little dog, Fortuné, was Hippolyte Charles, resplendent in his powder-blue uniform and scarlet sash.

8

A million kisses

'I have had the most difficult journey possible,' Josephine complained. 'I had a fever on mounting the carriage and was sad besides.'[1] Her six coaches of attendants, luggage, jewels and dresses rumbled through France. Hippolyte was her only consolation – he was returning as aide-de-camp to General Leclerc. By day, he and Josephine had to content themselves with smouldering looks and surreptitious touches of the hand, for they were escorted by Napoleon's brother, Joseph. By night, they took adjoining rooms at inns and slipped into each other's chambers.

Joseph did not notice the night-time creakings. He was preoccupied with scribbling away on the draft of a novel, and nursing a painful venereal infection. But Josephine's maid, Louise Compoint, one of the four servants accompanying her, did observe her mistress's behaviour, although she was distracted by a romance with the womanising General Junot. Certainly, they all saw Hippolyte was in love with Josephine and that he sulked every time she talked to anyone but him. Antoine Hamelin, a friend of Napoleon, felt unhappy seeing Bonaparte, already 'covered in a glory that he reflected on his wife', becoming the 'rival of a two-bit little man' who 'had nothing to offer but a good figure and the elegance of a wigmaker's boy'.[2]

Finally, two weeks after their departure, Josephine arrived at the gates of Milan to be met by huge crowds. She responded to the wild applause and tried to hide her misery that Hippolyte was set to leave for the army headquarters of Brescia. Napoleon was not there but he had decorated the Serbelloni Palace with flowers and filled the garden with new plants for her. The walls were decked with stolen Italian art.

A few days later, Napoleon arrived and the pair spent the third night of their married life together. Josephine was elegant in her clinging dress, and obviously not pregnant. The hero was so delighted to be in her arms again that he did not complain. She marshalled her charms to full advantage, flattering him, listening to his descriptions of military plans and pretending to be jealous of the Italian women. Napoleon was more obsessed than ever. He would often leap away from his papers and, as poor Hamelin blushed to report, play with her as if she were a child and 'overwhelm her with such rough caresses that I would go to the window'.[3] Then, four days after she arrived, Napoleon trundled off again to fight. 'I am dying of boredom here in the middle of the superb parties given to me,' Josephine bemoaned, missing the Talliens, Barras and her children.[4] Uncomfortable with the large household the Italians had given her, she discharged the staff and set up a much smaller establishment. Napoleon sent billowing letters of romance from the front line. He ranted about men who might admire her and waxed lyrical over her bodily delights. 'I thought that I loved you but now that I have seen you again, I love you a thousand times more,' he vaunted. 'Your charms burn my heart and my senses.' Josephine had heard it all before. He suggested she become more flawed, 'less beautiful, less gracious' and 'never be jealous, never cry, your tears carry away all reason and burn up my blood'.[5]

Napoleon's hysterical passion was no comfort for Josephine. She wrote to her aunt: 'My husband doesn't love me, he worships me. I think he will go mad. I have seen him only briefly, he is terribly busy.'[6] On 24 July, he gave Josephine her freedom from her gilded prison. He instructed her to come to Cassano. On the way, of course, she would have to stop at Brescia, and it would be her chance to see Hippolyte Charles. Napoleon declared his jealousy: 'I have been told that you have known for a long time and *very well* that gentleman you recommended to me for a business venture. If that was the case then you would be a monster.' He did not really believe it, but enjoyed creating a drama. He finished the letter, 'a thousand kisses everywhere, everywhere'.[7]

Josephine was on the way to Cassano when she and Hamelin spotted Austrian soldiers nearby. Napoleon ordered her to Peschiera, en route to Milan. The commander, General Guillaume, told her that he could not keep her safe and ordered her to leave immediately. She refused to do so until she had word from Napoleon. When he heard that the Austrians were moving towards the town, he sent Junot to tell her to travel to Castelnuovo, accompanied by dragoons. As they travelled, Junot saw an Austrian gunboat on a lake, turning to face its fire at them. He leaped from the carriage and pushed Josephine and her maid into a ditch. The two women had to crawl along under cover until the boat had passed. Hamelin was shocked that 'this woman so futile, so occupied with pleasures' could be courageous. 'Madame Bonaparte did not display one moment of weakness. Her only thoughts and worries were for the life, the glory, of her husband.'[8] At Castelnuovo, she threw herself weeping into Napoleon's arms. He then packed her and Hamelin off to Tuscany, again escorted by dragoons. In Florence, her house was invaded by eager locals, who had heard she was travelling with the dead body of her husband and wanted to see the corpse with their own eyes.

On 5 August, Josephine travelled through Tuscany and reached Brescia. After a decisive battle at Castiglione, Napoleon sent word for her to come to him at Cremona. Josephine pleaded exhaustion, unable to travel the twenty-five miles to her husband. She asked for one night in Brescia. That evening she had an intimate dinner with Hamelin and Hippolyte Charles. When the men were about to depart, she called Hippolyte back to attend to her. Hamelin later returned to retrieve his hat and a grenadier refused him entry. Josephine was back in Hippolyte's embrace.

One night was barely enough, but Josephine had to continue her journey. The next day, she and her husband met at Cremona and she was once more subjected to his passionate caresses. He set off again, not reassured. He accused her of writing to him as coldly 'as if we had been married for fifteen years'.[9] When no letters came, he went spiralling into a predictable rage. 'You are mean and ugly, very ugly, above all you are shallow. It is evil, to deceive a poor husband, a tender lover!'[10]

Josephine may have been a poor correspondent and dawdling with another man, but in Milan she played the wife of the great conquering Frenchman to perfection. She presided over balls and receptions and received delegations. They showered her with gifts, hoping she would win over her husband to their cause. The King and Queen of Naples sent a set of flawless pearls, the Duke of Modena offered gold worth thirty million francs if he were permitted to keep one Correggio painting. The Pope addressed her as his 'daughter in God' and gave her cameos.

Josephine still longed for Paris. 'All the Princes of Italy give me parties,' she wrote to her aunt. 'Well I would rather be a private citizen in France. I care not for honours bestowed in this country.' And yet she knew she was ungrateful in her hankering to be elsewhere. 'My husband is all day in adoration before me as if I were a goddess and there could not possibly be a better husband.'[11] She also wrote to Barras, ending most of her letters, 'Bonaparte sends you many messages; he still adores me.'

Two days after his majestic victory at Arcola, Napoleon was dreaming about Josephine's body. 'I am going to bed with my heart full of your adorable image,' he scribbled. 'I would be so happy if I could help undress you, small shoulder, small white breast, supple, very firm, the pretty little face and the hair tied up in a scarf *à la créole*. You know that I always remember the little visits, you know, the little black forest.' He hoped to return to Milan soon. 'I kiss it a thousand times and wait impatiently for the moment I will be in it. To live within Josephine is to live in the Elysian fields.' He finished with 'Kisses on your mouth, your eyelids, your shoulder, your breast everywhere, everywhere!'[12] She remained resolutely unconquered. Instead of waiting for her hero, she took the opportunity to hurry away to Genoa, no doubt to see Hippolyte Charles.

'I hope that in a few days you will be in my arms, and I will cover you with a million kisses, flaming like the equator,' Napoleon wrote on 23 November. Josephine did not receive the letter. On 27 November, he arrived at the Serbelloni Palace and dashed up the stairs to see his beloved. The bedchamber was empty. He was so shocked he almost fainted. When he came round, the servants told him she was in Genoa.

'I get to Milan, I fling myself into your room; I have left everything to see you, to hold you in my arms . . . You were not there, you were off somewhere or other in town.' He declared his heart was broken. 'The unhappiness I feel is incalculable.'[13] Next day, he wrote again.

While I give to you all my desires, all my thoughts, every second of my life, I submit to the power that your charms, your character and your whole person have over my poor heart. I am wrong if nature, unkind to me, has not given me the attraction needed to captivate you, but what I deserve from Josephine is respect, esteem and compassion.[14]

Napoleon gave full rein to his dramatic spirit, but there is no mistaking the sincerity of his feeling. Although he was too proud to believe that she would betray him, his painful cry 'nature has not given me attractions needed to captivate you' was a terrible admission for a man of his vanity. His despair was writ large on his body. A young general arrived in Milan and was shocked to find him 'haggard, thin, the skin sticking to his bones, the eyes shining with a constant fever'.[15]

On 7 December, Josephine finally returned. Once she was in front of him weeping on her knees, telling him she was true, he forgave her in an instant. He could not seriously believe she would be unfaithful. She threw a grand ball and he turned his mind to military planning. 'The army is without shoes,' Napoleon wrote heatedly, 'without pay, without clothes, the hospitals lack everything, our wounded are lying on the floors.'[16] It was the consequence of using companies like Bodin's: there was no flour and men were scouting in the hedges for food.

Despite the poor supplies, Napoleon's winter campaign was successful. The Corsican turned his attention to Austria. The Directory wished him to invade the country from the south, in order to meet the French Army of the Rhine. He advanced quickly towards Vienna, and was less than a hundred miles away by the end of March. On 26 March, he offered an armistice to the Austrians. He signed a treaty the following month, without writing to the Directory.

In May, keen to celebrate his victories, he moved his war court from Milan to the castle of Mombello, ten miles away. In Mombello, handsomely decorated with frescoes and luxuriously furnished, he instituted his own court, a carnival of Napoleon. His incredible charisma had cast a spell over his supporters, who had, as one of them put it, 'the sense of a future without limits'. His reception rooms were always crowded with generals, nobility and merchants from Italy, begging for the favour of a glance or a brief interview, and he dined in public like a king, allowing people to gaze on him. Josephine was always at his side and he delighted in her knack for performing the role of queen. She took the tributes with grace, led the ladies in the dancing and won over the enemy and the Frenchmen alike. Every week saw balls, receptions, dinners, hunting outings, as well as theatrical performances, operas with stars such as Madame Grassini, prima donna of La Scala, and boat outings on Lake Maggiore.

Napoleon spent some of the millions he had stolen on indulging Josephine at Mombello, and encouraged her to employ gardeners to lay out the grounds. To outsiders, they seemed the perfect couple. Napoleon took 'conjugal liberties' with his wife on journeys and jokingly threw 'pellets of bread at her during dinner'.[17] Josephine, noted a visiting poet, 'frequently caresses her husband and he seems devoted to her'.[18]

All the while, Madame Bonaparte was yearning for Hippolyte. The pint-sized dandy was often at Napoleon's side, as he had been promoted to one of his captains, but even Josephine did not dare conduct an affair while her husband was present. There were occasional surreptitious kisses and gifts, but these only made the pain worse.

She was more than happy to spend money keeping up the appearances Napoleon desired. Her debts were now running into the hundreds of thousands as she patronised the best dressmakers and bought nearly everything that was offered to her, too lazy and soft-hearted to haggle.

Josephine was loved, but her pug, Fortuné, had been barking at and threatening the other dogs at Mombello. 'I never knew a more horrible animal,' said Josephine's friend Laure Permond.[19] The little dog picked a fight with the cook's mongrel and the bigger animal savaged Fortuné to death. Josephine was distraught. It was a sad fate for the heroic pet who had run into Les Carmes prison to find his mistress. Napoleon was exultant at the death of his enemy, but sympathetic Hippolyte secretly bought her a replacement dog, a soft bundle she could embrace while she thought of her lover.

Napoleon hated the new animal. One day while out walking, he saw the cook trying to hide in the bushes. When he asked the reason for the man's bizarre behaviour, he was told that the cook was ashamed of his dog's crimes and that it was banned from the grounds of the palace. 'Bring him back, perhaps he will rid me of the new one too,' said Napoleon.[20]

Worse still for Josephine, the Bonaparte family had arrived and proximity was not breeding love. 'I have for him the most lively affection,' Napoleon wrote to her of his brother, just after their marriage. 'I trust he will obtain yours, he merits it.'[21] Poor Napoleon was ever hopeful. Divided over so much, the Bonaparte family were united in reviling Josephine. Joseph led their resentment, furious that her spendthrift ways drained Napoleon's purse. Hundreds of thousands of francs worth of confiscated gold and funds ended up in the pockets of the

Bonapartes, but still they complained. When Napoleon was made commander-in-chief in 1795, he had sent 60,000 francs to his mother, made Joseph consul in Italy and Lucien commissary with the Army of the North. His uncle, Cardinal Fesch (only six years Napoleon's senior, the child of the remarriage of his grandmother), left the priesthood to become a commissary, and in Mombello he was seizing artworks galore.

Joseph acted as the family banker, and was obsessed with money. His wife, Julie Clary, was a simple, modest woman, but unfortunately, as Désirée's sister, could hardly be Josephine's ally. The Bonaparte matriarch, Letizia, spoke Italian all the time and rarely managed a few words of French. Brought low by years of hardship, she was also preoccupied with money. When Napoleon complained, she would shrug, 'If ever all of you fall on my hands again, you will thank me for saving now.'[22] Letizia was, however, pleased by Josephine's act of concession at Mombello in always allowing her to enter a room first, although she was distressed by the lack of a child.

Elisa was the least troublesome of the sisters, a plain woman whose desperation for power was not as naked as that of her siblings. She had been forced to marry a Corsican officer, thanks to an absence of other suitors, but was little ruffled by her unhappy marriage. She tended to side with Lucien, but she was reasonably harmless, running an intellectual salon in Paris and supporting the author Chateaubriand against Napoleon's attempt to banish him. She hated Josephine but contented herself with sniping and complaining, rather than attempting to overthrow her.

For Letizia and the younger Bonapartes born after Napoleon's departure – Louis, Pauline, Caroline and Jérôme – life had been a struggle after the death of Carlo. Those early years of poverty had scarred them all and made them greedy for money. Louis was sickly, lazy and in the throes of gonorrhoea: paranoia, sores and delusions made him a man of 'harsh melancholy', as Josephine's lady-in-waiting put it.[23] Jérôme was the worst of all, a spoiled spendthrift who expected his brother to pay the bills. And then there was Napoleon's beautiful and aggressive sixteen-year-old sister, Pauline, Josephine's sworn enemy. Sensual and flirtatious, with a thick Italian accent and a frustratingly vague air, Pauline left a trail of chaos behind her. She loathed Josephine, stuck her tongue out at her in public if she felt like it, and tried to outdo her in diamonds and dresses. Pauline called her sister-in-law '*la vieille*' (the old lady) behind her back and every word about Josephine's beauty grated on her sensibilities. She tried to steal her patterns for gowns from her dressmakers and also attempted to find out her boudoir secrets. 'I am as good as she is,' she claimed. 'She is only more experienced than I am.' She was obsessed with the politician Louis Fréron, heavily associated with Thermidor, twenty-four years her senior and famous for his mistresses. On 14 June, Pauline was married off to the sombre General Leclerc, twenty-seven and very responsible. Napoleon hoped he might keep her out of trouble and away from Fréron. It made Pauline dislike Josephine even more, as she believed her to be behind the plan.

By September, Josephine was suffering, and even spending was no respite. She was told that Lazare Hoche had died of consumption at only twenty-nine. Hippolyte Charles had gone on campaign with General Leclerc and she heard that he had begun an affair with an Italian woman. She was very worried, for he still had her love letters. He had the power to expose her to Napoleon, his gloating family and a French public keen to hear scandal.

Back in France, the people were avidly following Bonaparte's victories. He was their hero, but the Directory was deeply unpopular. The royalists had won a majority in the Assembly of 1797 and the aristocrats were flocking back to the city and talking of restoring the King. Conspirators hung around corners and in clubs, wearing black velvet collars or wielding knotted handkerchiefs to show their allegiances.

Barras knew he was in a vulnerable position. Along with Talleyrand, he suggested that Napoleon might consider a *coup d'état* to show the Parisians who was in charge. The General shied from suppressing the popular will again, and gave the task to one of his generals, Pierre Augereau. The Directory put about rumours that a monarchist coup was imminent, and on 3 September Parisians awoke to find they were under military rule. Augereau's troops had laid siege to the Assembly, which was being held at the Tuileries. The next day, the deputies were arrested, newspapers were shut down and the elections were annulled. It was the end of the idealism of representation that had founded the Revolution of 1789. Over 160 captives described as 'enemies' were shot or deported. Ordinary Parisians cowered in their houses, shopkeepers refused to unfasten their shutters. The bloodletting was back.

In October, Napoleon confirmed the peace with Austria. Afraid of Vienna, the Republic of Venice invited him to visit in the hope of winning his protection. Unbeknown to them, France had secretly offered to cede Venice to Austria in return for Belgium and Lombardy. Aware that his visit would seem to Venice like tacit protection and that a refusal would pitch them into panic, Napoleon sent Josephine as his diplomatic representative.

The woman who had been a raw Martinique girl set off in style, after demanding a splendid collection of gowns paid for by army funds. The cost of her wardrobe could have paid for two or three months of the campaign. The huge entourage rumbled off to Venice and was met with ecstatic scenes inside the city. A hundred and fifty thousand people hung out of windows, throwing flowers to her and waving banners. She was as grand as Cleopatra. The following day, in a procession of hundreds of boats decorated with flowers, she went to dine in the open air at the Lido. The city authorities had spent weeks on the preparations. The highlight was a majestic evening of fireworks and another procession along the canal, followed by a grand ball at the Doge's Palace, where she was the guest of honour. On her return to Passirano, a delegation came to offer her 100,000 ducats if she could persuade Napoleon to favour Venice. Josephine received a handsome diamond ring for a speech she gave in their support. She smiled and nodded, entirely aware that Napoleon had already sold the city to Vienna.

In November, he departed Italy to debate the fate of Germany at Ratdstadt. Josephine returned to Paris. Throughout France, she received tributes to Napoleon as towns cheered her arrival and threw magnificent receptions. She smiled graciously – but her mind was elsewhere. Hippolyte Charles galloped after her and joined her at Nevers, his pockets stuffed with smuggled diamonds. Now that he did not have to follow Napoleon's commands, he could attend Josephine's whims as they idled across the countryside.

Napoleon arrived in Paris on 5 December, exhausted by his victories. He was shocked by his newly renovated home. Josephine had sent further orders from Italy asking the painter Jacques-Louis David to create a frieze in the salon, and she had been buying more mahogany furniture. The bill reached a huge 300,000 francs, scandalous when the house itself was only worth 40,000. It was fortunate that Napoleon had stolen millions of francs worth of gold from Italy. His general's income was a mere 15,000 francs a year, barely enough to fund Josephine's make-up.[24]

All Paris wished to celebrate him. Their street was renamed rue de la Victoire in his honour, and when Hortense arrived to see him she found 'people thronged in such vast numbers to cheer "The Conqueror of Italy" that the sentries stationed in the gateway of the house on the rue de la Victoire could hardly hold them back'.[25] Like many women, Madame de Staël had convinced herself that she was the hero's ideal companion. She wrote him gushing letters comparing him to Scipio and Tancred, described him as 'the most extraordinary genius ever seen', and complained he was married to an 'insignificant little Creole, quite incapable of understanding or appreciating his heroic qualities'.[26] The last thing Napoleon wanted was a strident, conspicuously clever woman such as Madame de Staël appreciating his heroic qualities, for he found the idea of women meddling in politics simply unbearable. Unfortunately, the more he ignored her, the more she swamped him with letters and later waylaid him at balls. When she first heard that Napoleon had returned, she dashed to his house. On being told that she could not enter because he was in the bath, she tried to push her way past, crying 'No matter, genius has no sex!'

Four days after the hero arrived, he was welcomed in a huge ceremony at the Luxembourg Palace. In front of crowds of spectators, Talleyrand presented 'the son and hero of the Revolution' to the Directory, declaring him a simple soldier who was uninterested in power. Barras thanked Napoleon for his presence and urged him to go on to conquer Britain.

Talleyrand intended one day to install himself as ruler, and hoped to use Napoleon as the military ballast to shore up his regime. He decided to cement his association with Napoleon by throwing a scandalously expensive ball to celebrate him, designed and overseen by Bélanger, a fashionable architect, who directed teams of carpenters and painters to remodel and decorate the Hôtel de Galliffet on the rue de Grenelle. Five hundred people were invited, all instructed not to wear any items of clothing from Britain. The ball was due to be held on 25 December and was to be dedicated to Josephine – but by the 24th, she had still not arrived.

She was spending her time with Hippolyte Charles, travelling slowly so that she could dine intimately with him and sleep longer in the mornings after their nights of passion. More in love with her handsome dandy than ever, she dreaded drawing close to the capital, where she would be separated from him and he would fall prey to other women.

Talleyrand postponed the ball until the 28th. The food and flowers had to be disposed of and reordered and hundreds of blossoming trees sent away. Servants gleefully pocketed fine breads and desserts from the untouched buffet. But since Josephine had still not appeared in Paris, Talleyrand postponed the ball once more.

On 3 January, she finally returned. Napoleon was furious, but she wept fetchingly and he forgave her. The ball finally proceeded. In the first courtyard the guests saw a great re-creation of a military camp, with soldiers from every regiment in the Army of Italy gathered around a fire. The reception rooms were decorated with stolen Italian art and Talleyrand himself stood at the centre of a staircase draped in myrtle. Napoleon and Josephine entered with Hortense, all plainly dressed, in stark contrast to the magnificent costumes of the other quests. The crowd fell silent at the sight of them. Just before the ball, fireworks shot into the sky and painted 'Vive la Republique' in flaming colours.

When dinner was called at 11pm, Talleyrand announced that he would revive, for a single night, the old custom in which the women were seated at the table while the men remained behind them, serving them with food and wine. Napoleon gallantly took up his position and impressed the company with his solicitousness. The meal's toast was to the 'Citoyenne who bears the name most dear to glory!' After dinner, Josephine was celebrated in a song as the 'dear companion' of the 'conquering hero'. Standing, cold and tired next to her already impatient husband, she had to smile beatifically as she listened to the voices proclaim 'By tending to his happiness/You acquit the obligation of France.'

However, Napoleon could not escape Madame de Staël. She captured him and demanded, 'Which woman in history do you most admire?' He retorted, 'The one who has borne the most children,' and marched abruptly away. 'Extraordinary man,' she exclaimed, undeterred.

The ball was unforgettable, even for blasé Parisians who were used to inventive entertainments. The tableaux were beautiful and the food divine, and it was the first night at which the company danced the new and risqué waltz. Napoleon, Josephine and Hortense departed at 1am, though the party was intended to continue until dawn. Poor

Talleyrand was then presented with hundreds of bills, made even bigger by Josephine's non-arrival. Bélanger 'begged the Minister to observe that the various delays occasioned by the late arrival of Madame Bonaparte caused a very large extra expense for items twice replaced like the 930 trees'. He also had to pay twice for painters, carpenters, masons, candlestick makers, engravers and gardeners – as well as massive sums for the buffet and musicians.[27]

Underneath the graciousness, Josephine was unhappy. She was uncomfortable with her new celebrity, missing Hippolyte Charles and suffering from Napoleon's fury over the bills for the renovations, as well as her lateness. When she heard her maid Louise Compoint had been having an affair with General Junot, she took out her temper on the girl. Josephine was very fond of her and the two had dined together more like companions than mistress and servant. But the news that she had been Junot's lover was too much and Josephine dismissed her.[28] Distraught, Louise began to plot her revenge.

9

'I am so distressed at being separated from him'

Napoleon was sure he was going to be poisoned. He employed someone to taste his food at all public events, took his own plate and glass to dinners, and kept a horse saddled and ready at the back of 6 rue de la Victoire. His friend, Bourrienne, declared that he had received a letter from a woman informing Napoleon that he would be killed. She was later found with her throat cut and her body mutilated.[1] He seemed to believe the threats to his life came from members of the Directory. Despite all the pomp and glory of the ball they had thrown for him, he was afraid of them.

'My health is ruined,' he complained to his brother. 'I can barely get into the saddle and need two years' rest.' He was exaggerating. He was living quietly in an attempt to win over the five Directors. They were teetering on a political knife edge and might turn against him at any moment. When he had boasted to Barras that the Italians wished to make him their king, he received a sharp response. 'You are right not to dream of any such thing in France for if the Directory was to send you to the Temple tomorrow, you would not find four people who opposed it.'[2] Barras had no qualms about threatening his protégé when he thought him too big for his boots.

The Directory was unloved. Inflation was rising and the Directors were seen as wealthy, corrupt and taking from the people. Napoleon despised them as weak, 'disturbed by the passions of the women, the children and the servants', but he had to pretend to be subservient to them.³ He could not glory in his success, as he had done in Italy. He refused invitations, sat in the shadows at the theatre and declined tributes, presented himself as a scholar, attending the Institut National des Sciences et des Arts. 'I shall bury myself in a retreat,' he declared. Talleyrand had pressed the Institut to accept him as a member, and Napoleon was delighted to be recognised as an intellectual rather than a military bruiser. He put it about that he and Josephine had become retiring scholars. Napoleon was merely biding his time. As he said to Bourrienne, 'I should overthrow them and be crowned king, but it is not yet time for that.'⁴

Josephine tended Napoleon's salon and invited poets, writers and scientists to the rue de la Victoire in order to bolster his pretence of being retired. In public, she played the consort so effectively that everyone was taken in by her husband's act. He 'shuns anything which might draw attention to himself', one newspaper noted. Meanwhile, his mind was working obsessively on his next conquest. 'This little Europe is a pinprick,' he wrote.' I must go to the Orient, all great reputations have been won there.'⁵

At the tender age of eleven at Brienne, he read of the campaigns of Alexander the Great, who had embarked to the Orient when he was only twenty. In 1789, Napoleon had been gripped by *Voyage en Egypte* by Constantin de Volney, a young Frenchman who had spent three years wandering the country in native dress – and when he met Volney on Corsica in 1792, he had questioned him intensely. In Italy at Mombello, inspired after dining with the French ambassador to Constantinople, Napoleon had dashed off a letter to the Directory declaring that it was time to take Egypt. He received no reply but he was not discouraged.

In July 1797, Talleyrand gave a speech before the Institut proposing an invasion of Egypt. A fortnight later, he was appointed to the role of foreign minister. Unaware that Talleyrand had raised Egypt in his lecture, Napoleon wrote to him. 'We must take Egypt,' he proposed. 'This country has never belonged to a European nation.' He asked for 25,000 men and eight or ten ships of the line.

France needed a conqueror of international might. The empire she had gained throughout the seventeenth century had been gradually lost to the British. Pondicherry and trading posts on the east coast of India were lost in 1761, Louisiana had been taken by the Spanish, and Britain took the Canadian colonies in 1763. Britain and France had fought over the West Indies. Britain had almost gained Martinique just before Josephine was born and there was bitter battle over France's other West Indian possessions, Guadeloupe and Saint-Domingue. France wished for an empire – and Egypt was a great prize. Napoleon planned to continue from Egypt to India, in the footsteps of Alexander. He would take scientists and philosophers and lead a voyage of discovery and cultural enrichment, as well as adding to France's imperial might.

Napoleon drew up careful plans, demanding 30,000 men and 3,000 horses. The Directory deemed the campaign impossible – the soldiers were needed to defend French interests in Italy. Aside from Talleyrand, the grey bankers of the Directory thought Egypt a romantic pipe dream. The warrior deputised Josephine to win them round. She sent letters, entertained them, hung on their every word – and turned the full force of her seductive personality on Barras. 'I wait in the hope that our friendship prompts you to sacrifice a quarter of an hour to come and see me, where you will find me absolutely alone. I hope, my dear Barras, that you will not refuse this mark of interest from a woman whom you care for.'[6] Josephine smiled, caressed, fluttered submissive eyelashes and lit candles for intimate suppers, but the men of the Directory were still unconvinced. Set on invading Britain, they sent Napoleon to survey the Channel ports in northern France and Belgium in February, leaving Josephine on her own again. She dined with Barras, saw Hippolyte and met with Bodin, earning money from his shady practices.

Napoleon returned on 21 February, earlier than she had expected. She wrote to Barras's secretary: 'Bonaparte has come back tonight. Will you, my dear Bottot, express to Barras my regrets that I cannot dine with him tonight. Tell him not to forget me. You know better than anyone how I am placed. Farewell, I send you my sincere friendship.'[7]

Josephine greeted her husband and it was all romantic reconciliation. Unfortunately, the haze of passion would not last long. In March, the newspapers erupted in fury over Bodin, his cheap horses and poor weapons, the exploited army and the French people who had been let down by the greedy businessman. The Bodin Company became the bête noire of the French people. Napoleon, like most soldiers, hated army profiteers, 'the scourge and leprosy of the service'.[8] He was stunned by suggestions that his wife had been linked to an organisation that had been revealed to be so corrupt. Unfortunately, the dismissed maid, Louise Compoint, chose that moment to revenge herself by spilling the beans about Josephine's relationship with Hippolyte. Normally, Napoleon would have paid no attention to a disgruntled servant, but now her words were yet another piece of evidence to Josephine's disadvantage.

Joseph struck fast. He went to Napoleon and told him that his wife had been working with Bodin, through Hippolyte Charles. The two brothers confronted her, with Joseph relishing every moment. They demanded to know if she was acquainted with Citoyen Bodin and if she had gained him contracts with the Army of Italy. Josephine denied it, and they moved on to more serious questions. Napoleon pushed his wife into a corner and asked if Captain Charles lived with Bodin at 100 Faubourg Saint-Honoré, and did Josephine go there every day?

She resorted to a typically dramatic response. She wept, railed and cried that if he wanted a divorce, he only had to say so. She bewailed her fate and said that he was distressing her, she pretended to faint and said she was cowering from his blows. She wrote to Hippolyte in panic, describing the ruthless interrogation.

> I said that what he was talking of meant nothing to me; if he wanted a divorce he had only to give the word; he had no need to use such means; and I was the most unfortunate of women and the most miserable.

Napoleon was won over, as delighted as ever by her dramatics and the tableau of her in tears, her rouge streaked over her face.[9] But he had not forgiven her entirely. He made it very clear to her that she would not be allowed out and she must never see Hippolyte again.

Josephine wept again and thanked her husband. But behind her tears, she was still desperately in love with Hippolyte.

> Yes, my Hippolyte, they have my unalloyed hatred; you alone have my tenderness and my love; they must see now, as a result of the terrible state I have been in for days, how much I abhor them; they can see my sadness – my despair at not being able to see you as

often as I wish. Hippolyte, I shall kill myself – yes, I wish to end a life that henceforth would be hopeless if it could not be devoted to you. Alas! What have I done to these monsters? But they are acting in vain, I will never give in to their disgraceful behaviour![10]

She was also thinking carefully.

Tell Bodin, I implore you, to say that he doesn't know me; that it has not been through me that he got the contracts for the Army of Italy; let him tell the door-keeper at No. 100 that when people ask him if Bodin lives there he is to say that he doesn't know him. Tell Bodin not to use the letters which I have given him for Italy until some time after his arrival when he needs them . . . Ah, they torment me in vain! They will never separate me from my Hippolyte![11]

These few incredible letters, found among Hippolyte Charles's papers, put her in a terrible light. Reckless and desperate to be with her lover, she said she would go clandestinely to Bodin's.

I will do everything to see you today. If I cannot, I will spend the evening at Bodin's and tomorrow I will send Blondin [a servant] to let you know the time when I can meet you in the garden of Mousseaux. Adieu, my Hippolyte, a thousand kisses, as burning as is my heart, and as devoted.[12]

I am going, my dear Hippolyte, to the country. I shall be back between half past five and six, to see you at Bodin's. Yes, my Hippolyte, life is a continual torture. You alone can make me happy. Tell me that you love me, and only me. I shall be the happiest of women.

Send me, by means of Blondin, 50,000 livres from the notes in your possession. Callot is demanding them. Farewell, I send you a thousand tender kisses. Tout à toi.[13]

Josephine's addiction to Hippolyte was pure danger. Underneath all her gentle smiles to Napoleon's generals and political friends, she was craving adventure and secret rebellion. The deception, the undercover assignations and the secrets were intoxicating.

Josephine's tears and cries about divorce won Napoleon round. He believed her, much to Joseph's fury, and bought the house in rue de la Victoire on 26 March for just over 50,000 francs. It would be foolish not to, since Josephine had spent 300,000 on the decorations. She was also fortunate. The Directory abandoned the plans to invade Britain. Napoleon was told he could advance to Egypt, and all his energies were now devoted to his new campaign.

The Directory set firm conditions with their brave young general. He could only have 25,000 men, he must raise the money for the expedition and he was forbidden from marching on to India. Talleyrand would assure the authorities at Constantinople that Napoleon had no aims to attack the Ottoman Empire, and merely wished to overthrow the Mamelukes of Egypt, allowing the French to trade in peace.

The Directory's decision threw Napoleon into a frenzy of activity, working day and night on planning the campaign. His way of raising the money was simple: he would steal from the countries he had 'liberated' from tyranny. Berthier, his chief-of-staff, travelled to Rome to rifle the Vatican, General Joubert did the same in Holland, and General Brune stole three million gold francs from the Swiss – the entire exchequer.

The greatest minds of Paris, including architects, artists, composers, astronomers, botanists, surgeons, literary scholars, printers, cartographers, zoologists and printers, were invited. The ships would be packed with everything from telescopes to chemistry sets. Napoleon even ordered one of the newest Montgolfier balloons – not to view enemy troop positions but in the hope of stunning the Egyptians into awe.

His official line was that he was aiming to invade Britain. Only his inner circle of generals and Josephine knew the truth. Even the Minister of War was kept in the dark. Indeed, some of the scholars refused Napoleon's invitation because they thought Britain too chilly and lacking in scientific potential. Josephine had to keep her mouth closed, and did not even tell Hippolyte of the plans. Hippolyte may have been her lover, but she was not prepared to betray her husband militarily – even if she could have profited from sharing such important information.

Stealing money, discussing balloons and drawing up strategies pre-occupied Napoleon completely, though he did attend to pleasing Josephine's children, finally winning over Hortense and offering to take

Eugène as an aide-de-camp. Josephine begged him to allow her to come too, telling him that her childhood on Martinique meant she would be accustomed to the heat. The Directory had commanded him to return in six months, but she knew that he had been suggesting he might stay six years, depending on the course of events. 'I shall colonize that country,' he said. 'We are only twenty-nine years old, we'll be thirty-five then.'[14] Bourrienne, who had been attempting to make himself useful to Napoleon since their schooldays at Brienne, received his reward. Napoleon appointed him his private secretary and took him to Egypt.

Josephine would be in a vulnerable position if Napoleon was away for longer than six months. She had grown jealous that he had become increasingly attractive to other women since his victories in Italy. The credit she was given by shopkeepers and bankers was contingent on her promise that he would be present to pay her debts. While he was travelling around the Orient, her lenders might very well call in their loans. As insurance, she begged Napoleon to buy the country estate of Malmaison, the beautiful house she had admired from her window when she lived at Croissy with Madame Hosten. Napoleon could see the appeal of a country estate and he agreed to view the house. The owners, the Couteulx du Molays, had bought the property in 1771 and thrown lavish receptions where they entertained members of the highest society and artists such as the great painter of Marie Antoinette's portrait, Elisabeth Vigée Le Brun. But aristocratic fortunes had declined after the Revolution and they needed to sell. Josephine loved the estate but the hero of France was scandalised by the asking price and told his wife to abandon her plans.

The house at 6 rue de la Victoire became overwhelmed by preparations for departure. Generals, messengers, scholars and artists were constantly at Napoleon's door as his brilliant mind oversaw the loading of thousands of men, horses and civilians, and all their equipment, onto vessels at six different ports. Time was of the essence: he needed to be in Egypt before the annual flooding of the Nile made campaigning impossible. On the evening of 4 May, the Bonapartes dined with Barras and saw *Macbeth* at the theatre. Then they departed Paris at four in the morning, too early for British spies to spot them leave. Napoleon and Josephine hurried to Toulon, arriving on 9 May. There she saw for the first time the French fleet bound for adventure.

One hundred and eighty ships stretched for miles, their masts swaying in the breeze.

The crown jewel, *L'Orient*, was Napoleon's flagship, the most powerful warship in the world. Made from 6000 oak trees, it was 214 feet long and had 120 cannons, and carried 2000 men.[15] Napoleon's fine chamber contained a library of nearly 300 books, carefully chosen by the poet Arnault. He had the Koran, the Hindu Vedas and Volney's *Voyage*. He also had a printing press, to make pamphlets declaring his excellence to the people of Egypt.

He assumed his position on the admiral's barge and boarded each warship to inspect it. After months of pretending retirement, Napoleon had his reward of pomp and grandeur in front of thousands. His soldiers cheered him, along with the scholars and their instruments (they were beginning to wonder if they were really going to Britain). Stowed away on the ships were also more than 300 women. Along with the washer-women and seamstresses, who officially accompanied the army, were the wives of officers, bundled up in men's uniforms while boarding and ensconced in cabins. Napoleon showed Josephine his quarters on *L'Orient* (including a special bed on rolling casters to assist with sea sickness, and 800 bottles of wine).

Bonaparte was not yet thirty and his mission to Egypt would be the first great seaborne invasion of the modern world. The following day, he inspected the troops and told them that the ideal of liberty of the Revolution meant France should conquer distant lands. If they succeeded, he promised, they would each be given six acres of land.

While he waited for a storm at sea to subside, Josephine still hoped he might allow her to come too. He agreed that she could join him later at Naples, once he had passed the British fleet under Nelson, which he knew was heading into the Mediterranean. Finally, on 19 May, the French fleet departed. Josephine watched from a balcony and wept as her husband left amid the firing of cannon, the shouts of the people and the music of the brass bands.

Napoleon set off towards Egypt, the conquering hero at the front of the fleet he had stolen from half of Europe to fund. For him, it was a time of hope and almost unbounded opportunity. On the journey over, he initiated conversations on topics from the age of the world to whether other planets were inhabited. Even the realm of space travel seemed open to him.

While Napoleon pondered alien life forms, Josephine followed his orders and waited at Toulon for two weeks for the news that the fleet had safely passed Sicily. She then set off for the spa town at Plombières to take the waters before travelling to Naples. On the way to Lyons, she wrote to tell Barras that General Brune, the French commander in Switzerland, was trying to break the government contracts held by the Bodin Company. 'Write on their behalf, I beg you, to General Brune,' she urged. 'Both you and I owe everything to them.'[16] She was still expecting Barras to protect her – and trying to help Hippolyte.

Plombières was a quiet town in the lush pine forests of the Vosges mountains in Lorraine, made up of small houses with balconies. Dating back to Roman times, the baths had been restored in the early seventeenth century. Since then, hundreds of well-heeled invalids had flocked to Plombières: rheumatic old women and gout-ridden men, along with dozens of frantic infertile women.[17] The local doctor, Johannes Martinet, ran a roaring trade and in 1791 published a book promoting the waters and their wonderful effects – *Observations sur quelques maladies chroniques et sur les effets des eaux de Plombières dans ces maladies*. He was an advertising genius holding out the promise of eternal youth. Josephine lodged in the Pension Martinet, with her maids and her huge wardrobe, took the waters and took promenades in the town. Plombières was a good place to prove her virtue to her husband. One visitor attended a ball and reported that there were sixty women to twelve men, and only four of the men were fit to dance.

Having learned from her previous mistakes, Josephine wrote eagerly to Bonaparte, sending the letters by courier to Barras to forward. 'I am so distressed at being separated from him that I cannot overcome my sadness,' she told him. 'His brother, with whom he corresponds so closely, is so horrible about me that I am always worried when I am far from Bonaparte.'[18] She dreaded Joseph. 'He is a vile, abominable person,' she wrote heatedly, 'some day you will know what he is like.'[19] She was still flirting with her former lover. 'I wish that the waters of Plombières could be prescribed for you,' she told Barras coyly, 'so that you could decide to come here and take them. It would be very kind of you to have an ailment in order to be able to cause me pleasure. I am very devoted to you.'[20]

The woman who had once infuriated Bonaparte with her failure to write was now scribbling every day. 'You know him and you understand how he would hate not getting news from me regularly,' she wrote to Barras. 'He says that I am to rejoin him as soon as possible and so I am hurrying to finish the cure.'[21]

The debacle with the Bodin Company had made Josephine feel nervous about her husband travelling without her, and she genuinely desired to go to Egypt, at least for a short time. And yet, after her cure, she planned to return to Paris for a few days, before setting out to Italy to meet the boat – it would have been hard to resist seeing Hippolyte.

Either way, she did not have a chance to prove her newfound devotion. On 20 June, two days after her letters to Barras, one of her maids called Josephine and her visitors to the balcony to see a little dog on the street. They all rushed to the balcony and it collapsed under their weight. The party fell twenty feet to the ground. One of her companions broke her leg and Josephine herself was badly hurt, for she was at the front and her visitors had landed on her. Her injuries were severe – she had a suspected broken pelvis and her spine was so bruised that she could not move.

The physician Martinet, a man more used to treating country burghers than the wife of the conqueror of Italy, promptly wrapped her in the bloody skin of a newly killed sheep, bled her, administered an enema and plunged her into a hot bath. Martinet sent daily reports to Barras, intent on ensuring the health of such an estimable patient. Poor Josephine was tormented by douches, hot baths, more enemas, poultices, plasters, leeches, camphor and compresses of brandy and boiled potatoes. Determined to make his fame out of the wife of Napoleon Bonaparte, he took notes of his treatments and would eventually publish everything in his *Journal physico-médical des eaux de Plombières*. Martinet informed her she had to stay there for two months, imbibing the waters and submitting to his treatments.

Hortense was rushed from school in Paris to find her mother an invalid and unable to feed herself. It was made worse by Napoleon's missives in which he said he could not live without her and reiterated the instructions to embark at Naples. 'I wish my health would permit me to depart now; but I don't see the end of my cure,' she wrote to Barras in July. 'I cannot stand upright for more than ten minutes without terrible pains in the lower back. I do nothing but cry. The doctors say that in a month I shall be cured.' She did concede that his letter had 'put balm on my bruises'.[22]

Nevertheless, Barras's letters and Martinet's enthusiastic baths and potions did the trick – or at least did not hinder a natural improvement. By August, Josephine had recovered and agreed to act as godparent, along with Barras, to Martinet's newborn daughter. On 15 August, she and Hortense arrived back in Paris. Pictures of Napoleon were suspended around the city. She was still hopeful of joining him in Egypt, if a ship could be found. But then a shocking piece of news came through. She wrote immediately to Barras. 'I am so worried about the news that has just come in via Malta that I must ask to see you alone tonight at nine. Give orders for no-one else to enter.'[23]

On 1 August, at Aboukir off the coast of Alexandria, Nelson had attacked the French fleet and all but four of Napoleon's ships had been sunk.

When British spies had seen the ships assembling at the French ports, they began to debate Napoleon's destination. The Minister for War and the British Consul in Livorno suggested Egypt. Earl Spencer, First Lord of the Admiralty, ordered the dispatch of Horatio Nelson, then Rear Admiral of the Blue, to the Mediterranean to ascertain Napoleon's destination. Thirty-nine-year-old Nelson, a genius for strategy and propaganda, set off, missing an arm, wounded in one eye and equipped with a pathological hatred of the French. Nelson had much in common with Napoleon, for he was also a social outsider and impatient with etiquette. He had been living in miserable retirement with his wife, making model ships and reading *The Times*, and he was hungry to be back at sea chasing his prey.

Napoleon was aware the British had been dispatched, but was too convinced of his own brilliance to worry. He avoided Nelson with ease, and on 11 June took Malta and raided the island's coffers. The Knights of Malta, the possessors of the island, were ageing and the 10,000 men who made up the garrison were not loyal and were unlikely to risk their lives to defend their masters. Napoleon banished the Knights and set about making the island into a modern state. He issued dispatches, abolished feudal privileges and freed 2000 slaves. Meanwhile, his men scoured the monasteries, churches and knightly properties for treasure. On 19 June, they set off once more, their trunks filled with gold.

On board, Napoleon pondered Islamic history and chattered about his wife. 'Josephine almost always formed the subject of our intimate chats,' Bourrienne noted. 'His love for her verged on idolatory.'²⁴ The thought of Josephine was a distraction from the awful conditions on board, for the meticulously planned food stores had been spoiled and the men were living on dry, wormy biscuits. When the fleet landed at Aboukir, Napoleon was concerned that Nelson might not be far behind. He demanded his men disembark immediately, but the sea was rough and many boats capsized. Already exhausted and broken, the soldiers began marching to Alexandria, spurred on by the thought of finding drinking water. Alexandria surrendered quickly and Napoleon's men won another victory over Mameluke troops at Shubra Khit, a village on the Nile. He commanded his battle-scarred men to continue on to Cairo.

If he had been missing Josephine on the boat, he was craving her in Egypt. In the calm after the victory over the Mamelukes, he had been boasting of his wife's excellence. General Junot had seen the men laughing behind their hands and felt Napoleon must be told the truth. A cynical philanderer, Junot had little belief in love. Most of all, he hated Josephine for dismissing Louise because of their affair, and he wanted revenge.

As Junot accompanied Napoleon past an oasis, he seized his moment. He told him that Josephine had continued her affair with Hippolyte and that all Paris knew it. Then he handed him a letter that proved the evidence. He reiterated that Louise had travelled with Josephine en route to Italy and she had seen everything. Napoleon fell into a state of shock: his face paled and his limbs began jerking. He beat his head with his fists. 'I have no wish to be the laughing stock . . . I will divorce her.' He cried out, 'Divorce – I want a public and sensational divorce.'

He dashed to Bourrienne and asked him the truth.

Josephine! – and I six hundred leagues from her – you ought to have told me. That she should have deceived me like this! – Woe to them! – I will exterminate the whole race of fops and puppies! As to her – divorce! Yes, divorce! A public and open divorce! ²⁵

Napoleon said he would write to his brother Joseph to pursue the divorce. 'I will not be a laughing-stock for all the idiots in Paris.'

Bourrienne attempted to quiet him, urging that it would be unreasonable to rely on hearsay evidence while so far away. He told him that it was unfair to accuse a woman who was not present to defend herself. As for divorce, 'it would be time to think of that hereafter'.[26] Napoleon eventually agreed to restrain himself from immediate action. His anger was subsiding. 'I would give anything if what Junot had told me was untrue, I love her so much.'[27] But it was clearly only a matter of time before he abandoned his wife. Night after night, Napoleon invited his stepson to his tent to bemoan Josephine's behaviour. Eugène was powerless in the face of his emotion. Josephine was ruined.

Napoleon turned his thoughts to battle. At Embabeh, they took on the Mamelukes again, and he sent home news of his great victory at 'The Battle of the Pyramids'. On 24 July, he entered Cairo. Instead of the opulence they expected, his men found 'shadowy houses often in ruins, even the public buildings seem like dungeons, shops are nothing better than stables'. Mercilessly, they complained that all the children were skinny and covered in flies.[28]

Napoleon requisitioned the palace of Elfi Bey on the edge of the city. Only recently renovated, the residence was a riot of marble, mirrors, damask curtains and silk-woven Persian carpets, with sunken baths on both floors. He settled in and sent the Directory his requirements for creating a properly French community in Cairo.

> 1st, a company of actors; 2d, a company of dancers; 3d, some dealers in marionettes, at least three or four; 4th, a hundred French women; 5th, the wives of all the men employed in the corps; 6th, twenty surgeons, thirty apothecaries, and ten Physicians; 7th, some founders; 8th, some distillers and dealers in liquor; 9th fifty gardeners with their families, and the seeds of every kind of vegetable; 10th, each party to bring with them: 200,000 pints of brandy; 11th, 30,000 ells of blue and scarlet cloth; 12th, a supply of soap and oil.[29]

Almost immediately, the conqueror ordered the building of hospitals and bakeries, made lit torches outside houses mandatory and forbade the burial of bodies inside the city walls. Declaring himself the liberator of the Egyptian people, he set up newspapers, threw balls and receptions and founded the Egyptian Institute for the scholars he had brought with him. The wives who had hidden themselves in uniforms now appeared openly, while the soldiers and scholars began to befriend the Egyptian women, even though they were rather shocked at their size (to compliment an Egyptian lady, they learned, one should say 'she was so beautiful, she could not get through the door'). The Egyptians complained that the Frenchmen were giving the women ideas about dominance – since they gave gifts and presents and 'pride themselves on their submission to women'.

Napoleon was still tormented by Junot's revelations. On 25 July, he sent Joseph a letter filled with despair. 'I have a lot of domestic problems for the veil is completely torn away. You are the only person left to me in this world,' he mourned. 'It is a sad state of affairs when all one's affection is concentrated in a single person. You know what I mean.' In words not dissimilar to those in his novel *Clisson et Eugénie*, he said he wished never to see Josephine again. 'I have had enough of people. I need solitude and isolation. Greatness no longer interests me. All feeling in me is dried up. At twenty-nine, everything is over.'[30]

Eugène wrote quickly to his mother.

My dear mama, I have so much to say to you that I don't know how to start. Bonaparte has been miserable for five days, as a result of a conversation with Julien, Junot and Berthier. Their words have affected him more than I would have believed. All I have heard amounts to this: that Charles travelled in your carriage until you were within three posting stations of Paris; that you met him in Paris; that you were with him at the Theatre of the Italians in the private boxes; that he gave you your little dog; that even now you are with him. Such, in scattered phrases, is everything that I have heard. You know, mama, that I don't believe a word; but what is certain is that the general is very upset. However, he redoubles his kindnesses to me. He seems to say, by his actions, that children are not responsible for the faults of their mother. Your son, however, chooses to believe that all this gossip has been manufactured by your enemies. Your son loves you as much as ever and is as eager as ever to greet you. I hope that when you do come all will be forgotten.[31]

Without Josephine there to fling herself weeping at his feet, Napoleon dwelled on her faults. The thought that everyone knew he had been shamed was deeply painful to him.

On 13 August, many of Napoleon's crew were offshore when Nelson arrived at Alexandria and most of the ships were undermanned. At three o'clock, Nelson took dinner and ordered fast action. At ten, *L'Orient* exploded into fire, killing hundreds of men. With it sank 600,000 livres in gold and diamonds stolen from Malta. Eleven warships were captured or lost and at least 1200 men were dead, with thousands more taken prisoner.

When the news of the attack on his fleet reached Napoleon, he received it 'without a flicker of emotion passing over his features'.[32] Holed up in his handsome marble palace in Cairo, he told his men that Britain might control the sea but France still had an empire on land, in the place where three continents joined. 'We are obliged to found a great Empire, and found it we will,' he announced. 'The sea, of which we are not masters, separates us from our homeland; but no sea separates us from either Africa or Asia.'[33] 'Everything is perfectly fine here,' he wrote airily to the Directory. He addressed questions of tax and property laws and made plans for further conquest.

The Battle of the Nile, as it became known, was an incredible victory for Britain. By the end of 1798, everyone in Britain and most people in Europe owned some sort of picture of Nelson in tribute, from cheap prints or his face on a tankard to expensive portraits. Women across the land draped themselves in Nelsonia, proudly wearing anchor necklaces, 'N' brooches and headbands and Nile-themed shawls. A popular print by the scabrous James Gillray showed a one-armed Nelson by the pyramids beating red, white and blue crocodiles with his truncheon made of 'British Oak'. The King and Queen of Naples, via the British Envoy's glamorous wife Emma, Lady Hamilton, begged the hero of the Nile to come to Naples to protect them. Lady Hamilton told him, 'I walk and tread in the air with pride to think I was born in the same land as Nelson and his gallant band.'[34] Nelson dashed to her – and out of Napoleon's way.

In Paris, Josephine continued her life blithely unaware that Napoleon knew of her infidelity. She frequented the friends her husband disliked. Barras, Thérésa Tallien and Juliette Récamier were often at her salons, along with the cream of society. Musicians and composers including Méhul and Cherubini, artists such as Gérard and Girodet, and Bernardin de Saint-Pierre, author of Napoleon's beloved *Paul et Virginie*, all came to her receptions. She also, dutifully, invited her sisters-in-law. The poet Arnault had fled Napoleon's company at Malta and travelled back to Paris. He found the delicate company of Josephine much preferable to rotten biscuits with her husband. She also saw Hippolyte Charles, flirted with handsome men and failed to write to Napoleon.

In October 1798, a Parisian newspaper reported that a French mail ship had been captured and letters written by Napoleon seized by the British. Among dreary lists of instructions and letters about domestic affairs from other officers was Napoleon's missive of 25 July, bewailing to Joseph that the 'veil is torn', and Eugène's to his mother telling her that Junot had told her secrets. After the success of the Battle of the Nile, the letters were a gift to the British, another indication of a weakness in Napoleon's armour. James Perry, the editor of the *Morning Chronicle*, grasped the scoop and printed sections of the letters on 24 November 1798. The readers goggled at Napoleon crying over his wife. They were not only read over the breakfast tables of London and Manchester. Unfortunately for Josephine, the *Morning Chronicle* was available in Paris. Before long, everybody knew of Napoleon's misery – and Josephine's terrible disgrace.[35]

10

'All I have suffered'

aul de Barras put pressure on the French newspapers not
to reprint the news about Madame Bonaparte. But copies
of the *Chronicle* passed hands and the rumours spread about
the marriage of the Bonapartes and Josephine's behaviour. She knew
she had been exposed. She grew desperate and terrified of the power
of Napoleon's family to destroy her.

Joseph was deeply gratified that his brother's letter to him had been
published. He refused to give Josephine money and laughed in her face.
When Louis Bonaparte returned from Egypt, he too declined to visit
her. In Paris, Josephine found herself shunned, mocked and ignored.
The French never received the letter. It still lies in the British Museum,
written across in Nelson's distinctive spiky hand, 'found on the person
of the courier'.[1]

Now that everyone knew about her infidelity, her creditors began
to call in their debts. She could not pay even the smallest bills.[2] She
tried to charm and influence the Directory and other men of power,
but this only gave her enemies more ammunition against her.

In his letter to Joseph, Napoleon had suggested he would keep 6
rue de la Victoire. Josephine knew it was her last chance to raise the
money she needed to buy a country property. Malmaison, the home
Napoleon had turned down, became invested in her mind with the
security she needed and the possibility of creating a rural retreat of
happiness in which Napoleon might fall in love with her all over
again. He would return, the great conquering hero, she would throw

herself at his feet and then he would pay her bills. She had ammunition of her own: Joseph had purchased the Chateau de Mortefontaine for 285,000 francs and she knew Napoleon would not want to be outdone.

Josephine visited Malmaison again with Hortense. She was particularly delighted by its beautiful situation amid lush green lawns, woodland and vineyards. She had always missed the foliage and flowers of Martinique, and Malmaison, she hoped, would be her chance to create gardens full of exotic plants. In October 1798, she asked her old friend Jean Chanorier, Mayor of Croissy, to approach the Molays about selling the property. All through that miserable winter of 1798–9, Josephine fretted and worried about money, had Barras fight off the debt collectors, borrowed funds and haggled through Chanorier.

Malmaison first appeared in the records in 1244 as a simple barn. By the fourteenth century, the site had become a substantial manor house, and it would remain in the same family until 1763. For Josephine, a typical example of the individual enriched by the Directory, buying it was staking a claim on history. Monsieur du Molay loved the house and could not bring himself to be involved in its sale (especially not to a *nouveau riche* wife like Josephine).[3] His wife took over negotiations. The women's drawn-out correspondence, with Chanorier acting as arbiter, is a testimony to female prowess, determination and business acumen. Neither party was prepared to give in easily.

In a letter dated 1 March 1799, Chanorier declared Malmaison to be not only 'the prettiest property I know', but also, as a working farm, exceedingly 'useful' in a financial sense.[4] He informed Josephine that Madame du Molay was asking for 300,000 francs and claiming that Bonaparte had agreed the price with a Molay relative who was 'prepared to testify to it'. He answered firmly. 'I told her that the General had only ever spoken of 250,000 francs; but that even if he had, the land would have decreased in value since then.'[5]

Josephine responded unequivocally. 'The price asked by Mme du Molay is too much,' she informed Chanorier. 'Whatever desire I might have had to come to an agreement over Malmaison, I am obliged to withdraw my interest. My last offer is 100,000 ecus [250,000 francs], for immediate occupation.'[6]

Then, on 17 March, she conceded.

My final offer, taking into account your opinion and the information you have given me, is 310,000 francs, to include everything and for immediate occupation. I firmly believe that I should not have to pay any more than this, and I'm keen to resolve the matter one way or another.[7]

Madame du Molay did eventually find Josephine's offer suitable. But she was not to be moved on easily. 'Poor Mme du Molay shuddered,' Chanorier wrote, 'when I told her that, being tired of Paris, if you purchased the property, it was quite possible that you would take up residence within a fortnight.' The Molays had asked to stay in one of the apartments in the farm until mid-July. 'That way, you could move in the day after you bought it.'[8]

For all her firm words, Josephine had been ruled by her heart. She later admitted that the final asking price amounted to well over 325,000 francs. Joseph had bought his grand chateau with 700 acres of land for much less. An undated letter from her to Barras, published in 1820 and recorded as being 'for Malmaison', suggests he helped her find the money to buy the house.

I was sure that this would interest you; I was no less sure that you would succeed. Here I am now certain of possessing a refuge, and thanks to this kindness, which is made all the sweeter by the grace with which it is offered, this refuge meets all my requirements, and I can allow my passions to flourish there. These are peaceful and pure tastes which in more prosperous times, I cultivated whimsically and which today I embrace wholeheartedly.[9]

With the furniture included in the price, Josephine could move in immediately. She did not waste a moment. She took occupation in April and immediately began planning a house-warming party.

Despite the Molays' modifications, the chateau needed sprucing up and was crying out for expansion. But the grounds were magnificent and the farm boasted a fine production of wine, a healthy wheat crop and a variety of livestock. Josephine was delighted at how she could 'freely breathe the country air'.[10] In years to come, the Île de Chatou on the edge of the property would be portrayed repeatedly by the Impressionists. The house was a sanctuary from Paris and yet it was only ten miles away.

If the solitude became too monotonous, Josephine would be able to access the capital in under an hour by coach.

She thought Malmaison the perfect place to hide from prying eyes. She invited Hippolyte Charles to visit her, at first in secret so that no one saw him arrive. Little by little, as his visits became more frequent and a routine began to establish itself, the couple became complacent. He even had his own bedroom next door to Josephine's. He spent whole weeks there, though he left when guests were expected.

The gossips repeated that a country neighbour had spotted Josephine and said, 'Poor Mme Bonaparte can be seen at dusk walking in her garden, leaning on the arm of a young man, probably her son.' Josephine, incredibly, was simply amused that the locals thought Hippolyte was her son. He was leading a precarious existence, engaging in the odd bit of shady business and still working with Bodin. Josephine too was receiving kickbacks from the profiteers. At a time when her enemies were collecting evidence against her, and the Bonaparte family looked forward to their ultimate triumph, her obsession with Hippolyte was very unwise.

He had a wandering eye, and she already suspected he had another lover. In February, she had written that she wished to see him. 'You can be assured, after this meeting, which will be the last, that you will no longer be tormented by my letters or by my presence. The respectable woman who has been deceived retires and says nothing.'[11] Still, they seemed to reconcile, and Josephine continued behaving with shocking risk. A general's wife should have avoided such potential scandal. But she loved Hippolyte's light-hearted air and his energy, and she could not give him up.

The Directory was beginning to fall apart. In June 1799, the ruthless intellectual former priest Emmanuel Sieyès had allied with Barras to expel the Directors he did not trust and brought in fifty-three-year-old Louis-Jérôme Gohier and two others in their place.

Josephine marshalled her beauty and her redecorated salon at rue de la Victoire to win over the men who would control Napoleon's career, and thus lure her husband back to her. Sieyès was dismissive of her, but Gohier was both eager to dine with her and sexually fascinated, although she was also close to his wife. A rising star was Joseph Fouché, a former cleric, pale-eyed and pale-faced and utterly without morals;

he too had dealt in army supplies. In July 1799, he became Minister of Police, tasked with quashing all criticism of the government.

Gohier advised Josephine that her relationship with Hippolyte compromised her in the eyes of the world, and she should either give him up or divorce Napoleon and marry him. She assured Gohier that they were just friends. She had no wish to be Hippolyte's wife, and he would not have married her anyway.

The War Ministry had launched an inquiry into the Bodin Company and discovered the poor horses, bribes and unpaid suppliers. Josephine was keen to save Hippolyte, now co-director, from disgrace. 'A report on the Bodin company is to be made today to the Directory, and I beg you to intervene for them,' she wrote to Barras. 'The firm is in such a bad way that it needs powerful sponsorship.'[12] Every time she gained her former lover's sympathy with her vulnerability, she also drove him to exasperation with her pleas to favour Bodin's dodgy dealings. He grew tired of her supplications. One evening, at dinner in the Luxembourg, Barras turned his back on her and spoke only to Thérésa Tallien. Josephine departed in tears, convinced that he believed she would be divorced by Napoleon on his return from Egypt.

Bonaparte soon heard of his humiliation in the British press and was bent on revenge. After attempting to amuse himself with dancers, he spotted pretty Pauline Fourès at a public balloon launch in the Ezbekiya Gardens. The wife of a lieutenant, twenty-year-old Pauline was a cheery, accommodating soul who had the slender figure Napoleon liked and looked well in her disguise of the uniform of her husband's regiment. She had long golden hair, a rose-petal complexion, a perky temperament and an eagerness for adventure. Lieutenant Fourès had come across her working in a milliner's shop in Carcassonne and married her just before setting off on campaign.

Napoleon ignored the balloon and stared at Pauline openly and without flinching – a tactic that many of his amours found disturbing. Junot was sent off to make a proposition to her. Unfortunately, he did so in coarsely practical language and Pauline was shaken. General Duroc was sent to make another attempt, bearing a handsome jewelled bracelet as a gift. The lady proved much more receptive.

On 17 December, Lieutenant Fourès was sent to take a letter to

Admiral Villeneuve on Malta and letters to the Directory in Paris, a journey Napoleon hoped would take three months or so. Fourès was refused permission to take Pauline with him. As soon as the husband's back was turned, Napoleon invited her and other officers' wives to a dinner at the palace. After dessert, an officer spilled coffee over her gown. Napoleon leaped to her rescue, ushered her upstairs to change, and neither returned to the dinner. She was soon living in a villa in the palace grounds, and dubbed Napoleon's 'Cleopatra'.

He treated the milliner's apprentice as a true companion. He admired her staunch determination to travel through Egypt with her husband and he was pleased by her vivacious personality. He flaunted her, hoping the news would get back to Paris. She presided at his dinner parties and accompanied him everywhere in his carriage. Napoleon forced seventeen-year-old Eugène to escort him and his new mistress around Egypt, until the poor boy begged to be excused.

On 24 December 1798, a week after capturing Pauline, Napoleon set off for Suez. He wished her a touching goodbye and told her to make a son while he was away. She had little time to engage in such an operation. He came back briefly after Suez, only to set off again in February on a grandiloquent expedition to Syria. He meant, eventually, to take on the Turks, who had declared war on France.

Pauline's husband was captured just outside Alexandria and was promptly returned to Cairo to embarrass Napoleon. Fourès was outraged by his wife's betrayal, but could do nothing. Napoleon pronounced the Fourès's divorce, leaving him free to enjoy Pauline. Her only fault was that she would not fall pregnant. 'What's to be done,' said the great hero, 'the silly girl . . . can't do it.' Pauline vehemently defended herself. 'Good God!' she cried. 'It's not my fault.'[13] She presumably meant that his cursory technique made conception unlikely.

Napoleon set off again, ever the adventurer. 'I saw myself on the way to Asia, riding an elephant, wearing a turban, attacking the English in India.'[14] The reality of the campaign was not so romantic. The men hated the conditions of the desert and suffered in the heat. At Jaffa in Palestine (now part of Tel Aviv), Napoleon's men were plied with alcohol to give them courage and then sent to massacre the garrison, including women and children. In the morning, Napoleon dispatched Eugène and another young aide, Crosier, to call for peace. Turkish soldiers holed up in a citadel told Crosier they would come down if their lives were spared. He brought all 4000 of them as prisoners.

Napoleon was furious with Crosier and Eugène. 'Have I any provisions to feed them?' he railed. 'What the devil can I do with them all?'[15] It was impossible to expect them to become loyal members of the French Army, and there were not enough troops to march them back. Napoleon ordered the men to be shot. For three days, his demoralised soldiers were forced to chase fleeing men into the sea and shoot them. Weeping children clung to the necks of their fathers as they too were killed and the sea turned red with blood.

The following day, the army was hit by bubonic plague. Napoleon refused to give in, declaring that any man who was afraid of the plague would immediately catch it. To prove his point, he visited a hospital and touched some of the patients and helped to lift others. He believed that if one had control over the mind, the rest would follow. The army progressed to Acre on the coast of Syria, but failed to take the garrison, which was protected by the British. Napoleon told his men to return to Cairo, after writing to the Directory that Acre was not worth seizing. He left behind 2000 wounded and plague-ridden soldiers. The British offered to take them on their ships, but Napoleon refused and the men were beheaded by the Turks almost as soon as the French left.

He wrote missives to the French full of praise for his incredible victories and barely mentioning the plague. 'We want for nothing here,' he exclaimed to the Directory, 'we are bursting with strength, good health and high spirits.' He had instructed that his men must be welcomed in Cairo like conquering heroes, with grand ceremony and bands playing. Napoleon was good at assuming the mantle of a victor, even if he did not deserve it and he hoped that the news of his celebration would reach France. 'We are masters of the entire eastern desert,' he wrote. 'If you could send us excess of 15,000 men, we would be able to go anywhere.'

He hurried back to the arms of Pauline Fourès and was disappointed to find she was not pregnant. He planned more victories. But then the British cunningly sent him a set of recent newspapers.[16] Napoleon was shocked at the news. France was under fire. Austria, Britain and Russia had banded together, the Austrians had pushed the French back over the Rhine, and the French had been forced to withdraw from much of Switzerland. Malta was blockaded and the French forces were being driven back through Italy. Most of the territory Napoleon had gained during his Italian campaign had been lost.

He scoured the newspapers, madly reading of the failures of his country. 'Italy is lost!!!' he cried. 'All the fruits of our victories have disappeared! I must depart.' France needed a saviour – and he was the man to do it. By 11 August, Napoleon was preparing to leave, abandoning his plague-ridden Army of the Orient under the command of Kléber, telling everybody but Bourrienne and his chief-of-staff that it was another expedition. He took Eugène with him but left Junot, still unable to forgive him for telling the truth about Josephine. He refused to let Pauline Fourès come, in case the British took the ship. 'You should think of my reputation; what would they say if they found a woman on board?'[17]

Once Napoleon had left Egypt, he was eager to get to France. At Corsica, the ships were stalled owing to a lack of wind. He stayed in his childhood home, saw relatives and his wet nurse and raged against the weather. 'I will be there too late,' he moaned. On 10 October 1799, he landed in France and was greeted by delighted crowds. The cannons fired in Paris to announce the news. People wept with joy and the theatres had to interrupt their performances so people could sing patriotic songs. In Cairo, governing from a palace, issuing edicts that had to be obeyed by a subject people, he had discovered a taste for tyranny and Empire. Instead of becoming emperor of Africa, he had changed his desire. In place of Alexander, his new model would be Julius Caesar, conqueror of Europe.

Throughout 1799, Josephine became increasingly nervous and unhappy. Exposed and guilty, she was afraid of Napoleon's return. 'I came to Paris, my dear Barras, meaning to see you, but I was told when I got there that you had a large party today,' she wrote. The woman who had thrived on admiration now wished to be private. 'Since moving to the country, I have become such a recluse that social occasions frighten me,' she told her former lover. 'Besides, I am so miserable that I do not wish to be an object of pity for others.'[18]

'Mama has bought Malmaison,' Hortense wrote to her brother in October 1799. 'She lives a very reclusive life there.'[19] She meant the letter to be read to Napoleon and for him to understand in how very retired a fashion his wife was behaving.

She has only given two big dinner parties since you both departed. The Directors and all the Buonoparte family were invited, but the latter always decline to come . . . Maman is, I assure you, very distressed that the family won't live on friendly terms with her, which must vex her husband whom she loves very much. I am certain that if Maman could have been sure of reaching him, she would have gone, but you know how impossible that would be.

Josephine herself, after presumably overseeing the letter, wrote that she wished for Eugène's return and that of Napoleon, 'especially if I find Bonaparte as he was when he left me; then I will be able to forget all I have suffered as a result of your absence and his.'[20] She was making a counter-strike: accusing her husband of neglect and absence. Luckily for her, Napoleon did not see the letter. He and Eugène were already on their way home.

11

'He owes me everything'

*O*n the night of 10 October, Josephine was dining with Gohier and his wife, discussing politics and Paris gossip. The cutlery and glasses clinked, the candles cast soft light, she smiled at Gohier's jokes and talked about dresses with his wife. Then an urgent message came through from Eugène that he had landed at Fréjus with Napoleon. Josephine leaped from her chair. 'I must reach him before his brothers can talk to him,' she cried. She made her hasty goodbyes, hurried into her carriage, collected Hortense and told her driver to speed south, in the hope of catching Napoleon at Lyons.

Josephine careened out of Paris, begging the coachman to push the horses as fast as he could. She did not know which route Napoleon would take and plumped for the route via Châlons. As she sped south, she saw that every village and coaching inn had been speedily decorated for the returning hero, with triumphal archways erected over the roads and illuminations strung across the houses. Each time they stopped to change horses, people crowded around their carriage, imploring Josephine to tell them 'if it was really true that the saviour (for that was the name that all France had given him) had returned', as Hortense recalled.[1] Finally they reached Lyons only to be told that the General had already left and was travelling to Paris on a different route. Napoleon had remained in Lyons for a while and the city had produced a quickly written new play, *Bonaparte at Lyon*, for him. Josephine had just missed him.

In shock, mother and daughter turned the horses around and raced through the night. The road back was nothing but a 'series of ovations' for him, and each was a bitter pill for poor Josephine.

Her worst fears had come true. Lucien and Joseph had travelled to meet Napoleon at Lyons. All the way to Paris, his brothers talked to him of Josephine's infidelity and her relationships with army profiteers.

Napoleon entered Paris to wild acclaim. The city sparkled with lights, bands played and men and women fainted. But he wanted only to see Josephine. Even though he was angry with her, he longed for her soft embrace and her perfumed body, to hear her gentle voice and to lie in her bed. He was ready to hear her defence. He expected a torrent of tears and then, when he deemed it fit, a passionate reconciliation.

But he arrived at their house at 6am and found her absent. Furious and miserable, Napoleon abandoned himself to melancholy in his lonely home. He believed that she must be with Hippolyte Charles, as everybody had said.

As soon as he was able, Napoleon called on Paul de Barras and declared he would divorce Josephine. Barras counselled patience and suggested he wait. The Directory would only be further undermined if their favourite general embarked on the embarrassing course of divorce.

Then Gohier, who was desperately fond of Josephine, told him that divorce was a 'black mark against the record of a man in public life'. He stressed to Napoleon how Josephine had rushed from their home to meet him, and told him that the public were more likely to trust a married man.[2] Napoleon, confused, turned to his family. Like vultures, they flocked to say she was away seducing her lover and he should divorce her immediately.

The next day, Jean-Pierre Collot, a banker, visited rue de la Victoire and begged Napoleon to forgive Josephine, for the moment at least. 'Think of France!' he cried. 'I will never forgive her!' railed Napoleon. 'How little you know me!' Collot, like Barras, suggested that a public separation would expose him to ridicule – 'you will be laughed at like one of Moliere's husbands' – and warned that he should not make any hasty decisions.[3] 'All this violence proves you still love her,' he argued. 'Do but see her, she will explain everything.'[4] Napoleon would not listen, avowing that people would grow bored with gossiping about him and his wife. 'My determination is fixed,' he said, 'she shall never again enter my house.'[5] Eugène, who had just arrived in Paris, attempted to speak to him, but Napoleon was adamant.

He visited Fortunée Hamelin and she also counselled caution. No man seen as a 'saviour' would be able to divorce, and he would become much less appealing to the public. But Napoleon was a wounded bear; he stormed home and told the maids to pack up Josephine's huge wardrobes of clothes.

Josephine arrived at 11pm that night, exhausted from travel and covered in dust and dirt from the journey. The porter told her that Napoleon would not see her and gestured towards her boxes of belongings, packed and ready for her to take away. Josephine and Hortense dashed past him and hurtled into the house. The servants did not dare stop them. A maid told them that Napoleon was in his dressing room and would not come out. Josephine wept and begged at the door, only to be told that he would not see her and he would never open the door to her again. She crouched on the last spiral of a narrow staircase, crying nosily and begging him to see her. She wept and pleaded for hours, her sobs echoing through the house. For the first time, Napoleon resisted her tears.

At nearly five in the morning, still weeping, Josephine stood, unable to credit that her tears had not succeeded. In a last-ditch attempt, she went to find Hortense and Eugène and implored them to assist her. They climbed the stairs in their nightgowns and wept outside Napoleon's room with her, pleading for mercy. He flung open the door and the tableau of his wife in tears with her two children, all three of them supplicating him for help, was too much to resist. Eugène and Hortense begged him not to break their mother's heart: 'ought injustice to take from us, poor orphans, whose natural protector the scaffold has already deprived us of, the support of one whom Providence has sent to replace him!'[6] Napoleon relented.

'I could not bear the sobs of those two children,' he later declared. 'I asked myself, should they be made victims of their mother's failings?'[7] He had come to see Eugène as his 'adoptive son' and Hortense was about to make her debut in society. His excuse for forgiving Josephine was that he could not bear to abandon her son and daughter.

Napoleon took Josephine to their bed and the reconciliation was complete. The next morning, Lucien arrived expecting some enjoyable complaining about Josephine and discussion of divorce. To his horror, he found the pair in bed together, his sister-in-law fully reinstated as the ruler of Napoleon's heart.

Josephine had been forgiven, but the balance in the marriage had shifted. Napoleon was now sure that she had been unfaithful to him. His success in Egypt, and his affair with Pauline, had made him more vainglorious and less dependent on Josephine. He would never again worship at her shrine; she would never again treat him so cavalierly. Without a child, she knew she was weak, and her exposure as an adulterer had made her realise that men of power and her friends alike would turn their backs on her if they felt her hold over him was slipping. When they had married, she had been the sought-after woman and few could understand why she accepted Napoleon's proposal. Now, he was seen as the saviour of France and she was a mere wife. Her position could be taken from her at any time.

His family were livid about the reconciliation. Her sister-in-law Pauline and the brothers were from then on 'at open war with Josephine'.[8] They would do anything to destroy her.

Napoleon claimed he had forgiven Josephine for the sake of her children. He was very fond of them. In Italy, not long after their marriage, he had written to her, 'Be sure to tell them that I love them as if they were my own. What is yours or mine is so mixed up in my heart, that there is no difference there.'[9] He told her that he thought Hortense 'entirely adorable'.[10] It was hard not to admire the pair: Eugène was dutiful and steadfast and had served him well in Egypt, and golden-haired, graceful Hortense was the jewel of Madame Campan's school, with a set of accomplishments worthy of Versailles. She was also rather terrified of Napoleon and would tremble when she spoke to him, and ask others to request favours on her behalf.[11] Such a display of fear could hardly fail to endear her to him.

But Napoleon was driven by more than mercy. He was also bent on political power and he needed his wife. Having a wife and step-children made him look reliable, and he also needed Josephine's soft skills of influence, her ability to please and flatter, her talents as a hostess and her hold over Barras, Gohier, Talleyrand and the others. Most of all, as a survivor of imprisonment, she gave legitimacy to his claim of protecting the Republic, while at the same time her aristocratic title persuaded the royalists into believing that her husband would espouse their cause. As Barras had said, she made him seem French.

Even in the stormy days after his arrival, Napoleon saw that the words of the informers who had written to him in Egypt were correct: the Directory was struggling. The populace of France, shouldering economic decline and distressed by the failures of the army in Europe, had lost faith in their government. The Directory was riven with rivalries and hatreds. Not one trusted another, and each member was trying hard to hold onto his position by ousting his rivals. The door was wide open for Napoleon to step in, adored by the people and, as a general, seemingly unsullied by politics. As Hortense put it, 'With Italy lost, the finances spent, the Directory devoid of energy and authority, the return of the General was seen as a favour from heaven.'[12]

The irascible Emmanuel Sieyès had been preparing a secret *coup d'état* to seize power by ousting his fellow Directors – Barras, Gohier and Jean-François Moulin. The fourth, Roger Ducos, he thought sufficiently spineless to follow him. He gained the confidence of Talleyrand, Joseph Fouché and Lucien Bonaparte. He needed only a general for military might. General Bernadotte, Minister for War, refused. General Joubert was killed in Italy, and both General Macdonald and General Moreau were reluctant to involve themselves in a political plot.

On 14 October, Sieyès was awaiting Moreau in his office at the Luxembourg Palace. Moreau arrived at the same time as a messenger delivering the thrilling news that Bonaparte had returned and was nearly at Paris. 'There's your man,' Moreau said and promptly departed.

Napoleon wanted more than to be the strongman for another man's political desires. He listened to Sieyès, nodded and then made his own plans to launch a coup. He employed Josephine to charm influential men and persuade them to espouse his cause – and to persuade Barras that he was still loyal to him. She obeyed gladly, keen to please, and planned dinners, receptions and intimate meetings. Six rue de la Victoire was a revolving door of politicians, ministers and generals all eager to dine on Josephine's delicate desserts and have her whisper in their ears. She flattered Barras and Gohier and lulled them all into a false sense of security about Bonaparte and his plans. As she did so, the Directory breathed its last.

Napoleon asked Barras what he would do if there was a coup to unseat the Directory. He refused to listen to the idea. Gohier made it clear to Napoleon that he thought him too young to be involved in government. Napoleon was left with no choice but to throw in his lot with Sieyès, although he despised him.

On 9 November, Napoleon got up at 5am and sent letters to favourable members of the Council of Elders, requesting their presence at the Tuileries at 7am (the rest would receive their letters too late, long after the voting had ended). Four hundred dragoons were already assembling there. He set about trapping the other Directors. 'Will you, my dear Gohier, and your wife have breakfast with me tomorrow at eight o'clock in the morning,' Josephine had written to her friend the night before. 'Do not fail: I must speak to you of interesting matters.'[13] Gohier thought 8am suspiciously early for Josephine, and sent his wife alone. She found Josephine's house full of soldiers, ready to arrest her husband and force his resignation.

Exploiting notions of an emergency and a rebellion, Napoleon arrived at the Tuileries at 8.30, surrounded by his generals. He addressed his troops, telling them the Directory had betrayed them. The Elders were essentially tricked into declaring the two legislative bodies – themselves and the lower house, the Council of Five Hundred – should move to Saint-Cloud. Napoleon thought it would be easier to pass a new constitution away from the centre of Paris. He had Gohier and another Director, Jean Moulin, arrested. Talleyrand went to Barras's house and told him that the others had resigned and he had no choice but to do the same. Napoleon gave him two million francs to bribe Barras. When Barras gave in without a fight, Talleyrand took the money for himself. At Saint-Cloud, Napoleon was criticised by the Elders, but the real violence came when he attempted to address the Council of Five Hundred, who were angrily questioning his actions. He was forced to flee for his life, but then sent in his troops, led by General Murat, to expel the Council from the Orangerie. The Council were forced to submit to the soldiers, and thus effectively gave over their powers to Bonaparte. 'It didn't go too badly,' he shrugged.[14] That night, he and Josephine slept with loaded revolvers under their pillows.

On 10 November, Napoleon asserted again that the Republic was in danger and he was the man to save it. He ensured that he was installed as a Consul, along with Emmanuel Sieyès and Roger Ducos, whom Napoleon secretly planned to oust very quickly. Almost unbelievably, thanks to his might, his clever plotting and the help of his wife, Napoleon

Empress Josephine in Her Coronation Robes,
by François Pascal Simon, Baron Gérard, 1807–8.

(*Above*) Josephine's childhood home,
La Pagerie, as it is now.

(*Below*) Alexandre de Beauharnais.

(*Right*) Hortense as a child.

(*Below right*) Eugène de Beauharnais,
Josephine's only son. Napoleon
made him viceroy of Italy.

(*Left*) Josephine visits her husband Alexandre at the prison in Luxembourg in 1794. Jean-Louis Victor Viger de Vigneau, 1867. (*Below*) A letter from Napoleon to Josephine.

(*Above*) Mme Thérésa Tallien. The glamorous heroine of the end of the Terror had three husbands and ten children by various lovers.

(*Right*) Paul Barras, handsome, rich, debauched and ruthless.

— ci-devant Occupations — or — Madame Tallien and the Empress Josephine dancing Naked before Barrass in the Winter of 1797. — A Fact!

Barrass (then in Power) being tired of Josephine, promised Buonaparte a promotion, on condition that he would take her off his hands:—Barrass had, as usual, drank freely & placed Buonaparte behind a Screen, while he amused himself with these two Ladies, who were then his humble dependents.—Madam Tallien is a beautiful Woman, tall & elegant.—Josephine is smaller & thin, with bad Teeth, something like Cloves.—it is naiddish to add, that Buonaparte accepted the Promotion & the Lady—now—Empress of France!

(*Above*) *Ci-devant Occupations! or Madame Tallien and the Empress Josephine dancing naked before Barras in the winter of 1797* by James Gillray, 1805. Both ladies, the cartoon declares, were Barras's 'humble dependents'.

(*Above*) The first known portrait of Napoleon by Andrea Appiani, 1797. He is 28.

(*Right*) *The Three Graces* by Antonio Canova, 1814, Hermitage.

*General Bonaparte
at the Bridge of Arcole*
by Baron Antoine-Jean
Gros, c. 1801.

Empress Josephine
by Robert Lèfevre, 1806.

The house at Malmaison.

View of the Wooden Bridge by Auguste Garnerey. The Garden at Malmaison.

View of the Salon de Musique, Malmaison by Auguste Garnerey, 1812. Josephine's picture gallery was her pride and joy

Josephine's dining room at Malmaison. She decorated the house in a mixture of Egyptian, Greek and Roman styles.

Josephine's Formal Bedroom at Malmaison. She lies between golden swans, an eagle watches over her bed and the ceiling is painted as the sky.

Josephine by Baron Antoine-Jean Gros, 1809.
A bust of Eugène is on her left, Malmaison lies
in the background and the hydrangea flowers
(Hortensia) symbolise her daughter.
Letters lie at her feet.

had moved from feted general to the most powerful man in France. Barras kicked his heels in his country seat of Grosbois. 'I see Bonaparte has tricked me,' he mourned. 'And yet he owes me everything.' The same was true for Josephine. Barras had cared for her, protected her and lent her money, and miserable exile was his reward.

'I found division reigning amongst all the authorities,' Napoleon declared, describing his return to France. 'They agreed only on this single point, that the Constitution was half destroyed, and was unable to protect liberty!' He announced that the Council of Elders had begged him to help them, since the 'men whom the nation has been accustomed to regard as the defenders of liberty, equality, and property', or the Directors, had been planning to restore the King. 'I was bound, in duty to my fellow-citizens, to the soldiers perishing in our armies, and to the national glory, acquired at the cost of so much blood, to accept the command.'

All lies, but believed. The men and women fighting for the fall of Louis XVI had hoped for a representative government. In 1799, they were given a tyranny. There would be no elections, but three Consuls and four Assemblies: every member of the Senate and the Council of State would be nominated by the First Consul, the Tribunat's members would be nominated by the Senate, while the Consul would also influence the Legislative Assembly. Bonaparte declared his plan: the First Consul would be appointed for ten years, and he would choose the other Consuls. The entire country would essentially be ruled by one man.

At three in the morning, Napoleon returned home to find Josephine in bed. He was fretting to Bourrienne that he had said the wrong thing. 'I like better to speak to soldiers than to lawyers. Those fellows disconcerted me. I have not been used to public assemblies; but that will come in time.'[15] Josephine begged his help for Gohier. 'What would you suggest, my dear?' he replied. 'He is respectable, but a simpleton. He does not understand me! – I ought, perhaps, to have him transported.'[16]

Bonaparte, clever as ever, lulled Sieyès into believing he would be First Consul. Josephine's smiling deference had backed up his plans. 'The Revolution is finished,' he announced on the last day of the year. Napoleon manoeuvred himself into position as First Consul, with two patsies, Jean Jacques Regis de Cambacérès and Charles-François Lebrun, as his colleagues. Sieyès was packed off with a pension to the country.

The General was now a little King. Josephine, the Martinique widow, was the Consuless. It had happened in the blink of an eye. Napoleon had achieved a shocking reversal of everything the French had fought for, and he had been allowed to do it because he had offered peace. With bands of royalists and Jacobins stalking the streets and black marketeers making fortunes, the people were desperate for order. But freedom to walk around the streets was unlikely with Talleyrand as the Foreign Minister and Fouché, brutal organiser of killings in Lyons under the Terror, as Minister of Police. Lucien Bonaparte was appointed Minister of the Interior. Napoleon, the dictator over all France, cheerfully voted himself a salary of 500,000 francs.

The Republicans were afraid of a monarchist restoration and believed Napoleon the man to save them. The royalists fooled themselves that he was simply securing the country before handing over to the exiled Louis XVIII. He offered men of influence more power. Deciding that the way to please the people was with the grandeur and pomp of royalty, he demanded carriages, palatial settings and officially announced that the names of address would no longer be citoyen and citoyenne but monsieur and madame. He believed the people would be easily pleased with pageantry and promises, and would give up their hope of representation to a man who offered peace and prosperity.

Napoleon decided the house in rue de la Victoire was too humble for a Consul and set Josephine and the maids packing up their belongings. They would move to the Luxembourg Palace. Josephine had often visited Gohier and Barras for dinners there. Her first meeting with Napoleon had been at an evening reception in one of its rooms. And yet she dreaded moving to its cold opulence. Built on the orders of Catherine de Medici, it was a brutal place of reputations briefly won and lost, and Josephine was already growing nervous about her husband's wild ambition. To console herself, she spent excessively on dresses, jewellery and furniture, and threw thousands of francs at Malmaison – still indulging her 'love of luxury grand enough to swallow up the revenue of ten provinces'.[17] She had also become newly careful of her own reputation: she informed her agents that she would have no further dealings with companies selling army supplies.

Napoleon was delighted with himself. Despite the privations, he had filled out a little and lost some of the skinniness of youth. In the early days, his hands had been ridden with scabies and dirty, but now they were rather beautiful, and in conversation 'he would often look at them with an air of self-complacency'.[18] Josephine had improved his dress and his accent had softened. He surrounded himself with servants in uniforms embroidered with gold.

By February, he decided himself so invincible that he and his wife should occupy the Tuileries Palace in the centre of Paris. With three pavilions, nearly 400 rooms and a long gallery, built by Henry IV, that linked it to the Louvre, the Tuileries was grand but decayed. Cheap streetwalkers sheltered with their clients under the shabby hedges outside. After Louis XVI and Marie Antoinette had been taken away in 1792, the Tuileries had fallen into terrible disrepair, looted and wrecked for its furniture and even the wood of the window surrounds. The stairs still bore spots of dried blood from when the Swiss Guards and courtiers had fought back against the coup. The dreaded Committee for Public Safety had met in the Queen's apartments. The main gate was inscribed with a warning, 'On 10 August 1792 royalty was abolished in France and will never return.' The gardens were overrun with sellers of lemonade and hot pies, catering for all the gawping sightseers and petitioners waiting to plead with the officials. The residence of every monarch since the mid-seventeenth century, it was to the people the symbol of Bourbon privilege and oppression. But Napoleon did not care. He wished to be King.

Today the Tuileries are no more, after a huge fire in 1870, but ghosts remain in the buildings of the Louvre and the gardens on the Place de la Concorde. Napoleon and his wife occupied apartments once lived in by the Gohiers. Josephine sat on chairs owned by her old friends and dined off their tables. She walked through rooms once occupied by Barras. She was living in a goldfish bowl: the newly and fashionably landscaped gardens had been made open to the public and had fast become a popular place for Parisians to take leisurely afternoon walks. They peered into the windows and knocked at the doors. Every time she went out she was dressed in rich gowns befitting her new status, transported in a carriage driven by six horses and accompanied by an escort of cavalry. The formality made her uncomfortable and she missed the rue de la Victoire. But still, she had won – over all those who had tried to unseat her, over the Bonapartes, and also over her husband.

Four years previously, Napoleon had clambered up the steps to toil at the Topographical Bureau of the Committee of Public Safety, a position he had gained thanks to Paul de Barras. The Revolution was barely ten years old, but for Napoleon it belonged to a different era. One of his first acts was to have the Revolutionary symbols daubed over the front of the palace painted over. 'I don't like to see such rubbish,' he said.[19]

He ignored the derelict rooms and the patches of damp. On their first night in the Tuileries, he swept Josephine into his arms, crying, 'Come, little Creole, get into the bed of your masters.'

Napoleon was officially installed at the Tuileries on 19 February. The carriages left the Luxembourg at 1pm to the stirring sound of military music and the beating of drums. As Napoleon and his retinue passed by, more than 3000 soldiers lined the streets and the crowds cheered. Josephine, in her customary flowing dress, had left the Luxembourg a little ahead of him, accompanied by Hortense. The populace gazed at their *Merveilleuse,* who was now the wife of the man they hoped would bring peace. After them came the Council of State, forced to use cabs because so few carriages were available – after they had been commandeered to load up the slaughtered dogs five years earlier. The registration numbers on the cabs were crudely concealed with pieces of paper.

It seemed as if all Paris had arrived to see Napoleon's grandiose parade, along with swathes of tourists. Josephine was enthusiastically cheered, but her inferior position was drummed firmly home, for she was not allowed to participate in the rituals. Instead, she was obliged to remain on a balcony to watch Napoleon perform the official ceremony and conduct his military review. Accompanied by Hortense and Napoleon's sister Caroline and other ladies, she gazed from above as he took the salute of his regiments and then the cavalry in a great show of martial might. Among the plumes and the pomp, he was a tiny figure.

Napoleon beamed and waved joyfully at his wife. Josephine responded in kind, her handkerchief clasped in her hand. After the review, he clambered up the stairs to take possession of Louis XVI's apartments on the first floor. 'I watched the siege of the Tuileries from there and the capture of that good Louis XVI,' he said, pointing out of a window to the house of Bourrienne's brother, 'but *I* will remain here.' That 'good Louis XVI' was his new model for grandeur, if not governance. He was utterly convinced of his right to live in the Palace.

Napoleon decreed Josephine should have Marie Antoinette's rooms on the ground floor. They had been used for civil administration and the Committee for Public Safety had met in her chamber. The new First Consul wished for the rooms to be returned to their earlier resplendence. Decorators and designers draped the chamber in blue and white silk with gold trimmings. Josephine decked the salon with violet taffeta, arranged Sèvres vases on the tables and displayed bronzes, hung the walls with paintings and brought in woodwork repairers to beautify the Queen's enormous mahogany bed.

Napoleon slept in the Queen's bed with Josephine, hardly ever returning to his own chamber. The whole Palace radiated splendour, but it was dark, cold and oppressively formal. Napoleon adorned it with statues of Hannibal, Demosthenes, Alexander and other great men. Josephine was miserable, ill at ease and longed for the informality of Malmaison. 'I was never made for so much grandeur,' she confided to Hortense. 'I will never be happy here. I can feel the Queen's ghost asking what I am doing in her bed.'[20] Napoleon had no patience with her unhappiness. He wanted her to fall at his feet, proclaim his excellence, offer sensual delights. And after the debacle of his return from Egypt, Josephine, walking on eggshells, had to keep her reservations to herself.

She was now the unofficial Queen of France. Napoleon had strict rules on how he wished her to behave. Thérésa Tallien, Fortunée Hamelin and all the others were banned. The First Consul hated Thérésa's flirtatious glamour and did not trust her or her husband, and kept them under permanent surveillance. He did relent for Madame Récamier – her banker husband was too wealthy to alienate. He instructed his wife that she should spend her time with those of aristocratic origin such as the Ségurs, the Caulaincourts and Madame de Rémusat.[21] On no account should she receive visits from men in her apartments, she was to dress far more modestly, and, most of all, she should refrain from politics. For Josephine, who was 'the sworn enemy of all forms of etiquette', life henceforward was to be fraught with strain.[22]

Napoleon was decided: women had been possessed of too much power. 'There is no feminine in the function of the Consul,' he said. 'We need the notion of obedience, in Paris, especially, where women think they have the right to do as they like.' As a young man in Paris just after the Terror, he had been baffled by the conspicuousness of women, their influence and conversation. He was paying them all back for snubbing him.

His ambition to rule in a world without women did not last long. He relied on his wife too much. He could not manage without her at his side on social occasions, and he needed her diplomatic skills and her ability to manipulate others into doing what he wished. When he was not in his office or at committees securing his position and drawing up laws, he wanted to be with Josephine.

She was constantly watched and always on show. As one courtier said, 'We turned their eyes towards the rising sun, Mme Bonaparte, who was installed at the Tuileries, where the apartments had been entirely refurnished as if by fairies.' She had 'already put on the airs of a queen', but a kind and gentle one.[23] Her every minute was planned. They were always together, and when he was not with her, Napoleon expected Josephine to ready herself in case he arrived. In the old days she had been free. Now, life was rather as it had been in Mombello – always the same.

Napoleon slept in her bedroom, leaving at eight for his own chamber, where he would bathe as Bourrienne read him letters and telegrams. He liked his bath boiling hot and often demanded more hot water from his servants. Bourrienne sometimes had to open the door to let in fresh air because he could not see through the steam. While Napoleon was being shaved, Bourrienne would read him the newspapers, paying attention to the news in the German and British papers but ignoring the French. 'Pass over all that,' Napoleon would say. 'I know it already.'[24] They would have a simple breakfast of chicken and onions before returning to drafting papers.

The Consul would usually join Josephine for a speedy lunch of twenty minutes or so – gobbling his food so fast that she had barely begun her first course by the time he had finished. He allowed more time for dinner, but generally did not eat until most of his work was finished, which meant Josephine often waited until past midnight for his presence.

Napoleon never ate much. 'I cannot help thinking that at forty I shall become a great eater, and get very fat,' he worried.[25] He thought excessively about his weight and accordingly often avoided food. And he never stopped exercising. While dictating he would sometimes walk back and forth for five hours, hardly noticing the time passing. As he walked, he stooped and clasped his hands behind his back. When he was deep in thought he often gave a quick shrug of his shoulders, and his mouth twitched from left to right as he came up with a new idea.

While Napoleon was working, Josephine attended to her correspondence and saw her dressmakers, milliners, portraitist and tradesmen. In the afternoon, she sat with her ladies and played cards or listened to a little music. Few guessed how dreary she found her new life. Her mien was always gay and pleased with what she saw, eager to greet people at the Tuileries and host endless dinners for up to 150 guests. She met thousands of people at home and abroad, all of whom expected a special word of recognition.

Josephine simply had to wait, beauteously dressed and perfumed, for the moment when Napoleon might burst through her doors without warning and demand tea.[26] He always came at five to watch her dress, and if he had a free moment he would dash downstairs to see his 'little Creole'. Sometimes he sat quietly, contemplating a military problem as she sat with him (in silence until he chose to speak). Other times, he would play his customary tricks on her, teasing and laughing, overturning her make-up pots, pulling her hair out of its style and pinching her. 'Do stop, Bonaparte,' she would say – for he wished to be treated as a naughty child. She worked hard to be his perfect companion, always ready to listen, to read, to go out driving with him and assume the soothing, unruffled mien that so pleased him. 'Josephine possessed an exact knowledge of the intricacies of my character,' he explained.[27] She was the only one allowed to call him 'tu' or Bonaparte.*

She was not allowed to feel tired at the midnight dinners or eat her lunch before he appeared. He expected her to be fully made up and coiffed, with no hint of fatigue or ill health, and perfectly gowned in exquisite French clothes that were not too revealing. He spent every night with her in an overheated chamber with the window firmly closed – neither liked the cold. 'We were a very bourgeois couple,' he wrote, 'sharing a bedroom and a bed', ensuring 'the wife's influence and the husband's dependency'. Josephine had cleverly persuaded him that occupying the same room would ensure his safety. 'I told him,' she said, 'that I was a very light sleeper, if any nocturnal attempt against

---

* Women of Josephine's class would ordinarily call their husbands by their surnames. Other family members would do the same – but Napoleon only allowed his wife to call him Bonaparte.

him was made, I should be there to call for help in a moment.'[28] Thanks to this, 'no action of mine escaped Josephine,' he said. 'She guessed, she knew everything, which was sometimes inconvenient for me.'[29]

She participated enthusiastically in the effort to fete Napoleon and shore up his image of himself as the ruler of a new world. She had befriended the painter Jean-Baptiste Isabey, former artist at Versailles, while he had been a teacher at Madame Campan's school. Josephine was fond of Isabey's studied style and introduced him to Napoleon, who saw no irony in the former artist of Marie Antoinette becoming his painter for hire. Isabey became Josephine's make-up artist and the key director of the appearance of Napolean's ceremonials, as well as the robes to show his greatness. In 1797 Isabey had created one of the first portraits of Josephine, a sketch of her in a white dress and head-kerchief, the ideal Republican heroine.

In public life, Napoleon was utilising Josephine's diplomatic skills, using her to win over aristocrats, crusty bankers and military men alike. She was by his side in dinners, balls and receptions and hosted grand occasions of her own. She supplied the dignity, grace and elegance that he lacked. Napoleon was 'deficient in education and in manners', Madame de Rémusat would explain, and had no idea how to enter or leave a room, make a bow or even how to stand up properly.[30] Josephine was acutely sensitive to social etiquette. But more importantly, she was equable and engaging where he was boorish. His way of showing friendliness was to pinch the ear or bash someone on the arm or call them a fool. Josephine was kind and her charm attracted 'many persons to his court whom his natural rudeness would otherwise have kept away'.[31] Her honeyed tones gained power and influence when his shouting failed. When Bonaparte arrived in the drawing room, all eyes were fretfully directed towards him to try and guess his mood. If she presided alone, everything was 'gaiety and ease'.[32]

Nothing in Josephine's upbringing had prepared her for such a life, but she quickly became the ideal consort. She had a knack for remembering people, her time as a mistress had schooled her in the importance of showing interest and attention to people who bored her, and she was truly skilled at using the right words to put everyone at their ease. Josephine was a human display of Napoleon's power: her gowns, her behaviour, her possessions and her art all proved his brilliance and wealth.

Even if Napoleon had kept to his original plan of excluding his wife from power, she received so many letters from people begging for her help that it was impossible to exclude her. Her correspondence in the months following the *coup d'état* is full of letters from influential figures requesting favours and promotions. Most of all, she was trying to help the émigrés – stripped of their wealth during the Revolution – restore their assets and clear their names from the list of enemies of the Republic.

Napoleon saw Josephine's postbag – and saw another way in which she could be useful to him. He needed the support of the royalists and the émigrés, for they had power, money and, his spies told him, support from Britain. One of his first acts as Consul was to abolish the law by which any returning émigré could be put to death. But allowing them to return would be seen as undermining the principles of the Revolution. Josephine was his device for covering his tracks. She would direct the policy, receive requests from the exiled aristocrats and apply to the ministers to have their names removed from the list of enemies of France. If Republicans demanded an explanation, he would simply say that his wife had too kind a heart.

Josephine was delighted to receive requests from the greatest families in France and entertain them in her salon. Previously so indolent, she read applications from morning until night. Napoleon even told Fouché, Minister of Police, to spy on her to ensure she did not go too far. She wrote letter after letter. 'Would you oblige me, citizen Minister, by speeding up the processing of citizen Michon de Vougy's forthcoming case with the commission of those inscribed on the list of emigrants,' she wrote to the Minister of Justice.[33] She also asked for favours – begging Fouché to 'receive favourably Mme Pasquier, one of my oldest friends'.[34]

Josephine assisted thousands of émigrés to return to France. They called her the embodiment of 'grace and goodness', she was respected and loved in equal measure for 'inexhaustible charity'.[35] In the first year alone, over 40,000 families were reunited. The returnees felt loyal to her husband and less likely to ally together to reinstall a king. She was particularly generous to the relations of her first husband, including her brother-in-law, François, who had been a member of the Army of the Princes at Koblenz, a group of young aristocrats who had plotted to invade France in 1792. Bonaparte was so led by his Josephine that he even gave François a diplomatic post. By 1802, nearly all exiles were permitted to return, apart from men who had fought against the French in foreign armies (unless, of course, they were François). They were not allowed to retrieve any property that had been seized by the government or army, but otherwise they had free movement in the country. Still, few of them liked the new, highly moralistic and repressive social regime Napoleon was leading. There was to be, as one returning émigré put it, 'no more flirting, no sentimentality, no godlessness, no more sparkling wit, no more easy relationships, no more joy'.

With the arrival of the émigrés, Josephine hoped that her husband might feel more sympathetic to the exiled Louis XVIII, son of the Dauphin and Maria Josepha of Saxony. The forty-five-year-old younger brother of Louis XVI was living in exile at Courland (modern-day Latvia) in a palace owned by Paul I of Russia. There he had written a biography of Marie Antoinette and attempted to create an opulent court like that of Versailles.

Not long after Napoleon's installation, Louis wrote to Josephine that he hoped she would use her influence to bring him back as monarch. To her husband, he was even more gaily optimistic, suggesting Napoleon use his military might to restore him to the throne. 'I wish you would act more quickly. You and I could secure the magnificence of France,' Louis plaintively wrote to the First Consul. 'You would have to climb over 100,000 corpses first,' Napoleon replied. He offered small consolation: 'I will gladly do what I can to make your retirement pleasant and undisturbed.'[36] Napoleon sent his answer to the press to be printed, much to the pleasure of the Republicans.

Josephine begged her husband to reconsider. After years of insecurity, she believed that a monarch was the only way to hold back the tide of bloodshed and Revolution, and she took Hortense to plead with her. 'I implore you, Bonaparte, don't go making yourself a King.' The Consul brushed off their tears. 'You see ghosts where there are none, my dear Josephine. You have been taken in by the Faubourg Saint-Germain,' he said, commanding her not to refer to the subject again.[37] 'They should return to their knitting and leave me in peace. But I don't hold it against them,' he said to Bourrienne.[38] An old snob to the core, Napoleon loved Josephine's links with the aristocracy and her passion for royalty. But he knew that the people still saw him as the protector of the Republic, a caretaker until the installation of a proper government, and he was determined to prove them wrong. 'To be at the Tuilieries is not enough,' he acknowledged to Bourrienne. 'I need to ensure that I stay.'[39] He would not be able to do so without Josephine.

Thanks to her guile and finesse, she had won. Napoleon now knew that he needed her. The rise of the Martinique girl, mocked by high society for her gruff accent and plump figure, seemed complete. Despite her spendthrift ways and failure to fall pregnant with an heir, she had become Napoleon's ideal wife, largely for propaganda reasons: her time in prison and her links to the aristocracy sparkled like the diamonds around her neck.

The British, who had laughed at the lovelorn Bonaparte's letters, shook their heads at her influence. In a caricature by an anonymous British artist, entitled 'Johnny Bull on the Look-out or – Bonaparte Detected Drilling His Rib, at the Play of King and Queen of England – Scene St Cloud' (1803), the couple's power roles are playfully subverted.[40] Johnny Bull is meant to represent England, while Napoleon and Josephine are seated on thronelike chairs. Josephine is larger and taller than Napoleon, and it is she who holds an orb and sceptre and wears a crown. Her pose is dominant, masculine, in charge.

Josephine was winning the battle to outplay Napoleon, but she was spending huge amounts of money to do so. He wished to see her in lavishly decorated apartments and desired her to be set apart from other women, always grandly dressed and covered in jewels. He wanted her followed in the haute couture magazines. Periodicals such as *Journal des Dames* and *Costume Parisien* would circulate pictures of the finery Parisian ladies were wearing, and they often reported on the styles of Madame Bonaparte. Once upon a time, European courts had looked to France as the leader of fashion. Napoleon wished those days to return.

After the simplicity of the post-Revolutionary dress, Napoleon dreamed of his wife as an *Ancien Régime* fashion plate. But still, he forbade brightly coloured gowns, declaring they made his head hurt. He hated dark gowns as well – he desired to see a graceful and slender woman in white. He threatened to burn her cashmere shawls, which were an incredible luxury, and forced her to wear woolly wraps made from properly French sheep. And she had to keep her weight down as he had an 'invincible hatred of a fat woman'.[41]

On the excuse of boosting the French silk industry in Lyons, the Consul banned the import of her cherished Indian muslin.[42] Whenever

Hortense and Josephine appeared before him, he would immediately ask, 'Is that muslin you're wearing?' They lied that it was St Quentin linen, but smiled despite themselves, and he would promptly rip the gowns into pieces with his hands.[43] Napoleon wished Josephine to wear modest necklines and demanded her clothing be made of more ostentatious fabrics, such as satin, velvet and taffeta. What she wore set the trend: women began wearing heavier clothes with straighter skirts and stiff bodices, raised their necklines and lengthened their sleeves.[44] When he spotted Madame de Staël at a ball in a low-cut gown, he bellowed, 'You must have nursed all your children yourself, Madame?'[45] Josephine's favourite high-waisted gown was a way for her to show off her still-impressive form without revealing too much skin. The shorter bodice of the 'Empire-line' gown was much closer to the neck and suited her figure entirely. Men, too, eschewed the more romantic look. They wore darker, thicker fabrics with a frock coat, tailcoat and straight waistcoat, very like military uniform. Josephine, however, still yearned for the fashions of her youth, the freedom of flowing dresses and natural hairstyles. She had been at her most beautiful in her mid to late twenties and spent the rest of her life trying to dress in similar fashion, even when it was very outdated.

The spectre of money reared its ugly head once more. When he returned from Egypt, Napoleon instructed Bourrienne to investigate his wife's debts. Bourrienne approached Josephine but found her reluctant to divulge the truth. Finally, after she became Consuless, she admitted to him that she was in debt for 1.2 million francs (around £12 million in modern-day terms). Bourrienne was scandalised and terrified at having to give his master such awful news.

Josephine begged for Bourrienne's help and he told Napoleon that the debts only amounted to 600,000 francs. Even that, for the First Consul, was a shocking sum. He seized her bills and roared with fury. Why, Napoleon fumed, had she needed thirty-eight new summer hats, all purchased in the space of a month, when she was in retirement at Malmaison? There was a bill of 180 francs for feathers and 800 for perfume. It was an outrageous amount when the average Parisian worker supported a family on 600 francs a year. In one year alone she bought 900 gowns, almost five times as many as Marie Antoinette. Josephine was spending hundreds of thousands of francs a year. Napoleon had already paid off the outstanding debt of about 300,000 francs for Malmaison, as well as funding the renovations for their old house in the rue de la Victoire, and his wife had spent twice that amount on fripperies.

Napoleon shouted, Josephine wept and pleaded and threw herself at his feet. Finally, he declared he would pay the debts. He did have some sympathy for her, for it was clear to anyone that many invoices were wrong – she had been hugely overcharged for certain items but had shown no interest in checking them.

Bourrienne had some difficult manoeuvring to do: he told the dressmakers, milliners, feather-makers, perfumiers and all the others that they should take half of what they were owed, saying that if they sued Napoleon might be forced from office and then they would receive nothing. Grumbling, the owners of the finest shops in Paris agreed. But they could not resist the siren call of Josephine's purse and soon presented her with more tempting delights, such as jewels, shawls, fabrics and trinkets. She bought everything without asking the price and promptly forgot what she had purchased.[46]

Napoleon could compel 'the toughest of characters, the most untameable of men' to do his bidding.[47] Yet he was powerless to curb Josephine's astronomical spending. In one year alone, receipts showed that she had purchased 520 pairs of shoes.[48] Her debts were not limited to tradespeople; she also borrowed money from friends. 'I have not forgotten your 50 louis,' she wrote to her friend and fellow Creole Madame de Krény in 1800, 'you will have them the day after tomorrow.'[49] As Bourrienne put it, her desperate need to spend money 'was almost the sole occasion for her misery'.[50]

Napoleon loved people to be in debt, since it was a way of keeping them in a state of dependence, but Josephine went too far: She was addicted to shopping. Having lost so much in the Terror, she was always afraid of being deprived again. She was also looking for control and security, and a way to forge an identity separate from Napoleon's demands. She could not stop buying things she did not need.

Even after he had cleared her arrears, Josephine almost immediately lurched back into debt. She resorted to very unfortunate methods to make money, notably sharing political information with men such as Talleyrand and Fouché for a price, as well as delving back into black-market army supplies.[51] She even revived her foolish contact with Hippolyte Charles, after trying to recommend his company for an army contract. 'I regret very much that I have failed,' she ventured, 'since I would have been so happy to prove to you that nothing will change my feelings of the tenderest and most lasting friendship for you.'

In seeing Hippolyte, Josephine took a terrible risk. Her motives were pure nostalgia, yearning for the days when she was younger, more hopeful, and not confined to the restricted role of wife of the First Consul. It is almost impossible that this contact went unseen, but Napoleon's spymaster Fouché protected her, as he was wont to do. She was wasting her time trying to prove her 'most lasting friendship'. As she confessed to Madame de Krény, Hippolyte was being cruel to her in an attempt to finally break it off.[52] She could not hold on any longer. The relationship was over. On Hippolyte's deathbed in 1837, he asked that Josephine's letters to him be burned. Five letters survived and in them lies the tale of the only woman who dared betray Napoleon.

Aside from spending her husband's money, she devoted every hour to being the perfect wife. She ornamented her apartments with tributes to Napoleon's glory, praised him excessively and proclaimed herself distraught when he departed her rooms. He deputised to her the task of entertaining visiting statesmen and keeping his allies on side, particularly those of noble origin. Many years later, Napoleon would admit that his marriage 'brought me closer to a group which I required for my plan of integration, which was one of the most vital principles of my government'. As he said, 'Had it not been for my wife, I should not have had an easy means of approaching it.'[53]

Although he despaired of Josephine's shockingly open purse, he loved her and could not be without her. She was popular with the elites of France and the people at large, and he knew she legitimised his rule. As he had to admit, his life had changed beyond measure since he had met her. 'To me, luck is a woman,' he said, and that woman was Josephine. 'He became accustomed to associate the idea of her influence with every piece of good fortune which befell him,' her friend Madame de Rémusat marvelled.[54] As he saw it, he had gained majesty with her and in order for his success to continue he would have to keep her by his side. 'I win battles,' he declared, 'but Josephine wins hearts.'

12

'The most beautiful thing in the world'

s Consuless, Josephine was writing letters, charming politicians and conforming herself to fit Napoleon's moods. Her heart was often miles away in Malmaison. While the First Consul was reconfiguring the very foundations on which the country rested, his wife began major restructuring and renovation of her country estate. In January 1800, the two young architects Charles Percier and Pierre-François-Léonard Fontaine were called upon 'to rebuild a badly constructed house which is falling into ruin and which was only built for a very ordinary person'.[1]

Percier and Fontaine kept a detailed notebook in which they recorded the modifications. This invaluable document gives a sense of the scale of the renovations. Entire sections of the house were demolished and rebuilt. Napoleon grumbled that his wife was spending too much money. Her attempt to evoke the look of military camps in the building was a failure. He dubbed a tent-shaped vestibule designed to house the domestic staff 'a fairground tent fit only for showing animals'.[2]

Malmaison was a home for entertaining, a place in which everything was sacrificed to these spaces. Josephine spent thousands on the salon, the dining room, the gallery and the billiard room on the ground floor. The architects remodelled them along classical lines with stucco columns and decorative panels, the best display for statues stolen from Italy. They created a music room, which Josephine decorated with her incredible collection of art. They renovated the dining room, replacing the ceiling and building an ingenious underfloor heating system. Louis Lafitte decorated it in Pompeian style. By July, Percier and Fontaine proudly noted, 'the dining room, billiard room and vestibule are nearly finished. The First Consul, who is back again, is pleased with the changes.'[3]

Next to the dining room was another tent-like meeting room. Beyond this stood Napoleon's office. Framed by imposing pillars (and a protruding kitchen pipe that annoyed the architects), the ceiling was decorated with a fresco of the figures of Minerva and Apollo and portraits of the hero. 'Mme Bonaparte desired to have paintings representing scenes from the general's life,' Fontaine noted.[4] Napoleon liked the paintings by Girodet and Gérard, especially since they were inspired by Ossian, the great ancient Gaelic bard – who had taken Europe by storm after the Scots poet, James Macpherson, had published poems he said he had found by Ossian, (actually written by Macpherson himself.) Napoleon was less enamoured by the pictures of him on the panels by Bidaut, Taunay, Dunouy and Thibault, and he demanded their immediate removal. The whole place was a tribute to Napoleon, covered in Greek and Roman decorations and ornamented with Egyptian trinkets. Josephine packed it full of heavy mahogany and gilt furniture made by Napoleon's favourite, Maison Jacob. Everything was meant to show grandeur and riches, and underline Napoleon's message that he was a new force for good, with connections to old traditions.

As with Percier and Fontaine, Napoleon's patronage changed the lives of the Jacob Brothers. The exquisite creations of their father, Georges Jacob, had adorned the royal palaces and the aristocracy fought to buy his work, but after the Revolution his workshop lay quiet. Under Thermidor, demand was soaring once more and his younger son François took over, and soon caught the attention of Barras and the Directors. Josephine filled her home with his furniture and by the time Napoleon was First Consul, François Jacob had to tempt his father out of retirement to help with Napoleon's demands for mahogany, gilt and bronze chairs, tables carved with his insignia, and chests and armoires so heavy with gold that they were wearing on the eye. Josephine spent millions on the work of Maison Jacob – including the most expensive item they ever made, her jewel cabinet, which was delivered in 1809.

Despite Napoleon's obsession with Versailles, in which bedrooms were public spaces as splendid as reception rooms, his home at Malmaison followed a bourgeois set-up: public rooms were resplendent and private rooms simple. Laure Junot, a regular guest at the chateau, was unimpressed, 'Our apartments consisted of a bedroom, a cabinet and a room for our maid,' she wrote. 'The furniture was very plain.'⁵ Until the end of the Consulate, Napoleon and Josephine shared a bed under a fresco of clouds blowing across a blue sky in a simply furnished room.⁶

By 1802, the now-jaded Percier and Fontaine had done their work and Malmaison had been radically transformed. Josephine turned her attentions to developing the grounds of her new home and buying land. She had purchased it with a rather measly 150 acres but by the end of her life the land had increased more than ten times over, with grounds stretching to the banks of the Seine. Percier and Fontaine created an area for sports and rebuilt the stables and outhouses. They erected extra buildings for staff and cottages for guests. Josephine had grand designs: she requested a pavilion and a roundabout to make it easier for dozens of coaches to attend at the same time. In 1801, after an attempt on Napoleon's life, she added sentry posts.

Josephine longed to reproduce the lush landscape of Martinique in her home and bought books on horticulture as well as thousands of plants. 'She wants us to work on the gardens, the waters, the conservatories,' Fontaine noted in 1800.⁷ He protested that her requirements were 'without measure and without limits'.⁸ Josephine, transported by romantic desires for rolling hills and free-flowing beds of flowers, clashed with Fontaine, who preferred a classical layout. He was infuriated when she hired the British gardener Howatson and then Jean-Marie Morel, both specialists in the *jardin à l'anglaise*, as she wished for a wilder look to her grounds than Versailles.

On 2 October, Napoleon appointed a new superintendent for the gardens in an attempt to curb the expense. It was hopeless. Josephine had become a woman obsessed by plants. In a letter to her mother, she asked for 'the trees and seeds of as many species as possible'. She filled the gardens with orchids and exotic magnolia trees from St Lucia and also exploited her husband's empire by collecting seeds from his representatives all over the world, including Africa, South America and the Middle East.

Josephine established connections with influential figures across the globe, sending off letters bursting with botanical knowledge and meticulous attention to detail. The year she moved into Malmaison, she wrote to General Lefebvre, 'I would therefore be delighted to receive some of the magnolias and the bushes which you possess in significant quantity. But I attach a condition: that is that you make use of me with the same freedom and that you demand from me just as unreservedly any of the plants which I possess which you desire.'⁹ She wrote to Monsieur Cazeaux, in November 1803, playing on his 'patriotic zeal' and asking for some of his plants and 'seeds from America'.

I wish to multiply the production of plants from this continent in France, since its temperature is similar to our own. In order to achieve this goal, of which I have no doubt you will recognise the value, I am dedicating a section of the grounds adjoining Malmaison to a nursery. Exotic trees and bushes which thrive in our climate are cultivated here. The First Consul is observing the development of this establishment enthusiastically. It is a new source of prosperity for France.¹⁰

Josephine was presenting her garden as the glory of France. In a letter to the prefect Thibaudeau she thanked him for the 'wonderful collection' of seeds he had sent.

It brings me such inexpressible joy to see these foreign plants multiplying in my gardens. I hope that Malmaison will soon offer a model of good culture and that it will become a source of riches for the departments. It is to this end that I am growing a large quantity of trees and bushes from Australian and American territories. In 10 years time, I want every department to possess a collection of precious plants from my nurseries.¹¹

Josephine exchanged seeds, ideas and cuttings, pressing the male owners of fine gardens to give her the plants she desired.¹²

Malmaison was her empire. As the botanist Etienne-Pierre Ventenat wrote in the foreword to *Le Jardin de la Malmaison* in 1803, she created 'an impressive reminder of the conquests of your illustrious husband'.¹³ She had gathered 'the rarest plants growing on French soil', which had never before left 'the deserts of Arabia or the burning deserts of Egypt'.¹⁴ Specimens arrived from Egypt and other countries Napoleon had been to on military campaigns. She even bought from the enemy, spending her husband's gold at the Hammersmith nursery Lee & Kennedy. 'Some plants have arrived for you from London,' Napoleon wrote in 1801.[15] She begged the ambassador in Britain to see if the King would sell her some of his plants. Even in times of war with Britain, when the rest of Europe was blocked from trading with it, much to the dereliction of their economies, Josephine still bought plants from Britain. Napoleon even allowed one nurseryman safe passage to bring over a particularly delicate tree.[16]

In 1800, he authorised the explorer Nicolas Baudin to undertake an expedition to Australia, instructing him to bring back plants and animals. He returned with thousands of treasures for the Consuless, including hibiscus, mimosas and other flowers from New South Wales and Tasmania, as well as eucalyptus trees. Josephine wished for an expert in Australian horticulture and appointed Felix Delahaye, who had restored Marie Antoinette's garden at Versailles and travelled to southwest Australia in 1791 with an expedition during which he had collected 200 plants.[17] Malmaison became a little Australia. All the sea captains were told to bring back flora for Josephine. In 1809, Napoleon sent over 800 plants and seeds from Schönbrunn in Austria.

'My garden is the most beautiful thing in the world,' Josephine said in 1813.[18] Malmaison was a fiefdom of rare and exotic plants from all over the world. She grew many species for the first time in Europe, some of which are now common in our gardens, including cactuses, rhododendrons, tulips, dahlias and double jacinths. 'There are so many rare plants from all parts of the world, that one might believe oneself to be in the tropics,' pronounced the Comtesse Potocka.'[19] From 1804, she cultivated roses and would eventually produce fifty varieties. She spent thousands on specimens and nurtured her own, using names that evoked beauty and sensuality, including *cuisse de nymphe emue*. She once spent 3000 francs on a single bulb. She had an exceptional collection of heather and grew jasmine from her native Martinique. By 1813, she could inform Eugène proudly that her garden was 'more visited by Parisians than my salon, since at this very moment that I am writing, I am told that there are at least 30 people walking in the garden'.[20]

Malmaison had something of the fairground or theme park about it. In 1802, Josephine built an exotic orangery full of pineapples and other fruits, which she served at her table. The following year she bought a fleet of pretty cows and opened a dairy, staffed by a cowherd imported from Switzerland and a team of dairymaids in Swiss costume. Marie Antoinette's Petit Trianon had been mocked and derided; now Josephine made one that was even grander and more kitsch, taking the bas-reliefs by Pierre Julien, along with the marbled furniture and porcelain from the Petit Trianon, to furnish it. Morel built a Swiss chalet and three similar constructions on the edge of the Saint-Cucufa pond as cattle sheds and a house for the herders. Josephine served the butter, milk and cheese at her table. In 1808, the King of Spain sent a present of 2000 prime Merino sheep and she set them wandering over her grounds. Parisian high society, as they had with Marie Antoinette, loved playing farm.

In 1805 Josephine opened her hothouse, designed by Jean-Thomas Thibault and Barthélemy Vignon. 'Vast and magnificent', as one visitor said, it was a 165-foot-long tropical paradise full of plants from around the world.[21] Huge trees over fifteen feet tall touched the glass ceiling, and dahlia, amaryllis and fruit trees perfumed the air. In the midst of it all was a bust of Jean-Jacques Rousseau, Josephine's model for gardening. His notions of freedom, emotion and feeling, the haven of love and the home were in absolute opposition to the stiffness of the Consul and the mannered formality Napoleon desired – but in her hothouse and gardens she could be as romantic as she wished. In a letter to one of her gardeners, she wrote to say that she would like her bust of Rousseau to be displayed so that the tendrils of the surrounding plants would trail around his head.[22] Rousseau, ornamented with greenery, was the king of her domain.

The biggest attraction of all was her zoo. Her animals roamed freely in the grounds at Malmaison and it was the most exotic menagerie in Europe. Few ships arrived in France from foreign climes without an animal for Josephine. Kangaroos hopped around the verdant gardens and emus nuzzled at the soil as the country neighbours gaped at Peruvian llamas. She had the first zebra in Europe, as well as a gnu, a chamois and golden pheasants from China. Gazelles trotted around and nibbled from the hands of guests, and flying squirrels swooped through the trees. Talleyrand gave her a monkey, which liked sealing letters with wax.

After surviving lengthy sea journeys, her animals flourished at Malmaison, unless Napoleon felt like using them for target practice (fortunately, he was a poor shot). Peacocks stalked the flowerbeds while her prized Australian black swans swam on Malmaison's canal and lake. They were the first to be seen in Europe and she was incredibly proud of them. Such were the spoils that came back from the Australian expedition that the Natural History Museum demanded a share, but the Minister of the Interior told them that Josephine came first.

Her most cherished animal was a female orang-utan possessed of a remarkably sweet nature. The little lady strolled about the house fully dressed and when anyone approached her, she pulled her coat over her legs and would 'assume a modest, decent air to welcome the visitor'. She always ate at table, using a knife and fork, and was particularly fond of nibbling on turnips. After dinner, she loved to cover her head with a napkin and then pull funny faces. When she fell ill and was put to bed, she:

> lay with the cover drawn up to her chin and her arms outside it, completely hidden by the sleeves of the dressing gown. If anyone she knew came into the room, she greeted him with an appealing look, shaking her head gently and pressing his hand affectionately.[23]

Nowhere else in France, or indeed Europe, could one see a llama grazing or an orang-utan eating turnips. Her visitors were delighted by great forests, lawns, beautiful waterways and the long canal full of boats and black swans. The whole place was a museum of curiosities. Josephine also collected stuffed animals and birds and placed them in cabinets all over Malmaison.

Troupes of gardeners, landscapers, designers, botanists and horticultural specialists followed Percier and Fontaine, throwing their hands up in dismay over the demands of the Consuless. Louis-Martin Berthault, who began work there in 1807, best understood Josephine's tastes. He created a temple of love, a monument to melancholy, a grotto made of rocks from Fontainebleau and an ornamental lake with a statue of Napoleon at its centre. Berthault positioned classical and Renaissance sculptures all around the park (perfect for the guests to play hide and seek). He widened the river to create another lake and added a salon to the side of the huge greenhouse that housed Josephine's tropical plants.

Decorated in the antique style, adorned with vases and heated by wood-burning stoves, her 'greenhouse' salon was an intimate place to talk with her guests. The centrepiece featured two 'beautiful *brèche violette* marble columns, 12 feet in height, with gilt capitals and bases', procured by the founder of the Musée des Monuments Français.[24]

Before long, Josephine became inseparable from her garden. Botanists even named plants such as *Lapageria rosea*, *Josephinia Imperatricis* and *Amaryllis Josephinae* after her. Trading on the idea of her garden as a reflection of her husband's battles, she said that three of the plants she grew – Lily of the Nile, Parma violets and Damietta roses – recalled Napoleon's military conquests.[25] She also planted a cedar tree on the property to commemorate the Battle of Marengo.

Creating a beautiful garden was often seen as the role of the consort. Maria Carolina, Queen of Naples, had caused her British Envoy, Sir William Hamilton, endless headaches in her quest for a truly British garden for her palace. But Josephine prided herself on knowing more about horticulture than Marie Antoinette or Catherine the Great, and she used portraiture to advertise her knowledge. In Baron François-Pascal-Simon Gérard's watercolour *An Allegory of Empress Josephine as Patroness of the Gardens at Malmaison* (c.1805–1807), she stands in front of Malmaison's famous hothouse. Similarly, Pierre-Paul Prud'hon's *Empress Josephine at Malmaison* (1805–1809) shows her looking relaxed and ethereal in the gardens, and it even depicts a *Josephinia Imperatricis* in the bottom right-hand corner. Eager to show off her excellence as a botanist, she took as her symbol the cornucopia, the classical symbol of abundance, prosperity, good fortune, peace and good government, and had it carved into many of her possessions.[26] The British caricatured her as an amateur botanist, with George Cruikshank producing *The Imperial Botany* showing a bosomy Josephine displaying her sunflowers to the beau monde – all have faces of powerful men and the Napoleon flower is much less healthy than the Wellington. The French snapped up pictures of her next to her plants and bought trinket cornucopias.

Josephine sought to publicise and record her gardens.[27] She asked Pierre-Joseph Redouté, formerly flower painter and drawing master of Marie Antoinette, to produce 120 colour plates in a two-volume work entitled *The Garden of Malmaison* (1803-1805), as well as eight volumes of *Liliaceous Plants* (1802-1816) by the botanist Etienne-Pierre Ventenat. She gave books away in an attempt to promote her gardens and encouraged Redouté to publish a survey of the roses in Malmaison. His

Roses (1817-1824) would make her gardens famous after her death. She covered her bedroom walls with flower pictures by Redouté and used them to decorate a giant bed she bought in 1812.

The gardens were an elaborate form of imperial propaganda and a consolation, as well as her stake at immortality and a reflection of the quest for power that her husband conducted with Josephine by his side. Her plants were also for her guests to admire while they wandered the grounds, talked politics, planned love affairs. Josephine claimed for herself the position of supportive consort, and assumed the role of the woman without intellect or political awareness. It was an act: few could have created such an imaginative and truly unique home. Informal, beautiful, welcoming and all ease and grace on the surface, Malmaison *was* Josephine. As Napoleon observed: 'Without you, Malmaison is too sad a place.'[28]

In the early days of the Consulate, Malmaison was practically the seat of government. She and Napoleon travelled to their country retreat whenever they could, and were always there for Saturday evening, all of Sunday and part of Monday. After meetings held to decide the Civil Code and foreign policy, Josephine would host grand receptions and fabulous dinners. As a hostess she meant, above all, for her guests to enjoy themselves. 'We chose our hour of rising,' recalled Madame Junot.[29] Breakfast was informal, around eleven at the earliest, and then the afternoons were to spend as they desired, with music, reading, games in the garden or simply wandering the grounds as the sounds of the harp and piano drifted over the grass. The company would gaze at the paintings and admire the incredible mosaic pictures from Florence, bronzes and Sèvres vases in the reception rooms. At dinner, Josephine provided a sumptuous spread, with her own butter, milk, fruits and meat, the table beautifully decorated with flowers and candles glowing above the young faces of Napoleon's court.

In the afternoons, Napoleon and Josephine would ride around in her barouche. 'When I am outside in the fresh air my ideas take a higher direction,' Napoleon said. 'I cannot understand how some men can work successfully if they are always inside, beside the fireplace, without communication with the sky.'[30] Visitors to Malmaison often saw him working outside, papers on his lap. Talleyrand once arrived to find Napoleon had 'established his office on one of the bowling greens'.

Everyone was seated on the grass which Napoleon did not mind in the least as he was wearing leather boots and kid breeches – and he is used to camping. But as for me in silk breeches and silk stockings – can you imagine me sitting on the lawn! I am full of rheumatism! What a man! It was as if he was in a camp![31]

On warm summer evenings Josephine would order dinner to be served outside, sometimes in tents to celebrate Napoleon's victories.[32] There would be hunts and, as Laure Permond, by then married to Junot, recalled, when Bonaparte 'felt in the mood' he would play games such as barre, 'which he vastly enjoyed, taking off his coat and running like a hare'. The Consul teased the animals, feeding the tame gazelle tobacco from his pouch and 'encouraging it to run at us and the horrid animal tore our dresses and often our legs'.[33] But his greatest pleasure was to see the younger ladies 'running beneath the leafy arches of the trees, all dressed in white.' Nothing touched him like the sight of a graceful woman in a white gown.[34]

On Sundays during the summer months there were balls in the salons, and guests in their finery spilled out onto the huge lawn of the property. There were concerts and games of blind man's bluff, chess, backgammon, cards, billiards and charades, which Napoleon hated losing. The company was young, fun-loving, wealthy, and life seemed full of possibility. Romantic liaisons were made under the trees, pursued beside the Greek statues, and broken by the lake of black swans.

'It was not difficult to be entertained,' Hortense remembered.[35] On Wednesdays, forty or fifty guests would be invited to dinner, and a hundred and fifty came for a theatrical performance overseen by the Consul. He would have his relations rehearsing for weeks, supervised the casting and spent thousands of francs on costumes and props. The theatre manager came over from the Théâtre-Français and drama coaches were hired in the form of the established actors Talma, Michot, Fleury and Mademoiselle Mars. As in royal courts throughout history, the family members took the important parts and the courtiers had to applaud them, no matter how bad they were. Fortunately, Hortense, who usually took the lead female roles, had a sweet voice and a facility for acting, unlike the rest. Bourrienne was given the longer parts on account of his good memory, Junot often played drunkards and stolid Eugène was landed with the footmen roles. Lucien declared the whole lot of them poor, but Bonaparte was delighted by their performances. As he wrote to Josephine cheerfully while she was in Plombières, Hortense was playing Rosina in *The Barber of Seville*.[36]

Napoleon initially told Fontaine to create 'a sort of portable theatre, which can be set up in the gallery at Malmaison, near the drawing-room'.[37] Then he ordered 'as economically as possible, a small hall, entirely isolated, in the direction of the farm'. It was not an economic design. Fontaine drew up a plan and an estimate, handed it to Bourrienne for a performer's view, and settled on a circular form, the seats divided into sections, with a pit, a row of boxes, a gallery, an orchestra, two small foyers and 'a smaller theatre with no machinery for intimate plays'.[38] On 12 May 1802, the architect recorded in his journal, 'the theatre of Malmaison has been used for the first time.'[39]

The actors played in front of consuls, minsters, senators and generals – and Napoleon. 'He would be there in his box, close beside us, and followed us with his eyes and at the same time with a more or less mocking smile, which terrified us all,' recalled Laure Junot.[40] 'After the spectacle, there was a crowd in the ground floor apartments for brilliant refreshments.'[41] The evenings ended at about midnight and quests clattered in their carriages back to Paris.

Malmaison was Josephine's crown, and Hortense, fresh from Madame Campan's, was its jewel. As Napoleon wrote to his wife in Plombières, 'your charming daughter does the honours of the house with perfection'.[42] She had inherited her mother's grace and elegance, along with her father's magnificent looks. Unlike her mother, she read widely, wrote poetry and also played the piano well, particularly her favourite sonatas by Haydn and Mozart and pieces by Gluck and Dalayrac. So accomplished were her musical compositions – which included *Le Bon Chevalier* – that they were performed and appreciated in other salons.[43] One of her compositions, *Va t'en guerrier*, was even turned into a military march at Napoleon's request.[44]

Josephine had been lazy at music and Napoleon could no sooner play than stand on his head, but they encouraged Hortense and Eugène to perform. She sang beautifully, putting great expression into the words, and her voice blossomed under the teaching of her Italian singing tutor, Bonesi.[45] Napoleon was always alert to improving his stepdaughter. On one occasion, he stopped her from reading aloud in mid flow and corrected her loudly.[46] But she needed little coaching. She was also a talented artist, and had benefited greatly from Isabey's tutoring. On one occasion at Malmaison, Hortense failed to make an appearance at dinner. When Josephine went to her daughter's room and found her drawing, she asked whether she was hoping to earn a living from her hobby. Astute for her age, Hortense replied: 'Mama, in the century in which we are living, who is to say that that might not happen?'[47]

Everyone thought Hortense destined for an auspicious marriage. Like Josephine, she was very affectionate and attached to her mother and brother. 'She is really angelic in disposition,' thought Madame de Rémusat.[48] She had also inherited her mother's talent for flirting. Madame Campan worried for her as she embarked on her new social life as Napoleon's stepdaughter. She warned that it would be a 'dangerous whirlwind', since many people wished to be friends only 'for their own advantage' because she was 'the person of the moment, with an awe-inspiring title'.[49] Madame Campan was right: Hortense was quickly surrounded by soldiers, ministers and diplomats eager for her attentions. She fell in love with Napoleon's former aide-de-camp, General Duroc. A romance blossomed – but Josephine had greater plans for her daughter. Napoleon declared that they could marry, with a dowry of 500,000 francs, but Duroc and she would have to leave for Toulon immediately after the wedding – 'I do not want any son-in-laws in my house' Napoleon said.[50] Duroc changed his mind, and Josephine sent her despairing daughter back to the round of dancing and balls.

When they were not entertaining, Josephine's routine at Malmaison seldom varied; she would spend the day corresponding about plants, surveying the house and the grounds, receiving visits and dining alone with Napoleon in the evening. He neglected his work to walk around the property and supervise the improvements, and amused himself by calculating the income from the grounds – including even the vegetables in the kitchen garden. 'That's not bad,' he said, looking at the profit of 8000 francs, 'but one needs a yearly income of 30,000 francs to live here.'[51]

'Napoleon loved Malmaison with a passion!' said one visitor.[52] 'Nowhere, except on the battlefield, have I seen Bonaparte happier than in the gardens at Malmaison,' wrote Bourrienne.[53] The Consul looked forward to his weekends there as eagerly as 'a schoolboy to his holidays'.[54] In a world in which he was always afraid of uprisings or rebels hungering for his blood, the Consul felt safe in Josephine's palace. Even in the later years, he still thought of Malmaison. In August 1809, while in Austria, he wrote, 'the pleasures of Malmaison, the beautiful greenhouses, the beautiful gardens cause the absent to be forgotten'.[55]

If the gardens were Josephine's display case for plants, the house was her frame for the art she chased at a cost of millions. The guests marvelled at pictures, statues and mosaics so beautiful that it was little wonder many had been locked up in the secret closet of the Pope. Even during the period of the Directory, she was an influential patron. From 1799, she amassed over 450 paintings, drawings and miniatures. By the time she died, there were over 3000 *objets d'art* at Malmaison (including works by old masters and contemporary artists, sculpture, furniture and other decorative objects). Josephine became one of the most important collectors of her time.

On a personal level, she loved the chase of collecting and spent money because it gave her a thrill. Like her garden, a museum of Napoleon's conquests, her gallery featured the finest paintings in Europe, taken by the brute force of her husband. 'I would have respected Mme Bonaparte more if she had simply said that all these works of art were taken by force at the end of a sword,' said Madame de la Tour du Pin.[56]

Catherine the Great had amassed art as an aggressive strategy, creating a collection that saluted Russia's power and wealth. With every painting she took from a vassal state, an enemy or a rival, she proved her country's magnitude. French consorts had previously patronised French artists, from the plump cherubs of Madame du Pompadour to Marie Antoinette's Sèvres. Josephine saw herself as the patroness of an Empire. As the wife of Napoleon, she knew it was her role to create a fabulous art collection to symbolise his power. It was also testimony to her independence, dedication and negotiating skills.

She kept up with trends in the art world and subscribed to a variety of journals. She used the most knowledgeable advisers in France, such as Dominique Vivant de Denon, director of the Musée Napoléon, the archaeologist Alexandre Lenoir, the curator and merchant restorer Guillaume Constantin, and the artists Pierre-Paul Prud'hon, Jean-Baptiste Isabey and Lancelot Turpin de Crissé, who became her chamberlain. She made the careers of many artists. 'How many she helped! How many received her support!' said her maid, Mademoiselle

Avrillon.[57] Once she had bought their works, commissions from Napoleon often followed, and everybody at court wished to use the same painters as Josephine.[58] The Consuless did not always pay her bills. She asked Antoine Hamelin, who was in Rome, to spend 100,000 francs on art for her, suggesting he could spend more if he saw items he liked. Two years later, he was still plaintively asking for his money.

Josephine owned great works from Italy taken by her husband, many French pieces, a good haul of Dutch and Flemish canvases and a few by Spanish and German painters. She had pictures by Rembrandt, Rubens, Gerard Douw, Metsu, Van Dyck, Ruysdael, Poussin, Lorrain, Bellini, Correggio, Raphael, da Vinci, Titian, Veronese and a number of marbles, bronzes, mosaics and antique vases from Egypt. She had family portraits, historical subjects, works inspired by Napoleon's military conquests, scenes from everyday life and mythology, still lifes and animal paintings. One of the most significant additions to her collection came in the form of the works confiscated by the French troops from the collection of the Hesse-Cassel family following the battle of Jena in 1806 (the owners had tried to hide them in a woodshack, but Napoleon's soldiers hunted them out). The glaring absence in her gallery was British paintings. Napoleon would simply not allow it – London plants were bad enough.

Josephine had initially planned to hang her paintings in the *salon de musique* (sometimes called the *galerie française*). She soon ran out of space. In 1806, Berthault designed a gallery of at least sixty-five feet in length, and its construction was completed in 1808. She threw a ball to celebrate the opening of the most magnificent room in all Malmaison. It was, said one visitor, 'so well built, so well painted and with such taste, so perfectly lighted from above, so well proportioned that one could not hope to see a more beautiful room'.[59] Two glass doors led to a huge double archway, and works lined the walls, with vases and bronzes crammed onto the tables, along with busts of Napoleon and herself.[60]

Josephine was a ruthless collector, yet the works she was most drawn to, as in her garden, were often romantic or sentimental about nature and rustic life, rather than congratulatory of Napoleon. She had emotive paintings by popular female artists and over thirty troubadour paintings – small, highly finished portraits of courtly love, such as François Fleury-Richard's *Valentine of Milan Mourning the Death of Her Husband, the Duc d'Orléans* (1802). Displayed at the Paris Salon of 1802, it reflected a craze for medieval style. One reviewer called it a 'triumph of marital love' and, rather ironically, Josephine snapped it up.[61]

She adored all things medieval, borrowing the look for her costume, collecting volumes on medieval culture and subscribing to the *Le Journal des Troubadours*.[62] She who had sold her favours for security spent hours staring at troubadour portraits, wrapped up in their notion of courtly tribute and men and women sacrificing themselves for love.

Many artists produced portrait busts of Josephine, and she loved the work of Antonio Canova, one of the most talented – if artistically conservative – of the day.[63] She became his primary French patron and commissioned five works by him between 1802 and 1814.[64] In 1804, the incorrigible Pauline Bonaparte tried to seize his attention by turning up in Rome and suggesting he sculpt her as a naked Venus – 'There was a perfectly good fire in the studio,' she said, hoping to see her statue famous across Europe. In retaliation, Josephine planned ever more beautiful sculptures.

In 1803, Josephine received a shipment of precious objects from the recent excavations at Herculaneum and Pompeii, a gift from King Ferdinand of the Two Sicilies. In 1809, Napoleon helped swell this collection even further by sending 180 Greek vases after his sister Caroline and her husband, Murat, were made King and Queen of Naples. Josephine filled the rooms with ancient vases, placed amphoras outside in the grounds and statues in the theatre.

The early years of the Consulate at Malmaison were a golden time for Josephine. She had something that was truly hers and she surrounded herself with the things she loved: plants, animals and art. Her home was an escape from the strict etiquette of the Tuileries, and the vultures circling to destroy her. She was a leader of style, a woman emulated and discussed, her every move charted. Her collection made her an arbiter of cultural taste. Men found her fascinating, women envied her. And yet there was one man who found her increasingly resistible. The First Consul had begun taking mistresses.

13

Scenes with Bonaparte

'*I* am so miserable,' Josephine wrote to her old friend Madame de Krény, 'every day there are scenes with Bonaparte, and for no reason. This is not living.' Josephine had found out why Napoleon was being cruel. 'Then eight days ago, I discovered that La Grassini was in Paris. It seems that she is the cause of all the pain I am suffering.'

Giuseppina Grassini, the tempestuous and divine twenty-seven-year-old contralto opera star, had caught Napoleon's eye in Mombello. In Milan, just before the Battle of Marengo, he watched her sing at La Scala and decided he must have her.

Before long, La Grassini was established in Paris in a house not far from the Tuileries. Josephine was in torment. She begged Madame de Krény to find out if Napoleon visited her or if La Grassini was smuggled into the Tuileries. 'I assure you my dear, that if I was at all mistaken, I would tell you . . . Try too to find out where this woman lives.'[1]

The details of where La Grassini lived or how Napoleon visited her could only cause Josephine distress, but she was desperate to find out. Still, she had to submit – and watch her rival perform at Malmaison.

'I am not like other men, and the ordinary laws of morality and rules of propriety do not apply to me,' Napoleon vaunted. Like tyrants throughout history, he imposed morality on the people while using his own position to pursue his sexual desires. He still needed Josephine, but after Egypt he knew he could find sexual satisfaction elsewhere. When Pauline Fourès returned from Egypt, he sent her money and arranged a marriage for her, but refused to see her. Now he was First Consul, celebrated and aristocratic women were flinging themselves at him and he had no need of a milliner's girl.

Napoleon openly dallied with actresses and aristocrats and everyone knew the reason: his sexual obsession with his wife had ended. Josephine was distraught when she discovered that the Bonapartes were pushing women into her husband's path, and wept bitterly to her ladies-in-waiting of her ill treatment. But there was little she could do. Her power over him came from her gentleness and the respite he gained in her rooms, but every time she challenged him, she lost a little of his affection. She had to understand that the price of Napoleon's love was her allowing his affairs.

Josephine's jealousy gave her much pain. But Napoleon's nights with his conquests bore no comparison with those he spent with her. He had been so wildly obsessed by their boudoir that he could think of nothing else. He showered her with kisses, craved her for hours and never tired of her. With the new mistresses, he was practical. The Consul would instruct that the lady be lying in bed, already disrobed, so that he did not have to bother watching her undress. The act of love was usually over in minutes. He took other women to slake his desire for power, not to fall in love.

There may have been one exception. The Duchesse d'Abrantès described Hortense as being 'truly charming at this time, with her slim waist, her beautiful blonde hair and her big, gentle blue eyes and her grace, utterly Creole and utterly French at the same time'.[2] Hortense's influence over Napoleon did not go unnoticed. Cruel gossip began that she was having an affair with her stepfather. The British gutter press leaped on the story, but it was also impossible for the French to resist: Napoleon seduced women, and she was beautiful and so close to him. Bourrienne declared he saw nothing in all his time with Napoleon to suggest 'a connection of the nature of that charged against him', which 'was neither in accordance with his morals nor his tastes'.[3]

Napoleon was under threat from the monarchists and the Jacobins alike, but he was more afraid of the former. 'My power depends on my glory, and my glory on my victories,' he said. For all his achievements, his position was by no means secure and he needed another military victory. 'Conquest alone can maintain me.'[4]

Early in May 1800, Napoleon hurried from the Palace, wishing goodbye to Josephine and telling her to keep his final destination secret. His aim was to rout the Austrian Army.

He set off across Europe, scribbling to Josephine as he went. 'I've had no letters from you,' he wrote, 'a thousand tender thoughts, my sweet little one.'[5] He was annoyed by her lack of response but no longer wished her to join him. 'Here is an example to be followed,' he told the other wives and camp followers. 'Citoyenne Bonaparte has remained in Paris.' The Consul and his men travelled over the St Bernard Pass and came down behind Austrian lines. On 14 June at Marengo, the Austrians fought back and by two o'clock in the afternoon, the French Army had been all but overcome.

On 20 June, Josephine was about to host a reception for dignitaries and members of the government when a messenger hurried into the room and told her Bonaparte had been killed and the army defeated. She refused to listen and continued to preside over the celebrations. Just as the dignitaries were about to go home (and the news was spreading about Bonaparte's fall), another messenger entered the room and laid two Austrian flags at her feet, both torn apart by bullets. He announced that the French had won and Napoleon had achieved a great victory over the enemy.

As Josephine later discovered, General Desaix had arrived in the nick of time with reinforcements, and the Austrian Army had fled. People poured into the streets, cannons fired, windows were hung with flags and illuminations. Napoleon returned to Paris, accompanied by his blood-stained men, on the anniversary of the fall of the Bastille. He announced the 'acclamations as sweet to my ears as the sound of Josephine's voice'.[6] Not everyone supported him. Madame de la Tour du Pin declared that the people were really unhappy.[7] 'I hoped that Bonaparte would be beaten, because it was the only way to put an end to his tyranny, but I did not yet dare admit this desire,' said Madame de Staël, no longer a passionate admirer.[8] Still, for Napoleon and his circle, Marengo made him a hero, the supreme ruler of Europe and the man who could never be unseated.

Thanks to General Desaix, Napoleon held his grip on the public imagination. The raggle-taggle return of the much-decimated Army of Italy in the autumn of 1801 barely dented his popularity. The would-be Louis XVIII, ageing and corpulent in Courland and hardly as appealing as a great general, was the only man who seemed able to challenge the British desire for territory. Napoleon set his minions to celebrating his victories in plays, tributes and art, the most significant of which was by Jacques-Louis David, former ally of Robespierre. His emotionally charged and hastily completed *Napoleon Crossing the Alps* (*c.* 1800) depicted the hero astride his rearing horse. 'Commemorate me!' the Consul cried to artists, musicians and writers. 'Celebrate me!' His ferocious censorship and Fouché's network of spies hardly fostered the climate for imaginative literature or art. François-René Chateaubriand and Madame de Staël were the only writers of note, and both were sent into exile. As Napoleon himself put it, the 'minor works of literature are for me and the great are against me'. Empire readers secretly lapped up translated British fiction, especially the gothic tales of Ann Radcliffe and novels of opposition.

In 1802, Madame de Staël published *Delphine* from exile and had more influence on the city than if she had hosted a hundred salons. 'The whole of Paris is behind closed doors reading Madame de Staël's new novel,' said the senator Pierre Louis Roederer.[9] Madame de Staël was disingenuous when she said there was 'not a word about politics in it'.[10] Set in 1790–92, the novel harked back to the idealism of the Revolution. As one character declares, 'Liberty is the chief happiness, the only glory of a social order.' A cruel and unscrupulous woman was portrayed as a version of Talleyrand. 'I hear that in her novel, Madame de Staël has described us both as women,' Talleyrand shrugged.[11] Bonaparte was furious that the police had not suppressed the book. He told her never to come back to Paris. Her son begged for her to be allowed to return and was firmly rejected. 'Women should stick to knitting,' said Napoleon.[12]

Josephine hated being left alone at the Tuileries, since Napoleon's family had now truly unsheathed their claws. Rather than being grateful that he had lifted them from virtual poverty to incredible wealth, the Bonapartes complained that he treated them unfairly – and continued to criticise Josephine's spending. 'On hearing my brothers and the impudence with which they daily demand new sums, you might think that I had spent their patrimony,' he bewailed.[13] Jérôme went to sea and disobeyed his brother by marrying an American shipowner's daughter, Betsy Patterson. When Napoleon declared she would not be allowed on French soil, Jérôme allowed the marriage to be annulled, on the promise of a kingdom, and Betsy fled to Britain, where she became a trophy wheeled out to declare the evil horrors of life with the insane Bonapartes.

Lucien was little better: he told everyone that he was responsible for the coup that had made his brother Consul. Napoleon believed he had published an anonymous pamphlet, *A Parallel between Caesar, Cromwell and Bonaparte*, and promptly sent him off as ambassador to Spain. Napoleon was infuriated by his siblings' failure to marry as he wished. Lucien refused a dynastic marriage with the Queen of Parma, instead marrying Alexandrine Jouberthon, the widow of a bankrupt speculator. When Napoleon chastised his brother because he had 'married a whore', Lucien shot back 'at least *my* whore is young and pretty'.[14] After he departed in a terrible temper, Napoleon gathered Josephine in his arms. 'It is painful to find in one's own family such stubborn opposition to interests of such magnitude. Must I, then, separate myself from everyone? Must I rely on myself alone? Well! I will suffice to myself, and you, Josephine – you will be my comfort.'[15]

At the age of thirty, the man who ruled all France could not control his family. Even the youngest, Caroline, would not do as he wished. Seventeen, blonde and only just out of Madame Campan's, she had fallen passionately in love with General Joachim Murat, a handsome, thuggish, vulgar man with a strong Gascon accent. Napoleon looked down on him, for he was an innkeeper's son, and thought him stupid, as well as hating him for boasting (untruthfully) that he had seduced Madame Bonaparte. But Murat, thirty-two and dripping with masculinity and ambition, was determined to marry Caroline. Napoleon refused and Josephine attempted to push his sister's cause. She had always tried hard with Caroline, sending her presents and fond letters when she was at school with Hortense, and now she saw her chance to be helpful.[16] Added to this, she knew Murat disliked her and she wanted to win him round. On 20 January 1800, Josephine's plan came to fruition: Caroline married Murat in an intimate civil ceremony at Mortefontaine, Joseph Bonaparte's grand estate.

Caroline was ecstatic. 'Her beauty was striking,' wrote the Duchesse d'Abrantès. 'She was fresh as a rose.' Her head was a little too big for her body, but her 'skin looked as smooth as pink satin'. She also had 'charming' teeth – unlike Josephine.[17] In encouraging the marriage,

Josephine had made a major mistake: together, the couple were not grateful to her but only strengthened in their mutual desire to unseat her.

Napoleon, annoyed at being outmanoeuvred, took his revenge on his wife. He gave his sister a very small dowry of 30,000 but supplemented it by taking a diamond necklace from Josephine's own jewellery box.[18] Josephine was furious. Not to be beaten, she hunted for an even more expensive replacement. She settled on a set of pearls worth 250,000 francs, designed by the fashionable jeweller Foncier, and which had once belonged to Marie Antoinette. Having identified her prize, Josephine found the money to buy it by asking General Berthier, Minister for War. It was a shrewd move. Berthier was anxious to stay in her favour, since he was hoping to get his Italian lover, Madame Visconti, accepted at the evening soirées at the Luxembourg.[19] Josephine always listened patiently when Berthier needed to discuss his emotional problems, and he was keen to show his gratitude. He promptly offered some army contractors payment for a hospital service in Italy – if they paid him kickbacks. The money flowed in and Josephine had her beautiful pearls. It was a story reminiscent of the Affair of the Diamond Necklace.

Josephine then had to fool Napoleon. He had an uncanny ability to remember each and every piece of jewellery in her collection. The necklace had to sit unworn in her jewellery box, shining painfully at her when she opened the lid. She turned to Bourrienne and begged him to help her, unable to face an impending party without her new pearls. She asked him to remain by her so he could tell Napoleon that the jewels had been long in her possession.

'How fine you are to-day!' said Bonaparte at the party. 'Where did you get these pearls? I think I never saw them before.' 'Oh! mon Dieu!' she replied, 'you have seen them a dozen times! It is the necklace which the Cisalpine Republic gave me, and which I now wear in my hair.' Bourrienne backed up her lie and Napoleon trundled off, satisfied.[20]

Madame de Rémusat felt it no exaggeration to claim that Napoleon 'despised women', for 'he regarded their weakness as unanswerable proof of their inferiority'.[21] His views found their most public expression in the form of the Civil Code, also known as the Code Napoleon.[22] Before the Consulate, there was no single set of laws, instead people were governed by local customs and charters, as in feudal times. He wished for one legal code that would define the lives of his people. The Code was Napoleon's monument, his attempt to show that he could not only be a great general but also a law maker and give 'a direction to the public spirit'.[23]

'My greatest victory was my civil government,' he would later say on the island of St Helena.[24] Even though he would occupy the role of a monarch – with even more powers than Louis XVI had enjoyed, thanks to his direct control over the army – Napoleon created the impression that his subjects were living in a world of post-Revolutionary equality.

The Civil Code was, on the face of it, founded on the principles that had driven the Revolution in 1789: equality before the law and the secularisation of the state. It put an end to privileges of birth and enshrined a meritocracy: government jobs should go to the most quali-fied. The ever-growing middle classes of France were pacified and convinced that the sacrifices of the Revolutionary era had not been in vain. The Code was meant to keep Napoleon's key supporters on side by abolishing feudalism and aristocratic rank, but doing everything to preserve the rights of wealthy men of property and implying they would only get richer. The rights of workers were irrelevant.

The losers in the Civil Code were women. Napoleon, unable to control his wife, sisters or mother, instituted harsh limits on the rights of women. The rights over property and money that they had previ-ously possessed were abolished and replaced with an emphasis on their duty to be obedient to their husbands and fathers, and they were awarded the legal status of minors. 'A wife must promise obedience and fidelity in marriage,' noted one of the articles. Acquiring a divorce was a relatively straightforward process for men, but complicated for women. A man could divorce a woman for adultery, but a woman could only do so if the mistress had been brought into the family home. An adulterous wife could be imprisoned for two years, and would only be released if her husband took her back. A straying husband simply paid a fine. Even the happily married were restricted: a wife's right to handle money was very much reduced, unless she was a registered trader.

In Cairo, Napoleon had seen the locals shocked by what they saw as the downtrodden state of French men. 'Women these days require restraint,' he declared. 'They go where they like, do what they like. It is not French to give women the upper hand.'[25] For Napoleon, the family should be treated in the same way as France. The country, he argued, 'must submit to despotism before the need for liberty is revived'. The Code promoted the family as the basic financial and social unit – and the way to keep the family together was through the submission of women.

The Code reflected Napoleon's political desire to bind the bourgeois to him, as well as his distrust of female power. By 1804, his grasp on France was complete, with backing from the military, the property-owning classes and the peasantry. The peasants supported him because they had bought confiscated land, the booming economy created more work and drove down the price of bread. The property-owning *nouveau riche* and businessmen, speculators, traders and bankers were delighted by their new protector. The upper echelons of the army lined their pockets with the loot they had obtained.

Is it possible to see Josephine's unreliable behaviour as partly responsible for this enshrinement of female inequality in law? Certainly, Napoleon saw himself as surrounded by women who had excessive power, but he was not only resentful of his wife. Women on campaign had only hindered operations, in his opinion, and the intellectual women of the salons, such as Madame de Staël, infuriated him with their interest in female equality. Most of all, his plans for French world domination needed a constant supply of young, fit men to be sacrificed to his aims, and women who hoped for independence or a life of intellectual or financial endeavour were a threat to this. There was a fear across Europe at the time that men and women, particularly those of the gentility and aristocracy, were becoming too enervated or frivolous to have children, and Napoleon saw the solution to this as reinstituting the proper gender roles. Paradoxically, he could not endure the sight of a pregnant woman and *enceinte* ladies were not welcome at his gatherings.[26] But he endlessly proclaimed that it was the duty of women to be mothers. As he had told Madame de Staël, the woman he most admired in history was the one 'who had the most children'.

Napoleon was always trying to impose proper gender roles on his courtiers. On one occasion, he marched up to Madame de Condorcet, the beautiful salon hostess. 'Madame, I do not like women who meddle in politics,' he announced. 'General, you are quite right,' she replied, 'but in a country where their heads are cut off, it is natural for them to want to know the reason why.'[27] 'Do you still like men as much as ever, Madame?' he demanded of Josephine's old friend, Aimée de Coigny. 'Yes, Sire,' Aimée replied, 'when they are polite.' Few others had the chance to get the better of him. 'The terror he inspires is inconceivable,' said Madame de Staël. 'One has the impression of an imperious wind blowing about one's ears when one is near that man.'

As well as bringing in civil reform and reminding everyone of his great military victories, Napoleon announced the return of the Catholic Church – but this time subordinate to the First Consul. 'Society cannot exist without inequality of wealth and inequality of wealth cannot exist without religion,' he had told Roederer. 'Religion is a kind of inoculation . . . The people must have a religion and that religion must be in the hands of the government.'[28] Only the Church could make inequality seem natural and make deaths in war seem less senseless. 'It is not we nobles who need religion,' Napoleon said loftily, 'but it is necessary for the masses and I shall establish it.'

Those who had fought for the Revolution were infuriated by the idea of reinstalling religion, but the ordinary people craved the old ways, with women in particular practising their religion in secret. Even the most cynical could see the benefits of resting every seventh day rather than every tenth.

On Easter Sunday 1801, the populace heard the bells of Paris ringing for the first time in ten years. Most churches were missing a few as Napoleon had requisitioned them for the war effort. At seven in the morning, in his carriage escorted by dragoons, hussars, grenadiers and Mamelukes, he essayed forth. Josephine followed behind and seated herself by her husband at the front pew of Notre-Dame. The ceremony itself was lacking in dignity. Both Josephine and Napoleon had forgotten the rituals of worship, and in fact the only members of the congregation who seemed to remember were ex-bishop Talleyrand and former priest Fouché. Everybody else stumbled, knelt at the wrong times and stood open-mouthed through the prayers.

Still, the point had been made. Loire peasants, Lyons market stall owners, Breton farmers and Dijon housewives poured into the churches. As in the old days, church became the place for the rich to show off their wealth. In some of the churches in the more fashionable areas of

Paris, there was barely a free seat on Sundays. After a grand ceremony to celebrate the return of Catholicism, Napoleon turned to General Bernadotte, now married to his jilted fiancée, Désirée Clary. 'Well, now everything was just as it had been before,' he said. 'Yes,' said General Bernadotte, 'except for two million men who died for liberty and who are no more.'[29]

Languishing in his luxurious Chateau de Grosbois in Val-de-Marne, aged forty-five and already exiled, Barras wrote letters to Napoleon and Josephine. 'Is this the reward for what you called my great services and for which you vowed eternal gratitude?' he demanded of Napoleon. 'When you were buried in Italy and your enemies attacked your republican glory, I defended you . . . and when your brothers were threatened, they came to me for help.'[30] The Consul did not reply.

Josephine had been Barras's companion and he had covered up her affairs, lent her money and kept the letters about her adultery out of the newspapers. She did not reply to his letters either. A year after Napoleon became Consul, Barras was arrested at Grosbois and deported to Brussels. His papers and letters to the Bonaparte family were confiscated, denying him the chance to prove his service ever again.

Of Josephine's former circle, only Juliette Récamier was still feted by society, thanks largely to the position of her banker husband. Foreigners, dignitaries and even the Bonaparte siblings came to her salons, where she performed the 'Attitudes', imitating the poses from Greek myths, borrowed from the performance of Emma, Lady Hamilton, wife of the Envoy to Naples – and by 1801 the flamboyant mistress of Horatio Nelson and mother of his baby daughter. A book by Friedrich Rehberg, with guidance on how to achieve Emma's attitudes, had sold like hot cakes across Europe. Juliette performed the poses Emma had used to captivate Nelson, the most terrible enemy of France, but she did it to promote herself as a heroine of the Consulate.

Napoleon was growing increasingly unpopular as his enemies understood he was not about to move aside for a new government or a king. 'Spy on everyone except me,' he told Fouché. His minister sent his policemen to follow people who had once been Napoleon's friends, ordering them to open the letters of half the population of Paris and bribe neighbours to inform on each other. Still, they were always one step behind the cells of dissent springing up across Paris.

On Christmas Eve 1800, Josephine was preparing to attend the premiere of Haydn's *Creation* at the Opéra. It was the event of the season and the performers had asked specially that Napoleon be present. Fouché had passed on a rumour to the Consul that there would be an attempt on his life, but he ignored it. He told Josephine she must be at her most beautiful and awe Paris's most fashionable elite. After dinner, at eight, the couple made their way outside to the carriages. Napoleon was to travel in one carriage, while Josephine, accompanied by Hortense, Caroline (who was eight months pregnant) and Napoleon's aide-de camp, General Rapp, would follow in the second. At the last minute, Napoleon gazed at his wife's outfit and decided it was not right. He declared the shawl from Constantinople did not suit her dress and hustled her off to change. The entire party had to wait while she hurried to her apartments to find a new shawl. By the time she returned, Napoleon had already left. She and her companions hastily boarded their carriage and set off for the performance.

As Napoleon's coach entered the rue Saint-Niçaise, the coachman was puzzled by a cart blocking their passage. As he turned into the next street there was a horrific explosion. Napoleon later said that it felt as though the whole carriage had been swept up by the sea and was being carried along by the waves.[31] Coming behind, Josephine and the other women were thrown to the floor of their carriage and the windows were smashed. Josephine fainted in shock, but fortunately the heavily pregnant Caroline took charge and remained calm. The roofs of surrounding houses fell in, glass was shattered and some of the horses bolted.[32] Accounts said as many as twelve civilians were killed and thirty people injured.[33] One contemporary illustration showed a small child being catapulted into the air and debris blown many feet high. In the second carriage, which was just a little way behind the first, glass lay all around and Hortense's dress was stained with blood from a cut to her hand caused by flying debris. Josephine was in tears.

The First Consul was the target of the bomb – and if he and his wife had left on time they would have been killed. Josephine, Napoleon, Hortense, Caroline and General Rapp were saved by an ill-matched shawl.

Napoleon continued on to the Opéra and, after hearing Josephine was safe, calmly took his place in his box. 'The rascals wanted to blow me up,' he shrugged.[34] The women arrived, pale and red-eyed, trying not to tremble as the audience greeted them with cheers and applause.

Napoleon maintained his unruffled demeanour only until the party returned home to the Tuileries. He demanded angrily that Fouché hunt down the Jacobins responsible and ordered that a number of former members should be deported. The minister's efforts to explain that intelligence suggested royalists had co-ordinated the attack fell on deaf ears.[35]

Josephine had to hide her distress as Napoleon did not like cowards. He was delighted at the way the bomb had bolstered his popularity and prompted 'extreme indignation in the populace'.[36] He proclaimed he had made a heroic escape.

Josephine was the Consuless, rich, celebrated, sought after and beautiful. Still, she worried about her future. She was Napoleon's love, the talisman he credited with his military successes and, as one of her friends put it, she was the 'woman whom popular suspicion regarded as his good angel'.[37] But the 'good angel' needed to have a child. At thirty-seven, she was not too old. Letizia had given birth to Jérôme when she was thirty-four, and only her husband's death the following year prevented her from having more children. Thérésa Tallien would have her tenth baby at the age of forty-two. But Josephine's body had been much weakened by her period of imprisonment during the Terror and her fall at Plombières had left her with a pelvic injury. The chemical treatments she would have used to prevent pregnancy while a mistress also had the long-term effect of reducing fertility. She was always lying to her husband about the frequency of her menstrual cycle.

Napoleon's family exploited Josephine's inability to have a child. One minute they told him to discard her because she was barren and next they teased him that he was the infertile one. Pauline Fourès had notably remained not pregnant and blamed Napoleon. If any actress or courtesan mistress of his said she was with child, his brothers claimed that they had seduced her. Josephine was not above suggesting that it was he who was responsible for their lack of children. He told her that her menses were irregular and not healthy, and she disingenuously replied that it made no difference.

Napoleon knew that he would be a laughing stock if he discarded Josephine and then failed to make his second wife pregnant. At the time infertility was generally seen as the fault of the woman, but there was a strongly-held theory that the more vigorous-looking the man, the better able he was to impregnate his partners. Napoleon was small, sallow and sunken. He suffered from seizures, due to an excess of nervous energy, and he fidgeted and scratched. Riven by digestive difficulties and suffering from headaches, he was hardly an inspiring figure of French manhood, even at the age of thirty-two.

'It is the torment of my life not to have a child,' Napoleon told Bourrienne. 'I plainly perceive that my power will never be firmly established until I have one.'[38] The majority of the population loved Napoleon and they wanted to see him with a son.

There had long been upsetting rumours that he was having an affair with Hortense. Now, the gossips declared, he might wish to have a child with her. Hortense wept bitterly but Napoleon was rather vain about the idea, saying such rumours only reflected the 'wish of the public that he should have a child', which only made Josephine feel more insecure.[39]

She was distressed by the gossip and hated Napoleon's repeated affairs. In desperation, she turned to the remedies of quacks. Napoleon decided she should travel to Plombières to attempt to renew her fertility in the waters, which he firmly believed had magic powers. There was hard evidence for their effects: Joseph's wife, Julie, had failed to fall pregnant for four years, but succeeded in late 1800 after a trip to Plombières.

Just before Josephine departed, Lucien Bonaparte took her for a private conversation. 'You are going to the waters,' he said. 'You must get a child by some other person since you cannot have one by him.' She was utterly shocked. 'Well,' he blithely continued, 'if you do not wish it, or cannot help it, Bonaparte must get a child by another woman, and you must adopt it, for it is necessary to secure an hereditary successor. It is for your interest; you must know that.' 'What, sir!' she replied. 'Do you imagine the nation will suffer a bastard to govern it? Lucien! Lucien! You would ruin your brother! This is dreadful! Wretched should I be, were any one to suppose me capable of listening, without horror, to your infamous proposal! Your ideas are poisonous; your language horrible!' 'Well, Madame,' he retorted, 'all I can say to that is, that I am really sorry for you!'[40]

Josephine set off to Plombières in anguish, escorted by a grand entourage of cavalry and aides. General Rapp, Hortense, Madame de

Lavalette and, less comfortably for Josephine, Napoleon's mother were accompanying her. Josephine wept and soon everyone was either suffering from a headache or travel sickness. Nothing went well. The inns were awful and their dinner on one night was 'spinach dressed with lamp-oil and red asparagus fried in curdled milk'.[41]

Fortunately, matters improved when they arrived. The town was illuminated, all the dignitaries were assembled and the cannons fired for them. Plombières was no longer a social desert. Josephine's visit in 1798 had made it fashionable and frequented by many, and Napoleon urged her to give balls and receptions and to continue nurturing social relations. No wonder the local Doctor Grosjean, who published a study on the medicinal properties of the baths in 1803, praised the 'salutary waters which Providence has bestowed upon our commune' – everyone was getting rich in Plombières.[42]

Napoleon was elated on her return. 'My wife's menses have started again,' he said. But his elation was short-lived. She failed to get pregnant. When Napoleon's sister Elisa hinted subtly that Josephine was the one at fault, Josephine reminded her that she already had two children, Hortense and Eugène. 'But, sister, you were younger then,' Elisa answered. Napoleon arrived in the room just as his wife burst into tears. 'There are some truths better left unsaid,' he remarked.

Josephine's many enemies were constantly plotting her downfall – and hissing to Napoleon that he should get a divorce. And so she embarked on the most ruthless act she had ever committed. In a desperate attempt to keep her husband to herself, she decided to sacrifice her daughter.

14

'My stepfather is a comet'

'I am his superstition rather than his love,' Josephine told a friend. 'He considers me one of the rays of his star.'[1] But wives needed to breed. She conjured up a plan. If eighteen-year-old Hortense married Louis Bonaparte, they could have a child and that child would be the heir to Napoleon and Josephine, a sharer in the blood of both of them.

She told Napoleon and he was delighted by the idea. Bourrienne was sent to break the news to Hortense. 'You know it is her great sorrow no longer to have a child,' he said to the teenager. 'I assure you intrigues are constantly being formed to persuade the First Consul to obtain a divorce. Only your marriage can strengthen the bonds on which depends your mother's happiness.'[2] He praised Louis, told her that otherwise she would have to marry 'some foreign prince' and talked of her debt to her mother.

Hortense was shocked. Like most girls of her age and class, she had expected her parents would try to arrange a marriage for her but believed they would also allow her to have a say in the matter, even though they had blocked her marriage to Duroc. She knew how highly Napoleon esteemed her and she could not imagine that he would ever give her to Louis. At twenty-three he was ugly, prone to wild paranoia and already tormented by gonorrhoea. He suffered cruelly from curvature of the spine, he stammered and was often ill. When he was well, he was idle, violent and neurotic.

All this might have been leavened if he was as dazzled by Hortense as every other man, but he barely acknowledged her and she believed he hated her because he despised her mother. He was interested in books and good with money, but that was little comfort.

Hortense pleaded with her mother and stepfather, but it was to no avail. 'It was a question of sacrificing my romantic fantasies for my mother's happiness,' she said.[3] As a child, while playing with jewellery with Madame de Rémusat, she had declared that she one day wished to be the owner of hundreds of diamonds. Now she would be wealthy, a princess, even a queen – but her heart was broken.

Josephine moved fast. She had to marry Hortense to Louis before the Bonapartes threw their customary spanners in the works. The family had to admit that Hortense was gentle, beautiful and accomplished, but they had no desire to link themselves further to Josephine.

Within a few months, on 4 January 1802, the entire clan was in the drawing room in the Tuileries, watching a white-faced and sick Hortense say her vows to Louis by a makeshift altar. Josephine had given her daughter a splendidly embroidered gown and a necklace and headpiece of diamonds, but Hortense insisted on a simple white dress and a string of pearls. She did not look at her groom and he avoided speaking to her. Pale and dignified, she received a religious blessing with her new husband. Caroline and Joachim Murat, who had married two years earlier, were also blessed.

The wedding night was dismal. Lucien had told Louis that the marriage was rushed because Hortense was already pregnant with Napoleon's child. That night, Louis tormented Hortense by reciting a list of her mother's lovers and criticising Josephine's behaviour. He then told her that if she gave birth to a child before the allotted nine months, he would banish her and never see her again. Hortense had to bear her situation. 'My stepfather is a comet of which we are but the tail,' she said. 'We must follow him everywhere without knowing where he carries us – for our happiness or for our grief.' She later received a beautiful gold and enamel watch from Josephine as a thank-you present. It was scant consolation.

Josephine had sacrificed her daughter to her ambition. The Bonapartes were furious. But still her position was not secure. She had told Napoleon that her great wish had been to see their union blessed, at the same time as that of Hortense and Louis and Caroline and Murat. A blessing, of course, would make it much harder to divorce her. Napoleon flatly refused.

Hortense became pregnant quickly. Even that was not joyous for her as she knew that, behind her back, people were accusing her of being pregnant at her wedding. The British press mocked the marriage and implied Napoleon was keeping his stepdaughter close so that he could continue the affair. In August, they suggested she had already had the child or was about to, implying it had been conceived before the wedding. Adamant to stop such 'scandalous rumours', Napoleon forced her to dance an energetic quadrille with him in public at an August ball.[4] From a man who hated the sight of pregnant women and thought the spectacle of them dancing one of the most disgusting things in the world, this was quite a gesture. It still did not stop the rumours.

To Josephine's delight, on 10 October Hortense gave birth to a son, Napoleon Charles, just a few days past the nine-month term. Napoleon declared the boy his heir – although he did not give him any such official status. Josephine felt safe – for the moment.

Was he Napoleon's son? Some thought him so, the British perpetuated the gossip that he was, and certainly Napoleon was much fonder of him than he was of Hortense's second son, Louis Napoleon. The Consul had long given up being faithful to his wife, but fond as he was of his stepdaughter, getting her pregnant was beyond even him. Josephine might have been desperate, but she could never put her daughter in her husband's bed to keep her position. And if the child had been Napoleon's, he would have been much less likely to still consider divorce – and to refuse Josephine her wish for a religious blessing.

In March 1802, Napoleon signed a treaty of peace with Britain at Amiens. The British economy was weakening due to the conflict, Pitt's government had fallen and the King was suffering from delusions. Weary of war, the ministers gave great concessions.

Amiens returned Martinique and Guadeloupe to the French and gave back territories to Holland and Spain. The treaty was a triumph for France and Napoleon's popularity soared. Towns and villages across France had been sorely tried by losing their young men to fight, and the people were tired of war. They looked forward to dominating the world through might rather than bloody battle.

In less than two and a half years, thanks to looted gold and terrorising campaigns in Italy and Europe, France had thrown off the misery of the days of the Directory. Napoleon poured money into the reconstruction of Paris, improving the parks and building bridges and roads. In 1803, one writer used one of Napoleon's visits to see the construction of a new canal to encourage the Parisian public to follow his example. Why, the author insisted, 'the First Consul himself' has visited the site, and 'his presence was a great encouragement for the workers'.[5] As Napoleon later said, 'I wanted Paris to become a town of two, three, four million inhabitants, something fabulous, colossal, unknown until our time.'[6] Tourists marvelled at the palaces, sampled the restaurants and filled their trunks with souvenirs. After the imprisonment of the King, the royal collection had become public property (aside from the paintings taken by Napoleon and Josephine), and in 1793 the Louvre had opened, with an exhibition of 537 paintings. The public crowded in to see the pictures once owned by the King, as well as those of the Church and nobility, and the Republic decreed 100,000 livres a year should be set aside for expanding the collections. They had not reckoned on Napoleon and his avarice for art. The Louvre closed for renovations from 1796 to 1801 and when it reopened, Napoleon crammed it with his stolen booty. In 1803, it was renamed the Musée Napoléon.

The British had been banned from France since 1792, and after the Amiens treaty they came in droves. When the British politician Charles James Fox came to visit in July, he declared one felt 'almost breathless expectation at the thought of seeing so celebrated a city'.[7] The luckiest might be presented to Josephine at one of her receptions or be shown the art at Malmaison. There, they were often rather surprised. Men, such as the stolid dramatist Edmund Eyre, were mesmerised by the Parisian ladies and their 'state of undress really immodest'.[8]

Josephine was thrillingly appealing to the British. When most queens were stolidly virtuous, she had been a kept mistress, veered close to being a courtesan and had been unfaithful to her husband. A British visitor said he had hardly arrived in the Palais de'Egalité, the traditional centre of prostitution in the city, when a man sidled up to him. Would he care to buy *The Licentious Life of Madame Bonaparte*?[9] Everyone was fascinated by the woman who held the mighty Bonaparte in such thrall.

Martinique paid for Josephine's grandeur. The conquered European countries suffered huge taxes but perhaps the biggest toll was levied on the newly regained Caribbean islands. In 1799, the Republic had ended slavery in Saint-Domingue (modern-day Haiti), but by 1802

Napoleon was reintroducing it, allowing more African slaves to be brought to the islands. Politically, he knew he could not push the French much harder – it was far easier to oppress colonies overseas. He wanted more money for his coffers and did not care how it was brought in. 'Bonaparte is very attached to Martinique and is counting on the support of the planters of that colony; he will use all means possible to preserve their position,' Josephine wrote to her mother in 1803.[10] She sent her presents, hoping she might come to Paris. 'You will like Bonaparte very much,' she assured her royalist mother. 'He is making your daughter very happy.'[11]

In August 1802, Napoleon was elected 'Consul for Life' by a massive majority. Only around 9000 of the 3.5 million men who voted had not plumped for him. He had become a king, yet with more power than a Bourbon had ever enjoyed, thanks to his direct control over the army. He steered his way between the Republicans and the royalists, offering concessions, promising favours and flattering everyone. As he said, 'There was not a party in France which did not build some special hope upon my success.'[12] For him, his people were children who could always be pacified with the promise of presents. And they rewarded him, putting as much faith in their Consul as if he were a miracle-worker. He was so convinced of his position that he had his birthday, 15 August – a date that was in Catholic countries the Feast of the Assumption of the Virgin – declared Saint Napoleon's Day as an annual public holiday. Within a few months, the mint was producing gold coins stamped with 'Napoleon Bonaparte: First Consul'.

Malmaison, he decreed, would no longer suffice. There had been hurtful suggestions that it was shabby and small. One British visitor declared it 'a poor old affair, washed yellow and backed by a good square patch of wood and planted without the least taste'. Bonaparte rejected Versailles as 'monstrous' and instead chose the Chateau de Saint-Cloud, only fifteen minutes by carriage from the Tuileries, a splendid chateau with extensive grounds overlooking the Seine.

Marie Antoinette had bought it from the Duc d'Orléans, for she thought the fresh air would be good for her children and wished for a property to leave to them after her death. She took what had been a home of the Orléans family and transformed it into her own pastel, feminine vision of beautiful interiors, with pale blue and green walls, drapes of white muslin and gilded sphinxes in her private apartments, golden furniture and bronze decorations. At the time, the idea of the Queen having her own palace was terribly shocking to the people, and there were rumours she would give it to the Austrian royal family. Overdecorated, overcoloured and spattered with gold, Saint-Cloud became for the French people a symbol of the corrupt and lavish Bourbon monarchy.

The contents of Saint-Cloud had been sold off after the Revolution. Now Napoleon reclaimed it for the nation, covered all the pastel colours with heavy gold wooden panels and imperial colours and filled the place with the formality Marie Antoinette had wished to escape. He stuffed the rooms full of Maison Jacob furniture, gilt ornaments, hangings and ornate mirrors. Napoleon's eyes could not stand bright lights or gaudy colours, so he had the mirrors draped in soft material and the lights shielded with gauze. Josephine had decorated Malmaison to pay tribute to him, with Egyptian figures and statues inspired by the Greeks and Romans. Saint-Cloud was similarly adorned with sphinxes, statues of Napoleon as a Roman hero and giant 'N's on the doorknobs and plates. Napoleon set his beloved Percier and Fontaine to work on plans. He spent six million francs on the building and huge sums on landscaping the gardens, adding fountains and cascades that rivalled those of Versailles.

Josephine was depressed by the move to Saint-Cloud. She loved Malmaison and found the new palace forbidding and gloomy, but to Napoleon it enshrined intimidating glory. The informality and lazy summer evenings of Malmaison were about to be a thing of the past. For Josephine, life as Napoleon's wife was soon all ritual and gilded furniture.

He saw no irony in occupying a folly of Marie Antoinette's that had once incensed the French people to murderous intent. Instead, he began planning a court that rivalled that of Louis XVI for splendour. Monarchs across Europe now prided themselves on their simplicity and lack of pomp. King George III in Britain was nicknamed 'Farmer George' for his humble interest in plants and his plain court at Windsor Castle. Napoleon, conversely, believed that the lessons of Marie Antoinette's fate were irrelevant to him and thought the populace more likely to pay tribute to the man who appeared in front of them adorned in gold. In place of the post-Revolutionary simplicity of the early days, he began to wear a uniform of a red velvet coat embroidered with gold and a sword inlaid with some of the crown jewels. As far as he was concerned, his people would be easily won over with the cheap gift of dress. Even the former Jacobins on his staff had not complained when he suggested they wore red velvet coats with a blue sash. 'I have only to gild the court dress of my virtuous Republicans for them to belong to me,' he crowed.

Napoleon felt that the naturally nostalgic French would welcome a new court and that it would encourage the royalists and aristocrats to his side. Unfortunately, he had little interest in the minutiae of courtly life. He turned to Josephine, who consulted Hortense's old headmistress, Madame Campan. Jeanne-Louise Campan had been First Lady of the Bedchamber to Marie Antoinette from 1786 until the storming of the Tuilieries in 1792, and thus was an expert in etiquette. Bows, curtseys, court dress and precedence became the hot topics of conversation. Napoleon took four prefects and Josephine had to appoint four ladies-in-waiting from aristocratic backgrounds. She chose Madame de Luçay and Madame Lauriston, whose husbands worked for Napoleon, and Madame de Talhouët, who probably gave information to the royalists. The fourth woman, twenty-two-year-old Claire de Rémusat, an old friend of Hortense, would appear to be the most loyal of all – although she wrote her memoirs of the court, later published by her son in 1880, in which Josephine's failings were laid bare.

Visitors were properly awed by the gilt, the excess and the fine liveries of the footmen. 'The household of the First Consul is increasingly taking on the appearance of a court,' said the Prussian ambassador. Swedish Count Armfelt decided the 'grandiose public splendour' hardly less lacking than Versailles. Napoleon was sometimes so confident that he simply wore his uniform waistcoat, sword, breeches, stockings and boots. He looked ridiculous among all the lustre and rich dress but nobody dared laugh.

Goldsmiths and jewellers worked day and night to keep up with orders. The needles of fine dressmakers and the brushes for painting gilt onto carriages were working overtime. In the winter of 1801, more than one million yards of satin and tulle were bought for ballgowns and receptions. Napoleon encouraged dances and masques, and reinstated the tradition of balls at the Opéra. It was good for trade, but also, as he put it, when people were dancing, they were not 'poking their noses into politics'.[13]

Despite his affairs, Napoleon was still fascinated by his wife. 'Bonaparte's superstition about his wife is very extraordinary,' commented one British visitor. 'When he came from St Cloud, though quite ill, she came with him to satisfy his feelings, and went to bed as soon as she arrived at the Tuileries.'[14] He depended on her, but in Saint-Cloud his rages were growing more severe. He shouted at her in public with the freedom with which he had once used to caress her. On one terrible occasion, he drove her to inspect a property he had acquired. On the way, Josephine saw a great ditch ahead. Already suffering from a migraine, she begged him to allow her to descend and make her way over the ditch on foot. Napoleon roared at her not to be such a child and whipped the horses to make them jump the ditch as fast as possible. The horses just made it, but the carriage shuddered and almost broke in half. Josephine burst into hysterical tears while Napoleon reproached her wildly for not trusting him. Such violent outbursts were becoming ever more common – but they were always followed by ardent sexual reunion. Josephine was often still resentful of his anger but she knew not to turn him down.

At Saint-Cloud, Napoleon and Josephine slept together every night as usual, allowing her the power of guessing his actions and thoughts. Then she threw a jealous scene about a mistress and Napoleon lost his temper. 'I resolved not to return to my subjugation,' he recalled.[15] He took up residence in a room across the corridor, though he spent many nights in her bed.

Although Josephine still had no official title, she was the queen of Saint-Cloud. She was expected to preside over the social life of the palace. As one of her ladies-in-waiting said, 'social events constitute the canvas which she embroiders, which she arranges and which give her a subject for conversation'.[16] Napoleon, who could often hardly bear the small talk and endless courses of banquets and receptions, would sometimes scuttle off on the excuse of business, leaving her to entertain the guests. He decided that all young women at the court should learn to make the 'Versailles Curtsey', a low dip, and perform it when he and Josephine entered the room for formal receptions. On other occasions, ladies would have to stand when Josephine entered the room, and again when she departed. Pauline and Caroline Bonaparte were spitting with fury at having to stand for Josephine – who sometimes threw them a sly smile as she floated by. The Revolutionary heroine was moving into the position of Marie Antoinette.

Josephine herself was rather unnerved by her new position. When ambassadors were presented to her, Napoleon commanded her to remain sitting, in the same fashion as the old queens of France. Josephine could not: she rose to meet them, holding out her hand. 'I feel that I was not born, my child, for such grandeur, and I would be happier in retirement, surrounded by those I love,' she wrote to Hortense. She had always been disquieted by Napoleon's wild ambition; now she was positively afraid. On one occasion, witnessed by Bourrienne, she came in her 'gentle and beguiling way', and settled herself on her husband's knee, 'caressed him and brushed her fingertips softly across his cheek and through his hair. Her words came in a tender rush. "Bonaparte, I implore you, don't go making yourself a king. It's that horrid Lucien who puts you up to such schemes. Please, oh, please, don't listen to him." Bonaparte laughed off her pleas. "You must be out of your mind, Josephine," he smiled.'

The most prestigious invitation of all was to one of Josephine's weekly dinners in her apartments. The guests would be received by the First Consul and his wife, seated on thrones. Josephine did not impress everyone – particularly the British. The writer Mary Berry thought her 'distinguished looking' but much older than her portraits. Another thought her rather ordinary. 'If chance had not placed her on a pinnacle, she would escape minute observation.'[17] Certainly her teeth – which gave her much pain – were in a dreadful state. All agreed, though, that Josephine's tact and grace worked wonders to smooth over her fading beauty and rather humble past. 'Her sense of the right word and the right action and her irresistible attraction convinced us all that she might have been born for the role fortune had given her.'[18]

Costume took up ever more time in her day. Napoleon, now sure that the way to rule was by stunning the populace with splendour, told her that she must outshine every woman present. 'Mme Bonaparte, who understood to a high degree the art of being well-dressed, set an example of the greatest elegance,' observed Laure d'Abrantès.[19] She bought spectacular outfits. One celebrated pink crêpe dress was covered entirely with real rose petals. A tribute to her love of roses, it was divine but she could not sit and could barely move. Another fine gown was made of toucan feathers, each one adorned with a pearl. She adored luxurious gloves and purchased over 1000 pairs a year.[20] When she desired a fresh pair, they would be brought to her on a silver tray.

Napoleon wished for his wife to look opulent, but he did not always comprehend the cost. On one occasion, Claire de Rémusat saw him lecturing Josephine that she should appear 'at her dazzling best in jewels and dress'. When she did not respond, he prompted, 'Did you hear me, Josephine?' 'Yes,' she replied sweetly, 'but then you will reproach me or even go into a tantrum and refuse to pay for my purchases.' She gave him such a gently flirtatious smile, 'the desire to please him so unmistakeably bright in her eyes that he would have had a heart of stone to resist her'.[21] She dreaded the times when she had to present her accounts to him. He railed that she spent excessively, gave too many presents, and did not understand the value of money. He used her spending to torment her, then compelled her to spend more.

Napoleon was trying to stake a claim to a court of spotless virtue, but he never criticised Josephine for her past. When he found out that Talleyrand had a mistress, Catherine Grand, a divorcée and former *demi-mondaine*, he forced him to marry her immediately, declaring that the diplomatic corps would protest at his behaviour. At the Tuileries, Napoleon berated Catherine in front of the whole company, saying she must atone for her immorality by behaving with dignity. 'In this respect, as in all others, I cannot do better than to model myself on Mme Bonaparte,' she replied. Talleyrand resented having to marry her: he found her annoying, she was losing her looks and his family thought little of her. Bonaparte, as Madame de Rémusat thought, 'took a malign pleasure in making Talleyrand marry'.[22] From then on, Talleyrand became an enemy.

The British were particularly fond of titillating gossip and the scabrous cartoonist James Gillray loved to recall Josephine's dubious past. He drew her and Madame Tallien dancing naked behind a gauzy curtain, with Barras enjoying the spectacle while drinking wine and a tiny Napoleon spying from behind. Barras, Gillray said, offered Napoleon promotion on condition he took Josephine off his hands, even though she was 'smaller & thin with bad teeth, something like Cloves'.[23] The *Progress of the Empress Josephine* showed her different incarnations: prisoner, Empress, Barras's mistress and 'loose fish' – or lady of low morals.[24] But few paid much attention. Only one visitor, Lord Morpeth, refused to let his wife be presented to her. But Napoleon did not see Josephine as his Achilles heel; for him, she was all grace and excellence, and the old days were long gone.

'Love is a singular passion, turning men into beasts,' Napoleon said. 'I come into season like a dog.'[25] Even though he was growing plump and had terrible manners, once he was made Consul for Life, he found it presented more sexual opportunity than he had ever imagined. In the autumn of 1802, he dismissed Bourrienne, declaring him guilty of financial corruption. He took the keys to his secretary's old room, adjacent to his study, and had it filled daily with fresh flowers. Actresses, dancers and *demi-mondaines* crept in to be his lovers. His skills of seduction had not improved, for he sat and stared at those he wanted until they blushed and gave in, dazzled by his riches and power. Mademoiselle Duchesnois, an actress from the Comédie-Française, was once shown to Bourrienne's former room by Napoleon's faithful valet, Constant. The Consul was working late in his study, and when Constant knocked on the door he cried out, 'Tell her to wait!' An hour later, Constant knocked again and he replied, 'Tell her to get undressed.' The actress did as she was bid and waited undressed. Constant knocked again and Napoleon cried: 'Tell her to go home!'[26]

Josephine was desperately jealous of her husband's many women and her teary questions only made him angrier. 'As soon as he acquired a new mistress,' wrote Claire de Rémusat, 'Bonaparte became hard, violent, pitiless towards his wife.' He told her the details and liked to show an 'almost savage surprise that she did not congratulate him'.[27] If she wept and complained, he turned on her ferociously.

Napoleon could never understand why his wife cared about his dalliances. 'She is always afraid that I will fall seriously in love,' he told Rémusat. 'Does she not know then that I am not made for love? It is not in my nature to surrender to any such overwhelming feeling. Why does she worry about these fancies in which my affections are not engaged?'[28] He was too busy to fall in love but he had plenty of time for fast seductions. After all, as he proudly told one mistress, he could often get the job done within three or four minutes. But Josephine, unable to bear his child and hated by the Bonaparte family, remembered his intense passion for her in the early days and dreaded him turning to another woman. Napoleon would point out that her past conduct gave her no right to complain, but she was still jealous, upbraiding him and weeping and paying spies to report back to her about his affairs.

Mademoiselle Duchesnois, like all the rest, did not last long. Soon Napoleon became entranced by her arch rival on the Paris stage, the fifteen-year-old actress Marguerite-Josephine Weimar, or Mademoiselle Georges. The grand battle between the divas captivated all Paris. Duchesnois was generally decided the better actress, although rather plain. Georges was no great tragedienne, but beautiful. In order to try and beat her rival, she went all out to capture the First Consul. An affair with Napoleon would catapult her to stardom.

Mademoiselle Georges met Josephine and watched her carefully, saying, 'It was impossible not to succumb in the face of that soft, mysterious charm.'[29] Cleverly guessing that the best way to capture Napoleon was to be as gentle as his wife, she feigned the mien of innocence. After she followed his summons to Saint-Cloud, flunkeys took her upstairs and then left her in a room 'with an enormous bed and heavy curtains of silk'. Napoleon arrived and she played the virtuous maiden for an hour or so, before claiming she could not help but give in to his charms.

Napoleon was delighted by his schoolgirl-age mistress. 'I am very fond of the name Josephine but I shall call you Georgina, if you'll allow me.'[30] With her he played the child, romping around the staircases and playing hide and seek behind the curtains. All Paris heard of the affair. When Napoleon visited her at the theatre, Josephine was humiliated and despairing. One night, they went to see Mademoiselle Georges play the lead role of Emilie in *Cinna*, a play written in 1639, which Napoleon favoured as it congratulated absolute power. The Roman Emperor Augustus has ordered the death of Emilie's father. She begs Cinna, who is in love with her, to kill Augustus. In the final act, Augustus challenges Cinna, and Emilie attempts to free him by saying she seduced him into it.

Georgina was ready for her stardom. At the dramatic high point of the play, she paused and gave the line: 'I have seduced Cinna, I shall seduce many more.' The crowd roared with delight, leaped up and turned to applaud Napoleon in his box. He smiled and puffed out his chest. Josephine's humiliation was dreadful.

One night, she was in her Yellow Salon with Claire de Rémusat, tormenting herself with the knowledge that Napoleon was in Bourrienne's chamber with Georgina. 'I cannot stand it any longer; Mlle George must be up there. I am going to surprise them.' She marched up the stairs with Claire following behind her. They nearly got there – and then thought they heard Napoleon's rather terrifying guard coming towards them. 'He'll kill us,' cried Josephine. Claire fled in terror and Josephine chased after her. When they reached the bottom of the stairs, they began to laugh and Josephine realised she had been deluded to think she could storm into the room.[31]

Some time later, one evening Josephine heard Georgina screaming in fear. She dashed to Bourrienne's room, along with valets and guards, only to find Napoleon suffering from a seizure and Georgina making her exit in a state of undress. She was terrified that the Consul had died and she would be blamed. Josephine stood there and saw with her own eyes the evidence in the rumpled sheets: her husband could find sexual passion with women other than her.

Napoleon stuffed 40,000 francs down Georgina's dress and set off in search of a replacement. He tried his hopelessly boorish seductions on every young woman he saw. Men found him naturally charismatic and fascinating, but he left women cold. Mademoiselle George had used his attentions for her advantage, but there were many women who had to submit because they had no protectors. Napoleon used them all for pleasure.

When General Junot and his young wife Laure came to stay at Malmaison, Napoleon promptly sent Junot away. He had known eighteen-year-old Laure since she was a child, and he had proposed to her mother, Madame Permond, before meeting Josephine. But such family connections did not dampen his fervour. At 5am, he entered Laure's room, sat on her bed, and read his morning correspondence. He gave her a pinch and she pretended to be asleep. He left the room. Laure begged her husband to disobey orders and remain with her that night. Next day, she locked the door and heard Napoleon rattling at it. Not to be dissuaded, he then set off to find a secret key. He burst into the room, ready for love, but found Junot in bed with his wife and exploded in fury.

Even when one woman fell out of favour, Josephine knew she was not safe. Another beautiful, adoring, younger mistress would soon be in her place. She knew Napoleon loved the way she presided over the court with grace and diplomacy, and that her presence mollified the royalists and the aristocrats. But she would no longer be his good-luck charm if one of his mistresses became pregnant.

'Ambition is never content, even at the summit of greatness,' Napoleon declared. The peace with Britain was fragile. He had deployed French troops to Holland, which contravened the treaty with the British. For his part, he was pitched into rage by the expansionist desires of the British and their irreverent newspapers. Day after day, he stared at caricatures of Josephine in a state of undress, jokes that Hortense was his mistress, and pictures of him as a pygmy with a giant nose. Lord Whitworth, the British Ambassador, calmly told Napoleon that the British press mocked everyone, but the constitution would not allow them to be silenced – which was not entirely true, since the newspapers were prevented from expressing pro-French opinion.

Napoleon detested Whitworth and he was personally annoyed by his impressive height of six feet. He demanded the British quit Malta and Whitworth replied that his government expected the Consul to give up on his aggressive policies of invasion. In March 1803, he lost his temper and raged at the ambassador in public with insults so terrible that Whitworth declined to repeat them in his letters. 'England wants war,' the Consul roared at the ambassadors of Russia and Spain. Within two months, Whitworth had left, the tourists fleeing behind him. The British seized all French and Dutch merchant ships near their coasts. On 18 May, Britain declared war on France once more, with the excuse that France had intervened in internal Swiss politics and sent troops to the country. Four days later, Napoleon declared all British men in France between the ages of eighteen and sixty would 'immediately be constituted prisoners of war', an act of capturing civilians that outraged international opinion.[32]

Simply, Bonaparte wanted to be at war with Britain again. Talleyrand was furious at the breakdown of the Peace of Amiens, his suspicions confirmed that Napoleon was only happy when he was sending his subjects into battle. As Madame de Staël put it, the 'natural restlessness of his character, independently from his need to dominate, is such that he could not be content with a mere thirty million people to govern and make happy'.[33]

It was a powder keg and Napoleon ignited it. 'In three days, granted favourable circumstances and foggy weather, I could be master of London, the Parliament and the Bank,' he boasted. Peace had not suited him; there were only so many days he could spend watching ladies curtsey. By June, he was in his element, bustling around newly-created camps for his forces and talking of erupting onto British shores. He had seen the newspapers mocking Lord Nelson for his desperate infatuation with Emma Hamilton and he thought his old enemy had lost his desire for blood. 'I will take you to London,' he boasted to Josephine, 'I wish the wife of the modern Caesar to be crowned at Westminster.'

While he was surveying his ships, Josephine wrote him a heartfelt letter.

All my sadness vanished, as I read your touching letter and the expressions of your feelings for me. I am so grateful to you for taking the time to write at such length to your Josephine. You cannot think how much joy you have given to the woman you love . . . I will always keep your letter which I press to my heart. It will console me for your absence, and guide me when I am near you, for I want to be always in your eyes as you want me to be, your sweet and tender Josephine, my life devoted only to your happiness.

When you are happy or for a moment sad, may it be upon my bosom that you pour out your joy or your grief; may you have no feelings that I do not share. All my desires amount only to pleasing you and making you happy . . . Adieu, Bonaparte, I will never forget the last sentence of your letter. I have it locked in my heart. How deeply it is engraved there and with what ecstasy my own has answered it! Yes, oh yes, that is my wish too – to please you and to love you – or rather to adore you.[34]

Josephine dreaded Napoleon venturing overseas. If he died, she would be completely unprotected, for there was no Barras to ask for help now. Fortunately for her, Napoleon changed his mind about invading when intelligence suggested he would need his armies to quell rebellion in his empire and fight back against Austria. Moreover, as he would not admit, his naval capacity was not equal to Britain's. The war situation changed to a game of stand-off and stalemate.

On 14 June, Josephine set off with Napoleon on a month-long royal tour, travelling through north-eastern France and the Low Countries. She was greeted by delighted crowds, who had turned out to see her as much as the Consul. For a month, she hosted receptions, and for the first time she was wearing the French crown jewels. Napoleon was given a pair of swans in Picardy, a gift that was from ancient times reserved for kings. He sent them back to Paris and let them swim in a lake at the Tuileries.

But he was growing more paranoid. In 1804, a Vendéan rebel leader was arrested and confessed to his captors that he and his co-conspirators had been plotting to assassinate the First Consul, and had only been waiting for a prince of royal blood to lead them. The government needed a scapegoat, and settled on the thirty-two-year-old Duc d'Enghien, nephew of Louis XVI and a commander in the army of the Prince of Condé, which had attempted to assist the Duke of Brunswick's invasion of France. Enghien was resident in the neutral Grand Duchy of Baden. Napoleon sent dragoons to cross the Rhine and seize him at his home. He was imprisoned at the Chateau de Vincennes near Paris – servants were already digging his grave near the dungeon.

The news spread quickly around the court and Josephine was horrified. She and her husband were at Malmaison at the time, and she hurried downstairs to find him serenely playing chess. Her royalist sympathies to the fore, she knelt before him and begged him not to execute the man. Her pleas were in vain. 'How harshly he repelled my entreaties!' she recalled. 'I clung to him! I threw myself at his feet!' 'Meddle with what concerns you!' he exclaimed angrily. 'This is not women's business! Leave me!' He pushed her off with a violence she had not seen from him since the time he had accused her of an affair with Hippolyte on the return from Egypt.[35] Later on, she tried again and he was even gruffer. 'Go away, you are only a child, you know nothing about politics.' That evening, Josephine was unable to pretend to be merry, and Madame de Rémusat, her lady-in-waiting, was pale. Napoleon demanded why she wore no rouge and she replied that she had not put any on. 'That could not happen to my Josephine,' he publicly pronounced. 'She knows that there's nothing more becoming to a woman than rouge – and tears.'[36] Later, he began to fondle Josephine brutally. Distressed but knowing better than to resist him, she allowed him to spend the night in her room.

Napoleon, by that point, hardly cared whether the stolid Duc was guilty or not. He was convinced that there was nothing like an assassination attempt to firm his hold over the people and garner more power.

The Consul was merciless. The Duc was sentenced to death, with no proper hearing. Less than a week after his arrest, on 21 March at two thirty in the morning Enghien was taken to the courtyard to be executed. He stood in the dark, his faithful dog still beside him. Holding a lantern near his heart to direct the fire, he did not cry out. He refused a handkerchief to cover his eyes, saying, 'You are Frenchmen, at least you will do me the service not to miss your aim.'

His dignity and courage awed the marksmen. They were told they could help themselves to his clothes and money, but they refused.

The news spread like wildfire across Europe. Napoleon had crossed into a neutral state and executed a man without proper trial. The wanton killing of a royal was not only a terrible reminder of the bloody Revolution and Terror, but many still believed the royals had been specially imbued by God. Josephine wept when she heard and struggled to control her feelings. 'I am a woman, you know, and I confess I could cry,' she repeated, over and over. She consoled herself that her husband was 'not naturally cruel, it is his counsellors and flatterers who have induced him to commit so many villainous actions'.[37]

Napoleon, delighted at his success, commanded Talleyrand to throw a ball to celebrate. 'The Duc d'Enghien was a conspirator like any other and he had to be treated as such,' he said. 'These people wanted to throw France into confusion and to destroy the Revolution by destroying me.' Allying himself with the Revolution was absurd, but he kept it up – 'I am the man of the State. I am the French Revolution. I say it, and I will uphold it.'[38]

His courtiers struggled to celebrate and foreign visitors stood in their finery, shaking their heads at the horror.[39] Just over a week after the death of the Duc, Napoleon went to the theatre. His habit was to dash to his box before Josephine's carriage arrived. This time, he needed her popularity. Pale and anxious, he entered with her, as she looked ahead, smiling as if nothing had happened. He was fortunate – this time. The people in the theatre erupted into shouts and cheers.

For the Parisians, who had read the false newspaper reports that cast Enghien as a conspirator, Napoleon had proved his excellence and strength once more.[40] 'I have forever silenced both royalists and Jacobins,' he crowed. The Jacobins were delighted; convinced now that he would never put a Bourbon on the throne. The royalists, shocked by his actions, realised they had underestimated him. But it was too late. Three weeks after that awful night when the bullets felled Enghien, the Senate assembled and duly declared that the Life Consul was now the Emperor. Josephine was indeed, as the Martinique fortune-teller had suggested, 'greater than a queen'.

15

'Your Imperial Majesty'

Napoleon's Empire was announced on 18 May 1804, to a twenty-one-gun salute. He was the only person at ease, receiving the senators as they stumbled between 'Citizen Consul' and 'Citizen Emperor'. Josephine visibly trembled when she was called 'Your Imperial Majesty'. She was now the Empress of France. Surely no mere actress could unseat her now.

Madame de Staël was shocked. 'For a man who had risen above every throne, to come down willingly and take his place amongst the kings!' Napoleon's supporters, particularly the working men who cheered his military victories, thought he could do no wrong. The liberals, who had deluded themselves that he was an heir of the Revolution, were scandalised. But the majority of the French were weary of bloodshed, afraid of the British threat, and desperate for security. Napoleon, a strong ruler who would brook no opposition, seemed their only option.

He had chosen Emperor as his title. King was impossible, but Emperor, he felt, would remind the French of the grandeur of Charlemagne, the Holy Roman Emperor. Unlike Charlemagne, however, he would not be travelling to Rome for the coronation. Pope Pius VII would have to come to Paris. Napoleon refused to listen to the disgusted complaints of his Council of State, many of them fanatical anti-clerics, about a religious coronation. The new Emperor assured them that his motivations were not vanity but to ensure the greatness of France by inspiring the people with pride and to put himself on the same footing as every monarch in Europe.

Sixty-two-year-old Pope Pius was reluctant to come, for he had been deeply distressed by Napoleon's treatment of the Duc d'Enghien. Cardinal Joseph Fesch was sent to persuade him. Fesch pleaded, he flattered, he offered gifts – and he gave a heavy-handed reminder of Napoleon's military strength. Pius gave in and agreed to come. As a thank-you, Napoleon gave Fesch a seat in the French Senate, the position of grand almoner of the Empire and the grand cordon of the Légion d'honneur.

Napoleon was the ruler of an Empire, but his family were proving as unruly as ever. On the evening he was proclaimed Emperor, he dined with them and they did nothing but attack him for not treating them well. He decreed that his heir would be Joseph, followed by his male descendants, and then Louis, followed by his descendants. Jérôme and Lucien, he decreed, should be ruled out of the line, since he did not approve of their marriages. Lucien's wife, the illiterate sister of an innkeeper, was hardly a woman who should be elevated to Napoleon's magnificent succession. Joseph and Louis were each given the title Prince of the Empire, a million francs a year, and an additional one third of a million francs a year in expenses. Their wives would be princesses – but this was too much for Elisa and Caroline, who would be without titles. The sisters screamed and railed as they accused their brother of condemning them to 'obscurity and contempt'.[1] Napoleon vainly puffed that he was Emperor and should be able to hand out honours as he liked. Letizia was incandescent that her title would be merely 'Madame Mère de Sa Majesté l'Empereur' and not 'The Imperial Mother' and declared she would not attend the coronation.

Napoleon gave in and allowed his sisters to take the title of Imperial Highness. They would be princesses, although their husbands would remain commoners. Pauline had the same privileges, but she was disdainful. As she pointed out, she was already a real princess since she was the wife of the Prince Borghese. Lucien was so furious to be excluded from the succession that he stormed off to Rome. The Bonaparte family were united in one wish: that Josephine would not become Empress. The thought of having to bow and curtsey to the whore from Martinique was simply too much. The family's hatred plunged Hortense into further suffering; her husband and his family never refrained from attacking her mother and listing her sins.

Napoleon expected Josephine to assume the role of the most splendid

Empress. The old days of informal gatherings and conversations with the public were over. 'She is a good, easy-going woman,' Napoleon told his Minister of the Interior. 'Her progress and her conduct will have to be dictated to her.' She now had fourteen ladies-in-waiting, copious jewels and a huge household. Most of her ladies were drawn from the old aristocracy, and complained about serving 'Madame Bonaparte' when her back was turned. One of her new ladies-in-waiting was Elisabeth de Vaudey, a pretty thirty-one-year-old blonde with a good singing voice and a passion for intrigue. She was fond of Josephine, but scornfully thought her 'need to open her heart, to repeat all that happens between herself and the Emperor, takes away much of Napoleon's confidence in her'. 'Josephine is like a ten-year-old child in her generosity, her frivolity and her rapid emotions, she can weep and be comforted in minutes.' Elisabeth thought she was as 'ignorant as most Creoles', but had acquired 'graceful manners' and wit, although she did admit that she was 'perfectly gentle and equable; it is impossible not to be fond of her'.[2] Josephine made a mistake in telling Elisabeth her secrets, for everything she said got back to the Emperor.

In July, Napoleon was due to travel to the coast to inspect the naval bases for another proposed invasion of Britain. Josephine, perhaps in a last-ditch attempt to fall pregnant, travelled to take the spa waters at Aix-la-Chapelle, the burial place of Charlemagne. The journeys to Plombières, eating spinach dressed in lamp oil en route, were a thing of the past. Napoleon set his ministers to creating a twenty-four-page directive on the Empress's triumphal progress, the style of her entourage, and what gifts she would offer.

As Madame de La Rochefoucauld and Josephine directed the packing of her gowns, all the mayors and shopkeepers along the way prepared gun salutes, rehearsed bands to play fanfares as she arrived, and strung illuminations across their towns. Josephine arrived in imperial magnificence (if not always exactly on time). She took four of her ladies, two women of the bedchamber, two chamberlains, a comptroller, a master of the horse, two ushers, ten footmen, coachmen and her own kitchen staff. At least seventy horses accompanied her carriage. It was grandeur all the way, and she was greeted with 'enthusiasm that erupted at the sight of the Empress in the towns through which she passed', in the words of Mademoiselle Avrillon.[3]

While inspecting the troops, Napoleon was very gratified to hear excellent reports of Josephine. At Charlemagne's tomb she was presented with a rather grimy bone said to be that of the Holy Roman Emperor. She declined it graciously, saying she had 'for her own support an arm as strong as Charlemagne's'. 'You are still essential to my happiness,' Napoleon wrote to her. To Josephine's joy, he then announced that he would meet her at Aix and accompany her party on a visit along the Rhine. 'I cannot wait to see you and to cover you with kisses. A bachelor's life is a horrid life and I miss my good, tender and beautiful wife.'⁴ He also wished to see Elisabeth de Vaudey. As the party progressed through the towns of the Rhine, Napoleon and Elisabeth began an affair. As always, a new romance meant he was even more irritable with his wife. One night, he hauled her out of bed in the middle of the night, demanding that she get dressed and attend him immediately, as if sleeping was an act of neglect.

Like queens and princesses throughout history, Josephine chose beautiful, graceful and accomplished ladies-in-waiting, only to find her husband attempting to seduce them. 'Every liberty which he takes pleases him as though it were a victory,' Madame de Rémusat observed.⁵ Unfortunately for the Empress, her old friend Juliette Récamier, who had long been able to withstand Napoleon's advances, had declined the role of lady-in-waiting (Napoleon later exiled her). Another Napoleon picked on was blonde twenty-year-old Anna Roche de La Coste, whose main task was to read to Josephine in her chamber. She gave in to Napoleon but refused to relinquish her lover, his chamberlain, Theodore de Thiard. The Emperor stumbled across them in bed together (no doubt notified by Fouché), and sent Thiard off to the Vatican. His attention was piqued by Anna's disinterest, and in front of everybody at court he gave her a seriously expensive ring, and demanded Josephine bring her to a state reception. Luckily, Anna soon fell out of favour and Napoleon amused himself by toying with Thiard and sending him on ever-more impossible missions.

When Napoleon and Josephine returned to Paris, he took up with Adèle Duchâtel, a golden-haired court beauty in possession of a complaisant older husband. Josephine was in paroxysms of misery at the affair. One day at Saint-Cloud, she saw Adèle secretly leave the room and she convinced herself that her rival was on her way to Napoleon. Madame de Rémusat tried to dissuade her, but Josephine was determined to find out what was happening. She hurtled up the stairs to

Napoleon's chamber, listened at the door and heard the voices of Adèle and her husband. She knocked and begged to be allowed in, and then burst through the door, ran to the bed and began upbraiding her husband. Adèle started crying and Napoleon was inflamed with fury, as she recounted to Madame de Rémusat, 'Bonaparte flew into so violent a passion that I hardly had time to fly before him and escape his rage. I am still trembling at the thought of it.'[6] Adèle fled and Josephine dashed away to her rooms, but he followed, screaming and shouting so loudly that the whole palace could hear. He threw every insult at her and smashed her furniture. Shrieking that she was now beyond redemption and that he had had enough, he ordered her to leave the palace immediately. He roared that he was tired of her spying and that it was time to think of his legacy, 'which demanded that he should take a wife capable of having children'.[7]

Finally confronting divorce, Josephine implored Hortense to try and win Napoleon round, but she declined. 'I cannot; Louis has forbidden it. My mother will only lose a crown and there are women more unhappy than she.'[8] Poor Hortense knew from experience that the Emperor was immoveable. 'Besides, her only hope lies in the influence she exercises over Napoleon by means of her sweet and gentle nature and her tears.' That evening, he sent for Eugène and told him he would divorce his mother. Eugène took the news with dignity. Rather than begging his stepfather to change his mind, he told him that it was his duty to accompany his mother, even if she wished to return to Martinique.

Josephine wept and pleaded with Napoleon to forgive her. Finally, he gave in and took her back into his bed – partly because he was so annoyed that his family had been delighted by the news of their argument. But he was still thinking of divorce. Like a coward, he hoped she might choose to leave. As he told her, 'I feel that I shall never have the strength to oblige you to leave me. I tell you plainly, however, that it is my earnest desire that you shall resign yourself to the interest of my policy and yourself spare me all the difficulties of this painful separation.'[9] Josephine, left to rely on her wits, conjured up a brilliant strategy: she bent her head in submission and said she would leave the minute she received a 'direct order from Napoleon to descend the throne'.[10] He could not bear to ask her and so the question remained unresolved.

Josephine, who had learned the lesson of her fury and jealousy, was now playing the most docile and obedient wife. Claire de Rémusat noted how her 'complete submissiveness and her attitude of unresisting victim' threw Napoleon into nervous uncertainty. His wife was jealous, too old to have children, and she had been faithless. But she had stood by him, married him when few other women would even talk to him and, perhaps most of all, she cared for him rather than his power. After Egypt, he declared he had forgiven her because of his love for Eugène and Hortense. Similarly, in 1804, he confessed he was very fond of his stepchildren (who, he said, never asked him for anything) and thought he owed Josephine kindness for their sake. 'My wife is a good woman who never does anyone any harm,' he sighed. He depended on her and doubted that any foreign princess could make him so content. When his minister Pierre Louis Roederer asked him what he planned to do, Napoleon was muddle-headed. 'It is only fair that she should be an Empress. If I was thrown into prison instead of ascending a throne, she would share my misfortune. She should share my grandeur,' he said. 'She will be crowned if it costs me 200,000 men!'[11] But he would make no firm decision.

While Josephine waited, and restrained herself from losing her temper, plans for the coronation were moving ahead. Napoleon was overseeing every aspect of the ceremony at Notre-Dame. To allow his procession full access to the cathedral, he ordered that some of the surrounding houses be demolished. He instructed Percier and Fontaine, along with Jacques-Louis David, to cover the exterior of Notre-Dame with board to hide the displeasing Gothic style. The interior would look less like a cathedral and more like a themed ball at the Tuileries. Workmen erected huge slabs of painted board, strung candelabra from the ceiling, decorated the floor with tapestries and rugs, and swathed velvet over the walls. David and Isabey were instructed to design the outfits for the men, and they selected the Renaissance style of Francis I of France. They meant to evoke a more heroic age, but the ruffs and doublets were not flattering to stocky Napoleon, or to many of his corpulent court.

The big question was whether Josephine would be crowned. Joseph told Napoleon repeatedly that it would be best for all concerned if Josephine sat in the pews and simply watched the ceremony. At the Tuileries there was a model of Notre-Dame, occupied by several hundred paper dolls to represent all the dignitaries who would attend the coronation. Isabey had created the model, rather than draw the series of events in pictures. The Emperor doll was purple and centre stage. But the Josephine doll had no official seating – she was moved around and sometimes left at the side of the model cathedral.

Napoleon decided that the icon of his reign would be the eagle of the Caesars, the bird of power and victory. Hunting for something suitably memorable to outdo the fleur-de-lys, he chose the bee to evoke Childeric, the fifth-century King of the Franks. When Childeric's tomb had been found by a mason in 1653, it had been filled with precious objects and over 300 gold bees. Napoleon felt that the bee – symbol of resurrection, immortality and royal authority – was another ideal icon for his reign. Fabric and carpet makers were at once set to weaving bees into every piece of material that would take them. He commissioned Fontaine to design an imperial state coach covered with stars, laurel leaves and bees and bearing an eagle and Charlemagne's crown at the top. Bees hovered and buzzed on the curtains, floor coverings, wall hangings, books and furniture of the Tuileries, in the workshops of dressmakers and jewellers, and across the apartments of the ever-loyal Josephine. She chose the symbol of the swan, graceful on the surface but scrabbling hard underwater.

The gossips were whispering that Josephine would not be requiring a particularly handsome gown for the coronation. The celebration was only weeks away and her position was still undecided. Her paper doll was without a home in the model of Notre-Dame. As the weeks progressed and Napoleon flirted with his mistresses, courtiers began to be openly rude to her. Everyone still laughed behind their hands at Josephine's humiliation over Adèle Duchâtel. The Bonapartes cut her dead and refused to stand when she entered the room. They were foolish. One night in November, frustrated with his demanding family and their pleasure in Josephine's fall, Napoleon made up his mind for good. As he watched her droop under their cruelties, he leaped up and in front of everyone went to his wife, seized her in his arms and stroked her like a child. 'The Pope will be here at the end of the month,' he said. 'He will crown us both. Start to prepare for the ceremony.' Josephine threw herself at Napoleon's feet.

Now she had to beg a favour from her dressmaker. Napoleon knew exactly how he wished her to appear and she had less than five weeks to perfect her costume. She would wear an elaborate white dress swathed in gold tulle and embroidered with golden bees, and there was to be a magnificent train of twenty-five yards of red velvet, adorned with yet more bees and bordered in ermine. Josephine's apartments were a flurry of great artists, all conferring with her on the design for the costume for her ladies as well as herself. There was talk of resurrecting the old hoop of Marie Antoinette, but Josephine refused, suggesting instead a tulle ruff around the neck – which corresponded perfectly to Napoleon's desire for a Renaissance look to the coronation (although some worried it evoked the terrifying Catherine de Medici).

Every dressmaker in Paris was working around the clock, gold thread was at a premium and fine embroiderers – who had fallen out of fashion in the Republic – could name their price. 'It seems like a dream or a story from the Arabian nights when I remember the luxury that was displayed at that period,' recalled Madame de Rémusat.[12] The population of the city seemed to double, people were repainting their houses, dancers at the Opéra were learning new ballets and delivery boys ran all over the city with food and drink for receptions. Notre-Dame was a hive of activity, so covered in embroidered hangings that one visitor thought God Himself would get lost there. Carts of furniture, cloth, jewels and fine glass and china arrived daily. The 'gaiety, anticipation and celebration in Paris then was unimaginable', Josephine noted.[13] The moneylenders did the best business of all. Each lady-in-waiting was given 10,000 francs to compensate for her expenditure and gowns, but they all spent much more, even four times that amount – a huge sum when the average wage was around 700 francs a year.

Not everyone was swept away with delight. The Bonaparte family began immediately on the counter-attack. The last queen of France to be crowned was Marie de Medici in 1610 – and her husband had been assassinated the next day. Did Napoleon want the same to happen? He tried to brush off their insinuations. Caroline, Elisa and Pauline were firmly told that they would be expected to carry Josephine's marvellous train of ermine and velvet, along with Hortense and Julie, wife of Joseph. The sisters practically fainted and Joseph roared that his wife, as a virtuous woman, could not carry Josephine's train. He complained that even when Marie de Medici had been crowned, a distant relative had carried her train, 'not the King's own sister'. Caroline led a hysterical strike of tears, pleadings and attempts at haranguing Napoleon into changing his mind. Finally, after suffering six days of constant complaints, he gave in and told his sisters that they would merely have to support the mantle during the ceremony. Each one would have a chamberlain to carry her own train. 'Only my family can exert such influence over me,' sighed Napoleon, the terrifying ruler of the French Empire brought low by his cross sisters – 'I've lost sleep over this.'[14] But although the sisters had escaped the public humiliation of playing Josephine's brides-maids, they had lost the bigger battle. The hated 'la Beauharnais', the reviled '*la vieille*' was to be crowned Empress in the eyes of the world.

Josephine's docile and gentle behaviour had, as Hortense predicted, won Napoleon to her side. But she was not satisfied. She wished for the religious blessing Napoleon had denied her.

After the wearisome journey from Rome, Pope Pius VII, elderly and infirm, arrived and was greeted by cheering Parisians. After welcome celebrations at Fontainebleau, Pius and his attendants took up residence in fifty-six rooms of the Tuileries and, having expected a nation of atheists, was quite stunned by the religious fervour. Everyone from Revolutionary generals to Jacobins flocked to his apartments, begging him to bless their belongings. As there were no rosaries on sale in France, Pius was confronted with watches, pens, scissors, purses and inkpots – and had to bless them all. He was followed wherever he went, and every morning huge crowds would appear under his balcony at the Tuileries, calling loudly for him to bless them.

It was only half consolation for some of the shocking demands Napoleon had made. The new Emperor had informed the Pope that the service would be radically changed and that he would have to walk into the cathedral rather than be carried on a litter – an unfair demand for vainglorious Napoleon to make of the elderly and infirm Pope.

On 1 December, the day before the coronation, Josephine made her move. She had left it to the last minute to minimise any possible discus-sion. She begged for a private audience with the Pope, and then, weeping, told him that her marriage had only been a civil affair. Poor Pius was shocked to discover that he had been on the brink of anointing the Emperor's concubine with holy oil. The idea that the imperial couple were living in sin was almost unbelievable, and he dug in his heels. Josephine had timed her attack superbly. Pius was annoyed at the constant humiliations he had received from Napoleon and, finally, he lost his temper. He had accepted having to walk into the cathedral,

he had given in to the curtailed ceremony, but he would not crown a
sinful pair of cohabitees as Emperor and Empress. If Napoleon and
Josephine were not married in a properly religious ceremony, he would
not preside over the coronation.

Napoleon had to relent. He could not postpone the coronation and
Pius was not to be moved. Cardinal Fesch was sent to arrange an
immediate marriage service. That night, snatching time from the preparations, at a makeshift altar hastily erected in Napoleon's study, the
Emperor and Empress were married by Fesch in a quick ceremony at
midnight. Their parish priest was not present, as was required, and the
attendance of witnesses was debatable – Josephine claimed two aides-
de-camp were present but Napoleon later denied they had been there.[15]
It was thus hardly legal – which was perhaps why Napoleon went
through with it without resentment. Josephine asked Fesch to give her
a written certification of the marriage. She thought it her sure-fire
protection against divorce.

16

'The King of Diamonds'

he second day of December 1804 was the coldest of the year. Freezing snow was followed by battering rain, but still the people took up their positions on the streets towards Notre-Dame. At the Tuileries, every moment had been dedicated to the forthcoming celebrations. Hairdressers had been at such a premium that many ladies had been coiffed the previous evening and forced to sleep upright to preserve their hairstyle. Some courtiers had not had time to go to bed. Josephine seized a few hours' rest, only to be woken before six so that Isabey could paint her face with the rouge Napoleon so loved. The hairdresser teased her hair into ringlets around a pearl and diamond diadem. Her ladies dressed her in the white satin gown, embroidered in gold, with a low neckline and the ruff as a collar. A diamond belt circled her waist.

Then Josephine had to wait. Napoleon's elaborate dress took over an hour longer than planned. He wore so many jewels that he looked like a walking mirror, and he had plucked the huge 'Regent' diamond from his sword and attached it to his hat. He was delighted by his appearance but, as expected, the Renaissance dress of a short coat over puffed knickerbockers was hardly flattering to his apple-shaped form. 'Perhaps successful on the drawing board,' commented one woman, 'it was unbecoming on the Emperor, who is short, fat and awkward.' More like an overdressed child than an awe-inspiring ruler, she thought he looked 'like the King of Diamonds'.

In high spirits, the King of Diamonds bounded down the stairs and, almost two hours late, left the Tuileries in the imperial state coach at 10am. Josephine was by his side, Joseph and Louis facing them, both similarly awkward in ruffs and stiff outfits that bore an unfortunate resemblance to fancy dress. Eight bay horses drove a Fontaine-designed riot of gold, bees and diamonds, with eight huge glass windows through which Napoleon and Josephine could clearly be seen. The spectators were more inquisitive than thrilled. 'I noticed there was no real enthusiasm anywhere,' Napoleon noted, although at least, he admitted, there was no active dissent. The state coaches rumbled through the narrow streets, with the ministers, the grand chamberlain, the Bonaparte princesses, the diplomatic corps all pretending dignity for the crowds. The people warmed their hands with hot pies and admired the horses.

As the imperial couple arrived at Notre-Dame the sun came through the clouds, and amid the roar of cannons Napoleon and Josephine stepped from their coach. Josephine had been fortunate that her husband had not forced her to dress in hoops and farthingales. Her clinging gown and gold decoration were an instant hit. Still, all the gold in the world could not hide her origins – 'What beauty!' recalled one. 'But for me, she would always be Barras's mistress.' Barras, in exile, had created them both, but neither Napoleon nor Josephine had a thought for him.

Inside the cathedral, the spectators had been waiting since the early morning, eating surreptitious sausages to keep warm. The elderly Pope had sat on his freezing throne for hours, offering prayer and begging God for a little mercy for what he was about to do. Napoleon had informed him that he and Josephine would not take the coronation communion. Poor Pius, once again, was humiliated by the irreligious nature of the man he had come to crown.

On arrival at Notre-Dame, the pair moved to a robing room to dress in the imperial robes. Napoleon attired himself as a Roman Emperor with a long satin gown and a mantle of purple, embroidered with bees and attached at the shoulder and the waist. He was crowned with a laurel wreath and carried a sceptre. Josephine donned a tiara of over 1000 diamonds set in platinum. After an hour in the robing room, the procession began with the heralds-at-arms, pages, grand master of ceremonies and Josephine's own equerries and chamberlains. General Murat bore her crown on a cushion and another carried her ring. The Empress herself was first to emerge, walking slowly forward under a canopy. Her huge mantle was carried by the five Bonaparte princesses. Despite the triumph of having their own trains carried, they were still resentful of following behind '*la vieille*' and not afraid to show it. They barely lifted the mantle and let it drag on the ground so that Josephine struggled to walk.

The Emperor appeared, his crown, sword, necklace and globe carried by his marshals. Impatient as ever, he was eager to get to the altar and used his sceptre to prod Cardinal Fesch to force him to hurry up. Although the procession had been excessively magnificent, the service itself was short and arranged so that only those closest could see. French kings had traditionally lain full length, face down in front of the altar, but Napoleon knew that doing so would only invite ridicule. He was wise: Josephine prostrate on the floor would have inspired dozens of cruel cartoons. Instead, after the Pope gave High Mass, Napoleon and Josephine would kneel at the altar for the Pope's triple unction of holy water on their heads and hands.

The Pope blessed the two crowns and placed them on the altar. Then, quick as a flash, Napoleon seized the biggest crown and popped it onto his head. It was an act of shocking affront and typical of the Emperor. The great showman had been planning it, borrowing from the Tsar of Russia, who had crowned himself, but the onlookers thought it all spontaneous. Sidelining the Pope altogether, he then took Josephine's crown and held it out, to signal her to come towards him. As Claire de Rémusat put it, she knelt with 'such simple elegance that all eyes were delighted with the picture she presented'.[1] He placed her crown first on his own head, and then on hers, over the diadem she already wore. Josephine burst into tears.

He was almost playful, as Josephine's lady recounted, 'He put it on, then took it off, and finally put it on again as if to promise her that she should wear it gracefully and lightly.'[2] Her carriage and bearing were so majestic that some of those watching became a little carried away. 'I have had the honour of being presented to many real princesses,' gushed Laure Junot, 'but I never saw one who, to my eyes, presented so perfect a personification of elegance and majesty.'[3]

The elegance and majesty came with a struggle. At the crucial moment, the Bonaparte sisters had their revenge. When Josephine walked up for her blessing, the sisters, all at once, loosened the mantle, threatening to let go. Josephine staggered backwards. Napoleon spotted it and whipped round to give his sisters a sharp reprimand. Ashamed, they huddled to resume their positions and Josephine carried on. After blessing the new rulers and completing Mass at the altar, the Pope retired to the sacristy – preferring not to witness Napoleon's civil oath to the Republic. To the presiding officers of the legislative bodies, and in resounding tones, Napoleon declared that he would 'maintain the integrity and territory of the Republic, to protect political, civil and religious liberties, and the irrevocability of national property'. Even during the ceremony, he was making plans that would contravene nearly every oath.

At 3pm, the newly crowned Emperor and Empress departed Notre-Dame, taking a longer route back so that even more Parisians could witness their grandeur. Their carriage was lit by five hundred pages carrying torches to allow everybody a proper view in the descending winter gloom. Every building was illuminated, and giant 'N's made from laurel leaves hung from the balconies. At the Place de la Concorde, a huge star stood at the spot where Louis XVI had been executed. 'Never have I seen on any face an expression of joy, of contentment, of good fortune, to compare with that which animated the figure of the Empress,' recalled Mademoiselle Avrillon. Royalists scoffed at Napoleon's sisters, 'who had left their laundry behind and now appeared in all their finery and diamonds to carry the train of Barras's former mistress'. Monarchists and Revolutionaries alike were scandalised by the elevations of, as Madame de Staël said, 'the bourgeois and bourgeoises of Ajaccio' (Napoleon's home town).[4] There was no returning.

Rather than a ceremonial dinner, the Emperor decreed that he would dine privately with his Empress. The Bonaparte family fumed, but could do nothing. Napoleon whisked Josephine into the private salon where he asked her to wear her crown for the meal, 'because no one could wear a crown with more grace'.[5] Josephine had won. Replete with success, she watched, with bitter irony, the courtiers who had snubbed her scrambling to please her. Confident in her position, she was now much more kindly disposed to the Bonaparte sisters and to the other members of her husband's entourage she distrusted. She bore their insults with patience, which only added to Napoleon's esteem for her.

His improper act of crowning himself became gossip across Europe, discussed in horror by scandalised royalists and all those he had exiled. The man's ambition knew no bounds. It also proved a logistical headache for Jacques-Louis David, the former Revolutionary who had been declared the court painter. He had been commissioned to produce the official portrait of the coronation. For months, David wrestled as he tried to show Napoleon crowning himself without making the picture appear ridiculous. After watching his master in torment, an apprentice suggested he paint Napoleon crowning Josephine – and the problem was solved. Napoleon approved the idea. Four years later, he and Josephine visited David's studio and the Emperor spent over an hour scrutinising every aspect of the picture. Much had been changed: Josephine and Napoleon were made to look younger and more statuesque, Madame Mère, who had left Paris in a temper, was painted into the congregation and the Bonaparte sisters, perhaps as a sop from Napoleon, were shown standing to the side, rather than bearing the mantle. Through David's alchemy, what had been a shocking insult to the Pope and usurpation of his role became refigured as an act of love and devotion from Emperor to Empress. Later, Napoleon railed that Josephine had indulged in 'little intrigues' in order to put herself in the centre of the painting. But at the time of viewing, he was most gratified. He told David that he was grateful to him 'for recording for posterity the proof of the affection I wished to give to the woman who shared with me the burden of office'.[6] Not even Napoleon was quite vain enough to wish the official portrait showed him crowning himself.

Once he had confirmed himself as Emperor, his hunger for absolute power increased daily. The Tribunate, the Senate and the Legislative Body remained, but they were thin pretences that existed to persuade the French that they were still living in a Republic. The Emperor coined a catechism for schoolchildren. When they were asked, 'What should one think of those who fail in their duties to our Emperor?' they should reply, 'According to the Apostle St Paul, they would be resisting the order established by God Himself and would deserve eternal damnation.' Napoleon liked religion when it suited him. At the beginning of January, he finally abolished the last remnant of the Republic: the Revolutionary calendar.

The new Emperor decreed everything from state policy to women's fashion. He desired his new court at the Tuileries to outshine every one across Europe for luxury and magnificence, and even outdo those of the Bourbon kings. For him, the court was useful to demonstrate his belief that he was the most terrifying ruler in history. Essentially, his guiding aesthetic was combining the style of ancient Rome with the brilliance and excess of Louis XIV, the Sun King, and Louis XVI. 'What I want above all is grandeur,' he said, 'what is grand above all is beautiful.' Napoleon's favourite architectural team of Percier and Fontaine were entrusted with transforming the Tuileries. He found the palace too 'bare and simple' (even though it had been redecorated since he arrived), and wished to erase all memories of the committees of the dull old Directory. Percier and Fontaine were instructed to make a new banqueting room, gallery and a great central staircase, hang the walls with thick silk brocades from Lyons, and cover the place in decorated panels. Gold bees and the imperial eagle flew across curtains and decorated mahogany furniture − some much the worse thanks to Napoleon's habit of hacking them with a penknife. He made plans for a theatre and a chapel. Visitor's eyes were dazzled by gilt, jewels and silver everywhere they looked. The stables contained 1200 handsome horses as well as dozens of carriages, all painted green. The annual budget for decorating and redecorating the imperial rooms and maintaining the palaces soared to six million francs. Napoleon had no time for theories that his court should reflect the aesthetic culture of Rome, which was perceived to be restrained. The days of the Revolutionary symbols on the front of the Tuileries, the austere interiors and the Committee of Public Safety were long gone. The glitter and the glamour worked to 'throw dust in people's eyes'.[7]

Napoleon ordered detailed rules of etiquette and precedence to be imposed on his courtiers, most of whom were in their twenties and thirties and too young to remember much of the *Ancien Régime*. The regulations of Louis XIV and his successors were pulled down from the library shelves. Madame Campan was questioned in minute detail, and anyone else who had been at Versailles was asked to rack their brains over life at the old court. A team headed by the Comte de Ségur produced a detailed volume, *Etiquette du Palais Impérial*, which gave exact rules on everything from where people should stand to how they should seat themselves at dinner. Napoleon established a huge household for himself, bigger than that of Louis XVI, with a grand almoner, a grand marshal, a grand equerry, a grand huntsman and a grand master of ceremonies. Josephine had an equally unwieldy staff of over a hundred, including twenty ladies-in-waiting, four more than Marie Antoinette.

She also had seventeen ladies of the palace, including ladies of the wardrobe and ladies of the bedchamber. All were overseen by her *dame d'honneur*, Duchesse Alexandre de La Rochefoucauld, a relative of Josephine's first husband. A Saint-Domingue heiress and an avowed *Ancien Régime* royalist in her late thirties, she was fond of making it clear that she was a merely deigning to be at the court – and she even cowed the Emperor into silence at times. Highly efficient, she kept Josephine's household running perfectly, overseeing the day-to-day needs, the visits, the work of the servants, and deciding on presentations and invitations.

The competition to serve Josephine was intense, particularly as Napoleon often recruited his mistresses from her household. She too had an almoner, chamberlain, equerry, another equerry overseeing the stables, lords-in-waiting, ushers, footmen and pages. There was really little point to such a huge household and most of the ladies and gentlemen had very little to do but sit about, complain and adjust their costume. It was one great self-serving machine: Josephine dressed three times a day to give them an occupation and whole occasions were held to give them something to anticipate. The purpose was the aspect of majesty and a vast, pleasing looking glass for Napoleon.

The Emperor was strictly formal. All the men of Josephine's household were to remain in her outer apartments, and if one needed to see her to receive orders, he should scratch at the door of the bedroom, where one of her ladies 'must always be in attendance, and seek permission to be introduced into her presence'. With the etiquette of 'scratching', the influence of Versailles was complete – courtiers there had been firmly instructed to scratch rather than knock at doors. There was no more Republican equality; instead, those at Napoleon's court behaved with the subservience of a courtier to a king. 'The Emperor is too grand for anybody to tell him the truth,' Josephine wrote to Eugène, 'everybody who surrounds him flatters him all day long'.[8] As Madame de Rémusat recalled, 'The fever of vanity seemed every day to lay stronger claim on of us.'[9]

Napoleon's obsessive interest in constructing a new world to surround him now extended to female fashion. Despite his own passion for seeing Josephine in diaphanous dresses and gauzy wraps, he demanded that ladies wore embossed gowns of lamé, brocade and satin, with mandatory velvet trains, all heavily embroidered in gold. As the men gleamed with medals, so the women must sparkle with jewels, and never wear the same gown twice. Laure Junot was firmly reminded of her duty at one court event. 'Madame, you have worn that dress several times. It is becoming, but we have seen it before.'[10]

Napoleon claimed he installed strictures on fashion to assist the French manufacturers. The result was very like the stiff grandeur of the court of Marie Antoinette, reproducing the strict repression and the cumbersome apparel that women had been so eager to throw off after the Revolution. The Empress sometimes rebelled against Napoleon by wearing trains of tulle or gauzy ensembles, but she was entirely obedient to his strictures about jewels and always wearing new outfits. She was clever at making a dress look different with shawls and accessories but, essentially, all her gowns were made to be worn once only. An inventory in 1809 found 49 grand court dresses, 676 gowns, 60 cashmere shawls and nearly 500 other shawls, 413 pairs of gloves and more than 200 pairs of silk stockings.

Josephine's coronation dress was the pattern for all her court gowns. She wore Empire-line waists with high embroidered collars and trains attached to the back. Her dressmaker, Leroy, was the mastermind and he quickly became the most in-demand designer in Paris. *Le Journal des Dames et des Modes*, the fashion bible of the day, was filled with pictures of Josephine, the most stylish woman in the country. Even passionately patriotic British women nursed secret desires for a French gown *à la* Empress.

Back in Britain, Lord Nelson and his mistress, Emma Hamilton, had set up home in Merton Place, near Wimbledon. They turned a rather ramshackle house into a tribute to his victories, with large 'N's on the walls, pieces of his ships over the staircase and fittings from crockery to crocus planters decorated with his name and image. What Nelson was doing on the domestic level, Napoleon wished to write large over his nation. There were 'N's and 'J's, eagles and swans everywhere. He placed the lion stolen from the column in the Piazza San Marco, Venice, in the middle of Paris and arranged the bronze horses in the Tuileries Gardens.

Napoleon set Percier and Fontaine feverishly making monuments to his great victories to remind everyone of his brilliance. He demanded a sixty-foot-high elephant inscribed with his victories be placed over the Champs-Élysées, facing towards the Tuileries (the plans for the elephant would eventually be replaced with those for the Arc de Triomphe). He was equally delighted with the idea of a column made from melted-down Austrian cannon in the Place Vendôme to commemorate the Grand Army. Percier and Fontaine scribbled out plans for towers, giant statues and more columns, each one unashamedly masculine in style, all situated to prove that the Emperor could never be dislodged.

Now Napoleon was Emperor, he was ever more determined to have a son. He asked Josephine to feign a pregnancy and then pretend she had given birth – he would supply a child, most probably from a mistress who was pregnant at the time. She agreed, but the chief physician refused to be party to such a deception. Certainly, it would have been nigh impossible considering the close quarters at which everybody observed Josephine and the number of spies on her staff. When this plan failed, her position was much weakened. When Napoleon and Josephine argued, usually after she had asked him jealous questions, he would counter by claiming he was not truly married to her. She would cry that she had the certificate of marriage. When Fesch was consulted, he agreed and said that the marriage was legal and validly solemnised. He advised Josephine to keep the certificate close.

As Emperor, Napoleon had become more brutal and aggressive than he had ever been. He was curt with his generals and courtiers and often attacked his servants. He once seized Berthier and banged his head against a stone wall, and kicked a minister in the genitals for presenting unappealing statistics. In the morning, during the ritual of dressing, he would sometimes throw nail scissors, brushes or boxes at the servants if he felt they prodded him too hard or dressed him in something he did not like. He slapped staff, pinched court ladies while he insulted them and pulled their hair, and loved to offend anyone he could in public. Despite his incredible power, he still derived a thrill from making his inferiors tremble with fear. He flew into tantrums and even kicked men in the stomach. As tyrannical as a medieval king, he screamed and shouted, complained and demanded, and everyone had to obey. Only Josephine could calm him with her soft hands and gentle words.

In the morning, Napoleon often woke up in pain, suffering from stomach spasms or a headache. As his servants tried to rub him down with eau de cologne and dress him, he tore off his clothes if they annoyed him, and slapped his valet for trying to put his coat on him. All the while, he was looking at police reports and the newspapers, bills and letters. When he was dressed, he doused himself with more eau de cologne – he got through sixty bottles a month – was given his handkerchief, snuffbox and tortoiseshell case of finely-cut liquorice. At nine, he would conduct a reception and private audiences with his officials, take breakfast at eleven, and then go to his study, pacing up and down as he dictated letters and orders to his secretary, Claude de Méneval, who had to create a new, faster form of shorthand to keep up. He would finish off by dictating a few articles for the newspapers and then stomp off to find Josephine. After lunch, he returned to giving audiences, meeting the Council of State or dictating further orders. After dinner, he might spend a short while in the Yellow Salon with Josephine and his generals and their wives, playing chess or billiards before retiring to his desk once more and working into the night.

When he undressed, he would oftentimes throw his clothes on the floor and hit the valet to purge his frustration. Unsurprisingly, he was a poor sleeper and would sometimes rise from his bed, plunge into a hot bath and call Méneval to take down yet more orders and commands for hours until he felt tired. When he himself wrote, he scribbled so fast and shook his pen so impatiently that the paper was covered in big blots of ink.

Napoleon had always bolted his food, but as Emperor he could scarcely bear to waste a moment eating. If he demanded a meal, he expected it and Josephine to be immediately in front of him. Fond of roast chicken and potatoes fried with onion, he would eat at the speed of light, often not bothering with a knife and fork. He preferred Josephine not to eat in his presence – which was fortunate, because she barely had the chance to do so. Intent that everything around him was hot with energy, he had a fire lit all the time and his courtiers and attendants often fainted from the heat. His skin was almost yellow, his digestion was terrible, he suffered from fits, and he coughed up blood. Sometimes he was so ill after eating that his courtiers found him lying down and groaning, with his head in Josephine's lap. His mind spun, even when he was trying to sleep, and he found that the only way to rest was by reciting army lists over and over.

Napoleon was impatient, brimming with nervous energy, and only ceaseless activity slaked his restless mind. Even when he maintained a

Josephine kneels to be crowned by Napoleon. David showed
Napoleon crowning Josephine – a neat solution, as a painting
of Napoleon crowning himself would have been ridiculed.

The Consecration of the Emperor Napoleon I and the Crowning of the Empress Josephine in the Cathedral of Notre-Dame de Paris on 2 December 1804 by Jacques-Louis David, 1807.

(*Left*) Napoleon's sisters at the Coronation.

(*Below*) Napoleon's mother at the Coronation.

(*Left*) One of Josephine's court gowns, 1805. The dress is elaborately embroidered with real silver thread.

(*Below*) Josephine's tiara.

Queen Hortense by Fleury-François Richard, 1815. Artistic, sensitive and beautiful, Hortense was doomed to misery when her mother compelled her to marry Louis Bonaparte.

Queen Hortense with her son, Napoleon Charles by François Pascal Simon, Baron Gérard, 1806. The little boy died a year later from croup. He was just four years old – and his death plunged Hortense into despair.

Imperial Botany – or a Peep at Josephine's Collection of English Exoticks, Captain Williams (attributed to George Cruikshank), 1814. Wellington (on right) and Prince Regent (as Royal Sun-Flower) grow strong while Napoleon (Crown Imperial) is a droopy weed.

(*Above*) The divorce settlement of
Napoleon and Josephine.

(*Right*) *Empress Marie-Louise with the King of Rome*
by François Pascal Simon, Baron Gérard, 1813.
Napoleon's longed-for son was fat and healthy –
the Emperor thought him destined to rule the world.

bove) The house at Navarre where Josephine lived when Napoleon married Marie-Louise.

cool mien in public, he was constantly fidgeting under his robes, taking snuff or pushing mint pastilles into his mouth. His armchair had to be changed every three months because he stabbed it to bits with his penknife. Beneath the imperial surface, he was still the little boy who had pulled chairs apart in school.[11] Josephine provided the calm and stillness that he could not derive from himself. When he sat for his portrait to commemorate the Battle of Arcola, he had fidgeted so much that Josephine had come to the studio and placed him on her lap in order to keep him still. Only she was allowed to pour his coffee after dinner and add sugar to it with a special gilt spoon. She was his refuge and he relied on her to be there when he needed her. As she later wrote to Caroline, 'The pride of women consists in submission and we should have no other power than such as a mild and gentle character imparts to us.'[12]

Napoleon was a genius at creating a cult of Empire, and for this the visual arts were vital. Everything was grist to his mill: the post-Revolutionary classical revival celebrating austerity and civic virtue became his mark of ingenuity. He preferred artists and craftsmen who had been beloved by the Bourbons, such as Isabey and the Jacob brothers. Jacques-Louis David, the man who had signed Alexandre's death warrant and would have signed Josephine's too – and refused to draw Louis XVI as he would not allow his pencil to reproduce the features of a tyrant – became Bonaparte's great ally and eulogised him again and again in paint. He portrayed him crossing the St Bernard Pass, turning his hero into Hannibal on a rearing horse, rather than a dreary mule as had been the case. His *Napoleon in His Study* had shown the First Consul hard at work in the early hours of the morning, and he painted the celebrated coronation portrait. But Napoleon never quite trusted David and favoured the work of his pupils, chiefly François Gérard, Antoine Gros and Jean-Auguste Ingres. Their work was unashamedly excessive and flattering, with Gros's *Napoleon at the Battle of Eylau* showing him tending to the dying, while Ingres's almost ridiculous *Napoleon I on his Imperial Throne* portrayed the plump little Emperor as a god – part Jupiter, part Augustus and part Charlemagne.

Napoleon was particularly fond of Pierre-Paul Prud'hon, who created romantic, sensual portraits of his wife. The Empire was a time for painters to become famous, but only if they agreed to lavish praise on the imperial couple. Gold and money poured into their workshops as they did the bidding of the Emperor.

Josephine took care of the matters of power that Napoleon could not bear. She heard petitions, patronised artists, planned dinners, fetes and celebrations and presided over receptions and tributes. Napoleon dreaded the evening dinners and balls. 'I am not made for pleasure,' he rued.[13]

Josephine's days rarely varied. In the morning, she and Napoleon often awoke together. His valet, Constant, would go to her apartments between 7 and 8am and sometimes find the pair still asleep. 'When the Emperor asked me for tea or for an infusion of orange flowers and started to get up, the Empress would say to him smilingly, "Must you get up already? Stay a little longer." His Majesty would answer, "You mean you are not asleep?" and he would roll her up in her blanket, giving her little taps on her cheek and on her shoulders, laughing and kissing her.'[14] Then her four maids would come in and busy themselves with the task of making her look like an Empress.

While Napoleon dictated his plans for conquest, Josephine was bathed and then her face was plastered with the heavy make-up Napoleon liked. He preferred an image that was more embellished than that of Versailles and, to the British, looked like the maquillage of courtesans. Her assistants smeared rouge in great tear shapes over her fine cheeks. She then put on her lace dressing gown as her hair was arranged by the hairdresser. As he created curls and tamed recalcitrant strands, Josephine's ladies brought in piles of gowns, shawls and hats for her to pick her attire for the morning – despite Napoleon's complaints – muslin and cambric in the summer and velvet and wool for the winter. Marie Antoinette had chosen her clothing similarly, except she had used a book of swatches and samples to keep track of her unwieldy wardrobe. Josephine changed every item of her dress three times a day and never wore the same pair of stockings twice. The whole operation of choosing outfits, picking them up from the baskets and trying them against her was a lengthy one. Eight dressers attended Josephine, while the Mistress of the Robes and the Lady of Honour regarded from afar.

The Empress was given an annual allowance of 600,000 francs to maintain her household and person, with a further 120,000 for charity. It was simply not enough. After she had dressed, merchants and shop-keepers would crowd into her apartments, along with artists, musicians and entertainers. She snapped up diamonds, shawls, silks, jewellery and trinkets, never asking the price and barely able to remember what she had bought. She commissioned portraits and bought books and ornaments and thousands of francs worth of gifts. In every fashionable shop in Paris, someone was making something for the Empress. The smallest gathering was an opportunity to order a new gown and she wore lace said to be worth 100,000 francs (one sixth of her yearly allowance). Even though she was hardly ever there, she spent thousands on furniture and plants for Malmaison. Napoleon fumed about her 'mad extravagance' but she would not listen. 'Every day I discover new instances of it, and it distresses me. When I speak to her – on the subject I am vexed; I get angry – she weeps. I forgive her, I pay her bills – she makes fair promises; but the same thing occurs over and over again.'[15]

Like any addict, the Empress always needed the new and forgot the old. She would sometimes pay 12,000 francs for a shawl and then use it as a cushion or a blanket for her dog. She would wear a superbly expensive gown for a day and then give it to her ladies or maids, who promptly sold it on. Mademoiselle Avrillon recalled that at Mainz, she and the other ladies had offered Josephine's old gowns as payment for the exquisite goods of the local tradesmen, who swiftly sold them to the local dignitaries. 'I remember a ball there at which the Empress might have seen all the ladies of a quadrille party dressed in her cast-off clothes – I even saw German Princesses wearing them.'[16] Everyone around Josephine was making a profit out of her.

After the shopkeepers had departed, she gave audiences and applied herself to her correspondence. She would also go through petitions and receive charitable requests. She wrote incessant letters requesting help for all types of supplicants. 'People get them from me by pestering me,' she explained to the Minister of War when he protested at the sheer number of notes of recommendation from her. At a quarter to ten she entered her Yellow Salon in order to take her morning meal with her ladies. Hers would be a much more leisurely affair than her husband's, with soup, entrées and roasts arranged across the table, followed by sweets. There was no formal dining room in the Palace (it was generally seen as a British custom), so a white cloth would be laid out on whatever table was indicated.

In the afternoon she received visitors, many of them émigrés demanding favours, and then would perhaps take a short walk. Later, as she did not read and had little interest in needlework, she often strummed her harp, apparently always the same tune. The waiting was interminably dull and Josephine sometimes found it difficult to bear. She once railed that she was little more than a 'bejewelled slave'.

By the late afternoon, she was back in her apartments, dressing for the evening ahead in her gold embroidered gown. Then she would wait to be called to dinner, which was supposed to be at six but would sometimes be delayed for three hours while Napoleon worked. On most evenings they dined together, for the quick twenty minutes it took him to wolf down his food and dash back to work. On Sundays, the dreaded Bonapartes came to dine. Official banquets and social celebrations were so replete with complicated dishes that they might take up most of the day. The custom of serving all the dishes together at the table was still in fashion, rather than the *à la Russe* fashion of eating courses in sequence. The tables of the Tuileries groaned under silver candelabra, foot-high tureens of soup and dishes of meat, fish and fowl served on Sèvres porcelain decorated with pictures of Napoleon's victories.

After dinner, the Empress would retire to her salon and spend the evening with her courtiers, talking or playing cards or billiards. She was not particularly fond of chess but she sportingly played whist and lotto with her visitors, ministers, ambassadors and ladies. Napoleon forbade playing for stakes, but when he was away she and her circle staked money, sometimes large amounts. Josephine also loved billiards. It was the only game in which the Emperor allowed her to beat him.

At ten, Napoleon might call her to read to him or join him in conversation – he was particularly partial to telling ghost stories. Her salon was connected to his room via a hidden staircase and he would often come to the door and tap on it as a signal that he needed her. Her ladies then had to wait for her in the salon until she returned. Invariably, by the time she arrived, they had fallen asleep, bent over the tables for support since they were not supposed to sit down. If she was to be alone for the night, she went to bed at around midnight – allowed, just for a few hours, to be free of rouge, with her hair undressed and her shoulders not weighed down by a heavy golden gown.

On days when Napoleon did not require her, Josephine saw her merchants and talked to her ladies. As one of her friends remarked, she could 'idle away her days doing nothing and yet never be bored with it'.[17] Her 'mania for having her portrait painted' meant that she was often sitting for artists or planning new compositions. She would give pictures of herself to anybody and everybody – friends, relations, courtiers and even her tradesmen. In her hundreds of commissioned portraits, she was ever young, beautiful, elegant and graceful, her mouth closed to shield her blackened teeth. Those who wished to please her adorned their houses with her delicate face. Such was the passion for her among the public that pictures were quickly transferred onto china, fans and cards, so even the poorest labourer could have the Empress over his fire.

Her apartments consisted of an antechamber, a first salon, a second salon and her own salon. In her private rooms, she had a bedroom, dressing room, boudoir and bathroom. In every one of the Emperor's palaces, the layout was the same, and the rooms were decorated in a similarly imperial manner, with stolid Jacob furniture, tapestries, gilding and drapes. As an Empress, she lived her whole day in public. Ladies and servants bustled around her rooms and everyone stared at her when she ventured out.

Josephine was naturally informal, and enjoyed conversation and befriending people when she travelled. This, Napoleon told her sharply, would have to stop. She should always be surrounded by 'splendour', escorted by infantry and cavalry and met by the tolling of bells rung by the town mayor or prefect. When she returned to Paris, she would be greeted by cannon and the courtiers would line up to pay homage. It was time she started behaving like an Empress. She missed Malmaison, where the plants grew unseen by her and her orang-utan wandered the grounds alone. Even while Napoleon was away, he wished her to keep up the imperial appearance, and that meant remaining in his grand palaces full of mahogany eagles and obeisant courtiers, rather than walking the grounds of Malmaison.

For most of the time, Josephine could not go anywhere at all. Her life was minutely constrained, every detail reported back to Napoleon. She sat, ornate and alluring, until he had finished his work in the evening and might come to dally away ten minutes with her. He relied on her emotionally but he also saw her as his essential helpmate. They divided the labour of imperial success. He stood for aggression, strategy, military triumph and tyranny, while she assumed all the roles he reviled: patron of art and beauty, manners and sympathy. Her kind heart and gentle words smoothed over his anger and fooled people into thinking that Napoleon had a more humane side. 'Nature,' he told his wife, 'has given me a strong and resolute character; she has made you of lace and gauze.'[18] Around Napoleon, the air fizzed and crackled; he was electric, intense and terrifying. Josephine created a bewitching spell of ease and pleasure. Most of his citizens and courtiers believed in the overall impression of humanity and harmony.

Josephine showed few signs of the will for independence she had once had. Her energy was invested in making herself Napoleon's elegant, perfect wife, ideally submissive, ready to respond to his every need. 'Josephine was invariably, unfailingly sweet with the Emperor,' recalled Mademoiselle Avrillon, 'adapting herself to his every mood, every whim with a complaisance such as I have never seen in anyone else in the world. By studying the slightest change in his expression or tone she offered him the only things he now required of her.'[19] She might be the married and consecrated Empress, but Napoleon, as she knew, did as he liked, and he would divorce her if he felt it necessary – especially for the chance of having a son. Few believed that she was still capable of having a child. She was forty-one and, as the doctors had told Napoleon, her menses had ceased.

And yet, he was fonder of her than he had been since Egypt. She was still the only person allowed to address him as 'tu'. He was eminently satisfied with his act of crowning her, and thus stealing authority from both the Republic and the Pope, and she was his evidence that he had practically usurped the role of God. Laure Junot recalled how she saw the Empress enter a room at Saint-Cloud, wearing clinging white muslin secured by medallions at the shoulder. Even though Napoleon professed to detest muslin, he went to her, kissed her on the shoulder and the forehead and took her to a mirror, so he could inspect her from all sides. 'Now, Josephine, I think I must be jealous, you must have some conquest in mind. Why are you so beautiful today?' She replied, 'I know that you love to see me in white and so I put on a white gown, that's all.' 'Very well then, if it was to please me, then you have indeed succeeded.'[20] He promptly kissed her again.

Napoleon remained entirely obsessed by her jewels and dress. He would regularly interfere in what she wore, pulling out her low-cut gowns from her wardrobe and tearing her shawl, even throwing it into the fire if he thought it ugly. He would erupt into her room and demand that she change her gown or jewellery, forcing her to try on outfit after outfit until he was content. Josephine was one of the few who could calm him when he was seized by temper. 'I care only for the people who are useful to me – and only so long as they are useful,' he said on St Helena.[21] He loved Josephine – but she was also beneficial to him.

The great Emperor was still jealous of Hippolyte Charles, and would never hear his name mentioned. On one occasion, he was walking with General Duroc and his face paled as he gripped Duroc's arm. Duroc thought he was about to faint and was going to hurry for help, but the Emperor silenced him furiously. In a passing carriage, Napoleon had seen Hippolyte Charles – the first time he had laid eyes on the dandy since Italy.

Napoleon guarded and worshipped his wife, but as Emperor he demanded a steady stream of beautiful young women trotting up the stairs to the chamber next to his. He refused to allow his wife or her spies inside. Constant would answer the door, saying firmly, 'I have orders to let no one in, not even her Majesty the Empress.' Actresses, courtiers, ladies-in-waiting, dancers and ladies of fashion, few refused Napoleon's call, even though his lovemaking was brusque and he lost interest almost as soon as he had conquered them. They were firmly instructed not to wear perfume and often had to wait for him undressed, so that matters could be speedily conducted. They hoped for jewels, influence and money, they were curious about the great man himself, and of course they wished to be proved more beautiful than Josephine.

Though Josephine resolved not to be jealous, she struggled, for not only did Napoleon conduct his affairs with flamboyant indiscretion, he also liked to acquaint her with every detail. As he fiddled with her make-up pots or vandalised her shawls, he would talk about his latest infatuation, praise her beauty and ask Josephine what she knew about her. Within a few days, he would be telling her of the conquest with, as Madame de Rémusat said, 'the most indecent openness'. Then he would describe 'the physical imperfections and anatomical peculiarities', as well as his thoughts on the 'performance' of the ladies – information he also shared with his male courtiers. Most of the women were half Josephine's age, and nothing was more painful than hearing of lissom bodies that had not yet aged, luxuriant hair when hers was thinning and growing grey, and faces that were always bright, even in the morning. He seemed to have no particular preference for brunettes or blondes. Any pretty girl would do.

Josephine also had to watch the progress of her husband's love affairs, as he would often attend her salon in the evening and play cards or talk with the lady in question, while his wife tried not to stare from the other side of the room. She pretended calm but she could hardly bear the jealousy and spent thousands on spies, much to the anger of her husband, who railed at how 'she humiliates both herself and me by surrounding me with spies'.[22] The Empress begged for information, even though it wounded her. She demanded her ladies-in-waiting write anonymous letters to Napoleon, reproaching him for his behaviour (wisely, the ladies secretly burned the letters after they had written them). When she knew he was with one of his mistresses, she would torment herself, weeping that she would be cast into oblivion and disgrace, forced out and divorced.

As he began to tire of his conquest and turn his eye to another willing actress or lady-in-waiting, he would ask Josephine to help him let the woman down gently and tell her she was no longer needed – the coward's way out. The price of Josephine's continued presence as Empress and consort was her willingness to forgive, even enable, Napoleon's affairs. His desire for women had become so well known that people would thrust pretty girls in his way in the hope of gaining influence, just as they had done with the old despotic kings. Courtiers sent their wives in the hope of finding out his plans. Napoleon had started offering thousands of francs as gifts to those he took for the night, and men were throwing their wives, lovers and even daughters at him for favours. Some women tried to seduce members of his entourage as a way of getting to him. But what he really wanted was the women who did not wish for him, whom he could slap, compel or browbeat into being his mistresses.

Napoleon claimed that they meant nothing, though some gained power from their new status. When a woman received particular favour from him, she naturally became a focus for courtiers and ministers demanding assistance. One Madame de X was a royalist spy, eager to undermine the Jacobins, and ready to 'abuse the indulgence' of the Emperor by taking action to further the exiled king's cause. As she knew, the way to please the ever-suspicious Napoleon was to tell him

gossip about plots against him. She invented tales against certain courtiers and 'many persons were ruined during her spell of favour'.[23]
Josephine was fearful of Madame de X and thought she had used her
influence to try and send Eugène on an impossible mission. But, once
more, when Napoleon grew weary of Madame's tell-tale tongue, he
asked Josephine to put an end to the affair. The Empress did so, telling
her rival in front of the whole court that the past would be forgotten.

The role of mistress to Napoleon was hardly enticing, for he was
too hardened to offer love to a susceptible woman and too ambitious
and sexist to give a determined one a chance to acquire power. The
actresses who could use the liaison to win publicity came off the best
of all. For, as Napoleon said, 'Women shall have no influence at my
Court; they may dislike me but I shall have peace and quietness.'[24] He
thought ladies 'ornamental at fetes and that was about all'.[25] He never
forgot his position as an excluded young man in the post-Revolutionary
years and he was not about to let women gain power now. 'Women
belong to the highest bidder,' he said, contemptuously. 'Power is what
they desire . . . I take them and then forget them.'[26] He sounded more
like an *Ancien Régime* roué than a great Emperor.

The Bonapartes were always seeking ways of luring Napoleon away
from '*la vieille*'. At the end of 1805, Caroline Murat introduced her
brother to Eléonore Denuelle, a tall, dark-eyed eighteen-year-old who
had also been a pupil of Madame Campan's (a fertile hunting ground
for mistresses to the Emperor). Her husband of only a few months was
in prison. Napoleon took a fancy to her and the Murats speedily
ensured her divorce and set her up as his lover. Caroline installed
Eléonore in her house just outside Paris so that Napoleon could visit
her whenever he pleased. Fashionable gossips felt sorry for Eléonore,
the virtual prisoner of the Murats, and decided her the victim of
'boudoir conscription'. She herself so dreaded the visits of the pale,
dull Emperor, who had nothing of interest to say, that she set the clock
in her bedroom half an hour forward whenever she heard he was on
his way.

Caroline installed Eléonore to distract Napoleon, and also in the
hope that the girl might fall pregnant. Josephine had been crowned
now, and Napoleon answered – when the family complained – that he
would only marry a new wife when Josephine died. Unfortunately for
them, she was still healthy and lithe and nowhere near death. The only

way they could drag Napoleon from her side was by proving that he could sire a child with another woman.

The family's hatred of Josephine was such that they were blind to their own advantage. If Napoleon divorced his wife and married another woman, any potential child would be his heir, and thus his brothers and their children would be displaced from the succession. To conserve their interests, they should have bitten their tongues and pretended esteem for Josephine. Simply put, they deluded themselves that Napoleon could not father a child, and so they continued in their campaign against his wife, thereby pursuing everybody's interests but their own.

The poor state of Hortense's marriage did not help her mother's cause. The couple were hopelessly out of sorts. Louis was growing sicker, and thus more irritable in everyday life. Even when they were not overtly at odds they spent time apart. At Saint-Leu, their country estate, she lived, as a visitor found, 'lonely, ill and always afraid of letting some word at which he might be offended escape her'.[27] Hortense loved music and drawing, and often entertained her old school friends at her salon, but nothing could console her. As she put it, 'I have wept greatly, but I have never caused others to weep.'[28]

Louis hated Josephine and told his wife that if she ever had any close discussion with her mother he would separate her from their son and shut her up in an out-of-the-way place – and warned that she must not tell Napoleon. He spied on her and attacked her. 'You are a woman, consequently a being all made up of evil and deceit,' he said. 'You are the daughter of an unprincipled mother; you belong to a family that I loathe; are these not reasons enough to suspect you?'[29]

When Louis was suffering from a skin disease he forced her to share his bed, even though the doctors told him not to do so. He even talked of lying in bed wearing the horribly dirty tunic of a similarly infected man as a cure, and said Hortense had to join him. Napoleon asked his brother to treat his wife more kindly and Louis refused, threatening to leave France. Hortense and her husband were ill matched and desperately unhappy, and far beyond the simplistic suggestions of patience and mutual understanding that both Josephine and Napoleon advised. Josephine sent a letter almost deluded in its naivety: 'Why show this repugnance to Louis? Instead of making matters worse with complaining, why not try patience and kindness?' She had been able to surmount

Napoleon's rages with gentleness, but that was because he had loved her. Louis had never loved Hortense. 'You wish that he resembled his brother but he must first have his brother's temperament.' The unhappy Hortense was given a practical solution: 'If poor Louis' digestion were better, he would be much more amiable.'[30]

'I hear no more of Hortense than if she were on the Congo,' sighed Napoleon. Her silence was because she was unhappy.[31] Underneath all the anger was Louis's resentment that he had been forced by his brother to marry the daughter of the witch Josephine. Paranoid and humiliated by the rumours that his wife had been his brother's mistress, he took his rage out on her. Napoleon had expected that the marriage would stop the gossip, but the British press and the anti-Napoleonic parties, as well as some courtiers, kept it going. After all, he seduced without compunction and Josephine had been an infamous mistress – why would Hortense be any different? She grew so distressed by the constant accusations that she even came to wonder if her mother believed them. 'How could you ever imagine that I share certain absurd, or perhaps, interested opinions?' Josephine wrote. 'Surely you cannot believe that I look upon you as my rival?'[32] Still, Napoleon did not restrain his eye from Josephine's family. He chased after her pretty blonde niece, seventeen-year-old Stéphanie de Beauharnais, another alumna of Madame Campan. That, for Josephine, was going too far and she began hunting for a husband for Stéphanie, preferably one living far from France.

Josephine still loved Malmaison. She continued to spend thousands on seeds and plants and bought more animals for her menagerie. But she was hardly ever there, and when Napoleon did agree to her visiting Malmaison, he was envious of what she loved. Sometimes, when seized by rage, he shot her swans, uprooted her plants and killed her pet animals. When she begged him not to shoot the animals during the breeding season, he was scathing. 'It seems that everything is prolific at Malmaison, except Madame.'

Josephine's spending on her household, jewels, ornaments, clothes and gifts, in modern terms, would be well over a million pounds. Indeed, it seems surprising that she did not spend more. Her wardrobe was spectacularly costly, her jewels ludicrous, and her apartments were filled with expensive knick-knacks: boxes, statues, ornamental books, vases and glass. Now that she was the Empress, she saw creating an art collection for the nation as one of her most important tasks and spent huge sums on paintings.

Despite Napoleon's passion for grandeur, he was still an old penny-pincher at heart and made frequent decrees to try and reduce spending, such as instructing that all the sheets in the courtiers' apartments should only be changed monthly. Josephine never economised and was too kind-hearted – or too indolent – to haggle with merchants pressing goods on her. As well as her gifts, her household and her charities, she also supported her family. She sent money to her mother on Martinique and pressed her to come to court, where she would have high status as the mother of the Empress. But Rose-Claire was distressed by Napoleon's act of making himself Emperor and she refused to come. She remained alone with her servants at La Pagerie.

Josephine's other relatives were not so wedded to principle. Her uncle Tascher came over, and she paid his debts and supported him and five of his children in the house on the rue de la Victoire, finding them positions at embassies. Her maternal cousins also accepted her invitation and were paid for, and she gave generous gifts to her god-daughter, Josephine Tallien. She also supported Euphémie Lefèvre, her maid and probable half-sister, who had come over with her to France; Euphémie soon bought a rather large property near Malmaison. Josephine also gave money to the family of her former husband – including his aunt and her daughter, his wet nurse, his illegitimate daughter and, most generously of all, his former mistress Laure de Longpré, who had once cruelly conspired with Alexandre against her. No doubt there was a superior pleasure in helping Laure. As Josephine wrote in the margin of one letter, 'this lady is very infirm'.

The word got around that those in need only had to ask Josephine for help. She gave money to poverty-stricken royalists and émigré aristocrats, as well as anyone who had ever served her. Her official charities were those expected from a consort: mothers, orphans, the sick and the old. In 1805, her annual donations had reached 72,000 francs and by 1809, they had soared to 180,000. These sums did not include the casual amounts given to supplicants who conveyed messages to her or charities she encountered while travelling.

Madame de Rémusat remarked that Napoleon 'encouraged people to be in debt because it kept them dependent'.[33] For him, Josephine's inability to stop spending was further evidence of her charming feminity, but he still rued her spending. In 1805, he declared that all merchants should be sent first to her comptroller, but she found ways of seeing them in secret. When the Emperor found her elderly milliner waiting in the blue salon he shouted for the guards, who dragged her away to be imprisoned. He quickly realised his error and sent a message to release her. But the poor woman's awful experience did not dissuade the others. Still the merchants flocked to the biggest purse in town.

One of Josephine's greatest expenses was jewellery. Marie Antoinette had been brought low by a diamond necklace, but it seemed that Josephine could appear covered in diamonds and no one would complain. One of her ladies-in-waiting claimed that her jewellery collection could have 'figured in a tale of Arabian nights', and it was certainly the finest in Europe.[34] Marie Antoinette's jewel box was too small for the Empress's sparklers. A favourite necklace of twenty-seven huge diamonds was the object of desire for Tsar Alexander, who bought it after Josephine's death. When celebrating the marriage of her niece to the Crown Prince of Baden, Josephine wore pearls in her hair valued at a million francs. She had the crown jewels of France, as well as Napoleon's excessive gifts of diadems, necklaces and bracelets – and every possible precious stone he could order back from his expeditions, including oriental rubies, stones from Brazil and ten necklaces of real pearls. The Jacob brothers made her an incredible jewel cabinet, designed by Percier and covered in gilt, bronze plaques and inlaid with mother-of-pearl. Now in the Louvre, it is a monster of French excess, with thirty drawers (many with secret locks, useful to ward off Napoleon's investigations), and the size of a small modern wardrobe. It was the most expensive item the brothers ever made – and still it was not big enough for her collection. In 1811, an inventory was made of Josephine's jewels, which assessed them as worth over five million francs. The 'good easy-going woman', the Martinique plantation daughter, had become the Imperial Empress, bowed under the weight of precious stones.[35]

17

'I have fulfilled my destiny'

In April 1805, Josephine was embarking on a plan to receive another crown. Earlier that year, a Milanese delegation had come to the Tuileries to ask Napoleon to be their king. He asked his brother, Joseph, who refused, since he did not wish to give up his claim on the French throne. The Emperor then suggested little Napoleon Charles, but his father, Louis, turned the honour down, declaring that he did not want to see his son set above him. Napoleon had to accept the crown, and eventually he and Josephine set off for Milan. She would be 'Her Majesty Queen of Italy'. After a week in Lyons of fetes and ceremonies, a bumpy ride over the Mount Cenis Pass, and a stop to see the Pope in Turin, they arrived in Milan.

Josephine walked in the procession but she was not crowned by her husband, as she had been the previous year. She watched, accompanied by her sister-in-law, Elisa, as Napoleon ambled along holding the crown and then placed it on his own head. 'God gives it to me,' he roared, 'woe to him who touches it.' He had demanded celebrations reminiscent of imperial Rome, and there was a day of chariot races and gladiator-style games. Then the Italians put their own twist on the celebrations: a woman went up in a balloon and threw flowers down over the new King and Queen. Nobles spent a whole year's worth of income on the fetes.

Napoleon's brothers and sisters sat at the coronation in silent fury, watching their most hated rival become Queen. He then informed them that Eugène would be Viceroy of Italy and adopted by Napoleon as a son of France. Caroline Murat fell ill and her husband broke his sword across his knee. Josephine, it seemed, was impossible to unseat.

She wept at the thought that her son would always be so far from her, and Napoleon upbraided her sharply. 'If the absence of your children causes you so much pain, guess what I must always feel. The affection which you display for them makes me feel bitterly the unhappiness of having none myself.' He immediately sent her to Lake Como to bathe and ready her body to have a child.

Napoleon travelled from Italy to inspect his army for the endlessly proposed invasion of Britain. He wrote cheerfully to Josephine, offering her the customary thousands of kisses. Josephine, too, was on her best behaviour, wisely restraining herself from upbraiding him about his affairs. She wrote to her son, 'No more jealous scenes now, my dear Eugène, I can truthfully say, and so we are both much happier.'[1]

Napoleon heard from Talleyrand that Austria was preparing to join Britain and Russia against France. The Emperor's spies told him that Prussia was also considering allying with Britain. He had to embark on immediate action. He decided to march into Austria, conquer them and then return to invade Britain. He was spoiling for a battle, after the womanish occupation of planning ceremonies and robes. A magnificent win over the Austrians was just what he needed to secure his position. After all, the route to his coronation had hardly been lined with cheering crowds. 'I have a fine army here and a fine fleet, everything I need to pass the time agreeably,' he wrote to his wife, who had travelled on to Plombières, 'only my sweet Josephine is missing, but I should not say that, in matters of love, women are best left in suspense, uncertain of their power.'[2] In September, he demanded 80,000 more conscripts.

He wished to depart alone for campaign, but Josephine returned to Paris and pleaded to be allowed to come too. At four in the morning, the imperial pair set off for Strasbourg in the Emperor's sleeping coach. They would travel for fifty-eight hours straight, stopping only to change horses. Napoleon was back on campaign but he never forgot the importance of grandeur as well as strategy. Even though he would remain there only briefly, the imperial apartments at the former Episcopal Palace in Strasbourg had been decorated to celebrate the Emperor, and the tireless Fontaine had sent furniture and silverware so that Napoleon could dine in proper style.

After four days of celebrations, he took a long bath and then set off again, on 1 October, leaving Josephine behind. She was to be his representative in Strasbourg, giving dinners and receptions, receiving the diplomats, and touring the hospitals as the wounded soldiers arrived from the front. She even presided over an initiation ceremony for a Strasbourg Masonic lodge, an honour reserved for the Empress. Bored and lonely, convinced Napoleon would take mistresses as he travelled, she consoled herself with buying art, plants, animals, dresses and toys. 'Rest easy,' he wrote. 'I promise you the shortest and most brilliant of campaigns.'³ It was not the campaigns she was worried about.

Napoleon sped fast, determined to reach the Austrians before the Russians arrived to ally with them. He set off in his carriage, with fifty-two more trundling behind. He was accompanied by General Berthier, and his most important supplies: a telescope, brandy, a compass, pens, ink and sealing wax. Dispatches were scribbled and flung from the window at an officer galloping beside the carriage. He also dashed off a letter to Josephine every day. The whole operation proceeded at such speed that meals were kept ready to serve at any minute, so whenever Napoleon decreed it was time to eat, he hopped down from his carriage, silver dishes were whipped out and the food was wolfed down, with his Imperial Guards surrounding him. The ordinary soldiers took their food from the people they passed, who looked, according to one soldier, like 'walking larders, hung about with long sides of bacon'.⁴

Winter was falling and the sleet and mud were so thick that Napoleon abandoned his carriage and travelled on horseback. Even as a pampered Emperor, he was still the old Bonaparte – oblivious to bodily needs, riding for ten hours without stopping, ploughing through driving rain without complaint. 'I have a slight cold,' he wrote to Josephine, with some understatement.

Napoleon and his army took the Austrians by surprise. They believed he was still on the French coast, fussing over his invasion of Britain. Their soldiers were surrounded and General Mack and his 50,000 men surrendered at Ulm on 20 October. With 1500 men dead, the French saw their losses as light. Napoleon dashed off a delighted letter to Josephine. 'I have fulfilled my destiny. I have destroyed the Austrian army,' he gloated. 'This will be the shortest, the most successful and the most brilliant of the campaigns I have fought.' He signed off, 'Adieu my Josephine, a thousand sweet kisses everywhere.'[5] His wife was not content, jealously looking for signs of neglect and still unhappy about mistresses. 'You should have more fortitude and confidence,' he sighed. 'You must be cheerful, amuse yourself.'[6]

Meanwhile, the plans to invade Britain by sea were limping on. Ever since the argument with Lord Whitworth, Napoleon had cherished plans to invade, but the fleet was never quite ready and he was never sure of the naval superiority he needed. One problem was that it was impossible to get the flotilla to sea on a single tide – it would take three tides, which would leave the ships vulnerable to attack as they waited. In August, he was ranting against Admiral Villeneuve, who had retreated to Cadiz rather than entering the Channel. Napoleon decided to replace him. In the hope of avoiding the shame of replacement, Villeneuve took the fleet out of Cadiz, and right into the arms of Nelson and his ships. The Battle of Trafalgar, on 21 October, was a tragic victory for the British. Horatio Nelson died from a shot in the shoulder, leaving Lady Hamilton to the nation as he took his last breaths. The death of Napoleon's great rival was small consolation for the French. The British celebrated the most magnificent naval victory they had ever enjoyed. The entire population bought Trafalgar brooches and Nelson mourning jewellery, the dignitaries wept at his funeral at St Paul's. Villeneuve was taken prisoner. When he was set free and returned to France, he stabbed himself to death.

Napoleon's hopes of invading Britain were finally over. As ever, he refused to accept the news and told the French press to make only a brief reference to Trafalgar. He did not write about it to Josephine and instead boasted about his successes. The incredible surrender of the Austrians at Ulm seized all attention in France.

On 22 October, Napoleon asked Josephine to travel to him in Munich, stopping in Baden and Stuttgart on the way. He had planned her first lone imperial progress in typically exhaustive detail. Accompanied by her ladies-in-waiting, her carriage would be followed by those carrying her chamberlains, her luggage and the imperial jewel case. She would ride his victory march through to Vienna, staying at the courts of the electors, princes and dukes who were his vassals. Every time she arrived in a town, she should be greeted by fanfares, cannons and the ringing of church bells. 'Be civil to all of them,' he wrote, 'but accept their homage as your due.'

Josephine charmed the conquered courts she visited with her gifts and her seemingly heartfelt thanks for displays of singing or fireworks, triumphal arches and odes in her honour. Napoleon was gratified by her success at smoothing over his rough victories. 'Have the grand fetes at Baden, Stuttgart and Munich made you forget the poor soldiers who live covered with mud, rain and blood?' he teased.[7]

Napoleon and his army battled on but the men were exhausted and supplies were low. He knew that the allies would see him as easy pickings, far from Strasbourg and leading a demoralised, hungry army. He made a daring plan to pretend that he was about to withdraw his armies in the hope that surprise would allow him to gain a victory. On 1 December, the eve of the first anniversary of the day he had been celebrated in the streets of Paris, he waited in silence with his men at the village of Austerlitz, crouched in the freezing cold. The weather was on his side. Mist descended and the French troops were hidden from enemy eyes. The Russians arrived and fell into the trap, deciding that the French were retreating.

As the sun broke through at eight in the morning, the order was given and the French charged at the Austro-Russians. Within three hours, the enemy army was in tatters. The Austrian Imperial Guard was smashed and by nightfall the Russians were retreating across an iced-over lake. Napoleon ordered his cannons to fire on the ice and declared that 20,000 men were killed. 'This is the happiest day of my life,' he told Méneval. He wrote to Josephine that it was 'the grandest of all those I have fought . . . more than 30,000 dead, a horrible sight'. He was also tired and 'my eyes have been rather bad'.[8] Fourteen-year-old Archduchess Marie Louise, daughter of the Austrian Emperor, burst into floods of weeping when she heard the news and wrote that the French Emperor was the 'Beast of the Apocalypse' and she hoped he would die that year.

The Russians retreated and Napoleon scurried on to Vienna, taking up residence at the palace at Schönbrunn, gratified to occupy yet another royal residence. On 5 December, Josephine reached Munich and heard of her husband's great victories. She was caught up in a round of celebrations that left her no time for writing letters. 'Mighty Empress! Not a single letter from you,' he complained. 'Deign from the

height of your splendour to concern yourself a little with your slave.'⁹
He was still reliant on her. A general wondered if Napoleon might
wish to firm his success by marrying an Austrian archduchess, but the
hero refused. 'The memory of Marie Antoinette is too recent.'¹⁰ Against
the advice of Talleyrand, who recommended allying with Austria in
order to intimidate Russia, Napoleon broke into pieces Austria and
those it had protected – to the benefit of his relations.

Eugène, he decided, would be married almost immediately to Augusta,
the eighteen-year-old daughter of the Elector of Bavaria, who was, he
noted, 'better looking than the portrait painted on the teacup I am
sending you'.¹¹ He informed his stepson of the decision, put the
announcement in the French newspapers and wrote to Josephine telling
her to arrange the celebrations. Eugène obeyed the instruction to 'set
out at all speed' and galloped from Italy, carrying the cup bearing a
picture of his fiancée. Josephine begged to be allowed to invite Hortense
to the wedding, but Napoleon was in too much of a hurry to wait for
her.

The Elector of Bavaria was very unhappy about the proposed
marriage. Complaining that Eugène was a commoner and that his
daughter was already engaged to her cousin, the Crown Prince of
Baden, he suggested that Napoleon divorce Josephine and marry Augusta
instead. The Elector's young second wife had once hoped to marry
the executed Duc d'Enghien, and she made little effort to be polite
to the Emperor.

Napoleon ran roughshod over their objections, and offered the jilted
Prince of Baden Stéphanie Beauharnais, Josephine's pretty niece. He
bribed the Elector by giving him the title of King of Bavaria at the
end of 1805, and decreed Eugène an Imperial Highness as well as
Viceroy of Italy and his officially adopted son. The wedding took place
three days after Eugène's post-haste arrival on 14 January 1806.
Fortunately, Eugène, a gentle and spirited man, was pleased by his
Princess and the two soon came to love each other. At the wedding,
Napoleon flirted with the young Queen of Bavaria and was convinced
she was in love with him – a high state of delusion.

Josephine was too wise to complain that the decision about her son's
marriage had been taken from her hands. With Eugène as the Emperor's
officially adopted son, there was a chance he might be declared heir.
It seemed impossible that Napoleon could divorce her after endowing

her son so munificently. She spent the first weeks of 1806 with him, celebrating his victories and cosseting his pride.

He returned from Austerlitz in January 1806 puffed up with his invincibility. Even the fact that Paris was in the grip of a financial crisis – after millions of government bonds had somehow disappeared – could not dent his self-confidence. He suspended the Minister of the Treasury and turned his attention to his favourite subject: his own glory. At thirty-six, he bestrode nations and ruled an Empire of many millions of people. He possessed almost all of Europe, save a few countries that annoyingly had resisted – including Spain, Britain and Sweden.[12] He was bloated, exhausted, a martyr to stomach pain and headaches, but he was the most feared man in Europe.

The King of Diamonds was full of ideas to make his court even grander after attending those of Austria and Munich. He decided that the court should immediately rehearse the ceremony of presentation. Josephine herself had not been presented, and now she was to preside over a presentation ceremony more tortuously detailed than that of Louis XVI and Marie Antoinette. The Emperor and Empress settled on their gilt thrones, flanked by the Bonaparte family on stools. Court officials and ladies-in-waiting advanced, bowing and curtseying. A lady due to be presented curtseyed at the door, then again a few steps on, then a third time in front of their Imperial Majesties – and then had to walk out backwards, with three further curtsies as she did so. Not long into the ceremony, Napoleon was growing desperately impatient, bouncing on his throne with annoyance and barely able to last to the end. Etiquette, he decided, was much better if carried out by somebody else. He was bored and purged his feelings by roaring insults at anyone he considered badly dressed.

It was all the Emperor's new clothes: foreign courts mocked the imperial court for its gold-splashed brashness, the ultimate in *nouveau riche*. Napoleon, a brusque fighter who cared little for the French people, saw himself as a virtual deity. As in the time of Louis XVI and his predecessors, there was a convention that the Emperor could make the sun shine if he wished, and so on fete days, even in the depths of winter, shivering courtiers in light dress would declare that it was not cold and it was not raining, even as their clothes and hair were soaked through. Everyone had to pretend around the fairy king Napoleon.

'The life I lead here is as fatiguing as it possibly can be, never a moment to myself,' Josephine wrote to Eugène. 'I go to bed very late and wake up early. The Emperor, who is very strong, copes very well with this busy life, but my health and my soul are suffering a little.'[13] The etiquette was punishing, 'a daily slavery'.[14] Napoleon was a precision individual and any misplacing of a foot, a movement too quick or an aspect of costume out of place could prompt a furious dressing-down.

Josephine later told her lady-in-waiting, Madame Ducrest, how much 'pleasure' she felt when anything interrupted 'the chains of court ceremony'.[15] Napoleon demanded a court of ostentatious ritual and procedure but had no patience to sit through any of it. He threw on his robes, barged through presentations and fidgeted through balls. He hated attending plays in the brand-new theatres in his palaces. The best actors in France, the most beautiful scenery, the funniest comedies and the most mellifluous music were brought out to please him, but he sat through each performance, hunched over, refusing to laugh. He then blamed the play for being a failure, and attacked his courtiers for not finding something that was truly amusing.

'Pleasure does not inhabit palaces,' wrote Madame de Rémusat. Napoleon's youthful court rather struggled with the dictates of raiment and behaviour. Some of the younger wives became so confused that they barely spoke to anybody, and girls fainted with fear at the thought of being presented to the Emperor. His habit of shouting at women or criticising their attire in front of everybody was terrifying. A woman without rouge was asked if she was just 'up from childbed', he noted the 'red elbows' of one, and mocked another for her ugly face.[16] The Emperor, so powerful, the ruler of millions, still took petty satisfaction from playground-style humiliation of women.

The man who pored over army lists at night had little interest in his court. He hardly ever remembered anyone's name and would stomp up to courtiers, demanding 'And what do *you* call yourself?'[17] Josephine smoothed things over in his wake. She remembered names, the details of people's health, families and homes and always had a kind word – she was the soft power, the woman who made her husband's excesses possible.

Everything turned on the minutiae of etiquette – 'a ribbon, a slight difference in dress, permission to pass through a particular door', as

Josephine's lady-in-waiting put it.[18] Those who had been at Versailles or in royalist company were much more at ease, and made a performance of laughing, smiling and behaving in an unaffected fashion. The Jacobins and Republicans were nervous and stiff, unaccustomed to court life and finding the ritual rather dreadful. Life was much easier for everyone when Napoleon galloped off for another military victory and Josephine presided in his stead. Certainly, they could all start playing cards for money.

Josephine smiled gracefully at the court but she was growing ever more uneasy. She thought that her rivals were whispering about her in corners and making plans to undermine her in front of Napoleon. She was also convinced her life was under threat. She would never be left alone and each time she fell ill with indigestion, she was sure she was being poisoned.[19] 'It is much to be hoped that the Empress will die,' the dreaded Fouché told Bourrienne. 'It would remove many difficulties.'[20] Josephine, fit and feeling herself a long way from death, worried about her food every time she ate. Napoleon shrugged off her concerns.

Josephine found consolation in the forthcoming marriage of her seventeen-year-old niece, Stéphanie – Napoleon's passion for her had given his wife much pain. Stéphanie found the stout, sleepy Prince of Baden very unappealing and demanded a king instead. Napoleon was rather delighted by her rebellion and the two were often seen giggling together at court. But the Prince could not be jilted and so Napoleon reluctantly gave Stéphanie the territory of Breisgau, a necklace worth 1.5 million francs and a huge trousseau, as well as calling her 'my daughter'. The wedding was one of the grandest the Tuileries had ever seen. A forty-person procession approached the altar – the bride in a silver-embroidered gown decorated in roses, hosts of ladies-in-waiting crowned with diamonds and flowers, and Bonaparte in Spanish costume. Josephine herself was resplendent in a gown covered in different shades of gold embroidery, the imperial crown and pearls worth a million francs. As the fireworks exploded that night over the Palace, Josephine congratulated herself on ridding herself of another rival.

Napoleon claimed he loved Eugène and Hortense because they never asked for anything. The same was not true for his family. Nothing he gave them was sufficient. He piled on the honours for his mother, giving her a court of two hundred, with nine ladies-in-waiting, a bishop and two sub-chaplains as her confessors and a former page of Louis XVI as her equerry. As her country home, she had a wing of the Grand Trianon and later a huge chateau near Troyes. Napoleon's sisters tried to outdo Josephine in their incredible spending. Pauline and Caroline would squander 15,000 francs on their gowns and then embellish them with diamonds and pearls. When Napoleon entered the room, flanked by his shimmering sisters, his mother in court dress and his brothers in their rich uniforms, they gave the impression of a united front. The reality could not be further from the truth. Napoleon's family was a party of incompetents, schemers and gangsters. They behaved as if Europe was theirs to carve up.

By 1806, Joseph was King of Naples and Sicily, Caroline and Joachim were Grand Duke and Duchess of Berg in Germany, and Elisa was Grand Duchess of Tuscany. Joseph desired a grander kingdom and the sisters wanted to be queens. They were poor rulers, although any ruler of Napoleon's vassal states was in an impossible position, since they had to implement repressive measures and punitive taxation commanded from Paris. As Viceroy, Eugène tried hard to defend the situation of the Italians and they esteemed him for doing what he could to improve their lot. He buried himself in papers and meetings. 'My son, you work too hard; your life is too monotonous,' Napoleon wrote to him. 'You must have some more gaiety in your home; it is necessary for your wife's happiness and your own health.'[21]

In 1806, he created Louis and Hortense King and Queen of Holland. The Dutch throne was a bribe. Louis had been refusing to allow Napoleon to decree their son heir to the Empire because he did not wish him to outrank him. Given the present of a kingdom, he agreed. Hortense wept bitterly when she was told by her stepfather that she must leave Paris. Her health was not good and she dreaded living with a husband whose hatred of her increased daily. She threatened that if the sufferings became too much she would retire to a convent, for she would have no difficulty 'relinquishing a crown of which she could already feel the thorns'.[22] She set off to Holland as if she was a victim about to be sacrificed.

She was right to be afraid. Louis initially demanded that she should have a fabulous court. Then, envious of her popularity, he changed his mind and made her accept a life of isolation, surrounded her with spies and constantly insulted her. Anyone talking to her about the merest trifle would be immediately pushed out of influence. Louis was a king endeavouring to be fair to his people, and tried to refuse the oppressive dictats from Paris. But to Hortense, he was unremittingly cruel.

Hortense had nothing to console her but painting and music, and the chance to lavish affection on her toddler son. Her close bond with little Napoleon made things worse: Louis was jealous and attempted to prise him away from her, much to the distress of the child. Hortense sunk into a state of lassitude and was so desperate for escape that she hoped the British might invade and take her prisoner.

By the summer of 1806, Napoleon was plotting again. After a long period of indecision, the King of Prussia had signed an agreement to ally with the Tsar of Russia. They then threatened to join with Britain if the French did not withdraw from their occupying positions in southern Germany. In August, the Prussians began to advance towards the French Army. Napoleon again decided on using the politics of pretence and put about a story that he did not wish to go to war because he was so comfortable in his luxurious palace. In reality, he was making minutely detailed plans for conquest.

Josephine, once more, vowed to go with him. When she received the information that he was about to leave, at four in the morning of 24 September, she dashed down the stairs and threw herself on him, begging to be allowed to come too. He ushered her inside his carriage and they set off. Josephine's ladies assembled the six carriages of clothes, equipment and jewels and followed a few hours later. She was to remain at Mainz while Napoleon set off again. He parted from her reluctantly, weeping, convulsing, then beginning to vomit. He looked powerful in his uniform – Marshal Massena said that he looked two foot taller when he put on his general's hat – but underneath he was suffering from an excess of fine living, and the thought of marching out into the cold was daunting. Still, he was the Emperor and was better and stronger than those weak kings who sent out their generals to do their work.

'I can't think why you weep, you do wrong to make yourself ill,' he wrote impatiently to his wife.[23] Left behind, she carried out her duties as Empress. She opened balls and receptions, listened to pleas and hosted delegations, visited the wounded and entertained German princes. She spent nearly 55,000 francs on gifts for the people she met. None of it made her smile. Napoleon sent frequent letters, ending with 'I love and desire you' and 'I love and embrace you'. But Josephine was miserable and spent every evening with her tarot cards, trying to see the future. She had reason to be worried: Napoleon's young mistress Eléonore Denuelle was six months pregnant. Josephine would not see her husband again for ten months.

One night, she called out to her ladies that the tarot cards had foretold a great victory. A few minutes later, the Emperor's page arrived with a letter bearing the news of the success. 'Never was an army more thoroughly beaten.'[24] He had won a decisive victory over the Prussians at Jena. The King and Queen took refuge in the east of Prussia and Napoleon entered Berlin in splendour, surrounded by his marshals and the Imperial Guard. He was delighted to prowl about the palace and prod the King of Prussia's belongings. He sat at the King's desk and took his sword and belt, as well as a very handy silver alarm clock, which he carried with him for years.

Napoleon blamed the Queen of Prussia for encouraging her husband to aggression. 'How unhappy are those princes who permit their wives to interfere in affairs of state,' he wrote, sharply. Josephine wrote back, expressing hurt. He replied, 'You seem displeased by my speaking ill of women. It is true that I detest scheming women. I am accustomed to ones who are kind, sweet and persuasive. It is your fault – you have spoiled me.'[25] But Josephine could not stop weeping and worrying. He offered more sympathy than he usually had for weakness. 'Talleyrand tells me you are always in tears,' he wrote after the arrival of his foreign minister in Berlin. 'You must be brave and remember you are an Empress.'[26]

Napoleon knew that Eléonore was pregnant but it was not earth-shattering news for him. He had never been convinced of her virtue and he suspected (correctly) that Joachim Murat had been seducing the teenager as well. In the midst of complicated military plans, he still wished for Josephine. In November, he closed the Prussian ports to British trade – a decree he would extend to all France's allies and vassal states. His hope was to starve Britain into surrender. As a plan, it would bring poverty and privation to an already battered Europe but he did not care. He would be master of the continent, and thus the world.

He did not stay long in Berlin. News came through that the Russians were marching through Poland towards him. He decided to set off into

Poland and crush the Russian army there, a daring plan considering his men were weary and homesick and had no greatcoats for the freezing Polish weather. When Josephine heard that her husband was advancing to battle once more, she was plunged into gloom. He sent her letters suggesting she might join him, and then changed his mind. By December, she was imploring him to allow her to come. 'I see that you have lost your little head. I wrote that you could come as soon as our winter quarters were decided,' he said. 'The greater one's position, the less one can choose and the more one must depend on events and circumstances.'[27] Josephine was growing frantic. 'There is only one woman for me. Do you know her? I could paint her portrait for you but it would make you conceited,' he wrote. 'The winter nights are long, all alone.'[28] She replied, desperately pained that she had dreamed he had found a woman he could love. Napoleon responded sympathetically. 'You say that your dream does not make you jealous, I think therefore that you are jealous and I am delighted. In any case you are wrong. In these frozen Polish plains, one dwells little on beautiful women.'[29]

Josephine pleaded with him to let her join him at Warsaw. 'Your letter made me laugh,' he wrote to her on New Year's Eve, travelling fast towards the capital. 'You idealise the females of Poland in a way they don't deserve.'[30] Later that day, he received a message telling him that Eléonore Denuelle had given birth to a son, Charles. Still convinced that Joachim had also been seducing the girl, he read the note and put it aside.

Unlike the rest of Europe, who saw Napoleon as a terrifying oppressor, the Polish saw him as a potential rescuer who would secure their independence from the Russians. The people had been dancing in the streets at the news that the French were drawing near and the ladies of influence established hospitals for the French wounded and palaces for the generals. On the same day, on the approach to Warsaw, Napoleon's carriage was surrounded by a crowd of people cheering for the French. A beautiful young woman with fair hair and blue eyes approached the carriage through the throng, after begging Duroc for help. 'We have been waiting for you to save us,' she gasped, in perfect French. Touched by her beauty and innocence, the Emperor gave her a bouquet of flowers from the coach. He kept waving his hat at her as the carriage drove away.

18

'I wish you would be more reasonable'

apoleon wrote a letter to Josephine. He no longer wished for her presence. 'I am inclined to think you should go to Paris where you are needed,' he told her. 'The roads are bad and not at all safe; I cannot expose you to so many fatigues and dangers. Go back to Paris for the winter.'[1] Josephine, alone in Mainz and tearful, harboured ominous thoughts, but Napoleon did not care. When he was not planning battle, he was thinking obsessively about the woman who had accepted his bouquet.

At home with her baby son, a young countess – Marie Walewska, beautiful and nearly twenty – was visited by a Polish dignitary. He told her he had heard of her triumph in grasping Napoleon's attention and invited her to a ball held in the Emperor's honour. Her husband, a nationalist count fifty-two years her senior, pressed her to attend.

In the youthful Countess Walewska, Napoleon had met his match. Even though her husband was over seventy-two, she believed in the validity of marriage vows. Young and idealistic, she had no desire to be a tyrannical Emperor's fleeting sexual conquest. She was intelligent and highly educated – by her tutor, Nicholas Chopin, father of the future composer – and spoke fluent French and was gifted at music, geography and history.

Marie's father had died when she was eight in a terrible massacre of independence fighters by the Russians. At sixteen and a half, she returned home from school and her mother accepted the suit of Anastase Walewski, the richest landowner in the area. Marie had little wish to marry him (his youngest grandchild was six years older than her) but she had little choice. In June 1805, she gave birth to a son.

Count Walewski was delighted by the attention his wife had received from Napoleon. She herself was rather afraid of the Emperor's intense response. At the ball, she wore a simple white gown, looking more like a peasant than a countess. Napoleon was fascinated by her and took her as a dancing partner, enthralled by her beauty, thrilled by her seeming virtue and stimulated by her obvious lack of interest in flirting with him. Next morning, he woke with his mind preoccupied by Marie. He scribbled off a letter. 'I saw no one but you, I admired only you; I want no one but you; I beg you to reply promptly to calm the ardour and impatience of N.' He sent the missive with General Duroc, along with a large bouquet of flowers.

Marie gazed at Duroc, who was waiting for a response, and replied: 'There is no answer.' The Emperor was shocked to receive no reply. As his valet recorded, 'he simply could not understand it; he considered himself irresistible to women, and I really believe that his *amour-propre* had been hurt'.[2]

That evening, Duroc returned with more flowers and another letter. This time, Napoleon tried a softer approach and summoned the old romantic words he used to deploy with Josephine.

Have I displeased you, Madame? I had hoped otherwise. Was it a dream on my part? Your ardour has cooled, while mine burns more and more fiercely. You have destroyed my peace! Oh give some little joy and happiness to the heart that longs to worship you![3]

For Napoleon, the siege had begun. He confessed a burning passion and pleaded with her to dine with him alone. He sent a red leather jewellery box, but Marie threw it to the floor in disgust. 'He must take me for a prostitute,' she said.[4] Napoleon would not be dissuaded. When his customary offers of favours and money were refused, he tried to blackmail her. If she attended him, he would look kindly on Poland. 'Your country will be dearer to me when you take pity on my poor heart,' he declared. 'Whenever I have thought a thing impossible or difficult to obtain, I have desired it all the more. Nothing discourages me . . . I am accustomed to seeing my wishes met. Your resistance subjugates me. I want to force you, yes force you to love me, Marie. I have brought back to life your country's name. I will do much more!'[5]

The Polish dignitaries told Marie she was their sole hope for independence. Only the Emperor could protect Polish independence from the Prussians, Russians and Austrians. Everyone had to try to please him – including her. Poor Marie – besieged by Napoleon and constantly attacked by her own husband and his political allies to give up her virtue – she was in an impossible position. Reluctantly, she agreed to attend Napoleon in private. She arrived, agitated and trembling, afraid of her fate. But Napoleon, busy working, said she should go to a palace apartment to take supper and rest. He carried on working until late. Then, when she was almost asleep, he burst into her room. He immediately began demanding details about the nationalist Polish nobles, as if she was an informer. Then he seized her and began forcing himself on her (his strategy had perhaps been that she would be nearly asleep and thus less resistant). She tried to fight back but he was merciless. 'Remember, if you push me too far the very name of Poland and all your hopes will be broken like this watch.'[6] He then threw a watch to the floor and smashed it to smithereens with his heel. Marie was so terrified that she fainted, and woke up to find Napoleon had taken her anyway. He had a different version – 'She did not struggle overmuch' he said.[7]

When Marie came round and began weeping, Napoleon treated her with kindness. 'You may be certain, Marie, that I will fulfil the promise I made you.' She passed on his words to her husband and the dignitaries. She had done her duty by her country, at some cost. Napoleon wrote to her again, this time addressing her as 'tu'.

Marie, my sweet Marie! My first thought is of you, my first desire is to see you once more. You will come again, won't you? You promised me you would. If not, then the eagle will fly to you. I shall see you at dinner, a friend tells me. Deign, then, to accept this bouquet, let it become a mysterious link which shall establish between us a secret union in the midst of the crowd surrounding us.[8]

Marie had become his mistress and she could not go back. Napoleon was so delighted by her that he called her to him constantly and tried his best to be gentle and kind. She was gradually won over by him and came to trust him. He admired her innocence, her patriotism and stringent virtue and valued her loyalty. Above all, he was a vain man and in Marie's interest in his ventures, he saw a flattering mirror of himself. For the first time since Josephine, he fell in love.

When he set off to East Prussia, Marie left her husband and little boy behind and moved to her mother's estate, ready to attend Napoleon whenever he called her. He wrote her romantic letters from every stage of his journey, promising her he would obtain a guarantee of Polish independence from the Tsar.

He wrote regularly to Marie – and also to Josephine. He was still encouraging her to return to Paris. 'Believe me, it is sometimes harder on me than on you to put off the happiness of our meeting. Say to yourself, it is proof of how precious I am to him.'⁹ But he was much less sympathetic with her low spirits than he had been before he met Marie. 'Be worthy of me, show more strength of character, I don't like cowards.'¹⁰ Despite his passion for Marie, he still wanted Josephine. 'I kiss you everywhere – everywhere – even on the little cousins.'¹¹

Josephine knew she had to obey him and return to Paris. Her spirits were so depressed that she struggled to maintain the grandeur and style of an Empress on her return journey. She arrived back to a gloomy city. The ban on trade with Britain and its Empire was causing great hardship. The peasants could not export their massive surplus of the harvest of 1808, and prices fell. The middle classes were without coffee, sugar, rum, chocolate and other goods from the West Indies. Everybody resorted to speculation, the black market and bribes.

The mood of despair did little for Napoleon's popularity – there was talk that the army had been suffering excessively and some of the men had committed suicide. People were saying that if the Austrians and Russians allied, Napoleon would not be able to overcome them. With so many husbands, sons and lovers away, the court was dreary and sad, with too many women cooped up together, all desperately hoping for news that their loved ones had survived.

Josephine found the Tuileries dispiriting and could hardly bear to preside over the round of court entertainments. Napoleon had no time for complaints. 'If you really wish to please me, you must live exactly as you live when I am in Paris,' he told her. 'Then you were not in the habit of visiting the second rate theatres.'¹² She asked him if she might receive Thérésa, now that she had married the Prince de Chimay and had, in her eyes, shaken off the association with Tallien (they had divorced in 1802). Napoleon sent a furious refusal. 'I find her more despicable than ever.'[13] Josephine needed the support of friendship. She had heard the news of his 'Polish wife'. Although she had little detail, she now understood that he had been dissuading her from joining him because he already had a companion. Her fears about beautiful Polish women had been realised and there was nothing she could do but try to behave as Napoleon wished. She held state receptions and dinners, attended galas at the Opéra and received ambassadors. But the smile on her face was painted. She wrote to Eugène that her heart was 'very sad at the long absence of the Emperor, in spite of his frequent letters'. The following week she wrote that if his absence went on longer, 'I do not know if I will find the courage to bear it.'[14]

Napoleon spent every spare moment organising equipment and accommodation, studying maps and sending out reconnaissance parties. On 11 February 1807, he attacked the Russians at Eylau. He won – but only just, and 20,000 French soldiers lost their lives. When the news of the loss arrived in Paris, the stock market plunged. Although the reports fudged the numbers, rumours of men dying in freezing conditions, stranded so far from home, travelled back anyway. Men began to flee Paris at the thought of another round of conscription into the army. Napoleon was predictably furious at his subjects' lack of faith. 'Never has France been in a better position,' he announced to Fouché. 'I repeat that the Bulletin exaggerates the losses . . . what after all are twenty thousand dead for a great battle?'[15]

His letters slowed and he wrote to Josephine apologising for not being in touch, 'knowing how much you worry'. She would not be allowed to come to him. 'I am just as anxious to see you as you are to see me, and yes, I do know how to do other things besides make war, but duty comes first. All my life, I have sacrificed everything to my destiny – tranquillity, pleasure and happiness.'[16] He wrote instructing her to be cheerful and throw banquets.[17] As he put it, and Josephine knew so well, 'An Empress cannot go where a private individual may.'[18]

Napoleon submitted to the weather and decided to wait until the thaw before progressing. He cheerfully told his wife that he had moved his headquarters to a 'very fine castle' in Finckenstein. 'I have several fireplaces, which is a great comfort to me: getting up often in the night,

I like to see the fire.'[19] He had reason for getting up after dark: Marie Walewska had joined him and he would visit her rooms at night.

Marie attended him patiently, turning to books when he was occupied with military plans. The Sultan of Turkey sent Napoleon thirty fine cashmere shawls, and rather than bundling them up for Josephine, he gave them to Marie. She accepted only one.

Josephine heard through her spies that the 'Polish wife' was at Finckenstein, and she wrote to Napoleon, hinting at her suspicions. 'I don't know what you mean about ladies with whom you say I am connected. I love only my little Josephine, good, sulky and capricious, who knows how to quarrel gracefully as in everything she does; for she is always sweet except when she is jealous, then she becomes a demon . . . But to return to those ladies, I hope the ones you have in mind have pretty pink rosebuds.'[20] Josephine was not fooled. Napoleon was reinvigorated by his new life with Marie. As he wrote to General Murat, his 'amorous drive had never been more vigorous'.[21]

Josephine knew that everyone at court had heard about the 'Polish wife'. The Bonapartes were being more openly rude to her than ever and Letizia refused to dine with her daughter-in-law on Sunday evenings. Rubbing their hands over Eléonore Denuelle's baby son, the Bonapartes felt sure they would trump their enemy.

On the evening of 4 May, four-year-old Napoleon Charles, living with Hortense and Louis in Holland, fell ill, of what was thought to be the croup after a bout of measles (it was more likely pneumonia or acute encephalitis, common consequences of measles). Doctors covered him with leeches and dosed him with powders, but he could not be roused and died in his mother's arms. Hortense was hysterical and could not be separated from his body until she fainted, her hands were prised away and she was carried to her rooms. When she came round, she was screaming with terror for her son and pleading to die. After a few days, she fell into a stupor. Unable to weep, talk or eat, she was paralysed by grief.

Josephine begged Napoleon to allow her to visit her daughter, but he refused. Now he was fondling his gentle Marie, his wife seemed a weak and whining harpy. 'You have had the happiness never to lose a child, but it is one of the pains and conditions attached to our miseries on earth.'[22] She was needed to maintain his status in Paris and he told her she should have more courage. 'I wish that you would be more reasonable,' he wrote, angrily. 'Would you wish to increase my unhappiness?'[23]

Josephine had always tried to make Napoleon the focus of her every waking moment, but now she was too tormented by grief to do so. She knew that the death of Napoleon Charles made her position very insecure. Napoleon had seen Hortense's son as his unofficial heir. With the child dead, Josephine suspected he would be more bent on divorce.

Napoleon had lost patience with her – and also, for the first time, with his beloved Hortense. 'Hortense is not being reasonable, she does not deserve our love since she only loved her child,' he blustered. 'Don't make my misery worse.'[24] He was utterly wrapped up in himself. Talleyrand suggested he mute his vainglorious behaviour in front of a delegation that had come to give him condolences on his loss, but Napoleon was impatient, saying he had 'not the time to waste on feelings and on grieving, like other men'.[25] Still, he did establish a prize of 12,000 francs – a huge sum – for the doctor who could write the best essay on how to cure the croup.

Josephine finally met her daughter in Brussels. Away from the memories of her son, Hortense made a slow recovery. Louis hurried to her, all differences forgotten, and tried to comfort her. Napoleon continued to harangue his wife about Hortense's failure to write to him. 'Why haven't you found her an occupation? Weeping won't do it!'[26] The party travelled on to take the waters at the Pyrenees, where the young husband and wife were kind to each other and Hortense fell pregnant again.

Napoleon commanded that Josephine was not to be told about a second piece of bad news. In June, her mother had died at La Pagerie. She was buried at Trois-Îlets in stately splendour, as befitted the mother of the Empress. Her body descended into the tomb to the ringing sounds of a military salute. The news came to Josephine through her informers and she was sunk into despair at the death of a mother she had not seen for so long. She was shocked when Napoleon decreed that the news should not be made public. He said that a month of mourning would only make the court unhappy and he could not brook anything that might threaten the round of celebrations of his brilliant victories. For Josephine, still pained over the loss of Napoleon Charles, it was another indicator that she was being pushed aside. She was wracked with headaches and found it difficult to sleep.

Napoleon was obsessed by military victory, and saw his battle against Russia as the most important of his career so far. The students at military colleges were called up eighteen months early and the German states were told to supply 100,000 men. His preparations were not in vain. On 14 June 1807, at Friedland, East Prussia, Napoleon and his men fought for two solid days in a snowstorm and gained a great victory, although 30,000 were lost on both sides.

The victorious Emperor sent his faithful courier Jacques Chazal – nicknamed 'Moustache' on account of his impressive facial hair – to give the news to the Empress at Saint-Cloud. Moustache rode so hard that his horse dropped dead in the chateau courtyard. The French, weary of battle and afraid of losing more men, cheered the victory but hoped there would not be further fighting. Napoleon felt aggrieved and convinced himself that only Marie really cared for his victories. He could not resist dictating another letter to Hortense. 'I wish you were more courageous,' read the Queen of Holland, sitting in her damp castle, alone and still grieving. 'Your mother and I had hoped to take up more place in your heart. I won a great victory on June 14.'

The Tsar of Russia requested an armistice and Napoleon agreed. He had no choice – his army was much depleted and men had been fleeing the draft in Paris. Eager to style himself as a wondrous peacemaker, he set off to meet the enemy at Tilsit in Prussia. Still, Josephine was failing to behave as he wished. 'I have received your letter of June 25 and I am hurt to see that you are entirely selfish and that you appear to be uninterested in my military success,' he wrote. 'I too long for our reunion, when destiny shall order it.'[27] Marie Walewska, gentle and biddable, was delighted beyond measure about his victory over the Tsar; by comparison, Josephine seemed like a monster of selfishness.

The plan was that the Tsar and the Emperor would meet on a raft in the River Niemen, near the town of Tilsit. 'Sire, I hate the English as much as you do,' was Tsar Alexander's first greeting to Napoleon. 'In that case, peace is established,' replied the Emperor.

'He is a pleasing-looking, young and kindhearted emperor,' Napoleon wrote to his wife, 'he has more intelligence than people usually give him credit for.'[28] Thirty-year-old Alexander was nervous, afraid of fighting, prone to mood swings and rather stupid. But he was outrageously good-looking and caricaturists painted him being admired by every lady from the Queen of Prussia to Nelson's Lady Hamilton. Practised in the art of deceit, he flattered Napoleon excessively. Dazzled, Napoleon began to ponder the Tsar's sister, twenty-year-old Grand Duchess Catherine. The sixth child and fourth daughter of Tsar Paul, she was vibrant, intelligent and one of the most eligible women in Europe. Catherine was her mother's pet and the Tsar's absolute favourite. He wrote her devoted letters about his affection and consulted her on political matters. If Napoleon seized such a prize, his position in Europe would be secure.

He asked for little from the Tsar other than Russia joining the Continental Blockade, the ban on trade with Britain. But he was cruel to Prussia. The nation would lose half its territory, pay huge reparations and accept a lengthy occupation. Queen Louise threw herself at Napoleon's feet to beg for mercy, but he was not merciful in victory. Instead, he looked down at her with disdain and asked if her dress was made from crêpe or Italian muslin. Her great effort to flatter amused him but did not win her anything. 'The Queen of Prussia is really charming, she wanted to make me her husband,' he wrote to Josephine. 'I didn't take any notice.'[29]

Napoleon, not yet thirty-eight, was all powerful. Britain seemed only a pipsqueak island, with a fading overseas Empire. Russia joining the ban on trade was a blow for Britain since their navy used Russian wood and supplies for their ships. The vast extent of the French Empire now presented a spectacle that rather resembled the 'dominion of the Romans and the conquests of Charlemagne'.[30] The Emperor now had forty-four palaces and Europe was subject to his whims. But even the rulers he scorned – deranged George III, the hated King of Prussia and all the pusillanimous princes – had the one thing he did not: a legitimate heir. As he later said at St Helena, he returned 'so certain of his destiny' that he knew divorce was inevitable.[31]

19

'Cold and often embarrassed'

'The Emperor since his return from campaign has behaved toward his wife in a cold and often embarrassed manner,' wrote the diplomat Prince von Metternich gleefully to Vienna. 'They do not share a bedroom. Many of his daily habits have changed.' Napoleon was preoccupied with his own brilliance, resentful of Josephine for not having sufficiently celebrated his victories – and thinking of a son.

His time with Marie Walewska had proved to him that he could indeed live with another woman in a domestic setting. He threw a magnificent party for his thirty-eighth birthday and began picking out ladies of the court for affairs. Believing they might have a chance to seize position, the women jostled for his affections more intensely than ever. But Napoleon wished his next wife to be a royal princess, with money, cachet and blue blood. Marriage to an Austrian or a Russian would make an alliance between his two enemies much less likely and a foreign princess would give him the regal status he craved, as well as the true grandeur that he felt the Tuileries lacked. The courtiers turned secretively to ponder a marriage. Talleyrand, Josephine's long-trusted ally, was now working against her. Her enemies' reasons were simple: as Fouché put it, 'Napoleon's brothers are disgracefully incompetent and we must prevent the return of the Bourbons.'[1] Lists were drawn up of possible royal brides and ambassadors competed to push the advantage of their own princesses, showing lovely miniatures and talking of sweet temper, grace, health and accomplishments. Talleyrand pushed for an Austrian princess, Fouché voted for Grand Duchess Catherine of Russia.

Josephine worried about her fate. 'If they should succeed in separating me from him, it is not the loss of rank I should regret,' she wrote to Eugène, 'sooner or later he would discover that those who surround him are more interested in themselves than in him and he would know how he has been deceived.'[2] Eugène replied that he had heard much about divorce in Munich and Paris, but felt sure that the Emperor would treat her kindly. 'He must treat you well, give you an adequate settlement and let you live in Italy with your children,' he replied. 'If the Emperor wishes to have children who are truly his there is no other way.'

After Mass one Sunday Fouché told Josephine that she should begin the 'inevitable sacrifice' of a divorce and allow Napoleon to have a legitimate son. Josephine was prepared. 'Did the Emperor direct you to tell me this?' The minister refused to answer and she responded with dignity. 'I see my link with the Emperor as written in the record of the highest destinies. I will never discuss the matter with anyone but him and I will never do anything without his orders.' She went straight to Napoleon and – bravely – demanded if he had directed his minister to speak. The Emperor declined all knowledge. 'You know very well I could not live without you,' he said. He then asked her what she thought of the proposal and whether she might 'take the initiative to help him make the sacrifice if he found it necessary'. Josephine told him she would not. 'Our joint destiny has been too extraordinary not to have been decided by Providence. Only you must decide my fate.'[3] She had thought carefully about what she would say. 'I am too afraid of bringing us both bad luck if, of my own accord, I should separate my life from yours.' It was a brilliant strategy. Napoleon seriously believed she was his good-luck charm and he dreaded losing his magic touch. He burst into tears and they clutched each other passionately. He returned to her bed once more.

Even though Napoleon could still fall back into Josephine's arms, he was angry about what he saw as her excessive grief over Napoleon Charles. When he first saw Hortense after his return, he lost patience. She was nervous and emaciated, tears glimmering in her eyes. 'Come, come, stop this childishness. You have wept enough over your son. It is becoming ridiculous . . . Be gay, enjoy the pleasures of your age and don't let me see any more tears.'⁴ He soon told her that he would not make her second child, Napoleon Louis, his heir, saying that would only prove the dreadful rumours that her first child had been sired by him. Hortense wept at his words and Napoleon was predictably angry. Once upon a time, he would have forgiven Hortense anything.

He found it easy to consider the reasons for a divorce when he was apart from Josephine – and ask his ministers to do his dirty work for him. When he saw her again, he could not help loving her. He watched her presiding gracefully over the court and doubted anyone could be a more befitting consort. 'I would be giving up all the charm she had brought to my private life,' he said to Talleyrand. 'She adjusts her habits to mine and understands me perfectly.' And even though he took his sexual pleasure elsewhere, he still needed her. 'I truly loved her, although I didn't respect her,' he said on St Helena. 'She was a liar and a spend-thrift but she had something that was irresistible. She was a woman to her very fingertips.'⁵

Although he could see the benefit in allying with Russia and marrying a Grand Duchess, his people might see it as betraying his duty to France. Most of all, there was no guarantee he could have a child with another woman. One police report from December of 1807 noted that the women of high society were saying that 'the Empress's sterility is not her fault, that the Emperor has never had any children; that his majesty's relations with several women have never borne fruit but as soon as these ladies were married, they became pregnant'.⁶

Napoleon was not in a position to do anything rash. His popularity was at its lowest ebb. The people were distressed by the huge losses of men in the recent wars. Theatres stopped the custom of the reading out of army bulletins because too many people screamed and fainted when they heard the news of the fatalities.

Men were doing everything they could to dodge conscription and, unlike in previous years, their families and friends did everything they could to support them. Some fled their homes, others were so desperate that they purposely caught syphilis or cut off one of their limbs. Many of those who did accept the draft tried to desert. There were huge riots protesting against conscription. If the economy had been strong, the people would have been more forgiving, but the wars in the East had been expensive and the ban on trade with Britain had wrought a terrible toll. The French, so proud of their country and so delighted by their military strength, were beginning to curse their Emperor. One in ten of all conscripts had deserted.

Napoleon's response to the resistance was to put plans to divorce on hold and clamp down hard on his people's remaining freedoms. He weakened the bodies left over from the Consulate. The Legislative Body would meet only a few weeks a year and the Council of State would simply be a listening board for his lengthy monologues. He had long controlled the content of the newspapers; now he suppressed all but four journals. He wished to go further – surely, he said, all the people needed were two papers: the official *Moniteur* and the *Journal des Dames* for the ladies. Spies were everywhere, intellectuals were censored and the press were firmly told not to mention politics. The man who had once tried to write a romantic novel now believed that the arts could undermine the state. 'You can make politics by talking literature, morality, art, anything in the world,' he said.[7] The Emperor of the Republic was now in the position of a military dictator.

Vainglorious and obsessed with outdoing Russia, Napoleon had decided that his entire court would move to the hunting chateau of Fontainebleau in the winter. While in Prussia, he had ordered the redecoration of the palace by his cherished Percier and Fontaine. No expense was spared: silk wall coverings, heavy furniture, tapestries and carvings. The throne room was entirely redecorated to promote the splendour of the Empire. Napoleon wished to take the court hunting as a way to recall and outdo the *Ancien Régime*. Unlike the Bourbon kings, he was poor at shooting and struggled even to hit Josephine's slow swans at Malmaison.

Josephine had once followed the hunt, as a young woman looking for protectors, but the Fontainebleau she returned to as an Empress was very different. One thousand two hundred people descended on Fontainebleau in the autumn, including all the Bonapartes and the entire Ministry of Foreign Affairs. Napoleon decreed that a hunt must take place three times a week, even in heavy rain. All the nobles and their households had their own hunting colours for riding coats – Josephine's was purple, and Napoleon ordered that Hortense put aside her mourning dress and wear blue and silver. The men would go on ahead to hunt, and then Josephine, unhappily resplendent in purple, would lead the trail of ladies in open barouches before presiding over the hunt breakfast. As a younger woman, she had found hunting exhilarating, but now she was cast down by the cruelty of it and hated the ritual her husband had imposed.

She was ill at ease, and the entire court was barely more cheerful. People found it hard to celebrate with the Emperor after so many military losses. Napoleon complained to Talleyrand in frustration that the court 'refused to be amused and sat around looking tired and sad with long faces'. As he saw it, he had given them the marvellous treat of Fontainebleau, and they repaid him with melancholy. He set up lavish entertainments celebrating his victories and decreed that every night would see a splendid ball in one of the princely apartments, conducted just as it had been in the Bourbon days. Still, his courtiers sat unhappily in their heavy robes. But it was his own behaviour that was reflected back at him. Paranoid about plots and whispers, he had become so remote that, according to Madame de Rémusat, 'no one could reach the Emperor except Josephine'. In the evenings he would dine with her, and then expect the entire court to assemble in the room designated for the ball. Josephine would enter and take her place, then a deathly silence fell until Napoleon entered, seated himself next to the Empress and 'with a forbidding expression' watched his courtiers dance. Nothing, recalled Laure Junot, could describe 'the magnificence, the magical luxury that now surrounded the imperial couple' – and the contrast between it and their downcast mood.

Once, Josephine had been able to lull hundreds of people into feelings of cheerful ease. Now she was unhappy and nervous, constantly sending her ladies to monitor the rumours about Napoleon's desire to divorce her. She could see that some courtiers were distancing themselves from her in preparation for a new Empress. She tried to obey Napoleon in everything.

At the end of the year, Napoleon's youngest brother, Jérôme, was made the King of Westphalia, with a country made for him out of parts of Prussia, Hesse and Brunswick. Princess Catherine of Württemberg was brought over at speed to marry him in a grand ceremony at court. One of the guests, a handsome widower, Crown Prince Frederick Louis of Mecklenburg-Strelitz, was captivated by Josephine, but she was too afraid of offending Napoleon to respond to his blandishments. Still, while Napoleon was away she went to the theatre with the Crown Prince. Napoleon was infuriated, declaring his wife a second Marie Antoinette and demanding his rival leave Paris within two days. Jérôme was a hopeless king, imposing huge taxes, seducing every woman in sight and plunging his treasury into debt.

The Bonapartes were as intent as ever on pushing Napoleon towards a divorce. But this only persuaded him to keep his wife – his family caused him endless distress and Josephine's presence soothed him. His beautiful younger sister Caroline Murat began an intense affair with the debonair General Junot. Only twenty-four, she was as hardened in her quest for power as her siblings. Annoyed that her husband had not been given a kingdom, her aim was to get Junot's support in her quest to depose her brother and put her husband in his place. Eventually, the affair soured and Caroline turned to the wily Austrian diplomat, Count Metternich. He also seduced Junot's wife, Laure, at around the same time, and when Caroline told her former lover, he set upon Laure with a pair of scissors and nearly killed her. With Jérôme behaving like a seducing satyr, Pauline taking a string of lovers and the Murats prompting crimes of passion, it was hardly surprising that Napoleon fled to the calm of Josephine's room.

Although Hortense was pregnant with her third child, her marriage was in an unhappy state. The brief reconciliation after Napoleon Charles's death forgotten, Louis treated her cruelly and she was losing her looks thanks to her sufferings. Napoleon tried to intervene. 'A King commands and seeks no one's counsel,' he wrote to his brother. 'In your domestic life you should display the paternal and effeminate character you show toward your government, and toward the government the severity you show your wife.'[8] Louis did not listen. He knew that the wind was blowing towards a divorce and he resented being stuck with the daughter of Josephine.

Napoleon was infuriating his ministers with his indecision over the divorce. On the one hand was a son, a royal liaison and a legacy. On the other was his Josephine, to whom he felt he owed respect for her long years of marriage to him and her support for his endeavours when everybody else saw him as a Corsican upstart. It would help if he could decide on his chosen fiancée, but he could not; instead, he read reports of various royal ladies and found none particularly engaging. At the end of the year, he travelled to Italy for a triumphal progress. He made his way without Josephine, carrying a list of twenty eligible princesses.

Josephine wrote to her son of her worries. 'My own defence is to live a blameless life. I no longer go out, I have no pleasures.' She blamed the grandeur. 'How unhappy do thrones make people, my dear Eugène!' she wrote. 'I would resign mine tomorrow, without any pain. For me the love of the Emperor is everything. If I should lose that, I would have little regret about anything else.'[9] To her deep distress, she heard that Napoleon had brought Marie over from Warsaw and installed her in a house on the Quai Voltaire. There, he visited her secretly and loved to play a game in which they disguised themselves as a bourgeois couple and he engaged the local shopkeepers in chat about the devilish Bonaparte. Josephine attempted to distract her husband by throwing one of her ladies-in-waiting in his way. He was happy to dally with a new woman, but he still visited Marie. Late at night, leaving Josephine alone, his carriage left the palace for the townhouse of the beautiful Polish girl with golden hair.

One evening in March 1808, Josephine was about to enter the Yellow Salon when she received word that Napoleon was ill. She hurried to his apartments and found him in court dress, prostrate in bed, wracked by stomach pain and weeping hysterically. She sat beside him and he pulled her into his arms. 'My poor Josephine, I can't possibly leave you,' he wailed. He demanded she get into bed with him and they made passionate love. She spent the night with him, although both were restless and slept poorly. That morning, she later found out, he had resolved on a divorce – but the thought of it was so painful it had made him ill. 'Why can't the devil of a man make up his mind?' cried Talleyrand when he heard the news of the reconciliation.

In March 1808, King Charles IV of Spain abdicated after an uprising and allowed his son to take his place. He hated his son, who had tried to depose him the previous year. In April he appealed to Napoleon for help – an unwise move. Napoleon sent Marie Waleswka home and commanded the entire Spanish royal family to meet him in Bayonne, on the French side of the Pyrenees. Once there, he sent for Josephine, for he required her gentle diplomacy to charm the Spanish party of the King, the Crown Prince, the Queen and the Prime Minister, who was both the King's favourite and said to be the Queen's lover. Napoleon had no desire to help them; instead he wished to persuade them into accepting his 'protection'.

Josephine played the role of gracious hostess, befriending the Queen and lending her clothes and jewels. A second rebellion broke out in

Madrid and Marshal Murat and his men suppressed it with savagery. Napoleon informed Charles IV that only he could save his life, and the King agreed to give the throne to the Emperor. Napoleon decreed Joseph Bonaparte would be crowned, and sent the Spanish royals to live under luxurious arrest. He then spent the last days in Bayonne relaxing with Josephine, pleased with a job well done. They ran hand in hand along the beach and swam in the sea. He played his usual tricks, throwing her shoes into the water and pushing her over in the sand. They were like young lovers on honeymoon.

On the way back to Saint-Cloud, Josephine performed as the Empress, receiving gifts, sitting as guest of honour at banquets and listening to speeches. Almost as soon as they reached the palace, Napoleon heard that there had been further uprisings in Spain and Joseph had fled to the frontier rather than be crowned. French troops had been defeated at Bailen in Spain. The rout of the seemingly invincible French troops was shocking news for all Europe, and Napoleon knew it would prompt Austria to attack. Josephine paid much more attention to the news that Hortense had given birth to a third son, Charles Louis, on 20 April. She hoped that another son might be a hold over Napoleon's heart.

In September, Napoleon departed to meet the Tsar in Germany. Before he left, he and Josephine played 'prisoner's base' with a few courtiers, a game in which players had to run to base before another player spotted them. Footmen with torches lit the Emperor and Empress running around in their finery in the dark, until Napoleon swept Josephine away, despite the protests of the others. His playfulness made her feel more secure. 'For the last six months he has been simply perfect to me,' she wrote to Eugène. 'So when I saw him leave this morning, it was with sadness at the parting but not concern about the future.'[10] But as soon as she left the room, courtiers again began gossiping about divorce. As everybody knew, before he departed the Emperor had ordered a diadem in Paris for a new Empress.

'I wish the Emperor Alexander to be dazzled by the spectacle of my power,' Napoleon decreed. He ordered all his German vassal kings and princes to attend his meeting with the Tsar at Erfurt, and adorned the palace in incredible style with paintings and ornaments sent from Paris. He brought French chefs to tend to the palates of the Russians, and the Comédie-Française, including Talma, its star, came to entertain them. Josephine, hitherto the great display of Napoleon's power, was absent.

There was good reason; he wished to awe the Tsar into allowing him his sister's hand in marriage. He saw himself as doing a great act for his country. 'It would be a real sacrifice for me. I love Josephine; I will never be happier with anyone else, but my family and Talleyrand and Fouché and all the politicians insist upon it in the name of France.'[11]

After his first meeting with Napoleon in Tilsit the previous year, the Tsar had arrived back in St Petersburg to find his family and ministers furious at his gesture of peace towards the Emperor. They were outraged by the harsh strictures imposed on Prussia and resented Napoleon's demand that any French citizen who had taken exile in Russia should be expelled. When the Tsar saw his darling sister again, he was even more dubious about the marriage. As he well knew, his mother, the Dowager Empress, would revile the idea of her beloved Catherine becoming the wife of the Emperor of France. Marriage to a divorcé was scandalous, Napoleon was a commoner and the merciless killer of so many Russian men, as well as the cruel aggressor of Prussia.

When the Tsar arrived in Erfurt, he was determined not to be beguiled by Napoleon. He enjoyed the daily hunting parties, receptions and balls, but offered no concessions. Napoleon made every effort to please, even letting his rival shine on the dance floor. 'The Emperor Alexander dances, but not I. Forty years are after all, forty years,' he wrote to Josephine.[12] The Emperor begged, promised and bowed low for the hope of the Grand Duchess's hand. 'I am very busy,' Napoleon told his wife. 'Conversations which last whole days and which do not improve my cold. Still all goes well. I am pleased with Alexander, he ought to be with me. If he were a woman, I think I would make him my mistress.'[13]

The Emperor's cause was actively undermined by Talleyrand, who was taking money from Austria to push its interests. On a personal level, he resented the forced marriage to his mistress Catherine Grand, whom he did not love. Politically, he had come to fear Napoleon's wild military ambition and believed that Europe could not be at peace if he were allowed to continue unchecked. Behind Napoleon's back, Talleyrand suggested to the Tsar that an alliance with Austria would give him more power and independence and stonewall Napoleon's rampant desire for territory.

Napoleon decided to put his cards on the table. 'Use any argument you like,' he told Talleyrand, begging his minister to persuade Alexander to hand over his sister. 'Tell him I will agree with him on any of his plans for the partition of Turkey.' The Tsar's spies were aware that no movements had been made towards a divorce, and Alexander used the knowledge to play for time. He told Napoleon he would happily give his consent, but that of another was needed – meaning Josephine. By remaining uncommitted, he got everything he wanted. In return for a promise to assist him if Austria declared war on France, Napoleon told him that he would not intervene if Russia invaded Finland or Turkey, and that the Tsar could do as he wished with Poland. Marie Walewska's sacrifice had been worthless.

Napoleon returned home to his wife and was embarrassed with her. She was suspicious of his actions but was too afraid to ask questions. After only ten days, he departed for Spain, asking her for a good-luck kiss. She pleaded with him, 'Will you never stop making war?' He replied evasively and refused to let her come too. 'It is not I who direct the course of events, I only obey them.' When she wrote to him of her concerns that Austria was growing more powerful, he was dismissive. 'You are in a black mood of depression,' he said. 'Austria will not make war on me . . . nor will Russia desert us. People in Paris are mad! Things are going splendidly here.'[14]

Napoleon was reaching a new low in popularity. The public were furious when they heard that he wished his armies to return to Spain to force the installation of his brother as King Joseph I. It seemed as if their men were being sent to die merely to give his brother a throne. Riots against conscription soared again, Napoleon was caricatured and detested, and courtiers considered moving their loyalties elsewhere. The vassal states were rebelling and Austria was growing braver.

He needed a huge army to subdue Spain, but he had no way of transporting supplies as the roads were so poor over the Pyrenees. He did not care and forced his men to march. He managed to drag them to Madrid, but when he heard that the Austrians were re-arming he immediately turned back. Even worse, more news came by courier – and through spies to every ambassador in Europe – that Talleyrand and Fouché, formerly mortal rivals, had been seen in open discussion in the Tuileries. They declared they were debating a provisional government in case Napoleon died. In fact, they had plans to overthrow him.

Napoleon returned to the Tuileries and screamed abuse in public at Talleyrand for three hours. 'You are nothing but shit in a silk stocking!'

he ranted. His minister did not reply. After the tirade, Talleyrand went to the Austrian ambassador and arranged to continue work for him – at a price of one million francs. Napoleon turned his attention to Fouché and told him that he wished to call up another half million men. Fouché warned him that this would be unwise. France was already at breaking point with a million men in the army – any more might push the people into a concerted riot against Napoleon.

The Emperor finally recognised that his position was desperately insecure. He also had disappointing news from Russia. Grand Duchess Catherine was engaged to the Duke of Oldenburg. He resolved to retain his wife. 'This year is an inopportune time to shock public opinion by repudiating the popular Empress. Already I am not loved. She is a link between me and many people, and she is responsible for attaching a part of Paris society to me which would then leave me.'[15]

The scales were falling from the eyes of the French. Napoleon, it seemed, had brought them nothing but warfare and suffering.

Austria was convinced that Napoleon was weak, his army overextended and lacking support at home. In April 1809, he heard that Austria had invaded Bavaria, a kingdom he considered a vassal, and decided on immediate action. He tried to leave without Josephine, but she heard the sounds of departure and dashed down the steps in her night gown, weeping as she threw herself into his carriage. Napoleon did not have the heart to send her away. He put his coat over her shoulders and ordered her luggage to be sent on later. Her victory was a hollow one. He left her in the palace at Strasbourg and sent her curt letters from the front. Hortense came to stay and brought her second child, Louis Napoleon, and the baby, Charles Louis. But it was little consolation. Josephine's only hope was that the Emperor was too distracted by battle to divorce her. 'I have only one passion, only one mistress – France,' Napoleon declared. 'I sleep with her, she never lets me down, she pours out her blood and her treasure; if I need 500,000 men, she gives them to me.'[16] But the French had fled his army and it was made up of men from the occupied states, the poor and the desperate. The old morale and strength of purpose were gone.

The Emperor had initial success and pushed on to Vienna. Once more, he moved into the Schönbrunn Palace and hoped for word from the Tsar. The two sides met in battle at Essling, not far from Vienna, and the result was a stalemate, although claimed by the Austrians as a victory. Both sides lost over 20,000 men. The news of the failed battle reached Paris and the stock market plunged again. The French no longer believed themselves invincible. They knew that one more defeat would bring the whole house of cards tumbling down as conquered states gained the courage to fight back and expel the French armies that occupied them.

In June, Napoleon encouraged Josephine to travel to Plombières and then return to Malmaison. She lived quietly. He did not write to her often and there were no letters demanding that she preside over court balls or visit the Opéra. She retreated to her flowers and plants and sank into despair.

Napoleon sent for reinforcements and, six weeks later, routed the Austrians at the Battle of Wagram. Fifty thousand men were killed. Napoleon returned to Schönbrunn the victor and set his ministers drafting a treaty with Austria. Marie Walewska, ever dutiful, wrote to Napoleon after the victory and asked to join him. 'Yes, come to Vienna,' he replied. 'I would like to give you further proof of the tender friendship I feel for you.'[17] He meant to offer her more than friendship. As soon as she arrived, he began spending every afternoon with her. At the beginning of September, Marie was confirmed as pregnant.

Josephine was doomed.

Marie was the first of Napoleon's mistresses whom he was sure had been entirely faithful to him. Unlike Eléonore Denuelle, she truly loved him and there had been no gentlemen callers. Napoleon was now certain that he could father a child. Marie's pregnancy secured his lasting affection for her, and meant the end of her three-year period as his mistress. As he told Lucien, 'Naturally I would prefer to have my mistress crowned, but I must be allied with sovereigns.'[18] He left Vienna resolved to divorce his wife and find a royal to marry.

Josephine was still at Malmaison when she received the news about Marie's pregnancy. It seemed to her like an avalanche of bad news, for the British had conquered Martinique and shed blood on the island. To her further distress, she heard that Pope Pius VII had been arrested for refusing to turn British ships away from the ports of Rome. The Pope had excommunicated the Emperor and refused to give up his temporal power. In return, he was bundled roughly into a carriage and taken from the Vatican to a house controlled by Napoleon in northern Italy.

Josephine knew there was nothing to save her. Excommunicated, Napoleon would care even less about breaking the blessing of his marriage or Josephine's coronation. Under French law, only the Pope could annul a royal marriage, but Napoleon clearly cared nothing for such a law. He needed a son to stay the ambitions of his family. And he no longer saw her as his talisman. The good luck she brought had dissipated – and perhaps someone else might grant him more. Laure Junot went to visit her with her daughter, and Josephine confessed she 'truly suffered' at the sight of the child. 'I know I will be shamefully dismissed from the bed of the man who crowned me, but God is my witness that I love him more than my life and much more than the throne.'[19] She no doubt hoped that the well-connected Laure would pass on such information at court. But there was little she could do to save herself. Napoleon was puffed up with pride at his mistress's pregnancy and convinced that a marriage could change his fortunes. He ordered his ambassador in St Petersburg to ascertain whether fifteen-year-old Grand Duchess Anna, the youngest sister of the Tsar, was physically ready to bear children. He wrote, reiterating that the Tsar could do as he wished with Poland, saying that the words 'Poland' and 'Polish' should be 'obliterated not only from any transaction but from history itself'.[20] Poor Marie, who had given up everything for him, was told to go back to her husband, heavy with the Emperor's child.

If Grand Duchess Anna was deemed too young, Napoleon had a second choice. Metternich in Paris had been intimating the excellence of seventeen-year-old Marie Louise of Austria, daughter of Francis I. She spoke good French and she was biddable, healthy and definitely ready for motherhood.

Napoleon wrote to Josephine saying that he was leaving Munich and would be at Fontainebleau on 26 or 27 October, and she should meet him there.[21] Unfortunately, the courier only reached her on the morning of the 26th, and when she arrived that evening, Napoleon was already waiting for her. She entered his study to greet him. He looked up briefly from his work and said, 'Ah, here at last?' She retired to her rooms – only to see that the door between her room and his had been sealed. The order, she was told, had come from the Emperor himself.

He was still unable to make the final break. Over the next distressing weeks, he dined with Josephine, but only briefly and she could not speak to him because there was always a gloating Bonaparte sibling sitting between them. In the evenings, Pauline threw him parties full of beautiful Italian women, but she did not invite Josephine. If Josephine said anything, he lost his temper. 'There was no more tenderness, no more consideration for my mother,' Hortense recalled. 'He became unjust, he tormented her.' In the old days Josephine had awaited Napoleon's night-time tap on her salon door with pleasure, for it was his request for her to read to him, soothe him or come to his bed.

In November 1809, the thought of such a tap pitched her into violent palpitations, breathlessness and feelings of dread. She could not bear 'to hear the confirmation of what she most dreaded to learn'.[22] The Emperor, able to batter countries into submission and send hundreds of thousands of men to their death, could not tell his wife he wished to divorce. Napoleon asked Hortense to tell her mother that the marriage was over, explaining it would 'remove a heavy burden from my heart' if she did so.[23] She said she could not. Eugène also refused.

Josephine saw all around her the evidence of her fate. The ladies of the court were openly dismissive of her, even daring to sit in her presence. The Bonapartes laughed in her face. She behaved with dignity, holding tight to her last days as Empress.

On 27 November, the court moved from Fontainebleau to Paris. Napoleon sent a telegram to Eugène asking him to join them immediately. There was urgent business he required completed before the end of the year.

20

'Like a wounded soldier'

On the evening of Thursday 30 November 1809, Josephine and Napoleon shared a miserable dinner. She struggled not to cry and could eat nothing. According to the Comte de Beausset, the palace prefect who was attending them, she looked the 'image of sadness and despair'. Napoleon's only words were, 'What time is it?' Before the Comte had a chance to reply, he rose from the table. Josephine followed him, her handkerchief over her mouth. The coffee arrived and the tray was offered to Josephine, so she could perform her task of pouring it for her husband. Instead, he took the tray, poured the coffee into his cup and added the sugar, staring all the time at his wife. She gazed back in horror. He drank down the coffee, handed the tray to the page and dismissed the Comte, shutting the door behind him. 'I saw in the expression of his countenance what was passing in his mind, and I knew that my hour was come,' Josephine said.

> He stepped up to me – he was trembling, and I shuddered; he took my hand, pressed it to his heart, and after gazing at me for a few moments in silence he uttered these fatal words: 'Josephine! my dear Josephine! You know how I have loved you! . . . To you, to you alone, I owe the only moments of happiness I have tasted in this world. But, Josephine, my destiny is not to be controlled by my will. My dearest affections must yield to the interests of France.'[1]

She fell into hysteria and began to cry out. The Emperor opened the door and the Comte saw her lying on the floor in tears. 'I seemed to lose my reason,' she later recalled. As Napoleon told him, he must help get Josephine to her chambers, alerting no one. The two men bundled the Empress down the stairs, the Comte stumbling over his sword, Napoleon too agitated to hold the candle still. In a state of nerves, almost weeping and breathless with emotion, he poured out his heart. Fortunately, since the Comte was a renowned gossip, Napoleon was near incoherent, 'National welfare,' he panted, 'violence to my heart . . . political necessity . . . took me by surprise . . . her daughter was to have prepared her' was all that the Comte could make out from the torrent of emotion.

Josephine kept up the tears and hysteria all the way down the stairs, except for one moment. She put her head close to the Comte and hissed, 'You are holding me too tightly.' The pair dropped her, none too gently, on the bed and Napoleon pulled the bell for her ladies to come. He then made a hasty exit. Josephine passed a night of despair and misery. The humiliation of the preceding days had been awful, the anticipation painful, but receiving the news itself was not a relief. 'With what eyes do courtiers look upon a repudiated wife! I was in a state of vague uncertainty worse than death until the fatal day when he at length avowed to me what I had long before read in his looks!'[2]

Napoleon summoned Hortense and told her to go to her mother. 'Nothing will make me go back on it, neither tears nor entreaties,' he cried. Hortense responded with the calm dignity that he had always esteemed. 'You are the master, Sire. No one will oppose you. If your happiness requires it, that is enough,' she said. 'She will submit and we will all go away, taking the memory of your kindness with us.' Napoleon looked at her in shock. He could barely speak. 'What! You are all going to leave me?' he cried. 'You are going to desert me? Then you don't care for me any more?' He had not truly accepted that he might never see them again. 'We cannot live near you any more,' said Hortense, with grace. 'It is a sacrifice that has to be made and we will make it.'[3]

Eugène arrived. 'We will all go away quietly,' he said. He told the weeping Napoleon that his first loyalty was to his mother. Devastated at the thought of losing all three, the Emperor repined that Josephine should stay at court and even said the divorce should be stopped. Eugène disagreed, for 'what was in his mind being known to us, the

Empress could not live happily with him'. Napoleon begged him to accept the Kingdom of Italy, but Eugène refused – he did not wish to be rewarded for his mother's despair.

'Alas! I had good reason to fear ever becoming an Empress!' Josephine cried.[4] The princely kings and vassals of Germany were arriving for a celebration of Napoleon's Austrian victories. Every night she had to smile at receptions and dinners attended by hundreds, regard military performances, and host the ladies at her court. In order to prepare the ground for the divorce, Napoleon decreed she must come to all official functions alone. She attended the fifth anniversary of the coronation, but did not travel to Paris with Napoleon or sit by his side in the cathedral. At the gala banquet that evening, the Emperor was escorted by one of his sisters. Josephine walked alone to the dais and sat quickly, her legs almost collapsing beneath her, barely able to smile in the face of her humiliation.

She kept her head high, but she knew that Napoleon was planning the ceremony of the divorce. She was at her most dignified in the final weeks of her role as Empress. Napoleon was less so, often in tears, declaring himself the plaything of fate, cruelly treated by his destiny – and yet attempting to take the marriage certificate from her. Many were on her side, most of all the shopkeepers and fine tradesmen of Paris. Josephine's wild spending had single-handedly supported many of the city's luxury goods makers.

Napoleon wished the ceremony of the divorce to be a court occasion, and all the courtiers jostled for an invitation and fretted over what to wear. Josephine feigned calm. The night before, when many were openly ignoring her, she gave a polite bow to all those who came up to acknowledge her. 'I doubt,' wrote Pasquier, the future chancellor, 'whether any woman could have acted with such perfect grace and tact.'

The night of the divorce ceremony was the grandest social occasion the court had seen for months. On 14 December, everyone flocked to the throne room, resplendent in jewels and finery. The Bonapartes, as Hortense noted, 'betrayed their joy by their air of satisfaction and triumph'.[5]

Josephine entered in a plain white gown, supported by Hortense. Napoleon was waiting for her, trembling so hard that his valet thought he might faint. The Emperor proclaimed the divorce. 'God only knows what this resolve has cost my heart,' he said. 'But there is no sacrifice beyond my courage if it is in the best interests of France . . . I have only gratitude to express for the devotion and tenderness of my well-beloved wife. She has adorned thirteen years of my life, the memory thereof will remain forever engraved on my heart.' He wept as he pronounced that he would wish her to retain the privileges of Empress.

It was Josephine's turn to speak. All the eyes of the court were upon her. 'With the permission of my dear and august husband, I proudly offer him the greatest proof of attachment and devotion ever given a husband on this earth.' She could not go on. Her words choked her and for the first time her courage failed her. After a minute of silence, she handed the speech to one of her attendants to complete. He too was tearful. 'The Emperor will always be my dearest love,' he said. 'I know how much this act, demanded by politics and wider interests, has crushed his heart.'

Napoleon, Josephine and members of the family signed the record of proceedings. Then, in front of everyone, Napoleon kissed Josephine, took her by the hand and led her to the apartments. Hortense battled to control her tears. Eugène fainted as soon as he left the throne room. He later referred to the time of the divorce as 'the most dreadful moment of my life'.[6]

Josephine was still trying to hold on to her old life. That night, her hair untidy, her face in distress, she arrived in Napoleon's bedroom. She fell on the bed, put her arms around him and caressed him. He pressed her to him. 'Allons, dear Josephine. I will always be your friend.' They wept together, and then he prompted her to leave. She spent the night alone.

Now the deed was done Napoleon offered a generous settlement. He said she would keep the title of Empress, retain Malmaison, be given the Elysée Palace in Paris, and an allowance of three million francs in gold. He had thought carefully about her household: she was to have thirty-six attendants, including nine ladies-in-waiting, four ladies of the bedchamber, chamberlains, a doctor and a knight of honour. But he worried that her presence in Paris would be unsettling to the people and the court. When he asked her to consider living in Italy she was horrified. He did not force the matter. Napoleon ordered her a Sèvres dinner service as a gift and gave her 4000 livres to 'do as much planting as you like' at Malmaison.[7] He pored over the inventory of her belongings, including a fourteen-page description of her wardrobe – ten pages of court dresses, 280 pairs of shoes, right down to chemises and camisoles and nightgowns. He did not demand from her any of the gifts he had given her, most notably the art collection at Malmaison. Josephine kept her spoils of war.

As quitting lovers tend to do, Napoleon pretended to himself that things could stay the same. He fussed over her title and asked archivists to search the previous royal records for questions of how to treat a divorced empress – which, of course, no previous court had entertained. He made the decision that Josephine would sit on the right of his throne and his new wife would be positioned on the left.

'I have drawn out the path that I must follow and I will not stray from it,' Josephine wrote. 'The arts and botany will be my occupations.'[8] Her departure from the Tuileries was a lengthy operation of packing her gowns, ornaments, books, pets and other belongings into carriages. On the morning after the ceremony, Napoleon came to embrace her and then hurried off, claiming he had to see to his duties. Accompanied by Hortense, the fallen Empress was taken in the early afternoon rain to Malmaison, with no Emperor to see her go. Napoleon went straight to Versailles and shut himself away in the Grand Trianon, far from his former wife. He tried to distract himself from grief by rehanging every painting. He was not so broken, however, to forget to demand Josephine's marriage certificate. She declined to give it to him.

'We were sad and silent all the way to Malmaison,' recalled Hortense. 'Her heart was heavy as she entered this place she loved so much.'[9] The next day, Josephine walked around the grounds in tears. Napoleon, in the Trianon, was equally despairing and finally could bear it no longer. He drove to Malmaison and he and Josephine walked hand in hand in the rain. Careful to keep up appearances, as he did not want any spies reporting to foreign courts that he still had relations with his wife, he did not enter the house or embrace her but told her of his distress and described to her how lonely he was dining on his own. That evening, he wrote to her, telling her to feel a courage he could not.

My dear, I found you today weaker than you ought to be. You have shown courage; it is necessary that you should keep it up and not subside into sadness. You must be contented and take special care of your health, which is so precious to me. If you are attached to me, and if you love me, you should show strength of mind and force yourself to be happy.[10]

However, he also sent her letters about his unhappiness without her. Claire de Rémusat begged her husband to ask the Emperor to 'moderate his expressions of regret'. Josephine was crying so hard that her eyesight was troubled: soon she could not bear any bright light and her vision was failing.

On 9 January 1810, the religious marriage between Napoleon and Josephine was declared void, on the basis that it had not been properly witnessed nor had the parish priest been present and Napoleon's consent had not been fully obtained. The last was a provision in the law for young girls forced into marriage against their will, not a great general on the brink of declaring himself ruler of all France. They were both now free, but the Emperor still could not put his former wife aside. He noted that there were few other visitors but him at Malmaison and promptly went around his court, asking everyone if they had visited the Empress. In response, carriages rumbled off full of courtiers eager to pay their respects to Josephine. Laure Junot visited and saw the drawing room, billiard room and gallery thronged with people. To reach Josephine in her gallery, guests had to pass through an antechamber filled with thirty footmen and a salon of four valets with swords, as well as ladies and attendants.[11] Sitting by the fireplace, under a portrait of Napoleon, she wore a simple dress and a green hood, which she drew over her face when she needed to hide her tears.

She kept Napoleon's study exactly as it had always been. She dusted it herself daily and showed her visitors everything – even the old armchair that he had cut with his penknife. She kept, as one put it, 'a veritable cult of the Emperor' and would not allow so much as a chair to be moved. It was a shrine to him; everything was left as it was when he had last been there, right down to a book of history, open at the page he had been reading.[12] His bed was still there, his coat of arms hung on the walls and items of his clothing were scattered around, just as if he was about to return. She always wore full dress, in case Napoleon arrived.

Josephine could not be consoled. 'Sometimes it seems as if I am dead and all that remains is a sort of faint sensation of knowing that I no longer exist.' Napoleon chastised her. 'Savary tells me that you are always crying: that is not good,' he wrote. 'I shall come to see you when you tell me you are reasonable, and that your courage has the upper hand.'[13] He was angry that the servants had seen her weeping. Malmaison, he wrote, 'is full of our happy memories, which can and ought never to change, at least on my side'.[14] On Christmas Eve, he visited her at Malmaison, and on Christmas Day invited her, Hortense and Eugène to dine with him at the Trianon. Even in February, Napoleon was pondering a meeting with Josephine at the country house of a friend. In the end he decided they should not be under the same roof for the first year after the divorce.

On 1 January, she called Madame de Metternich, wife of the diplomat, to meet her at Malmaison. Josephine suggested to her that only a marriage with an Austrian princess would make her sacrifice worthwhile. She hoped to prove to Napoleon that she only wished to help. He relented to her pleas to allow her to live at the Elysée Palace, where she would be nearer to him. But matters were already in hand for Austria.

In early February, Napoleon's ambassador in St Petersburg wrote describing the prevarications of the Tsar over giving his sister Anna in marriage. Napoleon hastily sent Eugène to the Austrian Embassy to ask for the hand of Marie Louise. Eugène, performing a task that weighed heavy on his soul, informed the ambassador that he must receive an immediate answer and the contract should be signed the following day. There was no time to consult Vienna. The ambassador had to accept and a jubilant Napoleon announced the news to the nation. He sent a missive to the Tsar informing him that he no longer required his sister's hand. At the exact same time, the Tsar wrote to Napoleon that Grand Duchess Anna was too young for marriage.

Eighteen-year-old Archduchess Marie Louise was given the shocking news: she was to be married to the man who had attacked her country, who was divorced, brutal and twice her age. Only five years earlier, she had written in her diary how much she wished him to die. Like Marie Walewska, she was told to sacrifice herself for the good of the state. Her father ordered a splendid trousseau of clothes and jewels and fretted that the marriage was bigamous in the eyes of religion, since the Pope had not annulled Napoleon's union with Josephine. Cardinal

Fesch assured him that the Pope was irrelevant and the decision of the French clerical authorities was sufficient.

Marie Louise had been prepared since childhood for a foreign marriage, and had been tutored in Spanish, English, Latin, Italian and French, the language of the enemy. Tall and fair, although no great beauty, she was well educated, with a fondness for reading and painting landscapes and was skilled at the piano and harp. Spirited and not easily dominated, she had been brought up to hate the French who had executed her great aunt, Marie Antoinette. Her mother had died in 1807 when Marie Louise was fifteen, and her father had soon married his cousin, Maria Ludovika, only twenty-three herself. Marie Louise was a much beloved, rather spoiled child – and now she was set to wed Napoleon, the bloodthirsty monster of terrifying reputation. In Britain, Lord Castlereagh drily remarked that 'a virgin must now and then be sacrificed to the Minotaur'.[15] The proxy marriage took place in Vienna, the banquets were thrown and the Archduchess departed for France.

Napoleon ordered a round of balls and receptions to celebrate his union with Marie Louise. Unfortunately, the public refused to play his game and the newspapers still followed Josephine. 'I told you to arrange that the journals do not speak of the Empress Josephine, but they do little else,' he railed at Fouché. 'See to it that they do not repeat this new publicity.'[16] The divorce had been a very unpopular move. With the break from Josephine, it was as if the Emperor had thrown his Revolutionary past aside. He had claimed the glory of the Republic and now he was divorcing to produce a hereditary line. Josephine was esteemed by the older generals and ministers who had participated in the Revolution, and the aristocrats and royalists saw her as their own. Marie Louise was Marie Antoinette all over again.

Josephine was loved – but she was lonely. Napoleon refused to allow her permission to come to the balls and dances to celebrate the wedding. The dignitaries were too occupied to visit her and Napoleon did not wish to do so. Every piece of news about the preparations for the arrival of the Archduchess was a blow to Josephine. All Paris seemed to be at the glittering receptions and dances, except for her. Napoleon asked Hortense to be a lady-in-waiting to the new Empress and she reluctantly accepted. Hortense was one of her few regular visitors, and she told her mother the details of the plans for the wedding.

Napoleon's first marriage had been conducted speedily during a break between composing military strategy, but was not blessed until the night before the coronation. His second marriage, he decreed, would be very different. He demanded that it follow in exact detail the wedding of Louis XVI and Marie Antoinette in 1770, and he poured over the archives and the records for the finer points. The Archduchess resembled her great aunt Marie Antoinette, thanks to her protruding Hapsburg lip, clear complexion and fine golden hair, although she was taller and more robust. Spies said she was clumsy, her bosom too large and her walk graceless. Her French was good but formal and she found small talk trying. She could not have been more unlike Josephine. But Napoleon did not care. He threw purses of gold at the wedding.

The hardened fighter was behaving like a young man in love once more. He took waltzing lessons and had new clothes made, ordered a huge redecoration of the palaces, and devoted hours to Marie Louise's trousseau. He had the contents laid out for him in the Tuileries and inspected court gowns, riding habits, ball dresses, shawls, shoes adorned with mink, diamond-encrusted fans and her exquisite satin and ermine wedding dress. The Chateau de Compiègne, where Louis XVI had met Marie Antoinette, was chosen as the place for the encounter between Emperor and Archduchess, and Napoleon had it entirely redecorated. He studied the etiquette for the reception of Marie Louise with as much care as his battle plans, and sent his sister Caroline, and a hundred attendants, to meet the Archduchess at Munich. Caroline was a disastrous choice: Marie Louise hated her, for she had taken the throne of her aunt, Maria Carolina of Naples, and Caroline detested the idea of her brother marrying. As the Bonapartes were now realising, their thirteen-year campaign against Josephine had not been in the family's interest, for if Napoleon produced a litter of children, their own would be thrust from the succession. They had underestimated Napoleon, hoping they might be able to marry him to a woman under their influence.

Marie Louise arrived in Munich to be treated icily by her dreadful sister-in-law. Suffering from a bad cold, she was not in the mood to pander to Caroline, and the two proceeded together in ill humour. In 1770, Marie Antoinette had been met on an island in the middle of the Rhine, stripped of her Austrian clothes and re-dressed in French gowns. She had given up all her belongings, even her beloved pug. Over forty years later, Caroline oversaw the ritual undressing and re-dressing of Marie Louise and insisted that her dog be sent back. Poor Marie Louise felt nothing but dread about marrying the man reputed across Europe as a beast.

Napoleon, for his part, tried to please his bride, sending regular missives assuring her of his affection. 'You will find a husband who wants your happiness above all else,' he told her, and then, 'Nothing now interests me but you.'[17]

The Emperor told Josephine that she would have to leave Paris for a chateau in Navarre before Marie Louise arrived. 'I trust that you will be pleased with what I have done for Navarre,' he wrote. 'You must see how anxious I am to make myself agreeable to you. Get ready to take possession of Navarre, you will go there on 25 March, to pass the month of April.'[18] The Archduchess was due to arrive on 27 March. Josephine, hardly able to stand the thought of such exile, did not leave until the very last minute, after Napoleon had departed to meet his bride. She left Hortense and Eugène, who were both due to attend the wedding.

Josephine and her ladies travelled to Navarre overnight. They arrived at nine to be greeted by the entire town, the mayor and a gun salute, dubbing her the 'Duchess of Navarre'. They were then escorted to the chateau. It was a truly frightful sight. So ugly that it was nicknamed locally 'the cooking pot' or *la marmite*, the two-storey building was sturdy and lumpen, topped with lead and unhappily situated at the bottom of the valley. Inside, the vast reception room was paved in marble and only lit by slits in the dome of the ceiling, so it was impossibly gloomy. The ceilings were so high that the rooms were hard to heat, the doors and windows would not close properly – and without the rugs, drapes and curtains of the Tuileries, hot-blooded Josephine was constantly cold, even though her staff hauled in huge loads of wood and twenty-one cauldrons of coal every day. The Empress found the other rooms small, the woodwork rotting and she was scandalised by the state of the grounds. The castle's situation in the dip of a valley meant that it was surrounded by puddles of rainwater. The garden had been laid out in the Chinese style, with criss-crossing canals and streams topped by bridges and pagodas, but the waterways had been severely neglected and the ground was entirely waterlogged. The walls of the palace smelled of damp. As her new lady, Madame Ducrest, put it, the building had been 'left a mere ruin'.[19] Josephine spent 100,000 francs on furnishings, but those obtained for her by one M. Pierlot were of poor quality – broken tables, torn armchairs and tattered curtains.

She wrote to Napoleon begging for repairs and furniture. Her household were horrified by the chateau, and some immediately demanded to leave, preferring to serve the new Empress. Those who stayed found the days passed so slowly that they seemed to last a lifetime. There was the occasional dinner for local dignitaries, but most evenings consisted of interminable games of patience or billiards, chequers with the elderly Bishop of Evreux, or a little needlework while one of the chamberlains read aloud. Josephine could not give up her addiction to telling fortunes, and she and her ladies whiled away hours with the tarot cards, attempting to find better fates than their own.

She sat in the chilly rooms of Navarre, ruing her fate but never uttering a word against Napoleon. She did not contact Paul Barras or Hippolyte Charles, or any other old friends – although Madame Ducrest suspected she had received Thérésa in secret at Malmaison. Her admirer, Prince Frederick Louis of Mecklenburg-Strelitz, raised the possibility of marriage, but she refused. Not only was she still in love with Napoleon, she also dreaded having to live abroad and make a new start in her mid-forties. Poor Frederick Louis was downcast. Although it would have been a comedown to the Empress to live with him in dreary Mecklenburg-Strelitz, the alternative was to remain in Navarre, listening to the tales of Marie Louise and her triumphs. Even worse, she heard rumours that Napoleon wished her to go into exile and never return to Paris.

'I have cried only occasionally for some time past,' she wrote to Hortense. 'I hope that the quiet life I lead here, far from intrigue and gossip, will strengthen me and that my eyes will get well.' There was nothing in the news to console her.

While Josephine languished, the marriage sped ahead. On the evening of 27 March, Napoleon arrived at the Chateau de Compiègne, counting the hours like the world's most eager bridegroom (even though he had been with an Italian mistress until the night before). Unable to wait any longer, he catapulted off to meet Marie Louise en route. He had his coachman flag down her carriage, then jumped in to embrace her. Unlike Louis XVI, who reported succinctly in his journal, 'Meeting with Madame la Dauphine', regarding his encounter with Marie Antoinette at Compiègne in 1770, Napoleon was determined to celebrate his decision.

At the Tuileries, kings and queens, courtiers, little girls with bouquets and assembled ladies had been waiting for hours. He pushed past them all and swept Marie Louise and Caroline upstairs, where he ordered supper for the three of them. He then demanded of his uncle, Cardinal Fesch, whether he and his new wife were properly married. Fesch told him they were married in a civil sense but not a religious one. That was enough for Napoleon and he bundled Marie Louise off to bed. He thought the evening had gone with a bang – and for the bride, it was not as bad as she had expected. 'She asked me to do it again,' Napoleon later said on St Helena.[20] Next morning, Hortense found Marie Louise's expression 'sweet but a little embarrassed'.[21]

Nearly a week later, Napoleon and Marie Louise were formally married in a blaze of festivities in Paris. The pair drove into the city followed by thirty-two carriages of their household. The fountains were running with wine and food was laid out across the route, but the people were not cheering wildly. Some spectators even mistook the fat little Emperor, resplendent in feathers and lace, for Marie Louise's governess. She stared out nervously at the people who had hated and murdered her great-aunt, with only the idealistic hope of a teenager to reassure her.

At the ceremony at the Tuileries, Hortense carried Marie Louise's train, along with the dreaded Bonaparte sisters and Joseph's wife, Julie, now the Queen of Spain. Elisa, Caroline and Pauline could hardly bear to hold the train and pretended to be ill. Marie-Louise's wedding dress suited her rather sturdy figure. 'Once she is properly dressed and arranged, she will be perfectly all right,' Metternich decided. Others noted that the bride was taller than the groom.

The Austrian Prince Schwarzenberg, who had been instrumental in the marriage negotiations, invited the court to a ball at his home. He erected a huge ballroom in his garden but, disastrously, when the evening was in full swing, gauze drapes caught fire from a candle and the blaze spread through the ballroom. Napoleon and Marie Louise escaped, but other guests perished, including Schwarzenberg's sister-in-law. Napoleon was terrified by the bad omen and was only mollified when his advisers declared that Schwarzenberg was the unlucky one. He had another piece of lucky news, not long after. On 10 May, Marie Walewska gave birth to a son, Alexandre Florian Joseph. Her husband, Count Walewski, agreed to acknowledge him as his child – accepting his responsibility for pushing his wife into Napoleon's arms, four years previously.

'I am not afraid of Napoleon, but I am beginning to think he is afraid of me,' Marie Louise told Metternich, with some pride. The Emperor was intimidated by real royalty, and Marie Louise, unlike the French, was not fearful of him and spoke to him with the courage of a confident teenager. The new Empress loved eating and Napoleon arranged lengthy banquets to please her, with fourteen choices of dessert. The bolted meals were largely a thing of the past – as was the work he carried out that had made them necessary. After the wedding, Napoleon revelled in his marriage and spent his days at hunts and his nights at balls and the opera, leaving his study papers untouched and even coming late to council meetings. He had no desire to go to Spain to command the army. He wished to be by Marie Louise's side, and indeed there was no other way for him to conceive his longed-for legitimate son. 'The Emperor is very much taken with his wife,' reported Metternich, 'and if the Empress continues to dominate him, she could render very great services to herself and to all of Europe. He is so evidently in love with her that his habits are subordinated to his wishes.'

After all, it was a long time – if ever – since Napoleon had been with a virgin. And yet, he did not let her share his bed as Josephine had. His excuse was that he could not bear her Germanic habit of sleeping with the windows open. In truth, he was afraid of ceding control. As he later said on St Helena, he had been afraid she would demand to sleep with him in his bedroom, for it was the way for a woman to have power over a man. Moreover, her allowance was exactly half that of Josephine's – 300,000 francs to live on and 60,000 francs for charity.

Marie Louise, a pampered daughter of royalty, expected more protection from the Emperor than he was willing to give. She was hauled out for propaganda reasons on her first imperial tour – of lands that had once been the possession of Austria. They visited Belgium, Holland and the Rhine, followed by dozens of coaches carrying kings, queens, viceroys, attendants and courtiers, ladies-in-waiting, trunks of dresses and boxes of gifts to be distributed. Austrian imperial progresses had never involved such pomp, and Marie Louise was miserable at the endless receptions and audiences, cross about the weather and suffering from headaches. Napoleon was angry and impatient with her and fumed when she was a failure at receptions. Poor Marie Louise was shy and often glacial, unable to make small talk and struggling to hide her boredom. On one occasion, when she went to launch a ship at Cherbourg, the Minister of Police wrote to the chief of her Imperial Guard escort, begging him to ensure she would be punctual and would smile and be gentle with those who approached her. 'For God's sake, my friend, no ice,' he implored.[22]

Unlike Josephine, Marie Louise did not obey Napoleon when he railed. 'Nearly two o'clock and the Emperor would not allow me to eat in the carriage! He said a woman should never have to eat. I was so angry and hungry that it gave me a fearful headache and so much bad humour that the Emperor was furious. I didn't care. If I return in another world, I would certainly not remarry.'[23] The Empress had reason to be hungry, tired and suffering from headaches, for by July she was pregnant with Napoleon's child.

Napoleon was thrilled by the pregnancy. Convinced he would have a son, he planned extensive celebrations, wrote down directives for the birth and christening, following exactly that of the Dauphin. The news put the seal on Josephine's end – despite all her hopes, there was no going back now or living under the same roof. Marie Louise had succeeded in her duty. As Napoleon put it, 'I have married a womb.' Now, finally, the decision that had caused him so much torment was proved right. He had been correct to divorce.

By this point Josephine had returned to Malmaison after Napoleon had at last relented. She had written on 19 April, thanking him for permission to leave the cookpot castle after only three weeks. 'I feared I had been entirely banished from Your Majesty's memory,' she said. 'I see that I am not. I am therefore less wretched today and even as happy as it is possible henceforth for me to be.' She was all humility. 'While I am at Malmaison, Your Majesty may be sure I will live as though I were a thousand leagues from Paris and Your Majesty will not be troubled in his great happiness by any expression of my own regrets.'[24]

She promised not to remain long at Malmaison but travel speedily to a spa. Napoleon's response was cool. 'I have received your letter of 19 April; it is written in a bad style.' He encouraged her to remember that he was still her friend.[25] She wrote back humbly begging his pardon.

There was not a word which did not make me weep; but these tears were very pleasant ones. I have found my whole heart again – such as it will always be; there are affections which are life itself and which can only end with it. I was in despair that my letter of the 19th had displeased you; I do not remember the exact expressions but I know what torture I felt in writing it – grief at having no news of you.[26]

Josephine's promise to live at Malmaison as if she was 'a thousand leagues from Paris' was not truthful. She still hankered after her old Paris life. She wished for invitations and balls, and dreamed of Napoleon's idea of him seated at court between both Empresses. She asked to meet the new Empress, but Napoleon told Hortense it would be impossible, for 'the Empress Marie Louise is alarmed by what she has heard of your mother's attractions and the hold she is known to have over me'.[27] The new Empress had wept when her husband had driven her past Malmaison and proposed they might visit.

Josephine was undeterred. She wished to befriend Marie Louise in an attempt to return to court. When Josephine sent a request herself, Napoleon refused. 'No, she thinks you are very old. If she sees you and your charms she would be worried, she would ask me to send you away and I would have to do it.' Marie Louise was predictably rude about her. 'How can he want to see that old lady? And a woman of low birth!'[28]

Josephine left Malmaison and took the waters with Hortense at Aix. Hortense was newly free – for her husband had abdicated his throne on 1 July, largely because he no longer felt able to pursue the oppressive regime Napoleon expected, notably the ban on trade with Britain. He had left Hortense in power, as regent for their eldest son, but after eight days Napoleon declared Holland part of the French Empire and removed his stepdaughter from the throne. She did not miss it. Separated from her husband, she travelled with her mother and spent time with her admirer, the Comte de Flahaut, a handsome soldier who may have been Talleyrand's illegitimate child. In 1811, in secret in Switzerland, Hortense gave birth to his child. Flahaut gave her happiness, flattered her and was solicitous. It was a brief return to the days when she had just graduated from Madame Campan's, the jewel of Malmaison and the object of a thousand admiring glances.

Josephine left Aix to travel to Switzerland, where she was generously cheered and offered presents and tributes. Madame Ducrest went to visit her in Geneva, at l'Hôtel d'Angleterre, and saw her feted at the Festival of the Lake, where she was transported by a boat drawn by two swans to the sound of fireworks and cries of '*Vive l'imperatrice!*' Unfortunately, such a reception had to be rewarded with largesse and Josephine next went to the local factories where, as Ducrest remarked, she spent hundreds of frances on souvenirs.[29]

'There is not the slightest doubt that the Empress has entered into the fourth month of her pregnancy, she is well and is very much attached to me,' Napoleon wrote to his former wife in September.[30] While she was in Italy, Claire de Rémusat wrote that Josephine should stay in exile. 'You will not without grief listen to the sound of so much rejoicing, relegated as you may be to oblivion by the whole nation.' Claire mentioned 'Marie Louise's jealous disposition', and evoked a tableau of family life at the Tuileries from which Josephine would be excluded. 'The Emperor will be caring for his young wife although still moved by his sentiments towards you . . . [he] asks of you one more sacrifice . . . Will you write the Emperor that the winter will be spent in Italy?'[31]

Napoleon, gleeful and addicted to grandeur as ever, announced that a son would be the King of Rome, a daughter the Princess of Venice. He asked the indefatigable Fontaine to draw up plans for a huge palace for his son, as 'the Palace of the King of Rome'. Apartments in the Tuileries were lavishly decorated and furnished with silver and heavy furniture, as well as an extensive library.

Josephine was permitted to return to France and arrived on 22 November at Navarre. She was pleased to see how the gardens had been completely renovated and drained according to her plans, with new flowers brought over from Malmaison. She enjoyed having a second garden to cultivate, and grew plants almost as rare as in Malmaison – as revealed in the *Description des plantes rares cultivées à Malmaison et à Navarre* (1812–1817), illustrated by Redouté.

Life was still a black hole for Josephine's money. She had her lady of honour, Madame d'Arberg, various ladies-in-waiting, including Madame de Rémusat, an almoner, equerries, chamberlains, a reader, ushers, a doctor and a secretary. At Navarre, Josephine met merchants and representatives of charities in the morning and took a walk or an accompanied drive around the grounds after lunch. At dinner, people sat where they chose and there was rarely an order of precedence in the carriages. She was exasperated at the hierarchy of her servants – at meals they were served on twenty-two different tables, since the cooks would not eat with the kitchen maids, nor would the servants who scrubbed the floors sit with those who lit the fires. Madame d'Arberg only managed to reduce the tables to sixteen.

Napoleon was as impossible to please as ever, for he demanded that she keep up the style of an Empress but with not quite enough money to do so. He wrote angrily that she should still behave as if she were in the Tuileries and her household gentlemen should not be allowed to wear frock coats. Instead they must display the court outfit of embroidered dress, swords and feathers. She must always, he instructed, travel with an escort. He did, however, allow her ladies free choice in their gowns, as long as they were green.

Josephine's spirits had lifted a little after the first shock of Napoleon's new marriage. The renovations to the house and gardens made life much more congenial. Madame Ducrest found a jovial household who stayed up late chatting and playing cards. The party ate late into the night, on special occasions dining off Josephine's Sèvres divorce present from Napoleon and a golden plateau given by the city of Paris on the day of the coronation. On one occasion, the household decided to play dress-up and Josephine gave them her feathery headdresses, cashmere shawls and gowns covered in gold embroidery. She herself had become careless of imperial trappings and wore simple crêpe dresses and caps or diadems of flowers rather than the weighty headdresses of the Empress. She preferred informal gatherings and begged the inhabitants of Evreux not to celebrate her birthday (they ignored her and illuminated the town all the same). When the Navarre waterways iced over, Josephine ordered sledges from Paris for her staff, and supplemented them by putting wheels on armchairs – unfortunate, as a wheel dropped off and Mademoiselle Avrillon broke her leg. On New Year's Day 1811, rather than giving presents (the custom in the early nineteenth century was to give presents then rather than at Christmas), Josephine declared she would hold a lottery for her jewels, giving away crosses, rings, brooches and pins. Despite the informality, people were still nervous of her. As Madame d'Arberg said, 'so few persons appear in their true character that Her Majesty is very partial to those who display any candour.'[32]

Eugène, too, welcomed the opportunity to throw off ceremony. When he arrived for a visit, he begged not to be announced so he could dash in without any of the company rising. He won over all the ladies and Madame Ducrest claimed it was 'impossible to display greater amiability, instruction or good nature'.[33] One of their favourite occupations with him was to have a competition as to which lady could hook the most fish in the little rivers around the castle – they would then have the chefs fry them up for dinner. The visits of Hortense were rather sadder, for she was despairing and in poor health.

Josephine dreaded the occasional journeys between Navarre and Paris, since Napoleon desired a true triumphal progress. She was so weary of it that on one occasion she told her ladies to dress humbly and tell everyone they encountered that the Empress had already passed incognito and she would then travel the next day. The ladies witnessed terrible disappointment in every town, for the burghers had all emerged in their costumes, the troops had been polishing their silver and shining their boots and young girls had dressed up in white, holding nosegays in their hands, only to be told that the Empress had already passed.

Still she was seen as a benefactor. 'There is no danger of annoying or importuning Josephine when we enable her to relieve the distressed,' Madame de Rémusat said. Josephine was constantly importuned by the suffering. On one occasion, a musician came to Navarre and was so bad in his attempt at imitating a quartetto of different instruments that the ladies-in-waiting could not restrain their laughter. Josephine gave him food and money and gently reprimanded her ladies for mocking 'a poor man who tried so hard to please me when he was dying with hunger'.[34]

On 20 March, Josephine was dining with Madame d'Arberg, having sent her household to a dinner with the Mayor of Evreux. She received an official dispatch and then heard the village bells ring out. A son had been born to Napoleon and Marie Louise. Briefly, pain spread across her features, and then she resumed her gracious manner and spoke of her pleasure at an event that gave her former husband such joy. She sent a courier with a message to congratulate her beloved Napoleon. Josephine's household hurried back from the dinner to attend her. Torn between hope for the Empire, Madame Ducrest wrote of 'a violent emotion of anger when I recollected that the woman who held her place was completely happy'. Josephine was serene with her household. 'I am well pleased to find that the painful sacrifice I made to France has proved of some advantage.'[35] She sent Napoleon a 5000-franc diamond pin and planned a great ball in celebration of the news.

Marie Louise had first begun to feel labour pains on the evening of 19 March. The courtiers, Bonapartes, ministers and grand officials had been waiting on standby – and the minute they heard the message from the Empress's lady-in-waiting, they donned their court dress and dashed to the appointed chamber.

At Marie Antoinette's first accouchement in 1778, the room had been so full of dignitaries that, as Madame Campan said, 'anyone might have fancied themselves in a place of public entertainment'.[36] The poor Queen fitted and fainted before a doctor demanded that space was made for her and the courtiers open the shutters. After such a fiasco, Louis XVI had ordered that most of the court wait outside to protect the Queen's health. Other royal consorts had rebelled against giving birth in public – Queen Charlotte in Britain allowed only members of the Cabinet and the Archbishop to wait in the adjoining room. But Napoleon, as ever, wished to return to the high point of Versailles – everything for him was theatre. Marie Louise's labour was as crowded with spectators as a court jousting match. Doctors and nurses flittered among courtiers, who were all standing to attention. Hortense was there as Marie Louise's lady-in-waiting and Eugène had been summoned by Napoleon. The labour was hard and gave great pain to the Emperor. The man who could shrug off the horrors of the battlefield was shocked by childbirth and dashed from the room. The doctor told him that the baby was breeched and might possibly only be saved by killing the mother, presumably by an ad hoc Caesarean section. Even though the whole point of the marriage had been to provide an heir, Napoleon did not hesitate. 'Save the mother,' he said. 'It is her right. We will have another child.'

Despite the difficulties, at 9.20am Marie Louise gave birth to a nine-pound boy. The doctors used forceps in the end, with Napoleon hiding in the bathroom. After the birth, the child lay unmoving for seven minutes. The Emperor gazed at his son, convinced he was dead. Finally, the child let out a noisy cry and Napoleon took his son in his arms.

The Bonapartes were by this point in an adjoining room, and Eugène watched with bitter satisfaction as both Caroline and Elisa burst into despairing tears at their loss of influence when the news came that it was a boy. Outside, cannon fire was telling all Paris that Napoleon had a child. It would be twenty-one rounds for a girl and one hundred for a boy. At the twenty-second, the people began dancing in the streets in the first spontaneous outpouring of enthusiasm for Napoleon since long before the coronation. The royalists, always hoping that there would be no heir, succumbed to hopelessness. Napoleon watched his people celebrate, tears running down his cheeks.

'My son is fat and healthy,' he wrote to Josephine. 'I trust he will continue to improve. He has my chest, my mouth and my eyes. I hope he will fulfil his destiny.'[37] Josephine pushed ahead her plans for a huge ball at Navarre, ordering a re-laying of the floor and repainting of the rooms, as well as deliveries of ornaments, flowers, furniture and food that kept the tradesmen of Navarre entirely afloat. Despite the extravagance, few would travel from Paris and the guests were mainly the stolid burghers of Navarre. In a silver lamé dress and diadem of diamonds, Josephine greeted them as if they were the highest nobility. The burghers danced and ate until four in the morning – delighted by the unforgettable ball of the Empress Josephine.

Again she begged Napoleon to allow her to return to Malmaison and sent Hortense to plead with him as well. He complained that he would offer her anything else. She could be governor of Rome or live in Brussels and hold a brilliant court. She wanted only Malmaison. Finally, he gave in and allowed her to return to her adored home and garden.

But her home was in the clutches of a financial crisis. Money had been embezzled from her accounts and the son of the Prince of Monaco, who was in charge of the stables, had sold off horses cheaply. Napoleon was furious with her. 'Consider how ill I must think of you, if I know that you, with 3 million francs a year, are in debt.' He told her to save as much as she spent every year. 'Look after your affairs, and don't give to everyone who wants to help himself.'[38]

He sent his treasurer to tell the Empress that she must moderate her expenses and keep accurate accounts. Marie Louise, she was told, was skilled in economy and never went into debt. Josephine wept at the lecture, doubly pained to be reprimanded by an official rather than Napoleon himself. When the Emperor heard that she had burst into tears, he was as moved by her as ever. 'You mustn't make her cry!' he said to the treasurer.

'I was annoyed with you about your debts,' he wrote to her, after hearing from Hortense that she had been weeping. 'Nevertheless, never doubt my affection for you, and don't worry any more about the present embarrassment.'[39]

Josephine did attempt to curb her expenses. Her comptroller rented out some of her land, tried to reduce the excessive spending on plants and attempted to claim some of her money from Martinique. But Josephine still spent wildly on clothes, hospitality, gifts and bequests. When she discovered that one of her gentlemen, the flirtatious Monsieur de Pourtales, had been courting the naive Mademoiselle de Castellane, she took the pair for a walk in the gardens. 'You possess nothing but your name,' she said to Mademoiselle de Castellane, 'M. de Pourtales is very rich; you cannot believe that he intends to marry you.' Confounded, Pourtales promptly announced that he would, and Josephine offered a dowry of 100,000 francs and the trousseau. She was very generous with her money and too old to change her ways. Napoleon had told her to set aside a million francs a year for her grandchildren. It was unlikely. She soon was in debt for over three million francs, despite her hefty allowance.[40]

'Tranquillity is such a sweet thing,' she wrote to Eugène. 'Ambition is the only thing that can spoil it, and thank God I do not suffer from the disease.' The excitement of the old days was gone. Even a year after the divorce, Josephine still cried bitter tears over her loss. When Bourrienne came to visit her at Malmaison, she could barely speak. 'I have drained my cup of despair. He has cast me off! Abandoned me! He conferred upon me the vain title of Empress only to render my fall the more marked.'[41] It was all dreadful and anyone who came to visit heard the same story again and again. She told Bourrienne:

> You cannot imagine, my friend, all the miseries I have suffered since that awful day! I cannot imagine how I survived it. You cannot conceive the pain I endure on seeing descriptions of his fetes everywhere. And the first time he came to see me after his marriage, what a meeting was that! I shed so many tears!

She was spending more than ever in an attempt to dull her pain. She shrugged when she was told to avoid milliners, dressmakers and jewellers. 'I ought, indeed to be indifferent to it all, but it is a habit.'[42]

She poured money into her home and Malmaison was consequently at its most beautiful, a true *chateau-musée*. In June 1813, Josephine wrote again to Eugène from Malmaison: 'The life I lead here is still the same, occupying myself only with my gallery and my plants.'[43] Her new gallery, built in the same year as the divorce, was, as Madame Ducrest said, 'one of the finest sights imaginable', and she had commissioned a proper catalogue of her art collection. Foreign visitors would travel especially to see her paintings and sculptures.[44]

Josephine wrote hundreds of letters pursuing the art she desired. Writing to Eugène's minister, the general treasurer of the Kingdom of Italy, she expressed thanks for advice he had offered on five paintings by Melizi, which he thought might be suitable for the gallery. 'I will also buy the two paintings by Mme Grimaldi,' she instructed.[45] 'All that I desire now is the painting [by Titian] which was shown to me on the evening of my departure. Be so good as to find out the asking price for me.'[46] She busied herself launching the careers of lesser-known artists, suggesting that the yearly art exhibition in Paris, the Salon, display a list of paintings by her favourite, M. Töpffer, 'of whose work you have seen several examples at Malmaison'.[47] Josephine herself, as a divorcée, was not allowed to go to the Salon. She commissioned from her beloved Canova *The Dancer* and *Paris*, but refused to allow *Paris* to go to the exhibition. If she could not go, why should her artworks?

In 1812, Josephine asked Canova to create a sculpture of the Three Graces for her. Euphrosyne, Aglaea and Thalia, the three daughters of Zeus, presided over banquets for the guests of the gods, and represented beauty, charm and joy. Josephine, commissioning such a sculpture in the evening of her life, surely had in mind her days with Thérésa and Juliette, the three graces of Paris, and the time of wonder when all was freedom and anything seemed possible.

Carved from a single slab of white marble, *The Three Graces* is a masterpiece of softness and beauty. On a visit to Canova's studio in Rome, the Duke of Bedford spotted the sculpture and fell in love with it. He was told there was no possibility of having it, for it was to go to the Empress herself. He was not the first art collector to be disappointed. To the chagrin of many collectors across Europe, Josephine came first.

Malmaison was a wonderland of exotic animals, art and plants, and it was expensive to maintain. Guests flocked there to sample the delights of the table and peer at the menagerie, and most of all to tour her works of art. It was the height of fashion to partake of her fabulous dinners, with bananas and pineapples from her greenhouses and her homemade ice cream. Josephine had brought in a special ice-cream maker from Italy, who created the exquisite 'glacé Malmaison', a raisin and liqueur-flavoured ice cream. Cheerfully ignoring the ban on trade with Britain, she even had a British attendant who served up Cheshire cheese and English muffins, which were rare excitements for the French.

For the children of Hortense and Eugène, Malmaison was a marvellous playground. As Louis Napoleon, later Napoleon III, recalled, 'I can still see the Empress Josephine in her salon on the ground floor, covering me with her caresses, and even flattering my vanity by the care with which she repeated my childish bon mots.' For, he said, 'my grandmother *spoilt* me in every sense of the word.' At Malmaison, 'we – my brother and I – were at liberty to do just what we liked. The Empress, who was passionately fond of plants and conservatories, allowed us to cut the sugar canes to suck, and was always telling us to ask for whatever we wanted.'[48] Josephine had not learned the lesson of her rotten teeth.

The sugar, the dinners, the muffins and the ice cream had their effect – she was growing larger. Laure Junot recalled that 'one special feature of her figure assumed really incredible proportions'. She was forced to wear boned corsets to keep her rapidly expanding bosom under control. 'They say you are as fat as a good Normandy farmer's wife,' Napoleon wrote cheerfully to her.[49]

Josephine's chamberlain, Comte Turpin de Crissé, paid tribute to her hospitality, describing a court where 'dignity, grace, wit, talents and good conversation made a seat of exile into a place of enchantment and a queen without a crown into a woman surrounded by real friends'.[50] The Comte was slightly biased. There was gossip that Josephine relied on him emotionally and that in 1810 she took a holiday with him, a single equerry and one lady attendant. Still, if there was an affair, it was short-lived. The Comte married in 1813 with Josephine's blessing.

On 8 June, the baby King of Rome was christened at Notre-Dame. The ceremony was a version of that of Louis, Grand Dauphin of France. Napoleon, as ever, seized the limelight and took the child from the arms of Marie Louise and raised him aloft to show the public, twice.

Josephine desired above all to see the King of Rome. She wished to touch the child who had cost her so many tears. Napoleon was very resistant, but he finally allowed her an hour, in secret. The little boy was taken to play at the summer palace of Bagatelle on the outskirts of Paris, and his governess, Madame de Montesquiou, allowed Josephine to hold him and kiss him. When Marie Louise got wind of the meeting, she was furious and made Napoleon promise never to permit it again.

Napoleon was happy in the Tuileries, eating desserts with his wife and playing with his son. He had also taken up with mistresses again, and brought Marie Walewska and her son, little Alexandre, to Paris. As he dressed up as a shopkeeper to visit her, presided over celebrations, and watched the King of Rome play with gilded rattles, the Empire was crumbling. Napoleon himself was plump and self-satisfied, indeed, more like a contented shopkeeper than the obsessive military genius once able to ride for ten hours straight. His Empire was in little better condition. Massively overextended, it was impossible to govern and police and the resentments in the vassal states were growing. Thanks to the rapacious behaviour of the French armies, states began their subordination full of grievances and distress, and matters only grew worse, with high taxes levied to pay for the price of occupation and also supporting Napoleon's vast expenditure at home. The people were shocked at his treatment of the Church, for he seized Church property and closed many of the orders, leaving monks and nuns with no choice but to beg on the streets. His extravagant behaviour (and that of Josephine) generated pure hatred, as the people struggled to pay taxes in order to keep him and his huge court in pampered luxury in Paris. France was no less restive than the vassal states. Scarred and traumatised after the Terror, the people had believed Napoleon would bring peace to the nation. Now, it seemed as if he was attacking countries for the sake of it – and his people could not see where his ambition would end. 'Soon Europe will not be enough for him,' wrote one, 'he will wish for Asia.'[51]

Across the Empire, conscription caused particular misery, now increased to encompass men from twenty to sixty years of age. Towns became ghostly places of only women, forced to take on all jobs because their menfolk were gone. The price of bread was soaring, there was widespread misery due to the Continental Blockade, and the thought of losing more menfolk was almost too much to bear. The conscription notices posted on street corners filled whole towns with despair, as people gathered to look for the names of their husbands and sons. But Napoleon, the sun of his own world, thought himself immune to complaints. 'I have three hundred thousand men to spend,' he said. The Tsar had recently begun trading with Britain and Napoleon saw his act as one of aggression. Determined to seize a significant military victory, he grew set on the ludicrous idea of invading Russia. He called up over 600,000 men from all over his dominions, from Italy to Poland, Denmark to Switzerland. Fat, sickly and pale, his huge torso balanced on tiny legs, suffering from a hacking cough and bladder problems, he dressed himself up in ermine and medals, styled himself as a leader, and demanded their allegiance.

Before departing for Russia, he visited Josephine for over two hours. She begged Constant to look after him, surprising the valet with her 'care for the man who had abandoned her'.[52] Napoleon left for Dresden, accompanied by Eugène, 300 carriages, and by Marie Louise. She was now his symbol of power and riches, his attempt in human form to awe his vassals. 'I leave St-Cloud and I go to Moscow, not out of inclination or to gratify myself, but out of dry calculation,' he said.[53] He lied: he yearned for glory.

In his usual vain fashion, Napoleon announced that he would conquer Russia in twenty days. But he and his men battled with the terrain. 'My health is fine,' he wrote to Marie Louise, and 'it is very hot'.[54] The heat of the plains was exhausting and the troops quickly ran low on supplies. The Russian serfs had expected that Napoleon would liberate them, and when he did not they actively tried to thwart him. As for the outnumbered Russian troops, they simply retreated and let the punishing land of Russia do their work for them. After two months, no battle had been fought and 150,000 men had fled, died of illness or heat exhaustion, or were too weakened to fight.

Napoleon pushed on and in September, the Russians and the French clashed at the village of Borodino. At the end, 44,000 Russians lay dead or wounded on the battlefield and Napoleon lost around 30,000 of his troops, including many generals. He declared himself the victor, and on 15 September he entered Moscow. The inhabitants had fled, aside from those too infirm to leave and the criminals and foreigners forbidden to do so. As Napoleon entered, the Governor of Moscow put torches to his house and distributed explosives to gangs of men to set the rest of the city alight, then sent the last few to destroy the fire-fighting equipment. Napoleon occupied the Kremlin and gazed at 'the mountains of red, rolling flames, like immense waves of the sea. Oh, it was the most grand, the most sublime, the most terrifying sight the world had ever seen!'[55] Certain that the Tsar would sue for peace, he wrote to Alexander demanding a treaty.

Alexander, squirrelled away in St Petersburg, did not reply. Napoleon sat in the Kremlin, dawdling over his meals to kill time, playing *vingt-et-un* with Eugène or trying to read novels. For the first time in his life, Napoleon was kept waiting. 'I shall fight to the last man in my Empire,' pronounced Alexander. 'Now it is Napoleon or me; we can no longer reign together.'[56] But really, there was no need to fight at all. As he knew, Napoleon could not remain in Russia forever, for he had a restive population at home. It was now too cold to march to St Petersburg. Less than a month after they arrived, the French slunk out of the city. The snows were beginning to fall.

'We seemed to be marching in a world of ice,' recalled one soldier. Temperatures fell to well below minus twenty degrees. Thousands of horses slithered on the snow and perished and the soldiers fell and died where they lay. 'The ravages of cold were equalled by those of hunger,' wrote one Württemberg soldier. No food was too rotten or disgusting to be eaten, and no dead horse, cat or dog was left untouched. Soldiers would watch a comrade grow weak, counting the hours until he fell to the ground and died. Then they would steal his belongings and eat his flesh. Men would even gnaw on their own bodies. 'All human compassion vanished,' the soldier recalled, men's minds were addled by the cold and 'dull despair and raving madness had taken possession of many and they died muttering, with their last breath, the most horrible imprecations against God and man'.[57] It was so cold that 400 men might gather around a fire at night and 300 would be dead in the morning. Those who did not die of hunger and despair were picked off by the Russian troops, who followed them through the countryside. French soldiers were impaled on stakes and thrown alive into cauldrons of boiling water. The peasants, brutalised and angry, tortured them by beating them with hammers and pushing stakes down their throats. Napoleon was unruffled. 'Small change,' he said, poking with his foot at the corpses on the ground.

He left his army on 5 December and hurried on ahead. He arrived at the Tuileries just after midnight on 19 December, in secret, slipping through a back door. He immediately ordered a round of balls and receptions to celebrate his return.

The Emperor paid no attention to the devastating dispatch sent by General Berthier, 'Sir, your army exists no more.' Out of the 600,000 men who had travelled to war, only 93,000 would stagger home. Many were not in a fit state to fight ever again and barely able to return to normal life. Two hundred thousand horses had died. Napoleon's insane plan to invade Russia was, as Talleyrand put it, 'the beginning of the end'.

General Caulaincourt, who accompanied Napoleon back to France, said – only half in jest – that the Prussians should take Napoleon prisoner and give him to the British to display in London like an animal in a cage. 'A man such as I does not concern himself about the lives of a million men,' Napoleon said.[58] The populace, by his estimation, needed to be forced to love him – just as he had always tried to force ladies to do the same.

He did not write to Josephine from Russia, and she spent the campaign in an agony of panic over her former husband and her son. Eugène, she knew, had been wounded, but there was little news of him. Marie Louise took pity on her rival and gave Hortense some of her letters from Napoleon to read and pass on details to her mother.

The Emperor went to visit Josephine on his return, but he did not invite her to the celebrations. Even if it had been appropriate, she was a reminder of the military success of better days. The first campaign he had undertaken since his marriage to Marie Louise had been a terrible, scandalous failure.

Josephine sat alone in Malmaison. Everyone else of fashion in Paris, it seemed, had been forced to attend what were nicknamed 'the wooden leg balls', because so many of those present were missing a limb. Those who went to the Tuileries found it a bitter diversion. 'In the midst of the general consternation, people were shocked to see the Emperor entertaining at the Tuileries,' wrote Major Raymond de Montesquiou, Duc de Fezensac. 'I shall always remember one of those dismal balls, at which I felt I was dancing on graves.'[59]

21

'More full of charm'

*B*y the beginning of 1813, the corpulent Empire and its even fatter Emperor were in trouble. Prussia had joined with Russia against France and a campaign in Spain had been a failure. 'The Emperor was invincible no longer,' the Duc de Fezensac rued. The Emperor himself was also weary. 'The late hours, the hardships of war, are not for me at my age,' he said. 'I love my bed, my repose, more than anything, but I must finish my work.'[1]

Napoleon's enemies were not only external. Joachim and Caroline Murat, eager to keep their throne at all costs, had signed a pact with Vienna. Joseph had failed to impose order on Spain. However, unlike his turncoat siblings, Louis was still faithful to the man who had given him power and position. He wrote to Napoleon offering to return to France and stand by his side. 'My husband is a good Frenchman, he has proved it by returning to France at the point when all of Europe has turned against it,' said Hortense.[2] She too, despite everything that Napoleon had done to her, was still loyal to the Emperor.

The allies could see chinks in Napoleon's armour. On 22 November 1813, Eugène was visited by an aide of the King of Bavaria, his father-in-law. He offered Eugène protection if he deserted Napoleon. Eugène refused. 'It is not to be denied that the Emperor's star is beginning to wane, but that is only another reason why those who have received so much from him should remain faithful.' He wrote to Napoleon to say he had told Bavaria that he would not 'commit such a despicable act; that I would, until my final breath, remain true to the oath that I made to you'.[3]

The enemy troops were drawing near to Paris. Josephine's guards at Malmaison had fled and she had only sixteen wounded soldiers in their place. She still refused to quit the city. On 28 March 1814, Hortense sent her a message telling her that Marie Louise was about to flee. With Napoleon away fighting, Marie Louise was Regent and she had been refusing to leave. She was told that she and the court must leave for Blois – and that the Emperor would not wish her or her son to be captured by the enemy. 'I would prefer my son to be killed rather than see him brought up in Vienna as an Austrian prince,' she said.[4] She reluctantly said she would depart, 'very angry . . . especially when the Parisians are showing such eagerness to defend themselves'.[5]

The following day, Josephine travelled to Navarre, her diamonds sewn into her petticoat. 'I don't know if it is possible to express how unhappy I am,' she wrote. 'I have had courage in the many sad situations in which I have found myself; I can bear these reversals of fortune; but I do not know if I have enough strength to bear the absence of my children and the uncertainty of their fate.'[6] She did not have long to wait. Hortense and her children fled to her two days later, with the news that Paris had surrendered. The Emperor was under house arrest at Fontainebleau.

In Paris, the Champs-Élysées was filled with bearded Cossacks, dressed in blue trousers and tunics, squatting by the road as they mended their clothes or polished their weapons. They slept outside, their horses tethered to trees. Aside from a little looting, they behaved perfectly – and the citizens of Paris lined up to inspect their new visitors. Marie Louise begged her husband to be allowed to join him in Fontainebleau, but, sunk into a depression, he wrote to her only to pay out a million francs each to his mother, Joseph, Jérôme, Pauline, Louis and Elisa. Once they received the money, they hurried off. 'No one loves you as much as your faithful Louise,' she said. When he would not direct her, she took matters into her own hands and set off to interview her father. She was soon seized and kept by the Austrians.

Josephine was heartbroken to hear the news that the Emperor had signed his agreement of abdication on 6 April. The portly long-exiled Louis XVIII would be king in his place. Her spies told her of Napoleon's low spirits and inability to take action. 'How I have suffered in the way in which they have treated the Emperor,' she wrote to her son. 'What attacks in the newspapers, what ingratitude on the part of those upon whom he showered his favours! But there is nothing more to hope for. It is finished, he is abdicating.'[7]

The allies in Paris were behaving like kings. In mid-April Josephine returned to Malmaison, and the Tsar paid a visit the following day. Hortense arrived and was shocked to see the courtyard full of Cossack soldiers and attendants. They told her that Josephine was out walking with the Tsar of Russia. Hortense met them and was introduced, but she was cold with the Tsar until Josephine reminded her of their precarious position. After the visit, the Tsar wrote a warm letter and asked to come again. Josephine was unwilling, but Napoleon advised her to receive the Tsar, for 'the future of your children depends upon it'. She ordered new gowns and set her household polishing the furniture and arranging flowers.

She did everything to try and please the Tsar. On taking tea with her, he pointed to a cup bearing her portrait and asked if he could have it. She told him that he could buy a similar cup anywhere, and instead gave him a large antique cameo – showing Alexander the Great and Philip of Macedonia – which had been a gift from Pius VII on her coronation. 'I wish to give you something which is not to be found anywhere else and which sometimes will make you think of me.'[8]

The Tsar set the trend. All the allied leaders desired to come to Malmaison, taste the ice cream, see the orang-utan and gaze at the stupendous art collection. Josephine had become a trophy, just as Cleopatra had been for the Romans. Josephine smiled graciously as she was treated like a spoil of war, but her heart was breaking. 'I cannot be reconciled to Bonaparte's fate,' she wrote to Hortense. He had been a brutal killer, a ruthless dispatcher of soldiers and civilians alike, but to her he was her husband, her man of bravery and skill. Her future as a captive beauty of the allies was hardly appealing. 'At times I have fits of melancholy enough to kill me,' she said.[9]

On 16 April 1814, Napoleon wrote the last existing letter to Josephine, while he waited to be sent abroad. 'In my retirement, I shall substitute the pen for the sword,' he told her, saying he would tell the truth about his reign. 'I have showered benefits on thousands of wretches! What did they do in the end for me? They have betrayed me. Yes all of them except our dear Eugène, so worthy of you and me,' he rued. 'Adieu, my dear Josephine. Resign yourself as I am doing and never forget one who has never forgotten and will never forget you. P.S. I expect to hear from you when I reach Elba. I am far from being in good health.'[10] On 20 April, he left Fontainebleau, accompanied by fourteen carriages and an escort of Polish soldiers. Josephine could hardly bear the news that her husband had been bundled off to the obscure island of Elba, twelve miles off the Tuscan coast. He lied about his supporters: Marie Walewska had rushed to Elba, along with his mother and Pauline, and Marie Louise had desperately tried to attend him. But he thought only of Josephine.

The letter from Napoleon plunged Josephine into despair. On 3 May, fat and fifty-nine, Louis XVIII entered Paris and was declared King. Louis-Philippe Crépin produced a painting of the King 'lifting France from its ruins'. Josephine's world had nearly disappeared. She still entertained the Tsar, always dressed in her finery as she accompanied him past the shrubs from St Lucia and the flowers from Syria and into the greenhouse that pleased him so well. On 14 May 1814, she caught a cold while out walking with Alexander. On 23 May, she received the King of Prussia and the Grand Duke Constantine, even though she felt weak. 'She seemed to me to have a mere cold and her health was usually so good that I was not at all concerned,' Hortense remembered.[11] Josephine's doctor was equally sanguine. She refused to be cowed and hosted dinner and a small ball on the 25th for the Russian grand dukes, opening the dancing with the Tsar. She then insisted on walking around the grounds with him, wandering past the beautiful plants in the moonlight. By the end of the evening, her fever was high, she had a rash and she felt very unwell.

Hortense fussed around her with mustard plasters, but nothing worked. On the 27th, the Tsar sent his own doctor. Josephine greeted him politely and with dignity. 'I hope his interest will bring me luck,' she said. The Tsar – who seemed to have little else to do in Paris other than visit Malmaison – was due again on the 28th for dinner. Josephine oversaw the preparations from her bed, to the despair of her doctor, who wished her to rest. He came out of Josephine's chamber to tell Hortense that her mother was very ill.

On the 28th, the Tsar came to see her but she was too frail to receive guests and unable to speak. She was struggling to breathe, dropping in and out of consciousness and in great pain. The doctors agreed that there was little hope. Josephine sent away all those who came to console her. Worried that she might infect her family, she even begged Hortense to leave. Her daughter remained outside, and heard from the lady-in-waiting that Josephine occasionally uttered words in her delirium: 'Bonaparte . . . island of Elba . . . King of Rome'.[12] Next morning, the former Empress, always aware of the need to appear in splendour, asked her attendants to dress her in a pink satin morning gown with matching ribbons, and put on her jewels in case the Tsar came to visit. At eight o'clock, Hortense and Eugène went to wish her goodbye.

'When she saw us, she held out her arms with great emotion and uttered something we could not understand.' Ornate in pink and rubies, she received the last rites at 11am. Josephine struggled through her last breaths, and at noon, the Empress, Napoleon's 'little Creole', died, two months short of her fifty-first birthday.

The cause of death was probably pneumonia. But in simple terms, she no longer wished to live. Without Napoleon, reduced to the trophy of the allies, she could see little estimable in her future. Her maid, Mademoiselle Avrillon, said 'she died of grief'. She had not the spirit to live under occupation. 'What fine tact, what kindness and moderation, she possessed,' said Madame du Cayla, the youthful favourite of Louis XVIII. 'Her very dying, just now, is a proof of her good taste.'[13]

Napoleon received the news of Josephine's death from a newspaper. In shock, he hid himself away in a dark room and refused all food. 'No woman was ever loved with more devotion, ardour and tenderness,' he wrote, 'only death could break a union formed by sympathy, love and true feeling.'[14]

Josephine lay in state in the foyer of Malmaison for three days in her coffin of lead and mahogany. Twenty thousand members of the public attended to see the great Empress. Her beautiful, seductive eyes were closed and her mouth was touched by a smile. The bells of the nearby parishes tolled throughout the day.

The capital had rejoiced to be liberated from Napoleon, but they mourned his Empress. Some said she had been poisoned, and the puppet king, Louis XVIII, put out an announcement praising her to quell unrest.

The news of the death of Mme de Beauharnais has provoked general sadness. This woman was born with sweetness and something genuinely good in her manner and in her spirit. Sadly, during the terrible times of the rule of her husband she was forced to take refuge against his brutalities in her love of horticulture . . . She alone amongst the milieu of this Corsican upstart spoke the language of the French and understood their hearts.

On Thursday 2 June, Josephine's coffin was taken to the church at Rueil, followed by local representatives and Imperial Guards. Behind them walked a lone footman carrying a silver casket on a cushion. Inside was the Empress's heart. The pall-bearers were Alexandre de Beauharnais's brother François and his uncle Claude, the Grand Duke of Baden, and Comte de Tascher, Josephine's cousin. Eugène, Hortense and their children walked behind the coffin. Behind them followed a long procession of courtiers and dignitaries of the imperial regime, diplomats and friends. Thousands of people watched and cried as the Empress passed by. The church, entirely draped in black, was so full that only those with invitations could attend. The rest remained outside, weeping for their old Empire, their Revolutionary past and the woman herself.

In 1815, when Napoleon returned to France in an attempt to recapture his lost Empire, he hurried to Malmaison and pressed those who were with her in her final hours to tell him of her words. 'I still seem to see her walking along the paths and collecting the flowers that she loved so much,' he said, wandering the gardens. 'Poor Josephine! She was truly more full of charm than any other person I have ever known. She was a woman in the fullest meaning of the word: capricious and alive, and with the best of hearts.'

Epilogue

*I*f Josephine had lived longer, she would have seen Napoleon back in her home, perhaps restored to her arms. 'She had her failings of course,' he said, 'but she at least would never have abandoned me.'[1] Marie Louise, once so devoted, quickly forgot her husband. In the summer of 1814, she went to take the waters at Aix-les-Bains, and Metternich ensured she was escorted by Albrecht von Neipperg, a seducer extraordinaire. She fell in love with him and eventually bore him three children. She sent Napoleon a formal greeting for the New Year of 1815, and never wrote to him again.

By the winter of 1814, Napoleon was planning to attack the allies. Disappointed that matters had remained the same with the restored Louis XVIII on the throne, the people were beginning to remember the Emperor with fondness and they resented the allied troops. Divisions among the allies only encouraged Napoleon to launch an attack. 'You were not made to die on this island,' said Letizia – and on 26 February 1815, Napoleon set off with 650 men of the guard, 100 Polish soldiers and further volunteers. The European ministers had been in Vienna, discussing how to carve up the Napoleonic Empire, when they heard the unbelievable news. The former Emperor had landed in France. On the night of 19 March, Louis XVIII fled the Tuileries. Napoleon settled into his old home and even called Fouché back as Minister of Police (a mistake, as he was in the pay of the allies). The ever-loyal Marie Walewska returned too. But outside Paris his enemies were coming together. Napoleon decided on a pre-emptive strike and hurried to Belgium.

On 15 June, the Duchess of Richmond threw a lavish ball for the allies in Brussels. As the people danced, the news came through that Napoleon was advancing. The men left to fight, still in evening dress. Three days later, Napoleon was comprehensively defeated at the Battle of Waterloo and fled towards Paris. On 22 June, he abdicated in favour of his son and moved to Malmaison, where Hortense performed the honours of the table. 'I will go to Malmaison: I can live there in retirement with some friends, who most certainly will come to see me only for my own sake,' he said.[2] Marie Walewska and her son came to visit him, along with other mistresses, including Madame Duchâtel, and his nine-year-old son by Eléonore Denuelle, Charles, Comte Léon. Napoleon wandered Malmaison in a state of depression, remembering his Josephine.

King Louis XVIII, restored by the allies, cheerfully said that Napoleon had been a good tenant and kept the Tuileries looking well. They all thought that would be his only legacy. Napoleon could not stay in France. He asked for exile in Britain, believing that the British principle of fair play would mean he was humanely treated, and when he arrived at Torbay, crowds of sightseers came to catch a glimpse of him. The Prince Regent, the Prime Minister and the Secretary of State for War claimed him as a prisoner of war and informed him he would be sent to St Helena in the Atlantic Ocean, between Africa and South America, and a very long way from anywhere. He was told he could take three officers and twelve soldiers and would be treated as a general on half pay. 'I am not a prisoner but the guest of England,' he complained, but to no avail. To be placed for life on an island within the tropics, cut off from all communication with the world was, he thought, quite 'horrible'. He declared he would have preferred the Tower of London.[3]

Napoleon was put under virtual house arrest on St Helena, and amused himself with maths puzzles, gardening and dictating his memoirs. The hero for whom, as Bourrienne said, 'all Europe was too small' and who had exhausted himself with his victories, now had years of rest.[4] He could not bear it. By March 1821, he was severely unwell and in April his condition deteriorated. In delirium, he cried that he saw the Empress:

I have just seen my good Josephine but she would not embrace me. She disappeared at the moment when I was about to take her in my arms. She was seated there. It seemed to me that I had seen her yesterday evening. She is not changed. She is still the same, full of devotion to me. She told me that we were about to see each other again, never more to part. Do you see her?[5]

Ten days later, on 5 May, he died, uttering his last words: '*France, armée, tête d'armée, Josephine*'. At the very end, he thought of his Empress.

After the death of their mother, Hortense and Eugène were orphans. 'My courage is gone!' Hortense said. 'Alexander will soon forget the promised protection, and then I shall have to struggle alone with my two children against the hostilities people will heap on me for the sake of the name I bear.'[6] But Tsar Alexander did remember his pledge and pressed Louis XVIII to create her Duchess of Saint-Leu. When Napoleon returned in 1815, she supported him and thus was banished from France when he was finally defeated. She travelled in Germany and Italy before purchasing a chateau in Switzerland. Her relationship with the Comte de Flahaut continued until after Napoleon's brief restoration, but then he moved to Britain and in 1817 married Margaret Elphinstone, daughter of Napoleon's mortal enemy Admiral Lord Keith and a friend of Princess Charlotte, then heir to the British throne. Hortense and Flahaut's son, Charles Auguste, was sent to live with his paternal grandmother. Hortense lived in her Swiss chateau with her third son, Charles Louis Napoleon Bonaparte. Her second son died in his brother's arms in 1831 at the age of twenty-seven, of what seems to have been measles. Charles Auguste became a successful Paris businessman, earning a huge fortune from sugar-beet factories. Hortense died in 1837, at fifty-four, worn out by grief. She was buried next to Josephine in the Saint-Pierre-Saint-Paul Church in Rueil.

Still, Hortense won in the end. The child born just a year before Napoleon divorced her mother, Charles Louis, became Napoleon III in April 1852. In 1853, he married Eugenie de Montijo, a pretty Spanish-born aristocrat, after seeing her at a ball. When he was overthrown after the failure of the Franco-Prussian War, they took refuge in Chislehurst in Kent. She died almost forty years after her husband, in 1920, after witnessing the world change in ways that Josephine could never have imagined.

★   ★   ★

Eugène continued as sensible and stoic as ever. After the fall of Napoleon, he retired to Munich and obeyed the strictures of his father-in-law, Maximilian of Bavaria, to keep out of French politics – although all his surviving children, except for his second daughter, bore the middle name of Napoleon (feminised with a second e for the females). Astonishingly, he succeeded in gaining 700,000 francs from the Bourbons as compensation for his mother's seized property. His six children (he lost one daughter, Caroline, in infancy) made auspicious marriages. His eldest daughter, Josephine, became Queen Consort to Oscar I of Sweden, the son of Désirée Clary and General Bernadotte. Josephine, like her grandmother, loved gardening and was a patroness of art, and always worked hard to promote her husband's politics. Out of all the marriages, the most magnificent was that of his third daughter, Amelia, who became Empress of Brazil. Her husband was so struck by her appearance that he apparently collapsed with emotion when he first saw her as her boat docked in Rio. Like her grandmother, she was renowned for her elegance, her gentle behaviour at court, and her skill at hosting social events, a reputation that remained until her husband's abdication in 1831. Eugène's youngest son, Maximilian, married the eldest daughter of Tsar Nicholas II, Grand Duchess Maria. In the end, someone at least seized a Grand Duchess. Eugène died at the age of forty-two in 1824. His descendants remain in many European royal families.

Thérésa (Tallien) retired to the Prince de Chimay's estates in the Netherlands, where she lived until 1835, leaving behind ten children fathered by four men – her first husband, Tallien, the banker Ouvrard and Chimay. Jean Lambert Tallien fell into poverty and finally had to accept a pension of 100 sous a month from Louis XVIII. He died of leprosy in 1820.

Some of the discarded mistresses perhaps had the happiest time. The free-spirited La Grassini became mistress to the Duke of Wellington in Paris, much to the shock of the newspapers. Pauline Fourès lived contentedly, surrounded by exotic birds in the home Napoleon bought for her in Paris. She wrote a novel, *Lord Wentworth*, and died in 1869.

Marie Walewska remarried in 1816 but died the following year, shortly after the birth of a son. Alexandre, her son with Napoleon, became Napoleon III's ambassador to Britain. At a London reception, a lady guest enthused about his striking resemblance to his 'distinguished father'. 'I had no idea, Madame,' he replied, 'that you were acquainted with the late Count Walewski.'

Napoleon's family took up occupation in Italy, welcomed by the Grand Duke of Florence and Pope Pius in Rome, still alive and willing to forgive the Bonapartes their slights. Italy had been thoroughly and cruelly conquered by the Bonapartes, its artworks and palaces looted, but still their people provided refuge for the family behind the ambition. Letizia had returned with Napoleon to France from Elba, but he had forbidden her to accompany him to St Helena. She died in Rome in 1836. Pauline died of consumption in Florence in 1825 at the age of forty-five. Elisa died in Trieste at forty-three in 1820. Her death particularly affected Napoleon on St Helena and he cried that she had 'shown me the way'.[7] Louis died alone in 1846 in Livorno. Caroline was arrested by the Austrians after a failed attempt to regain the Neapolitan throne. Freed, she lived with Elisa in Trieste, married a British general and died in Italy of cancer in 1839. She was the only Bonaparte family member to attend the funeral of Hortense at Rueil, a token of respect to a schoolfriend she had done so much to undermine and destroy.

Lucien and Joseph changed their loyalties and became preoccupied with installing Hortense's son on the throne as Napoleon II. His death in 1831 put an end to their hopes. Lucien turned to writing bad novels and died in Viterbo, Italy, in 1840, and Joseph died in 1844 at the grand age of seventy-six, after a spell in New York and New Jersey, living off the proceeds of the stolen Spanish crown jewels. The luckiest of all was Jérôme, Napoleon's least favourite sibling. He fought at Waterloo and lived long enough to see the ascent of Napoleon III, and thus received the rank of a French prince. He died in 1860 in a chateau in Villegenis and was buried in Les Invalides – the only Bonaparte to die in France.

Cardinal Fesch, who had fallen out with Napoleon for taking the side of the Pope, retired to Rome after Waterloo and remained there until he died in 1839. He kept intact his incredible collection of around 16,000 pictures, much of it looted from the Italian campaign.[8] He left more than a thousand pieces to the Bonaparte home town of Ajaccio on Corsica, including works by Botticelli, Bellini and Titian. Some he left in Lyons and the rest were sold in Rome after his death. They now hang in museums and private homes all over the world. Five paintings are in the Wallace Collection in London, including two Greuzes, and works including Michelangelo's *The Entombment* and Raphael's *Mond Crucifixion* are in the National Gallery.

Napoleon's much desired son, the 'King of Rome' or Napoleon II, lived a miserable existence as the captive of his grandfather in Vienna. On 21 April, just before he died on St Helena, Napoleon wrote him a lengthy letter. 'My son should not think of avenging my death. He should profit from it,' he announced. 'Let my son bring into blossom all I have sown.' He was quite sure that the Bourbons would fall after his death and he saw the little King building an Empire. 'He ought to establish institutions which shall efface all traces of the feudal law, secure the dignity of men,' he wrote. 'He should propagate, in all those countries now uncivilised and barbarous, the benefits of Christianity and civilisation.'[9] It was not to be. The King of Rome died of tuberculosis in Vienna at the age of twenty-one.

When Josephine died, Eugène inherited Malmaison and sold the Hesse-Casell paintings to the Tsar in 1815. In 1819, there was a huge house sale at Malmaison. Interested parties could buy antique busts and statues, Etruscan vases, granite columns, boxes, dresses, shawls, lace, collars and feathers, *objets d'art*, tables and even two mummies, one male and one female. The buyers spilled in to buy a little of the Empress's greatness. Josephine's treasures were dispersed across the world, her flower paintings lost, her fine furnishings broken and burned. Occasionally her belongings come up at auction and sell for huge sums. The Tsar took many of her paintings and sculptures, with most now in the Hermitage, although some of the paintings have since disappeared.[10]

Josephine died before she could see the sculpture of the Three Graces she had commissioned from Canova. The Duke of Bedford, who had desired it when it had been on display in the studio, immediately demanded it. The Tsar also wished to own it. Eugène claimed it for France. *The Three Graces* escaped the rapacious coveting of the Duke and the Tsar and remained in Eugène's possession until his son, Maxmillien, by then married to the Grand Duchess Maria, took it to the Hermitage. The Duke of Bedford had Canova make a copy – something that Josephine would never have allowed if she were alive – and it was installed at Woburn Abbey in 1819. It is this version that is alternately displayed in the Victoria and Albert Museum and the National Galleries of Scotland.

*   *   *

Over the years, Malmaison and its fine gardens fell into decline. All the furniture was stripped from the house and sold at auction. The roses were trampled, the remaining animals killed or sold off to homes that did not love them so well. In 1828, after Eugène's death, his widow sold Malmaison to a Swedish banker, Jonas Hagerman. In 1842, Queen Christina of Sweden took over the house and used it as a country residence. In 1861, Napoleon III, who had such fond memories of nibbling sugar cane in the gardens, demanded she sell the house to him. He opened it as a museum to coincide with the 1867 World's Fair. The house and gardens were damaged in the Franco-Prussian War of 1870 and the state sold it in 1877 to an estate agent, who sold off the land.

In 1896 a philanthropist, Daniel Iffla, bought the chateau and some of the land and donated it to France in 1904. The museum was opened in 1906.

Malmaison is now a story of grandeur and neglect in one, the remembrance of power and a reminder of how quickly it fades. The rolling estates have been eaten into by the development of Paris. For long years Josephine's picture gallery echoed emptily, the roses all dead. Now, once more, it is visited and enjoyed. If you walk into the gallery and look out onto the rose gardens you might imagine yourself a guest at one of Josephine's parties, watching as she walks towards you over the grass.

Notes

Prologue

1. Barras, *Mémoires*, II, p. 61.

1. *La Pagerie*

1. R. Pichevin, *L'Impératrice Joséphine*, p. 64.
2. J.B.T. Chanvalon, *Voyage à la Martinique* (1763), p. 38.
3. Pichevin, *L'Impératrice Joséphine*, p. 44.
4. Stuart, *Josephine*, p. 7.
5. Normand, vol. I, p. 6.
6. Pichevin, *L'Impératrice Joséphine* p. 26.
7. Antonia Fraser, *Marie Antoinette*, p. 62.
8. Jean Hanoteau, *Le Ménage Beauharnais*, p. 67.
9. Comte de Montgaillard, *Souvenirs* (Paris, 1895), p. 277.
10. Le Normand, *Historical and Secret Memoires*, pp. 19–20.
11. *Le Thai*, 30 May 1797.
12. Aubenas, *Histoire*, I, p. 92.
13. Frédéric Masson, *Josephine*, p. 104.
14. Masson, *Josephine*, p. 75.
15. Hanoteau, *Le Ménage Beauharnais*, p. 80.
16. Hanoteau, *Le Ménage Beauharnais*, p. 51.

2. Sophistication

1. Hanoteau, *Le Ménage Beauharnais*, p. 35.
2. Hanoteau, *Le Ménage Beauharnais*, p. 28.
3. Hanoteau, *Le Ménage Beauharnais*, p. 28.
4. Hanoteau, *Le Ménage Beauharnais*, p. 76.
5. Hanoteau, *Le Ménage Beauharnais*, p. 78.
6. Now that Marie-Josèphe-Rose is in Paris, I have chosen to refer to her as Josephine – for it is now that her life truly begins.
7. 'Les Registres Paroissiaux de Noisy-le-Grand', *Bulletin de la Société de l'Histoire de Paris* (1894), p. 126.
8. Hanoteau, *Le Ménage Beauharnais*, p. 87.
9. Hanoteau, *Le Ménage Beauharnais*, p. 34.
10. Hanoteau, *Le Ménage Beauharnais*, p. 37.
11. Hanoteau, *Le Ménage Beauharnais*, p. 85.
12. Hanoteau, *Le Ménage Beauharnais*, p. 55.
13. Hanoteau, *Le Ménage Beauharnais*, p. 102.
14. Hanoteau, *Le Ménage Beauharnais*, p. 87.
15. Montgaillard, *Souvenirs du Comte Montgaillard* (Paris, 1895), p. 85.
16. Hanoteau, *Le Ménage Beauharnais*, p. 52.
17. Hanoteau, *Le Ménage Beauharnais*, p. 103.
18. Hanoteau, *Le Ménage Beauharnais*, p. 124.
19. Hanoteau, *Le Ménage Beauharnais*, p. 125.
20. Hanoteau, *Le Ménage Beauharnais*, p. 130.
21. Hanoteau, *Le Ménage Beauharnais*, p. 130.
22. Hanoteau, *Le Ménage Beauharnais*, p. 137.
23. Hanoteau, *Le Ménage Beauharnais*, p. 149.
24. Hanoteau, *Le Ménage Beauharnais*, p. 151.
25. Hanoteau, *Le Ménage Beauharnais*, p. 152.
26. Hanoteau, *Le Ménage Beauharnais*, p. 162.
27. Hanoteau, *Le Ménage Beauharnais*, p. 162.
28. Masson, *Josephine*, p. 117.
29. Hanoteau, *Le Ménage Beauharnais*, p. 171.

3. 'Beneath all the sluts in the world'

1. Archives Nationales, Paris, Y 13,795.
2. Hanoteau, *Le Ménage Beauharnais*, p. 183. In Mme la Comtesse C. D'Arjuzon, *Joséphine contre Beauharnais* (Paris, 1906).

3. Hanoteau, *Le Ménage Beaharnais*, p. 184.

4. Hanoteau, *Le Ménage Beauharnais*, p. 201.

5. Victor du Bled, *La Société française du XVIe au XXe siècle* (Paris: Perrin, 1901), p. 312.

6. Mme de Rémusat, *Mémoires*, vol. 1, p. 34.

7. Mme la Comtesse C. D'Arjuzon, *Josephine Contre Beauharnais*, pp. 13–19.

8. In D'Arjuzon, *Joséphine contre Beauharnais*, p. 65.

9. Aubenas, *Impératrice*, I, p. 151.

10. Fersen coincidentally wrote to Marie Antoinette as Josephine.

11. Jacques Janssens, *Josephine*, p. 86.

12. Queen Hortense, *Mémoires*, I, p. 30.

4. Revolution

1. Fraser, *Marie Antoinette*, p. 281.

2. Kybalová and others, pp. 223–230.

3. Madame de Staël, *Considerations sur la Revolution française*, p. 101.

4. J.W. Croker, *Essays on the Early Period of the French Revolution* (1857), p. 121.

5. Madame de Staël, *Considerations sur la Revolution française, part 2*, p. 248.

6. Klinckowstrom, *Le Comte de Fersen & la Cour de France*, vol. 1, pp. 208–9.

7. Josephine, *Correspondance 1782–1814*, eds. Chevallier, Catinat & Pincemaille, p. 16.

8. *Memoirs de Madame de La Tour du Pin*, p. 177.

9. William Cohen, *The French Encounter with Africans*, p. 115.

10. Masson, *Josephine de Beauharnais*, pp. 186–7.

11. 17 January 1794, Josephine to the Committee, Josephine, *Correspondance*, ed. Chevalier, p. 17.

12. Masson, *Josephine de Beauharnais*.

13. Masson, *Josephine de Beauharnais*, p. 210.

14. Queen Hortense, *Mémoires*, vol. 1, p. 34.

15. Josephine to Hortense, *Correspondance*, p. 19.

16. Grace Elliott, *Journal of My Life*, p. 188.

17. Josephine to Hortense, *Correspondance*, p. 19.

18. Manuscripts Collection, La Pagerie Museum, Martinique.

19. Memoirs and Correspondence of the Imperatrice Josephine, collected by Regnault (Paris, 1820).

20. Georgette Ducrest, *Mémoires sur l'Impératrice Joséphine: La Ville, la cour et les salons de Paris sous l'Empire* (Paris, 1828), vol. 1, p. 55.
21. Ducrest, I, p. 59.
22. Ducrest, I, p. 59.

5. 'The height of good manners to be ruined'

1. Quoted in the *Magnificent Comedy*, p. 92.
2. Josephine to Mme La Pagerie, 20 November 1794, *Impératrice Joséphine, Correspondance*, p. 23.
3. Impératrice Joséphine, *Correspondance*, p. 26.
4. *Lettres inédites de Madame de Staël à Henri Meister*, eds. Usteri & Ritter, pp. 45–9.
5. Baron de Frénilly, *Recollections*, p. 136.
6. Baron de Frénilly, *Recollections*, p. 136.
7. *Correspondance de Napoléon 1er rassamblée dans les ouvrages publiés par les soins de Napoléon III 1858–69.*
8. 1 January 1795, *Impératrice Joséphine, Correspondance*, p. 28.
9. G. De Sainte-Croix de la Roncière, *Joséphine Impératrice*, p. 98.
10. Talleyrand, cited in Kybalová and others, p. 240.
11. A. Aulard, *Paris sous la Reaction Thermidorienne*, III, p. 180.
12. Ducrest, I, p. 332.
13. Frénilly, *Mémoires*, p. 65.
14. *Barras et son temps*, p. 205.
15. Lever, *de Sade: A Biography* (1993), pp. 514–15.
16. Pasquier, *Histoire de mon temps*, I, p. 118.
17. Stuart, *Josephine*, p. 64.
18. Barras, *Mémoires*, II p. 104.

6. 'What strange power you have over my heart'

1. Bertrand, *Cahiers*, II, p. 85.
2. Bertrand, *Cahiers*, I, p. 55.
3. Bourrienne, *Mémoires*, I, p. 75.
4. Bertrand, *Cahiers*, II, p. 198.
5. Bertrand, *Cahiers*, I, p. 66.
6. Bertrand, *Cahiers*, I, p. 75.

7. Bertrand, *Cahiers*, p. 78.

8. Rousseau, *Du Contrat Social*, II, p. 358.

9. Rémusat, I, p. 143.

10. Bertrand, *Cahiers*, III, p. 65.

11. Rémusat, *Mémoires*, I, p. 144.

12. Masson, *Napoleon inconnu, papiers inedits*, II, p. 286.

13. 12 August 1795, Joseph Bonaparte, *Mémoires*, I, p. 142.

14. Joseph Bonaparte, *Mémoires*, I, p. 144.

15. McLynn, Napoleon, p. 87.

16. McLynn, Napoleon, p. 85.

17. Bourrienne, *Mémoires*, II, p. 145.

18. There is much debate about Bonaparte's height – and some suggest he was as small as five foot two. The average height for a Frenchman at the time was about five foot six and many men make critical comments about his size. It should also be remembered that the aristocracy were thought to be taller; by saying that Bonaparte was small, people were declaring him low-class.

19. Napoleon, *Correspondance*, ed. Chevallier et al, I, p. 64. To Joseph.

20. Elliott's memoirs are unreliable but this seems very likely.

21. Napoleon, *Correspondance*, ed. Chevallier et al, I, p. 65.

22. Barras, *Mémoires*, pp. 57–9.

23. de Staël, *Correpondance*, II, p. 65.

24. Marmon, *Mémoires*, II, p. 52.

25. Josephine to Napoleon, 28 October, *Impératrice Joséphine, Correspondance*, p. 31.

26. Chantal Bonazzi, *Lettres d'amour à Josephine*, p. 45.

27. Bonazzi, *Lettres d'amour*, p. 52.

28. See Kate Williams, *England's Mistress*, p. 254.

29. Bonazzi, *Lettres d'amour*, p. 85.

30. Bertrand, *Cahiers*, p. 65.

31. Rémusat, *Mémoires*, I, p. 247.

32. Josephine to Mme Renaudin, 6 September 1796, *Josephine, Correspondance*, p. 47.

33. Bertrand, *Cahiers*, p. 86.

34. Ducrest, I, p. 137.

35. Girod de l'Ain, *Désirée Clary*, p. 91.

7. 'The single object in my heart'

1. Bertrand, *Cahiers*, p. 67.
2. Bonazzi, *Lettres d'amour*, p. 86.
3. 14 March 1796, Bonazzi, *Lettres d'amour*, pp. 49–50.
4. Napoleon, *Lettres d'amour à Josephine*, pp. 51–2.
5. 3 April, Napoleon, *Lettres d'amour à Josephine*, pp. 54–5.
6. 3 April, Napoleon, *Lettres d'amour à Josephine*, pp. 54–5.
7. 5 April, Napoleon, *Lettres d'amour à Josephine*, pp. 55–6.
8. 7 April, Bonazzi, *Lettres d'amour*, p. 66.
9. Bonazzi, *Lettres d'amour*, p. 67.
10. 24 April, Napoleon, *Lettres d'amour*, p. 66.
11. 24 April, Napoleon, *Lettres d'amour*, pp. 63–4.
12. 24 April, Napoleon, *Lettres d'amour*, pp. 63–4.
13. Napoleon, *Lettres d'amour*, p. 65.
14. 29 April, Bonazzi, *Lettres d'amour*, p. 61.
15. 15 June, Bonazzi, *Lettres d'amour*, p. 60.
16. 15 June, Bonazzi, *Lettres d'amour*, p. 80.
17. 3 April, Bonazzi, *Lettres d'amour*, p. 56.
18. Marmont, *Mémoires*, I, pp. 87–8.
19. 13 May, Bonazzi, *Lettres d'amour,* p. 62.
20. 26 June, Bonazzi, *Lettres d'amour*, p. 60.
21. 17 April, Napoleon, *Lettres d'amour*, p. 61.
22. Duc de Raguse, *Mémoires de Maréchal Marmont*, I, p. 187.
23. 8 June, Bonazzi, *Lettres d'amour*, p. 70.
24. Arnault, *Souvenirs*, p. 392.
25. 26 June, Bonazzi, *Lettres d'amour*, p. 80.
26. Hastier, *Le Grand Amour de Josephine*, p. 70.
27. *Souvenirs et mémoires, recueil mensue; de documents* (Paris, 1898), I, p. 55.
28. Henry Foljambe, p. 188.
29. Napoleon, *Correspondance*, II, p. 72.
30. McLynn, *Napoleon*, p. 147. In tearing the Catholic art out of context, Napoleon was denying religion. Also, Britain might have had a superior naval power, but its art was unimpressive landscapes, horses and dogs hung on the Briton's walls, and dreary Benjamin West was in charge of the Royal Academy.

31. Bonazzi, *Lettres d'amour*, p. 75.

32. Napoleon, *Lettres d'amour*, pp. 74–5.

33. Napoleon, *Correspondance Generale*, I, p. 43.

8. *A million kisses*

1. Josephine, *Correspondance 1782–1814*, p. 45.

2. Antoine Hamelin, *Douze ans de ma vie*, pp. 11–12.

3. Hamelin, *Douze ans de ma vie*, p. 15.

4. Josephine, *Correspondance 1782–1814*, p. 45.

5. 17 July, Bonazzi, pp. 93–4.

6. Josephine, *Correspondance*, p. 45.

7. 21 July, Bonazzi, p. 97.

8. Hamelin, *Douze ans de ma vie*, p. 19.

9. 17 October, Napoleon, *Lettres d'amour*, pp. 112–13.

10. Napoleon, *Lettres d'amour*, pp. 113–14.

11. Josephine to Mme Renaudin, 6 September 1796, *Correspondance*, p. 47.

12. 21 November, Bonazzi, *Lettres d'amour*, p. 123.

13. 27 November, Bonazzi, *Lettres d'amour*, pp. 127–8.

14. 28 November, Bonazzi, *Lettres d'amour*, p. 129.

15. Tulard and Garros, *Itineraire de Napoleon*, p. 89.

16. 19 November, 1796, *Correspondance*, II, p. 1201.

17. Miot de Melito, *Mémoires*, II, pp. 174–5.

18. Carron de Nisas, *Mémoires*, I, p. 78.

19. Abrantes, *Mémoires*, p. 66.

20. Bourrienne, *Mémoires*, I, p. 45.

21. 24 April, Napoleon to Josephine, Bonazzi, *Lettres d'amour*, p. 70.

22. Masson, *Napoleon Inconnu: Papiers Inédités*, p. 203.

23. Rémusat, *Mémoires*, I, p. 131.

24. Bourrienne, *Mémoires*, I, p. 150.

25. Hortense, *Mémoires*, p. 65.

26. De Staël, *Des Circonstances actuelles qui peuvent terminer la Révolution et des principes qui doivent fonder la République en France*, p. 122. Emmanuel de Las Cases, *Mémorial se Sainte Hélène, 1823–1824*, II p. 195.

27. Michel Poniatowski, *Talleyrand et La Directory*, p. 89.

28. Bertrand, *Cahiers*, Janvier-Mai, 1829, p. 98.

9. *'I am so distressed at being separated from him'*

1. Bourrienne, *Mémoires*, I, 565.
2. Lucien Bonaparte, *Mémoires*, II, p. 342.
3. McLynn, p. 153.
4. Bourrienne, *Mémoires*, I, p. 343.
5. Bourrienne, *Mémoires*, I, p. 87.
6. Impératrice Joséphine, *Correspondance*, p. 87.
7. Masson, Josephine, p. 124.
8. Bertrand, *Cahiers*, p. 67.
9. Mme de Rémusat, *Memoirs de Madame de Rémusat 1802–1818*, I, p. 247.
10. L. Hastier, *Le Grand amour de Joséphine* (Paris, 1955), pp. 152–4.
11. Hastier, *Grand Amour*, p. 153.
12. 17 March 1798, Josephine to Hippolyte Charles, Josephine, *Correspondance*, p. 60.
13. Josephine to Hippolyte Charles, Josephine, *Correspondance*, p. 60.
14. Bourrienne, *Mémoires*, II, p. 67.
15. *L'Orient* should have carried 1000 men but it was crammed – which made for poor conditions.
16. Masson, *Josephine*, p. 128.
17. Adrien Grosjean, *Nouvel essai sur les eaux minérales de Plombières* (Paris, 1803), p. 7.
18. Josephine, *Correspondance*, pp. 66–7.
19. Masson, *Josephine*, p. 131.
20. Masson, *Josephine*, p. 130.
21. Josephine, *Correspondance*, pp. 70–1.
22. Masson, *Josephine*, pp. 137–8.
23. Masson, *Josephine*, p. 142–3.
24. Bourrienne, *Mémoires*, I, p. 241.
25. Bourrienne, *Mémoires*, I, p. 322.
26. Bourrienne souped up his memoirs after the event and, like most memoirists, inserted himself more, so there is a possibility he might not have been there. But his picture of Bonaparte is correct: he was devastated.
27. Bourrienne, *Mémoires*, I, p. 322.
28. Morand, *Lettres sur l'expedition de Egypte*, 19 September 1798, pp. 171–2.
29. Bourrienne, *Mémoires*, I, p. 200.
30. British Museum, Add MSS, 23003. Also, see *Mémoires et Correspondance du Roi Joseph*, ed. Du Casse, I, p. 189.

31. Masson, pp. 139–40.

32. Desvernois, *Mémoires*, p. 134.

33. Napoleon, *Correspondance*, XXIX, p. 457.

34. Williams, *England's Mistress*, p. 232.

35. *Morning Chronicle*, 24 November 1798.

10. *'All I have suffered'*

1. British Museum, Add MSS, 23003.

2. Rémusat, *Mémoires*, I, p. 65.

3. Hubert, *Malmaison*, p. 14.

4. Hubert, *Malmaison*, p. 14.

5. Hubert, *Malmaison*, p. 14.

6. Impératrice Joséphine, *Correspondance, 1782–1814*, ed. by Bernard Chevallier, Maurice Catinat and Christophe Pincemaille (Paris: Payot, 1996), letter 115, 2 March 1799, p. 82.

7. Impératrice Joséphine, *Correspondance*, letter 116, 17 March 1799, p. 82.

8. Hubert, *Malmaison*, p. 14.

9. Impératrice Joséphine, *Mémoires et correspondance de l'Impératrice Joséphine* (Paris, 1820), pp. 154–5.

10. Impératrice Joséphine, *Correspondance*, letter 126, 24 June 1799, p. 87.

11. February 1799, Impératrice Joséphine, *Correspondance*, p. 81.

12. Gavoty, *Les Amoureux*, 23 June, p. 279.

13. Bourrienne, *Mémoires*, II, p. 296.

14. Bertrand, *Cahiers*, I, p. 234.

15. Bourrienne, *Mémoires*, I, p. 300.

16. They were from June, the most recent they had.

17. When she found out the truth, she took Junot as a lover and then General Kleber, who was infuriated to be left in charge of the Army of the Orient by a commander who had failed even to consult him or take his leave.

18. Impératrice Joséphine, *Correspondance*, letter 131, 30 September 1799, p. 89.

19. *Les Beauharnais et L'Empereur. Lettres de l'Impératrice Joséphine et de la Reine Hortense au Prince Eugène* (Paris, 1936), pp. 125–6.

20. Impératrice Joséphine, *Correspondance*, p. 56.

11. *'He owes me everything'*

1. D'Abrantès, *Mémoires*, 1, p. 265.
2. Maurice Lescure, *Madame Hamelin*, p. 54.
3. Bourrienne, *Mémoires*, II, p. 5.
4. Bourrienne, *Mémoires*, II, p. 7.
5. Bourrienne, *Mémoires*, II, p. 120.
6. Bourrienne, *Mémoires*, I, p. 344. Bourrienne's words were probably exaggerated, but this was the type of melodrama that Napoleon liked.
7. Bourrienne, II, p. 10.
8. D'Abrantes, *Mémoires*, II, p. 92.
9. 18 July, Napoleon to Josephine, Bonazzi, *Lettres d'amour*, p. 105.
10. 24 April, Napoleon to Josephine, Bonazzi, *Lettres d'amour*, p. 166.
11. Bourrienne, II, p. 102.
12. D'Abrantès, *Mémoires*, 1, p. 265.
13. Gohier, *Mémoires*, II, p. 2.
14. Bourrienne, I, p. 199.
15. Bourrienne, *Mémoires*, I, p. 250.
16. Bourrienne, *Mémoires*, I, p. 252.
17. Lever, *de Sade*, p. 514.
18. Bourrienne, *Mémoires*, I, p. 155.
19. Bourrienne, *Mémoires*, I, p. 355.
20. Hortense, *Mémoires*, p. 187.
21. Jules Bertaut, p. 135.
22. Ducrest, p. 33.
23. Memoirs de Mme de la Tour du Pin, p. 85.
24. Bourrienne, *Mémoires*, I, p. 352.
25. Bourrienne, *Mémoires*, I, p. 354.
26. As her lady-in-waiting put it, 'the idleness of a Court life makes the day seem a hundred hours long' (Rem, p. 131).
27. Bertrand, *Cahiers*, p. 345.
28. Rémusat, 1, p. 61.
29. Bertrand, *Cahiers*, p. 365.
30. Rémusat, 1, p. 5.
31. Ducrest, 1, p. 33. Mme de Rémusat, 1, p. 29.
32. Bourrienne, *Mémoires*, I, p. 450.
33. Impératrice Joséphine, *Correspondance*, letter 152, p. 99.
34. Impératrice Joséphine, *Correspondance*, letter 153, p. 99.

35. Ducrest, 1, p. 33.
36. Bourrienne, *Mémoires*, I, p. 420.
37. Bourrienne, *Mémoires*, I, p. 430.
38. Bourrienne, *Mémoires*, I, p. 463.
39. Bourrienne, *Mémoires*, I, p. 460.
40. See Kiefer, *Empress Josephine*, p. 29.
41. Bourrienne, *Mémoires*, I, p. 345.
42. Kybalová and others, p. 243.
43. Hortense, *Mémoires*, cited in Hamilton, p. 120.
44. Kybalová and others, p. 243.
45. Christopher Herold, *Mistress to an Age*, p. 104.
46. Rémusat, *Mémoires*, II, p. 300.
47. Ducrest, 1, p. 12.
48. Alexandra Gerstein, 'Josephine at Malmaison', in *France in Russia*, p. 12.
49. Impératrice Joséphine, *Correspondance, 1782–1814*, ed. by Bernard Chevallier, Maurice Catinat and Christophe Pincemaille (Paris: Payot, 1996), letter 166, 1800, p. 106.
50. Bourrienne, *Mémoires*, I, p. 200.
51. Bertaut, p. 132.
52. *c.* Oct–Nov 1799, Josephine, *Correspondance*, p. 93.
53. *Le Mémorial de Sainte-Hélène*, in Kiefer, p. 26.
54. Rémusat, 1, p. 13.

12. *'The most beautiful thing in the world'*

1. Hubert, *Malmaison*, p. 17.
2. Hubert, *Malmaison*, p. 17.
3. Hubert, *Malmaison*, p. 18.
4. Hubert, *Malmaison*, p. 17.
5. Hubert, *Malmaison*, p. 20.
6. 'Le décor intérieur', *Musée National du château de Malmaison*, p. 85.
7. Gerstein, 'Josephine at Malmaison', p. 15.
8. Gerstein, p. 15.
9. Impératrice Joséphine, *Correspondance*, letter 140, 1799, p. 94.
10. Impératrice Joséphine, *Correspondance*, letter 209, 23 November 1803, p. 137.
11. Impératrice Joséphine, *Correspondance*, letter 213, 19 March 1804, pp. 142–3.

12. Impératrice Joséphine, *Correspondance*, letter 213, 19 March 1804, pp. 142–3.

13. Ventenat, *Le Jardin de Malmaison*, p. 88.

14. Ventenat, *Le Jardin de Malmaison*, p. 89.

15. To Josephine at Plombières, Bonazzi, *Lettres d'amour*, p. 161.

16. Napoleon made his old principal at Brienne head of the Library.

17. Jill, Duchess of Hamilton, *Napoleon, the Empress & the Artist*, p. 114.

18. Impératrice Joséphine, *Correspondance*, letter 485, 14 June 1813, pp. 348–9.

19. Hubert, *Malmaison*, p. 32.

20. Impératrice Joséphine, *Correspondance*, letter 485, 14 June 1813, pp. 348–9.

21. Fontaine, 1 July 1802, cited in Gerstein, p. 16.

22. *Lettres Intimes*, letter X, p. 179.

23. Hubert, 1989, pp. 34–5.

24. Fontaine, 1 July 1802, cited in Gerstein, p. 16.

25. Evangeline Bruce, p. 306.

26. Kiefer, pp. 12–16.

27. In 1805, she opened the property to members of the Institut de France and administrators of the Musée National d'Histoire Naturelle, publishing an invitation in the *Maison encyclopédique*.

28. *Lettres de Napoléon à Joséphine*, réunies et préfacées par le Dr Léon Cerf (Paris, 1928), p. 57.

29. Laura Junot, Duchess of Abrantès, *Autobiography and Recollections of Laura Duchess of Abrantès (widow of General Junot)* (Bentley, 1893), p. 407.

30. Hamilton, p. 118.

31. Hamilton, p. 118.

32. This was recorded in Fontaine's journal on 2 July 1800. Cited in Bernard Chevallier, *Le Château de Malmaison, des origines à 1904* (Paris: Réunions des musées nationaux, 1989), p. 279.

33. Hamilton, p. 119.

34. Bourrienne, *Mémoires*, I, p. 525.

35. Stuart, p. 285.

36. Napoleon to Josephine, 1 July 1802, Bonazzi, pp. 118–202.

37. Hubert, *Malmaison*, p. 23.

38. Hubert, *Malmaison*, p. 22.

39. Hubert, *Malmaison*, p. 22.

40. Hubert, *Malmaison*, p. 23.

41. Mme Junot, cited in Hubert, 1989, p. 23.

42. Napoleon to Josephine, 19 June 1802, Bonazzi, p. 25.

43. François Jarry, *Hortense de Beauharnais* (Paris: Giovanangeli, 2009), p. 66.

44. *Memoirs de Queen Hortense*, I, p. 2.

45. Jarry, 2009, p. 59.

46. On this account, see Hubert, 1989, pp. 24–5.

47. Jarry, 2009, p. 66.

48. Mme de Rémusat, *Memoirs of Mme de Rémusat*, trans. by Mrs Cashel Hoey and John Lillie (London, 1880), II, p. 323.

49. Mme Campan, letter to Hortense, cited in Jarry, 2009, p. 62.

50. Bertaut, p. 140.

51. Bourrienne, *Mémoires*, I, p. 213.

52. Bourrienne, *Mémoires*, I, p. 525.

53. Bourrienne I, p. 200, of Hamilton, p. 115.

54. Bourrienne, *Mémoires*, I, p. 200.

55. 31 August 1809.

56. Marquise de La Tour du Pin, *Journal d'une femme de cinquante ans (1778–1815)* (Paris: M. Imhaus & R. Chapelot, 1914), II, pp. 219–20, cited in Pougetoux, p. 93. Scholars now suggest that much of Josephine's collection was acquired legitimately, yet it is undeniable that she had more power to buy, more access and people sold to her because they were afraid of her husband (Pougetoux, pp. 93–4). The Louvre wanted her pictures, but had to satisfy themselves with copies.

57. Carol Solomon Kiefer, *The Empress Josephine: Art & Royal Identity*, exhibition catalogue (Mead Art Museum, Amherst College, Amherst, Massachusetts, 2005), p. 34.

58. Kiefer, p. 33.

59. Hubert, 1989, p. 33.

60. On the gallery, see Gerstein, p. 17.

61. *L'Observateur au muséum ou la critique des tableaux en vaudeville* (Paris, 1802), p. 17.

62. Kiefer, p. 41.

63. She also collected works by Pierre Cartellier.

64. Gerstein, p. 22.

13. *Scenes with Bonaparte*

1. Impératrice Joséphine, *Correspondance*, letter 156, 9 July 1800, p. 101.

2. Duchesse d'Abrantès, cited in Bertaut, p. 134.

3. Bourrienne, *Mémoires*, II, p. 102.

4. Bourrienne, *Mémoires*, I, p. 450.

5. Bonazzi, *Lettres d'amour*, p. 201.

6. Bourrienne, *Mémoires*.

7. Madame de La Tour du Pin, *Mémoires*, p. 346.

8. De Staël, *Dix années d'exil*, p. 94.

9. Pierre Roederer, *Ouevres*, V.

10. De Staël, *Correspondances Générale*, IV, p. 306.

11. Paul Gautier, *Madame de Staël et Napoléon*, p. 103.

12. Bourrienne, *Mémoires*, VIII, p. 101.

13. Queen Hortense, *Mémoires*, p. 69.

14. Jean Savant, *Tel fut Napoléon*.

15. Rémusat, I, p. 219.

16. Jules Bertaut, *Impératrice Joséphine* (Paris: Le Club du Livre d'Histoire, 1956), pp. 130–2.

17. Duchesse d'Abrantès, cited in Bertaut, p. 130.

18. Bourrienne, *Mémoires*, I, p. 464.

19. Bertaut, pp. 130–1.

20. Bourrienne, *Mémoires*, I, p. 500.

21. de Rémusat, *Memoires*, I, p. 11.

22. On the Civil Code, see Patricia Mainardi, *Husbands, Wives, and Lovers: Marriage and its Discontents in Nineteenth-Century France* (New Haven and London: Yale University Press, 2003), pp. 12–18.

23. Bertrand, *Cahiers*, p. 177.

24. Bertrand, *Cahiers*, p. 169.

25. McLynn, *Napoleon*, p. 256.

26. Bourrienne, *Mémoires*, I, p. 384.

27. De Staël, *Considérations*, p. 339.

28. De Staël, *Dix Années d'exil*, p. 105. See also Bourrienne, *Mémoires*, II, p. 30.

29. Madame de Staël, *Dix années d'exil*, p. 130.

30. Savant, *Tel fut Napoléon*. Barras, *Mémoires*, II, p. 65.

31. *Documens particuliers (en forme de lettres) sur Napoleon Bonaparte, sur plusieurs de ses actes jusqu'ici inconnus ou mal interprétés* (Paris, 1819), p. 103.

32. Louis Lumet, *Napoléon 1er, Empereur des Français* (Paris, 1908), p. 67.

33. *Documens particuliers (en forme de lettres) sur Napoleon Bonaparte, sur plusieurs de ses actes jusqu'ici inconnus ou mal interprétés* (Paris, 1819), p. 104.

34. Memoirs of General Count Rapp, p. 19.

35. *Documens particuliers (en forme de lettres) sur Napoleon Bonaparte, sur plusieurs de ses actes jusqu'ici inconnus ou mal interprétés* (Paris, 1819), p. 104.

36. *Documens particuliers (en forme de lettres) sur Napoleon Bonaparte, sur plusieurs de ses actes jusqu'ici inconnus ou mal interprétés* (Paris, 1819), p. 104.

37. Rémusat, *Mémoires*, I, p. 56.

38. Bourrienne, *Mémoires*, II, p. 130.

39. Bourrienne, *Mémoires*, II, p. 65.

40. Bourrienne, *Mémoires*, II, p. 54.

41. Bourrienne, *Mémoires*, II, p. 55.

42. Grosjean, p. 4.

14. *'My stepfather is a comet'*

1. Bruce, *Napoleon and Josephine*, p. 64.

2. Hortense, *Mémoires*, 1, p. 55.

3. Hortense, *Mémoires*, 1, p. 73.

4. Bourrienne, *Mémoires*, II, p. 145.

5. Anonymous, *Paris et ses modes ou les soirées parisiennes* (Paris, 1803), p. 19.

6. Bertrand, *Cahiers*, p. 45.

7. Charles James Fox, *Memoirs of the Latter Years of the Right Honourable Charles James Fox*, pp. 188–285.

8. Edmund Eyre, *Observations Made at Paris during the Peace* (London, 1803), p. 54.

9. Yorke, *Letters from France*.

10. Josephine, *Correspondance*, p. 138.

11. Josephine to Mme La Pagerie, 1803, BN, 9324, National Archive, Paris.

12. Rémusat, *Mémoires*, I, p. 50.

13. Bourrienne, *Mémoires*, I, p. 630.

14. Bertie Greatheed, *An Englishman in Paris*.

15. Bertrand, *Cahiers*, IV, p. 65.

16. Fojambe, p. 209.

17. Bruce, *Napoleon and Josephine*, p. 335.

18. Ducrest, I, p. 277.

19. Duchesse d'Abrantès, cited in Ludmila Kybalová, Olga Herbenová and Milena Lamarová, *The Pictorial Encyclopaedia of Fashion*, trans. by Claudia Rosoux (London: Paul Hamlyn, 1968), p. 227.

20. du Bled, p. 272.

21. Rémusat, *Mémoires*, I, p. 344.

22. Rémusat, *Mémoires*, I, p. 137.

23. James Gillray, *Ci-Devant Occupations*, 1805.

24. Thomas Rowlandson, *The Progress of the Empress Josephine*, 1808.

25. Bertrand, *Cahiers*, p. 65.

26. Constant, *Mémoires*.

27. Rémusat, *Mémoires*, II, p. 231.

28. Rémusat, *Mémoires*, I, p. 142.

29. Marguerite Joséphine Weimer, called Mlle George, *Mémoires inédits de Mademoiselle George*, p. 29.

30. Edith Saunders, *Napoleon and Mademoiselle George*, p. 55.

31. Rémusat, *Mémoires*, II, p. 321.

32. Some of these prisoners were held until Napoleon abdicated in 1814.

33. Madame de Staël, *Dix Années d'exil*, p. 94.

34. Masson, *Madame Bonaparte*, p. 65.

35. Bourrienne, *Mémoires*, II, p. 145.

36. Rémusat, *Mémoires*, I, p. 191.

37. Bourrienne, *Mémoires*, II, p. 150.

38. Rémusat, *Mémoires*, I, 2087.

39. Ducrest, *Mémoires*, 1, p. 59.

40. See *Documens particuliers (en forme de lettres) sur Napoléon Bonaparte, sur plusieurs de ses actes jusqu ici inconnus ou mal interprétés* (Paris, 1819), p. 106.

15. 'Your Imperial Majesty'

1. Rémusat, *Mémoires*, I, p. 255.

2. Fojambe, p. 209.

3. Avrillon, *Mémoires de Mlle Avrillon, première femme de chamber de l'impératrice, sur la vie privée de Joséphine, sa famille et sa cour*, p. 69.

4. Savant, *Napoleon et Joséphine*.

5. Rémusat, *Mémoires*, I, p. 5.

6. Rémusat, *Mémoires*, I, p. 306.

7. Rémusat, *Mémoires*, I, p. 305.

8. Rémusat, *Mémoires*, I, p. 309.

9. Rémusat, *Mémoires*, I, p. 309.

10. Rémusat, *Mémoires*, I, p. 313.

11. Roederer, *Oeuvres*, I, p. 214.

12. Rémusat, *Mémoires*, I, p. 315.

13. D'Abrantès, *Mémoires*, I, p. 215.
14. D'Abrantès, *Mémoires*, I, p. 216.
15. Rémusat, *Mémoires*, I, p. 247.

16. *'The King of Diamonds'*

1. Rémusat, *Mémoires*, II, p. 65.
2. Rémusat, *Mémoires*, II, p. 131.
3. Duchesse d'Abrantès, *Memoirs of Madame Junot, Duchesse d'Abrantès*, II, pp. 347–8.
4. Gautier, *Madame de Staël et Napoleon*, p. 168.
5. Rémusat, *Mémoires*, II, p. 65.
6. Bruce, *Napoleon and Josephine*, p. 373.
7. Rémusat, *Mémoires*, I, p. 263.
8. Josephine, *Correspondance*, p. 217.
9. Rémusat, *Mémoires*, I, p. 293.
10. D'Abrantès, *Mémoires*, p. 82.
11. Madame de Staël, *Dix années d'exil*, p. 95.
12. Ducrest, I, p. 255.
13. Rémusat, I, p. 122.
14. Constant, *Mémoires*.
15. Bourrienne, *Mémoires*, II, p. 150.
16. Avrillon, *Mémoires*, p. 103.
17. Rémusat, *Mémoires*, I, p. 234.
18. Bourgeat, *Lettres*, p. 67.
19. Avrillon, *Mémoires*, p. 156.
20. Rémusat, *Mémoires*, II, p. 145.
21. Bertrand, *Cahiers*, p. 75.
22. Rémusat, *Mémoires*, I, p. 350.
23. Rémusat, *Mémoires*, I, p. 357.
24. Rémusat, *Mémoires*, I, p. 132.
25. Remusat, *Mémoires*, II, p. 64.
26. Sutherland, *Walewska*, p. 40.
27. Rémusat, *Mémoires*, I, p. 402.
28. *Memoirs of Queen Hortense, Mémoires de la Reine Hortense*, p. 4.
29. Rémusat, *Mémoires*, I, p. 224.
30. Ducrest, I, p. 57.
31. Napoleon to Josephine, 14 August 1804.

32. Ducrest, I, p. 57.
33. Rémusat, *Mémoires*, II, p. 65.
34. Rémusat, *Mémoires*, I, p. 40.
35. Rémusat, *Mémoires*, I, p. 35. Bourrienne, *Mémoires*, II, p. 20.

17. *'I have fulfilled my destiny'*

1. Hanoteau, *Les Beauharnais et l'Empereur.*
2. Napoleon, *Lettres d'amour*, p. 174.
3. Rémusat, *Mémoires*, I, p. 437.
4. Alistair Horne, *Napoleon: Master of Europe*, p. 378.
5. Bourgeat, *Napoléon: Lettres à Josèphine.*
6. 27 October 1805, Napoleon to Josephine, Bonazzi, *Lettres d'amour.*
7. 10 December 1805, Napoleon to Josephine, Bonazzi, *Lettres d'amour*, p. 175.
8. 2 December 1805, Bonazzi, *Lettres d'amour*, p. 123.
9. 19 December 1805, Napoleon to Josephine, Bonazzi.
10. André Castelot, *Napoléon.*
11. Napoleon, *Correspondance de Napoleon I.*
12. By 1811, he ruled 44 million people.
13. Josephine, *Correspondance*, p. 185.
14. Rémusat, *Mémoires*, II, p. 55.
15. Ducrest, I, p. 193.
16. Hortense, *Mémoires*, I, p. 47.
17. Rémusat, *Mémoires*, I, p. 333.
18. Rémusat, *Mémoires*, I p. 294.
19. See *Mémoires* of Lucien.
20. Bourrienne, *Mémoires*, I, p. 345.
21. Napoleon to Eugène, *Correspondance*, XVII, p. 938.
22. Rémusat, *Mémoires*, I, p. 198.
23. 5 October 1806, Napoleon to Josephine, Bonazzi, *Lettres d'amour.*
24. 16 October 1806, Napoleon to Josephine, Bonazzi, *Lettres d'amour.*
25. Savant, *Napoleon et Josephine*. 6 November 1806, Napoleon to Josephine, Bonazzi, *Lettres d'amour.*
26. 1 November 1806, Bonazzi, *Lettres d'amour*, p. 157.
27. 3 December 1806, Bonazzi, *Lettres d'amour*, p. 158.
28. 2 December 1806, Bonazzi, *Lettres d'amour*, p. 159.
29. 3 December 1806, Bonazzi, *Lettres d'amour*, p. 160.
30. 31 December 1806, Bonazzi, *Lettres d'amour*, p. 161.

18. *'I wish you would be more reasonable'*

1. 7 January 1807, Napoleon to Josephine.
2. Christine Sutherland, *Walewska*, p. 68.
3. Walewski Archives.
4. Walewski Archives.
5. Walewski Archives.
6. Bruce, *Napoleon and Josephine:* Josephine correspondence, p. 200, from the Walewski Archives.
7. Bertrand, *Cahiers*, p. 145.
8. Napoleon to Marie Walewska, Napoleon, *Correspondance*, ed. Chevallier, p. 85.
9. 11 January 1807, Napoleon to Josephine, Bonazzi, *Lettres d'amour.*
10. 18 January 1807, Bonazzi, *Lettres d'amour.*
11. Bruce, p. 343.
12. Napoleon, 25 March 1807, Bonazzi, *Lettres d'amour*, p. 267.
13. Bruce, *Napoleon and Josephine*, p. 407, from the Archives Nationale in Paris.
14. Josephine, *Correspondance*, p. 200.
15. Hanoteau, *Les Beauharnais et l'Empereur.*
16. 27 March 1807, Bonazzi, *Lettres d'amour.*
17. 17 March 1807, Bonazzi, *Lettres d'amour.*
18. 25 March 1807, Bonazzi, *Lettres d'amour.*
19. 2 April 1807, Bonazzi, *Lettres d'amour.*
20. 10 May 1807, Bonazzi, *Lettres d'amour.*
21. Bruce, *Napoleon and Josephine,* p. 410.
22. Napoleon, 14 May 1807, Bonazzi, *Lettres d'amour*, p. 283.
23. Napoleon, 14 May 1807, Bonazzi, *Lettres d'amour*, p. 283.
24. 26 May 1807, Bonazzi, *Lettres d'amour.*
25. Rémusat, *Mémoires.*
26. 2 June 1807, Bonazzi, *Lettres d'amour.*
27. Bourgeat, *Napoléon: Lettres à Joséphine,* 3 July 1807.
28. Napoleon, 25 June 1807, Bonazzi, *Lettres d'amour*, p. 297.
29. 7 July 1807, Bonazzi, *Lettres d'amour*, p. 204.
30. Bourrienne, *Mémoires*, III, p. 150.
31. Bertrand, *Cahiers*, III, p. 51.

19. *'Cold and often embarrassed'*

1. Bourrienne, *Mémoires*, p. 65.
2. Josephine, *Correspondance*, p. 217.
3. Rémusat, *Mémoires*, II, p. 234.
4. Bourgeat, *Napoléon: Lettres à Joséphine.*
5. Bertrand, *Cahiers*, p. 145.
6. Maurice Guerrini, *Napoleon and Paris*, p. 183.
7. Bourrienne, *Mémoires*, VIII, pp. 101–16.
8. Napoleon, *Correspondance de Napoleon I.*
9. 10 February 1808, Josephine, *Correspondance*, p. 219.
10. Josephine to Eugène, 22 September 1808, Josephine, *Correspondance*, p. 229.
11. Caulaincourt, *Mémoires.*
12. Napoleon, Bonazzi, *Lettres d'amour*, p. 312.
13. Napoleon, Bonazzi, *Lettres d'amour*, p. 313.
14. Napoleon, *Correspondance*, ed. Chevallier.
15. Cardinal Fouché, *Mémoires*, p. 87.
16. FM, 412. Bertrand, *Cahiers*, IV, p. 56.
17. Bruce, *Napoleon and Josephine: An Improbable Marriage*, p. 438, from the Walewski Archives.
18. Rémusat, *Mémoires*. Martinique would remain British until 1814.
19. D'Abrantès, *Mémoires*, p. 182.
20. Normand Caulaincourt, *Mémoires* p. 456.
21. 22 October 1809, Bonazzi, *Lettres d'amour*, p. 207.
22. Ducrest, I, p. 244.
23. Hortense, *Mémoires*, p. 117.

20. *'Like a wounded soldier'*

1. Bourrienne, *Mémoires*, III, p. 64.
2. Bourrienne, *Mémoires*, III, p. 56.
3. Hortense, *Mémoires.*
4. Bourrienne, *Mémoires*, III, p. 115.
5. Hortense, *Mémoires.*
6. Ducrest, I, p. 207.
7. Imperatrice Josephine, *Lettres*, p. 240.
8. *Les Beauharnais et L'Empereur. Lettres de l'Impératrice Joséphine et de la Reine Hortense au Prince Eugène* (Paris, 1936), p. 81.

9. Hortense, *Mémoires*.
10. Napoleon, Bonazzi, *Lettres d'amour*, p. 359, December 1809.
11. Ducrest, I, p. 171.
12. Ducrest, II, p. 28.
13. Napoleon, *Lettres d'amour*, p. 360.
14. 17 January 1810.
15. Hortense, *Mémoires*, p. 175.
16. Castelot, *Joséphine*.
17. Napoleon, *Correspondance*, ed. Chevallier, p. 78.
18. Napoleon, Bonazzi, *Lettres d'amour*, p. 381.
19. Ducrest, I, p. 89.
20. Betrand, Cahiers, IV.
21. Hortense, *Mémoires*, p. 315.
22. Philip Mansel, *The Court of France*, p. 121.
23. Martineau, *Marie-Louise*, p. 78.
24. Bourgeat, *Napoléon: Lettres à Joséphine*, 19 April 1810.
25. Napoleon, 20 April 1810, Bonazzi, *Lettres d'Amour*, p. 382.
26. 22 April 1810, Bonazzi, *Lettres d'amour*.
27. Hortense, *Mémoires*.
28. Napoleon Letters, Bruce, p. 455.
29. Ducrest, I, p. 158.
30. 14 September 1810, Correspondence, ed. Chevalier, p. 166.
31. Masson, *Joséphine Répudiée*, pp. 199–201.
32. Ducrest, I, p. 239.
33. Ducrest, I, p. 206.
34. Ducrest, I, p. 283.
35. Ducrest, I, p. 214–15.
36. Fraser, *Marie Antoinette*, p. 155.
37. Napoleon, 22 March 1811, Bonazzi, *Lettres d'amour*, p. 395.
38. Napoleon, Bonazzi, *Lettres d'amour*, p. 396.
39. Napoleon, Bonazzi, *Lettres d'amour*, p. 397.
40. Gerstein, p. 12.
41. Bourrienne, *Mémoires*, III, p. 120.
42. Bourrienne, *Mémoires*, III, p. 140.
43. Impératrice Joséphine, *Correspondance*, letter 485, 14 June 1813, pp. 348–9.
44. Pougetoux, p. 94.
45. Impératrice Joséphine, *Correspondance*, letter 464, 25 September 1812, p. 336.
46. Impératrice Joséphine, *Correspondance*, letter 464, 25 September 1812, p. 336.

47. Impératrice Joséphine, *Correspondance*, letter 468, 13 October 1812, p. 339.
48. Baron d'Ambès, *The Intimate Memoires of Napoleon III*, ed. and trans. by A. R. Allinson (London: Stanley Paul & Co., 1933), I, p. 54.
49. Napoleon, Bonazzi, *Lettres d'amour*, p. 397.
50. Mansel, *The Court of France 1789–1830*, p. 121.
51. François-René Chateaubriand, *Mémoires*, p. 269.
52. Constant, *Mémoires*.
53. McLynn, p. 510.
54. Napoleon, *Correspondance*, ed. Chevallier, V.
55. Betrand, *Cahiers*.
56. Fairweather, p. 408.
57. Jakob Walter, *Diary of a Napoleonic Foot Soldier*, trans. (London: Penguin, 1991). CH, p. 202.
58. Bertrand, *Cahiers*, p. 145.
59. Duc de Fezensac, *Mémoires*, p. 254.

21. *More full of charm*

1. Caulancourt, *Mémoires*, p. 234.
2. Masson, *Joséphine répudiée*, p. 306.
3. Masson, *Joséphine répudiée*, p. 308.
4. Bonaparte, *Mémoires*, p. 445.
5. Napoleon, *Correspondance*, ed. Chevallier.
6. *Correspondance*, ed. Chevallier, I.
7. *Correspondance*, ed. Chevallier, II, p. 64.
8. *Memoirs of Queen Hortense*, p. 179.
9. Bourrienne, *Mémoires*, IV, p. 30.
10. Josephine, *Correspondance*, ed. Chevallier, p. 208.
11. Hortense, *Mémoires*, II, p. 103.
12. Hortense, *Mémoires*, II, p. 106.
13. Hortense, *Mémoires*, II, p. 193.
14. Betrand, *Cahiers*.

Epilogue

1. Bourrienne, *Mémoires*, IV, p. 150.
2. Bourrienne, *Mémoires*, IV, p. 100.
3. Bourrienne, *Mémoires*, IV, p. 135.

4. Bourrienne, *Mémoires*, IV, p. 150.

5. Napoleon, *Correspondance*, XXXII, 340.

6. Hortense, *Mémoires*, I, p. 194.

7. Bourrienne, *Mémoires*, II, p. 145.

8. He had offered Louis XVIII the paintings if the Bonaparte family were permitted to return to France, but he was refused.

9. Napoleon, *Correspondance*, XXXII, 250.

10. However, of the 68 paintings Alexander acquired, many have now been dispersed to other museums, and 15 have disappeared entirely. Alexander Babin, 'Le Voyage Pittoresque from Malmaison to St Petersburg', in *France in Russia*, pp. 25–8.

Acknowledgements

So many new letters and documents have emerged and yet popular notions still persist of Josephine as feather-brained, lacking intellect, without ambition. In the summer of 2008 I rented a flat near the Musée de Cluny in Paris and spent every day in the Archives Nationales, studying Josephine's letters and the memoirs of her friends and enemies. It became clear that her reputation as excessively 'feminine', lacking intellect or ambition, was a carefully cultivated power play on her behalf, which worked perfectly until the very end. This was the Josephine I wanted to explore in this book. Josephine's own propaganda of the gentle consort occupied only by trivialities is very seductive. But in a merciless time, she had to be tough to survive – and her letters lay bare her ruthless determination. It feels fitting that she chose a swan as her symbol, a bird which appears graceful but is scrabbling under-neath the surface – and has a pretty unforgiving bite.

I am indebted to all those who have edited the letters and diaries of Josephine and her circle, and who have written on her life and those of her associates. The current project of the Fondation Napoléon, led by Victor André Masséna, Prince d'Essling, to publish Napoleon's full correspondence – with letters omitted from the earlier volumes – is a joy to all Napoleon scholars. Ten volumes have been published to date, with four to come, and they have been invaluable to me – as they will be to researchers in the future.

My work would not have been possible without the efforts of archivists to conserve the papers of Josephine, Napoleon and her circle, and I am very grateful to them all. The generosity of other scholars is always humbling. I am indebted to those who have written books that have transformed our view of Josephine and her circle – and been very helpful to me with advice, insight and help. Bernard Chevallier, to whom anyone who works on Josephine is always greatly indebted, Jill, Duchess of Hamilton, who was always full of generous encouragement (and kindly loaned me her book), Andrew Roberts, Munro Price, Paul Strathern, Flora Fraser and the generous Mlle Mountjoly at the Musée de la Pagerie, Martinique, have all been very welcoming, and Andrea Stuart was very kind. Sandra Gulland's work is always inspiring. A welcome grant from the Society of Authors allowed me to consult the Archives in Martinique. Working in the Fondation Napoléon, Malmaison Archives and Archives Nationales has been an incredible privilege – and I am very grateful to all the staff.

I am very grateful to everyone at Hutchinson and Random House, who have always been this book's greatest support. Thank you to my wonderful editor, Jocasta Hamilton at Hutchinson, who has been full of patience, imagination, kindness, enthusiasm and brilliant ideas. Thank you to the truly marvellous Susan Sandon, Richard Cable and Gail Rebuck for their very kind support - and thank you very much, Susan, for the lunches! Paul Sidey commissioned the book and I am sorry he was not there to see it through, but I hope he enjoys it – he did so much for me earlier in my career. Paulette Hearn and Catherine Gaffney have shepherded *Josephine* kindly and patiently through the production process and Anna Swan was a copy-editor with an eagle eye that put me to shame. Amelia Harvell has done splendid things – as always – thank you. And thanks to Jeanette Slinger who makes coming to the office such a pleasure.

My parents and friends have put up with repeated absences – thank you. Marcus and Persephone have kindly endured a house full of books on Josephine and done so much to support me – with love and gratitude, thank you for everything.

Listing all the papers, articles and books I consulted would use up pages and exhaust the reader's patience. My research focused on the letters of Josephine and her circle. The following is a select bibliography of my sources.

Bibliography

Fonds Napoléon, Archives Nationales, Paris
Fonds Masson, Bibliothèque Thiers, Paris
Malmaison Archives, Malmaison, Paris
La Pagerie Archives, Musée de la Pagerie, Martinique
Archives, Bibliothèque Schoelcher, Fort de France, Martinique

Abrantès, Laure Junot, Duchesse d', *Histoire des Salons*, 6 vols (Paris: Ollendorff, 1837-8)
Abrantès, Laure Junot, Duchesse d', *Mémoires Complets et Authentiques de Laure Junot, Duchesse d'Abrantès: Souvenirs Historiques sur Napoleon, la Révolution, le Directoire, le Consulat, l'Empire, la Restauration*, 13 vols (Paris: J. De Bonnot, 1967-8)
Adams, William Howard, *The Paris Years of Thomas Jefferson* (New Haven, Conn., and London: Yale University Press, 1997)
Alexander, R. S., *Napoleon* (London: Arnold, 2001)
Alméras, Henri de, *Barras et son temps* (Paris: Albin Michel, 1930)
Alméras, Henri de, *La vie Parisienne sous le Consulat et l'Empire* (Paris: Albin Michel, 1909)
Ambes, Baron de, *Intimate Memoirs of Napoleon III*, translated by R. Allinson (London: Stanley Paul & Co, 1933)
Arnault, Antoine-Vincent, *Souvenirs d'un Sexagénaire*, 4 vols (Paris: Dufey, 1833)
Arneville, Marie-Blanche de, *Parcs et Jardins sous le Premier Empire* (Paris: Librairie Jules Tallandier, 1981)

Asprey, Robert, *The Rise of Napoleon* (London: Little, Brown, 2000)

Aubenas, Joseph, *Histoire de l' Impératrice Joséphine*, 2 vols (Paris: Plon, 1857)

Aulard, Alphonse, *Études et Leçons sur la Révolution Française*. Seconde Serie (Paris: Alcan, 1902)

Aulard, Alphonse, *Paris pendant la reaction thermidorienne et sous la Directoire*, 5 vols (Paris: Cerf, 1898-1902)

Aulard, Alphonse, *Paris sous la Consulat*, 4 vols (Paris: Cerf, 1903-9)

Aulard, Alphonse, *Recueil des Actes du Comité de Salut Public*, 28 vols (Paris: Imprimerie Nationale, 1899-1951)

Avrillon, Marie, *Mémoires de Mlle Avrillon, première femme de chambre de l'impératrice, sur la vie privée de Joséphine, sa famille et sa cour*, ed. Maurice Dernelle (Paris: Mercure de France, 1969)

Bainville, Jacques, *Bonaparte* (Paris: Éditions, 1931)

Banbuck, Cabuzel Andréa, *Histoire politique, économique et sociale de la Martinique sous l'ancien regime* (Paris: M. Rivière, 1935)

Barbe, Jean-Paul, and Bernecker, Roland (eds) *Les Intellectuels Européens et la Campagne d'Italie, 1796–1798* (Münster: Nodus, 1999)

Barras, Paul-François-Jean-Nicolas, Vicomte de, *Mémoires de Barras, Membre du Directoire*, ed. George Duruy, 4 vols (Paris: Hachette, 1895-6)

Baudot, Marc-Antoine, *Notes Historiques sur la Convention nationale, le Directoire, L'Empire et l'exil des votants* (Paris: Frères, 1893)

Bausset, Louis-François-Joseph, Baron de, *Mémoires anecdotiques sur l'intérieur du palais et sur quelques événements de l'Empire depuis 1805 jusqu'au Ier mai 1814 pour server à l'histoire de Napoléon*, 2 vols (Paris: Baudouin Frères, 1827-9)

Beauharnais, Eugène de, *Mémoires et Correspondence Politique et Militaire du Prince Eugène*, 10 vols (Paris: Lévy Frères, 1858-60)

Beauharnais, Hortense de (Reine Hortense), *Mémoires de la Reine Hortense*, 3 vols, ed. Prince Napoléon (Paris: Plon, 1928)

Beauregard, Charles Albert Costa de, *Un homme d'autrefois* (Paris: Plon, 1877)

Béranger, Pierre-Jean de, *Ma biographie, ouvrage posthume de P.-J. Béranger* (Paris: Perottin, 1857)

Bernard, J. F., *Talleyrand: A Biography* (London: Collins, 1973)

Bertaud, Jean-Paul, *1799. Bonaparte Prend le Pouvoir. La République meurt-elle assassinée?* (Brussels: Éditions Complexe, 1987)

Bertaud, Jean-Paul, *Le Duc d'Enghien* (Paris: Fayard, 2001)

Bertaud, Jean-Paul, Alan Forrest et Annie Jourdan (eds), *Napoléon, le monde et les Anglais. Guerre des Mots et des Images* (Paris: Autrement, 2004)

Bertaut, Jules, *L'Impératrice Joséphine* (Paris: Livre Club D'Histoire, 1956)

Berthier, Louis-Alexandre, *Relation des Campagnes du Général Bonaparte en Egypte et en Syrie* (Milan, 1800)

Bertrand, Génèral, Grand Maréchal de Paris, *Cahiers de Sainte-Hélène*, ed. Fleuriot de Langle (Paris: Sulliver, 1949)

Bigarré, Auguste, *Mémoires du Général Bigarré: 1775–1813* (Paris: Grenadier, 2002)

Blanc, Olivier, *Last Letters: Prisons and Prisoners of the French Revolution*, tr. Alan Sheridan (New York: Andre Deutsch, 1987)

Blanning, T. C. W., *The French Revolutionary Wars, 1787–1802* (London: Arnold, 1996)

Blanning, T. C. W., *The Origins of the French Revolutionary Wars* (London: Longman, 1986)

Blaufarb, Rafe, *The French Army, 1750–1820. Careers, Talent, Merit* (Manchester: Manchester University Press, 2002)

Blumer, Marie-Louise, 'La Commission pour la Recherche des Objets d'Arts', *Révolution Française*, 87 (1934): 62-88, 124-50.

Boigne, Louise-Eléonore-Charlotte-Adélaïde d'Osmond, Comtesse de, *Mémoires de la Comtesse de Boigne, née d'Osmond*, 2 vols, presented and annotated by Jean-Claude Berchet (Paris: Mercure de France, 1999)

Bonaparte, Joseph, *Mémoires et Correspondance Politique et Militaire du Roi Joseph*, 10 vols (Paris: Perrotin, 1853-4)

Bonaparte, Lucien, *Mémoires de Lucien Bonaparte, Prince Cannino, écrits par lui-même* (Paris: Charles Gosselin, 1836)

Bonaparte, Napoléon, *Clissold et Eugenie* (Paris: Lévy, 1841)

Bonaparte, Napoléon, *Correspondance Générale, publiée par la Fondation Napoléon*, ed. Victor André Masséna, Prince d'Essling, 10 vols to date (Paris: Éditions Fayard, 2002-13)

Napoleon Bonaparte, *Correspondance Inédite, Officielle et Confidentielle*, 7 vols (Paris: Pancoucke, 1819-20)

Bonaparte, Napoléon, *Correspondance de Napoléon I publiée par ordre de l'Empereur Napoléon III*, 32 vols (Paris: Plon, 1858-70)

Bonaparte, Napoléon, *In the Words of Napoleon: The Emperor Day by Day*, ed. R. M. Johnston (London: Greenhill Books, 2002)

Bonaparte, Napoléon, *Napoléon, ses opinions et judgments, sur les homes et sur les choses* (Paris: Dufey, 1838)

Bonaparte, Napoléon et Joséphine, *Correspondance, Lettres Intimes*, Textes réunis par Jean-Michel Laot, Préface de Bernard Chevallier (Paris: Pierrelongue, 2012)

Bonnet, Jean-Claude (ed.), *L'Empire des Muses: Napoléon, les Arts et les Lettres* (Paris: Éditions Belin, 2004)

Bordes, Philippe, *Jacques-Louis David: Empire to Exile* (New Haven and London: Yale University Press, 2005)

Bouillé, Louis-Amour, *Souvenirs et fragments pour server aux memoires de ma vie et de mon temps: 1769–1812*, 3 vols (Paris: A. Picard et Fils, 1906-11)

Bourhis, Katell le (ed.), *The Age of Napoleon: Costume from Revolution to Empire 1789–1815* (New York: Metropolitan Museum of Art, 1989)

Bourrienne, Louis-Antoine-Fauvelet de, *La Vie privée de Napoléon, par Bourrienne, son secrétaire intime*, 10 vols (Paris: Frères, 1831)

Bouvier, Félix, *Un Amour de Napoléon* (Paris: Gougy, 1900)

Boyer, Pierre-François, *Historique de Ma Vie* (Paris: Vouivre, 2001)

Bresler, Fenton, *Napoleon III: A life* (London: HarperCollins, 2000)

Breton, Guy, *Histoires d'amour de l'histoire de France* (Paris: Éditions Noir et Blanc, 1955)

Broers, Michael, *Europe Under Napoleon, 1799–1815* (London: Arnold, 1996)

Broglie, Victor, duc de, *Souvenirs, 1785–1870* (Paris: Calmann Lévy, 1886)

Brookner, Anita, *Jacques-Louis David* (London: Chatto & Windus, 1980)

Brown, Howard G. and Judith Miller (eds), *Taking Liberties, Problems of New Order from the French Revolution to Napoleon* (Manchester: Manchester University Press, 2002)

Bruce, Evangeline, *Napoleon and Josephine: An Improbable Marriage* (London: Weidenfeld & Nicolson, 1995)

Burney, Fanny, *The Journal and Letters of Fanny Burney, Madame D'Arblay, 1791–1840*, 12 vols, ed. Joyce Hemlow et al (Oxford: Oxford University Press, 1972-84)

Cailaincourt, Général de, Duc de Vincence, *Mémoires*, 3 vols (Paris: Lévy, 1933)

Campan, Mme, *Correspondance inédited de Mme. Campan avec la Reine Hortense* (Brussels: J. P. Meline, 1835)

Campbell, Neil, *Napoleon at Fontainebleau and Elba* (London: Maclachan, 1869)

Carrington, Dorothy, *Portrait de Charles Bonaparte. D'après ses écrits de jeunesse et ses memoires* (Ajaccio: Piazolla, 2002)

Casanova, Antoine, *Napoléon et la Pensée de son Temps* (Paris: Boutique de l'Histoire, 2000)

Castelot, André, *Joséphine* (Paris: Perrin, 1964)

Castelot, André, *Napoléon Bonaparte* (Paris: Perrin, 1960)

Castelot, André, *Napoléon et les Femmes* (Paris: Perrin, 1998)

Catalogue des tableaux de sa majesté l'Imperatrice Joséphine dans les galleries et appartements de son palais de Malmaison (Paris: Didot Jeune, 1811)

Catinet, Maurice, 'Joséphine et ses Livres', *Livres Précieux du Musée de Malmaison*, Exhibition Catalogue (Paris: Éditions de la Réunion des Musées, 1993)

Chanvallon, Thibault Baptiste de, *Voyage à la Martinique* (Paris: Frères, 1763)

Chastenay, Victorine de, *Mémoires 1771–1815* (Paris: Perrin, 1987)

Chaudonneret, Marie-Claude, *Fleury Richard et Pierre Révoil: La Peinture Troubadour* (Paris: Arthena, 1980)

Chateubriand, François-René, *Atala/René*, tr. Irving Putter (Berkeley: University of California Press, 1980)

Chateubriand, François de, *Mémoires d'outre Tombe*, 2 vols (Garnier: Paris, 1989)

Chauleau, Liliane, *Dans les îles du Vent: la Martinique (XVIIe-XIXe siècle)* (Paris: L'Harmattan, 1993)

Chauleau, Liliane, *La Vie aux Antilles Françaises au temps de Victor Schoelcher* (Paris: L'Harmattan, 1990)

Chevallier, Bernard, *L'art de Vivre au Temps de Joséphine* (Paris: Flammarion, 1998)

Chevallier, Bernard, *Château et Domaine des Origines à 1904* (Paris: Réunion des Musées, 1989)

Chevallier, Bernard, *Douce et Incomparable Joséphine* (Paris: Payot, 1999)

Chevallier, Bernard and Christophe Pincemaille, *L'Impératrice Joséphine* (Paris: Payot, 1996)

Chevaillier, Bernard, Maurice Catinat and Christophe Pincemaille (eds), *L'Impératrice Joséphine, Correspondance, 1782–1814* (Paris: Payot, 1996)

Chevallier, Bernard et al, *Josephine, the Great Love of Napoleon*, Exhibition

Catalogue, The Stewart Museum (Montreal: The David M. Stewart Museum, 2003)

Chevrier, Edmond, *Le Général Joubert, d'apres sa Correspondance* (Paris: Fischbacher, 1884)

Chuquet, Alphonse, *La Jeunesse de Napoléon*, 3 vols (Paris: Colin, 1897-9)

Clary et Aldringen, Prince Charles de, *Trois mois à Paris lors dur marriage de l'Empereur* (Paris: Frères, 1914)

Cobb, Richard, *Death in Paris, 1795–1801* (Oxford: Oxford University Press, 1978)

Cobb, Richard, *The French and Their Revolution* (London: John Murray, 1998)

Cohen, William B., *The French Encounter with Africans: White Response to Blacks, 1530–1880* (Bloomington: Indiana University Press, 1980)

Cole, Hubert, *Josephine* (New York: Viking, 1963)

Constant, Louis, *Mémoires sur la Vie de Napoléon*, 6 vols (Paris: Lévy, 1830)

Cooper, Alfred Duff, *Talleyrand* (London: Phoenix, 1997)

Copies of Original Letters from the Army of General Bonaparte in Egypt, Intercepted by the Fleet under the Command of Admiral Lord Nelson, 3 vols (London: J. Wright, 1798)

Coryn, Marjorie, *The Marriage of Josephine* (London: Hodder & Stoughton, 1945)

Cronin, Vincent, *Napoleon* (London: HarperCollins, 1971)

Daney, Sidney, *Histoire de la Martinique, depuis la colonisation jusqu'en 1815*, 6 vols (Fort Royal: 1846-7)

DeLorme, Eleanor P. (ed.), *Josephine and the Arts of Empire* (California: Getty, 2005)

DeLorme, Eleanor P., *Joséphine: Napoleon's Incomparable Empress* (London: Abrams, 2002)

Denon, Dominique-Vivant, *Voyages dans la Basse et La Haute Egypte pendant les campagnes de Bonaparte*, 2 vols (Paris: Lévy, 1807)

Desgenettes, Nicolas-René Dufriche, *Souvenirs de la fin du XVIIIe siècle* (Paris: Lévy, 1835)

Desvernois, Nicolas-Philibert, *Mémoires du Général Baron* (Paris: Plon, 1898)

Dinelli-Graziani, Marie, 'Le Cardinal Fesch (1763-1839), un grand collectionneur, sa collection de peintures' (Thèse de doctorat d'histoire de l'art, Université de Paris I, Panthéon Sorbonne, Centre Ledoux, 2005)

Documents particuliers (en forme de lettres) sur Napoléon Bonaparte, sur plusieurs et ses actes jusqu'ici inconnus ou mal interprétés (Paris: Lévy, 1819)

Doublet, Pierre-Jean, *Mémoires Historiques sur l'invasion et l'occupation en Malte en 1798* (Paris: Plon, 1883)

Ducrest, Georgette, *Mémoires sur L'Impératrice Joséphine, ses Contemporains, la cour de Navarre et de la Malmaison,* 3 vols (Paris: Lévy, 1828)

Dwyer, Philip (ed.), *Napoleon and Europe* (London: Longman, 2001)

Dwyer, Philip, *Napoleon: The Path to Power, 1769–1799* (London: Bloomsbury, 2007)

Elliot, Grace Dalrymple, *Journal of My Life During the French Revolution* (London: R. Bentley, 1859)

Ellis, Geoffrey, *Napoleon* (London: Longman, 1997)

Englund, Stephen, *Napoleon: A Political Life* (New York: Scribner, 2004)

Erickson, Carolly, *Josephine: A Life of the Empress* (London: Robson, 1999)

Eyre, Edmund, *Observations Made at Paris during the Peace* (London: Bell, 1803)

Fain, Agathon-Jean-François, Baron, *Mémoires du baron Fain: premier secrétaire du cabinet de l'Empereur* (Paris: Plon-Nourrit et Cie, 1908)

Fairweather, Maria, *Mme de Staël* (London: Constable, 2005)

Fezensac, Duc de, *Souvenirs Militaires de 1804 à 1814* (Paris: Plon, 1863)

Fontana, Biancamaria, *Benjamin Constant and the Post-Revolutionary Mind* (New Haven, Conn.: Yale University Press, 1991)

Forrest, Alan, *Conscripts and Deserters: The Army and French Society during the Revolution and Empire* (New York: Palgrave, 1989)

Forrest, Alan, *Napoleon* (London: Quercus, 2011)

Forrest, Alan, Karen Hagemann and Jane Rendall (eds) *War Memories: The Revolutionary and Napoleonic Wars in Modern European Culture* (Basingstoke: Macmillan, 2012)

Forster, Elborg and Robert (eds and trs), *Sugar and Slavery, Family and Race: The Letters and Diary of Pierre Dessaless, Planter in Martinique, 1808–1856* (Baltimore: Johns Hopkins University Press, 1996)

Fouché, Joseph, *Mémoires de Joseph Fouché, duc d'Otrante,* 2 vols (Osnabrück: Proff, 1824)

Fox, Charles James, *Memoirs of the Latter Years of the Right Honourable Charles James Fox* (London: Wood, 1811)

Fraser, Antonia, *Marie Antoinette: The Journey* (London: Weidenfeld & Nicolson, 2001)

Fraser, Flora, *Venus of Empire: The Life of Pauline Bonaparte* (London: John Murray, 2009)

Frénilly, Baron de, *Mémoires de Baron de Frénilly,* 3 vols (Paris: Frères, 1850)

Furet, François, and Denis Richet, *French Revolution,* tr. Stephen Hardman (London: Weidenfeld & Nicolson, 1970)

Garaud, L., *Trois Ans à la Martinique* (Paris: A. Picard et Kaan, 1895)

Gautier, Arlette, *Les Soeurs de solitude: la Condition Féminine dans l'esclavage aux Antilles du XVIIe au XIXe siècles* (Paris: Éditions Caribéennes, 1985)

Gavoty, André, *Les Amoureux de l'Impératrice Josephine* (Paris: Librairie Arthème Fayard, 1961)

Genlis, Comtesse de, *Mémoires* (Paris: Lévy, 1828)

George, Mlle (Weimer, Marguerite Joséphine), *Memoires inédits de Mademoiselle George* (Paris: Plon-Nourrit et Cie, 1908)

Gerstein, Alexandra, Alexander Babin, Tamara Rappe and Bernard Chevallier, *France in Russia: Empress Josephine's Malmaison Collection,* Exhibition Catalogue, Hermitage Museum (London: Courtauld, 2007)

Gilles, Christian, *Madame Tallien: la Reine du Directoire* (Biarritz: Atlantica, 1999)

Girod, François, *La Vie Quotidienne de la Sociéte Créole* (Paris: Hachette, 1972)

Girod de L'Ain, Gabriel, *Désirée Clary, d'apres sa Correspondance inédite avec Bonaparte, Bernadotte et sa Famille* (Paris: Hachette, 1959)

Gohier, Louis-Jérôme, *Mémoires de Louis-Jérôme Gohier, President du Directoire au 18 Brumaire* (Paris: Bossange, 1824)

Goldworth, John Alger, *Paris in 1789–94: Farewell Letters of Victims of the Guillotine* (London: George Allen, 1902)

Goldsmith, Louis [attrib.], *The Secret History of the Cabinet of Bonaparte; including his Private Life…* (London: Wright, 1810)

Goldsmith, Louis [attrib.], *The Secret History of the Court and Cabinet of St Cloud,* 2 vols (London: Wright, 1845)

Goncourt, Edmond and Jules, *Histoire de la Société Française pendant le Directoire* (Paris: G. Charpentier, 1879)

Gough, Hugh, *The Newspaper Press in the French Revolution* (London: Macmillan, 1988)

Gourgaud, Gaspard, Baron, *Journal de Sainte-Hélène 1815–18,* 2 vols (Paris: Frères, 1899)

Gouyé Martignac, Gérald, and Michel Sementéry, *La Descendance de Joséphine, Impératrice des Français* (Paris: Christian, 1994)

Grandjean, Serge, *Inventaire après Décés de l'Impératrice Joséphine à Malmaison* (Paris: Réunion des Musées Nationaux, 1964)

Gronow, Captain, *The Reminiscences and Recollections of Captain Gronow, 1810–1860*, abridged by John Raymond (London: Bodley Head, 1964)

Gulland, Sandra, *The Last Great Dance on Earth* (London: Hodder Headline, 2001)

Gulland, Sandra, *The Many Lives and Secret Sorrows of Josephine B* (London: Hodder Headline, 1999)

Gulland, Sandra, *Tales of Passion, Tales of Woe* (London: Hodder Headline, 2000)

Hamilton, Jill, Duchess of Hamilton and Brandon, *Napoleon, the Empress and the Artist: The Story of Napoleon, Josephine's Garden at Malmaison, Redouté and the Australian Plants* (East Roseville, New South Wales: Kangaroo Press, 1998)

Hanoteau, Jean, *Les Beauharnais et l'Empereur: Lettres de l'Impératrice Joséphine et de la Reine Hortense au Prince Eugène* (Paris: Plon, 1936)

Hanoteau, Jean, *Le Ménage Beauharnais: Joséphine avant Napoléon – d'après des correspondances inédites* (Paris: Plon, 1935)

Harris, Robin, *Talleyrand: Betrayer and Saviour of France* (London: Murray, 2007)

Hastier, Louis, *Le Grand Amour de Joséphine* (Paris: Chastel, 1955)

Hearn, Lafcadio, *Esquisses Martiniquaises* (Paris: Plon, 1887)

Hibbert, Christopher, *The French Revolution* (London: Penguin, 1982)

Hibbert, Christopher, *Napoleon: His Wives and Women* (London: Harper-Collins, 2002)

Hilton, Lisa, *Athenaïs: The Real Queen of France* (London: Little, Brown, 2002)

Hobsbawm, E. J., *The Age of Revolution: Europe 1789–1848* (London: Abacus, 1962)

Horne, Alistair, *Napoleon: Master of Europe, 1805–7* (London: Weidenfeld & Nicolson, 1979)

Hubert, Gérard, *Malmaison* (Paris: Réunion des Musées Nationaux, 1989)

Hunt, Lynn, *Politics, Culture and Class in the French Revolution* (London: Metheun, 1984)

Hurel, Roselyne, and Diana Scarisbrick, *Chaumet, Paris: Deux siècles de creation* (Paris: Musée Carnavalet, 1998)

Imbert de Saint-Amand, Arthur Léon, *La Citoyenne Bonaparte* (Paris: E. Dentu, 1883)

Iung, Théodore (ed.), *Lucien Bonaparte et ses Mémoires, 1775–1840*, 3 vols (Paris: G. Charpentier, 1882-3)

James, C.L.R., *The Black Jacobins: Toussaint L'Ouverture and the San Domingo Revolution* (London: Secker and Warburg, 1980)

Janssens, Jacques, *Joséphine de Beauharnais et son Temps* (Paris: Berger-Levrault, 1963)

Johnston, R. M. (ed.), *In the Words of Napoleon: The Emperor Day by Day* (London: Greenhill Books, 2002)

Jonquière, Clément de La, *L'Expedition d'Egypte 1798–1801*, 5 vols (Paris: Charles-Lavauzelle, 1899-1907)

Jourdan, Annie, *L'Empire de Napoléon* (Paris: Flammarion, 2000)

Jourdan, Annie, *Louis Napoleon: Roi de Hollande* (Paris: Flammarion, 2010)

Kahane, Eric H., *Un Marriage Parisien sous le Directoire* (Paris: Éditions le Carrousel, 1961)

Kale, Steven, *French Salons: High Society and Political Sociability from the Old Regime to the Revolution of 1848* (Baltimore: Johns Hopkins, 2004)

Kauffmann, Jean-Paul, *The Dark Room at Longwood: A Voyage to St Helena* (London: Harvill Press, 1999)

Kelly, Linda, *Women of the French Revolution* (London: Hamish Hamilton, 1987).

Kiefer, Carol Solomon, *The Empress Josephine: Art and Royal Identity* (Amherst, Mass: Mead Art Museum, 2005)

Kielmannsegge, Comtesse de, *Mémoires de la Comtesse de Kielmannsegge sur Napoléon 1er*, 2 vols, tr. Joseph Delage (Paris: Éditions Victor Attinger, 1928)

Knapton, Ernest John, *Empress Josephine* (Cambridge, Mass: Harvard University Press, 1963)

Kunstler, Charles, *La Vie Privée de l'Impératrice Joséphine* (Paris: Hachette, 1939)

La Diplomatie du Directoire et Bonaparte (Paris: Payot, 1951)

Lacour-Gayet, G., *Talleyrand, 1754–1838*, 4 vols (Paris: Payot, 1928-34)

Lacroix, Paul, *The XVIIIth Century: Its Institutions, Customs and Costumes: France, 1700–1789* (London: Bickers and Son, 1870)

Laing, Margeret, *Josephine & Napoleon* (London: Sidgwick & Jackson, 1973)

Lajer-Burcharth, Ewa, *Necklines: The Art of Jacques-Louis David after the Terror* (New Haven, Conn., and London: Yale University Press, 1999)

Larrey, Baron Hippolyte, *Madame Mère*, 2 vols (Paris: Plon, 1892)

Las Cases, Emmanuel-Auguste-Dieudonné, Comte de, *Le Mémorial de Sainte-Hélène*, 2 vols, ed. Gérard Walter (Paris: Gallimard, 1956)

Lavalette, Antoine-Marie Chamans, Comte de, *Mémoires*, 2 vols (London: H. Colburn & Bentley, 1831)

Lee, Debbie and Peter J. Kitson, *Slavery, Abolition and Emancipation: Writings in the British Romantic Period*, 8 vols (London: Pickering and Chatto, 1999)

Lenôtre, G., *La Maison des Carmes* (Paris: Perrin, 1933)

Lentz, Thierry, *Le Grand Consulat: 1799–1804* (Paris: Fayard, 1999)

Lescure, Maurice, *Madame Hamelin* (Paris: L'Harmattan, 1995)

Lever, Evelyne, *Marie Antoinette; The Last Queen of France*, tr. Catherine Temerson (London: Piatkus, 2000)

Lever, Maurice, *Donatien Alphonse Françoise, Marquis de Sade* (Paris: Pauvert, 1991)

Lieven, Dominic, *Russia Against Napoleon: The Battle for Europe 1807–1814* (London: Allen Lane, 2009)

Luca, Anne Sandrine de, 'La Noblesse du Premier Empire Français: L'identité nobiliare réinventée' (These de Docteur en Droit, Histoire du droit et des institutions, Université de Perpignan, 2005–6)

Lumet, Louis, *Napoleon 1er, Empereur des Français* (Paris: Lévy, 1908)

Lyons, Martyn, *France under the Directory* (Cambridge: Cambridge University Press, 1975)

McClellan, Andrew, *Inventing the Louvre: Art, Politics and the Origin of the Modern Museum in Eighteenth-Century Paris* (Cambridge: Cambridge University Press, 1994)

McLynn, Frank, *Napoleon* (London: Cape, 1997)

Mackau, Annette de, *Correspondance d'Annette de Mackau, comtesse de Saint-Alphonse, dame du palais de l'impératrice Joséphine, 1790–1870*, ed. Chantal de Toutier-Bonazzi (Paris: S. E. V. P. E. N., 1967)

Mainardi, Patricia, *Husbands, Wives and Lovers: Marriage and its Discontents in Nineteenth-Century France* (New Haven and London: Yale University Press, 2003)

Mallet du Pan, Jacques, *Mémoires et correspondence pour servir à l'historie de la Révolution Française* (Paris: Amyot et Cherbulliez, 1851)

Malraux, André, *Vie de Napoleon par lui-même* (Paris: Lévy, 1930)

Mansel, Philip, *The Court of France 1789–1830* (Cambridge: Cambridge University Press, 1988)

Mansel, Philip, *The Eagle in Splendour: Napoleon I and His Court* (London: Philip, 1987)

Marchand, Louis-Joseph, *Mémoires de Marchand, Premier Valet de Chambre et Exécuteur Testamentaire de l'Empereur* (Paris: Éditions, 1985)

Marmont, Maréchal, duc de Raguse, *Mémoires de 1792 à 1841*, 9 vols (Paris: Perrotin, 1857)

Marquiset, Alfred, *Une Merveilleuse, 1776–1851* (Paris: H. Champion, 1909)

Martin, Andy, *Napoleon the Novelist* (Cambridge: Polity, 2000)

Martin, P., *Histoire de l'expedition Francaise en Egypte*, 2 vols (Paris: Lévy, 1815)

Martinet, Johannes Florentius, *Journal Physico-Médical des Eaux de Plombières* (Remiremont: Dubiez, 1798)

Masson, Frédéric, *Joséphine de Beauharnais, 1763–1796* (Paris: Ollendorff, 1913)

Masson, Frédéric, *Joséphine, Impératrice et Reine, 1804–1809* (Paris: Ollendorff, 1899)

Masson, Frédéric, *Joséphine Répudiée, 1809–1814* (Paris: Ollendorff, 1901)

Masson, Frédéric, *Mme Bonaparte: 1796–1804* (Paris: Ollendorff, 1920)

Masson, Frédéric, *Napoléon et sa Famille*, 13 vols (Paris: Albin Michel, 1897-1914)

Masson, Frédéric, *Napoléon dans sa Jeunesse: 1769–1793* (Paris: Société d'Editions, 1907)

Maugras, Gaston, *Delphine de Sabran, Marquise de Custine* (Paris: Plon-Nourrit et Cie, 1912)

Mauguin, Georges, *L'Impératrice Joséphine: anecdotes et curiosités* (Paris: J. Peyronnet, 1954)

Mélito, Miot, Comte de, *Memoirs of Count Miot de Mélito*, 2 vols, trs. Cashel Hoey and John Lillie (London: Sampson Low, 1881)

Metternich, Clément, Prince, *Mémoires, documents et écrits...*, 8 vols (Paris: Plon, 1880-84)

Michel, Marianne Roland et al, *The Floral Art of Pierre Joseph Redouté* (Greenwich, Conn: Bruce Museum, 2002)

Millet, Pierre, *Souvenirs de la Campagne d'Egypte* (Paris: Plon, 1903)

Miot, Jacques-François, *Mémoires pour Servir a l'Histoire des Expeditions en Egypte and Syrie* (Paris: Demonsville, 1804)

Montgaillard, Maurice, Comte de, *Souvenirs du Comte de Montgaillard* (Paris: Ollendorff, 1895)

Montholon, Comtesse de, *Souvenirs de Sainte-Hélène 1815–16* (Paris: Ollendorff, 1901)

Morris, Gouverneur, *The Diary and Letters of Gouverneur Morris*, ed. Anne Cary Morris (London: Kegan Paul, Trench, & Co., 1889)

Mossiker, Frances, *Napoleon and Josephine: The Biography of a Marriage* (London: Victor Gollancz, 1965)

Murat, Joachim, *Lettres et Documents, 1767–1815*, ed. Prince Joachim-Napoléon Murat et Paul le Brethon, 8 vols (Paris: Ollendorff, 1908-14)

Nasica, Tommaso, *Mémoires sur l'enfance et la jeunesse de Napoléon 1er jusqu'au l'age de vingt-trois ans* (Paris: Dupont, 1965)

Ober, Frederick, *Josephine, Empress of the French* (New York: Grafton, 1901)

Oman, Carola, *Napoleon's Viceroy: Eugène de Beauharnais* (London: Hodder & Stoughton, 1966)

Orieux, Jean, *Talleyrand ou Le Sphinx incompris* (Paris: Flammarion, 1998)

Ouvrard, G.-J., *Mémoires de G.-J. Ouvrard*, 4th edn, 2 vols (Paris: Moutardier, 1827)

Paris et ses modes ou les soirées Parisiennes (Paris: Bon, 1803)

Pasquier, Étienne Denis, *Mémoires du Chancelier Pasquier*, 2 parts, 6 vols (Paris: Plon, 1893-5)

Pichevin, R, *L'Impératrice Joséphine* (Paris: Plon, 1909)

Plessix Gray, Francine du, *At Home with the Marquis de Sade* (London: Chatto & Windus, 1999)

Potocka, Comtesse de, *Mémoires, 1794–1820*, ed. Casimir Stryienski (Paris: Éditions, 2005)

Pougetoux, Alain, *La Collection des Peintures de l'Impératrice Joséphine* (Paris: Réunion des Musées Nationaux, 2003)

Prendergast, Christopher, *Napoleon and History Painting* (Oxford: Oxford University Press, 1997)

Price, Munro, *The Fall of the French Monarchy* (Basingstoke: Macmillan, 2002)

Price, Munro, *The Perilous Crown: France Between Revolutions* (Basingstoke: Macmillan, 2007)

Rand, Richard (ed.), *Intimate Encounters: Love and Domesticity in Eighteenth-Century France* (Princeton, N. J., Princeton University Press, 1997)

Rémusat, Claire-Elisabeth Jeanne Graviaer de Vergennes, Comtesse de, *Mémoires de Mme de Rémusat 1802–1808*, 3 vols (Paris: Calmann Lévy, 1880)

Ribeiro, Aileen, *The Art of Dress: Fashion in England and France 1750–1820* (New Haven and London: Yale University Press, 1995)

Ribeiro, Aileen, *Facing Beauty: Painted Women and Cosmetic Art* (New Haven and London: Yale University Press, 2011)

Ribeiro, Aileen, *Fashion in the French Revolution* (London: Batsford, 1988)

Roberts, Andrew, *Napoleon and Wellington* (London: Weidenfeld & Nicolson, 2001)

Roberts, Andrew, *Waterloo: Napoleon's Last Gamble* (London: Weidenfeld & Nicolson, 2006)

Roederer, Pierre-Louis, *Oeuvres du Comte P.–L. Roederer*, 8 vols (Paris: Firmin, 1853-9)

Sainsbury, John, *Catalogue of a Collection of Cameos …* (London: Wright, 1843)

Salvi, Claudia, *Pierre – Joseph Redouté le Prince des Fleurs* (Tournai, Belgium: La Renaissance du Livre, 2001)

Savant, Jean, *Tel fut Napoléon* (Paris: Fasquelle, 1953)

Schroeder, Paul, *The Transformation of European Politics* (Oxford: Oxford University Press, 1994)

Scurr, Ruth, *Fatal Purity: Robespierre and the French Revolution* (London: Chatto, 2006)

Sorel, Albert, *L'Europe et la Revolution Française*, 8 vols (Paris: Plon, 1893-1904)

Staël, Anne-Louise-Germaine, Madame de, *Correspondance Générale de Madame de Staël*, ed. Beatrice W. Jasinski and Jean-Jacques Pauvert, 6 vols (Paris: Éditions, 1960)

Staël, Anne-Louise-Germaine, Madame de, *Dix Années d'Exil* (Paris: Fayard, 1996)

Strathern, Paul, *Napoleon in Egypt: A Clash of Cultures* (London: Jonathan Cape, 2007)

Stuart, Andrea, *The Rose of Martinique: A Life of Napoleon's Josephine* (London: Macmillan, 2004)

Sutherland, Christine, *Marie Walewska: Napoleon's Great Love* (London: Weidenfeld & Nicolson, 1986)

Thiébault, Général Baron, *Mémoires, publiés sous les auspices de sa fille*, 5 vols (Paris: Plon, 1893-5)

Thompson, J. M, *Napoleon Bonaparte: His Rise and Fall* (Oxford: Blackwell, 1958)

Tour du Pin, Marquise de la (Henriette-Lucie Dillon), *Journal d'une Femme de Cinquante Ans, 1778–1815*, 4 vols (Paris: Imhaus & Chapelot, 1914)

Tourtier-Bonazzi, Chantal de and Jean Tulard (eds) *Napoleon. Lettres d'amour à Josephine* (Paris: Fayard, 1981)

Tulard, Jean, *Dictionnaire Napoléon* (Paris: Fayard, 1987)

Tulard, Jean, *Les Thermidoriens* (Paris: Fayard, 2005)

Volney, Constantin, *Voyage en Egypte et en Syrie*, 2 vols (Paris: Frères, 1787)

Wagener, Françoise, *L'Impératrice Joséphine, 1763–1814* (Paris: Flammarion, 1999)

Wagener, Françoise, *La Reine Hortense, 1783–1837* (Paris: J.C. Lattès, 1992)

Williams, Kate, *England's Mistress: the Infamous Life of Emma Hamilton* (London: Hutchinson, 2006)

Woloch, Isser, *Jacobin Legacy: The Democratic Movement Under the Directory* (Princeton: Princeton University Press, 1970)

Young, Arthur, *Travels in France* (London: Bell, 1899)

Zamoyski, Adam, *1812, Napoleon's Fatal March on Moscow* (London: HarperCollins, 2004)

Index